Algorithmic Strategies for Solving Complex Problems in Cryptography

Kannan Balasubramanian
Mepco Schlenk Engineering College, India

M. Rajakani
Mepco Schlenk Engineering College, India

A volume in the Advances in Information Security,
Privacy, and Ethics (AISPE) Book Series

Published in the United States of America by
    IGI Global
    Information Science Reference (an imprint of IGI Global)
    701 E. Chocolate Avenue
    Hershey PA, USA 17033
    Tel: 717-533-8845
    Fax: 717-533-8661
    E-mail: cust@igi-global.com
    Web site: http://www.igi-global.com

Library of Congress Cataloging-in-Publication Data

Names: Balasubramanian, Kannan, 1968 August 15- editor. | Rajakani, M., 1983- editor.
Title: Algorithmic strategies for solving complex problems in cryptography / Kannan Balasubramanian and M. Rajakani, editors.
Description: Hershey, PA : Information Science Reference, an imprint of IGI Global, [2018] | Includes bibliographical references.
Identifiers: LCCN 2017012038| ISBN 9781522529156 (hardcover) | ISBN 9781522529163 (ebook)
Subjects: LCSH: Data encryption (Computer science)--Mathematics. | Computer algorithms.
Classification: LCC QA76.9.D335 A44 2018 | DDC 005.8/24--dc23 LC record available at https://lccn.loc.gov/2017012038

This book is published in the IGI Global book series Advances in Information Security, Privacy, and Ethics (AISPE) (ISSN: 1948-9730; eISSN: 1948-9749)

British Cataloguing in Publication Data
A Cataloguing in Publication record for this book is available from the British Library.

All work contributed to this book is new, previously-unpublished material. The views expressed in this book are those of the authors, but not necessarily of the publisher.

For electronic access to this publication, please contact: eresources@igi-global.com.

Advances in Information Security, Privacy, and Ethics (AISPE) Book Series

Manish Gupta
State University of New York, USA

ISSN:1948-9730
EISSN:1948-9749

Mission

As digital technologies become more pervasive in everyday life and the Internet is utilized in ever increasing ways by both private and public entities, concern over digital threats becomes more prevalent.

The **Advances in Information Security, Privacy, & Ethics (AISPE) Book Series** provides cutting-edge research on the protection and misuse of information and technology across various industries and settings. Comprised of scholarly research on topics such as identity management, cryptography, system security, authentication, and data protection, this book series is ideal for reference by IT professionals, academicians, and upper-level students.

Coverage

- Cookies
- Privacy-Enhancing Technologies
- Data Storage of Minors
- IT Risk
- CIA Triad of Information Security
- Telecommunications Regulations
- Global Privacy Concerns
- Internet Governance
- Access Control
- Network Security Services

IGI Global is currently accepting manuscripts for publication within this series. To submit a proposal for a volume in this series, please contact our Acquisition Editors at Acquisitions@igi-global.com or visit: http://www.igi-global.com/publish/.

Titles in this Series

For a list of additional titles in this series, please visit: www.igi-global.com/book-series

Detecting and Mitigating Robotic Cyber Security Risks
Raghavendra Kumar (LNCT Group of College, India) Prasant Kumar Pattnaik (KIIT University, India) and Priyanka Pandey (LNCT Group of College, India)
Information Science Reference • copyright 2017 • 384pp • H/C (ISBN: 9781522521549) • US $210.00 (our price)

Advanced Image-Based Spam Detection and Filtering Techniques
Sunita Vikrant Dhavale (Defense Institute of Advanced Technology (DIAT), Pune, India)
Information Science Reference • copyright 2017 • 213pp • H/C (ISBN: 9781683180135) • US $175.00 (our price)

Privacy and Security Policies in Big Data
Sharvari Tamane (MGM's Jawaharlal Nehru Engineering College, India) Vijender Kumar Solanki (Institute of Technology and Science Ghaziabad, India) and Nilanjan Dey (Techno India College of Technology, India)
Information Science Reference • copyright 2017 • 305pp • H/C (ISBN: 9781522524861) • US $210.00 (our price)

Securing Government Information and Data in Developing Countries
Saleem Zoughbi (UN APCICT, UN ESCAP, South Korea)
Information Science Reference • copyright 2017 • 307pp • H/C (ISBN: 9781522517030) • US $160.00 (our price)

Security Breaches and Threat Prevention in the Internet of Things
N. Jeyanthi (VIT University, India) and R. Thandeeswaran (VIT University, India)
Information Science Reference • copyright 2017 • 276pp • H/C (ISBN: 9781522522966) • US $180.00 (our price)

Decentralized Computing Using Blockchain Technologies and Smart Contracts Emerging Research and Opportunities
S. Asharaf (Indian Institute of Information Technology and Management, Kerala, India) and S. Adarsh (Indian Institute of Information Technology and Management, Kerala, India)
Information Science Reference • copyright 2017 • 128pp • H/C (ISBN: 9781522521938) • US $120.00 (our price)

Cybersecurity Breaches and Issues Surrounding Online Threat Protection
Michelle Moore (George Mason University, USA)
Information Science Reference • copyright 2017 • 408pp • H/C (ISBN: 9781522519416) • US $195.00 (our price)

Security Solutions and Applied Cryptography in Smart Grid Communications
Mohamed Amine Ferrag (Guelma University, Algeria) and Ahmed Ahmim (University of Larbi Tebessi, Algeria)
Information Science Reference • copyright 2017 • 464pp • H/C (ISBN: 9781522518297) • US $215.00 (our price)

701 East Chocolate Avenue, Hershey, PA 17033, USA
Tel: 717-533-8845 x100 • Fax: 717-533-8661
E-Mail: cust@igi-global.com • www.igi-global.com

Table of Contents

Detailed Table of Contents

The field of cryptography has seen enormous changes ever since the invention of Public Key Cryptography by Diffie and Hellman. The algorithms for complex problems like integer factorization, Discrete Logarithms and Elliptic Curve Discrete Logarithms have improved tremendously making way for attackers to crack cryptosystems previously thought were unsolvable. Newer Methods have also been invented like Lattice based cryptography, Code based cryptography, Hash based cryptography and Multivariate cryptography. With the invention of newer public Key cryptosystems, the signature systems making use of public key signatures have enabled authentication of individuals based on public keys. The Key Distribution mechanisms including the Key Exchange protocols and Public Key infrastructure have contributed to the development of algorithms in this area. This chapter also surveys the developments in the area of identity Based Cryptography, Group Based Cryptography and Chaos Based Cryptography.

Chapter 2

The integer factorization problem used in the RSA cryptosystem, the discrete logarithm problem used in Diffie-Hellman Key Exchange protocol and the Elliptic Curve Discrete Logarithm problem used in Elliptic Curve Cryptography are traditionally considered the difficult problems and used extensively in the design of cryptographic algorithms. We provide a number of other computationally difficult problems in the areas of Cryptography and Cryptanalysis. A class of problems called the Search problems, Group membership problems, and the Discrete Optimization problems are examples of such problems. A number of computationally difficult problems in Cryptanalysis have also been identified including the Cryptanalysis of Block ciphers, Pseudo-Random Number Generators and Hash functions.

Chapter 3

Kannan Balasubramanian, Mepco Schlenk Engineering College, India

Many variations of the Diffie-Hellman problem exist that can be shown to be equivalent to one another. We consider following variations of Diffie-Hellman problem: square computational and Square decisional Diffie-Hellman problem, inverse computational and inverse computational decisional Diffie-Hellman problem and divisible computational and divisible decisional Diffie-Hellman problem. It can be shown that all variations of computational Diffie-Hellman problem are equivalent to the classic computational Diffie-Hellman problem if the order of a underlying cyclic group is a large prime. We also describe other variations of the Diffie-Hellman problems like the Group Diffie-Hellman problem, bilinear Diffie-Hellman problem and the Elliptic Curve Diffie-Hellman problem in this chapter.

Chapter 4

Kannan Balasubramanian, Mepco Schlenk Engineering College, India
Mala K., Mepco Schlenk Engineering College, India

This chapter focusses on Secure Key Exchange protocols executed among a group of parties, called group key exchange (GKE) protocols. Authentication and Key Establishment are very important in any secure communication. Authentication is generally based on long-term keys which can be associated with identities. To associate identities with long-term keys, we can assume the existence of a public-key infrastructure (PKI) which provides parties with some mechanisms for secure key registration and secure access to long-term keys of prospective peers. In most cases, there is also a need for some temporary keys. The Group Key Exchange protocols can be classified as Centralized, Distributed or Contributory. A few toolkits such as Spread and Cliques for the implementation of Group Key Exchange Protocols are also discussed.

Chapter 5

Kannan Balasubramanian, Mepco Schlenk Engineering College, India

Cryptographic Hash Functions are used to achieve a number of Security goals like Message Authentication, Message Integrity, and are also used to implement Digital Signatures (Non-repudiation), and Entity Authentication. This chapter discusses the construction of hash functions and the various attacks on the Hash functions. The Message Authentication Codes are similar to the Hash functions except that they require a key for producing the message digest or hash. Authenticated Encryption is a scheme that combines hashing and Encryption. The Various types of hash functions like one-way hash function, Collision Resistant hash function and Universal hash functions are also discussed in this chapter.

Chapter 6

Sumathi Doraikannan, Malla Reddy Engineering College, India

Digital Signature is considered as an authentication tool of electronic records. The main benefits of the digital signature are cost, security, time stamping, non-repudiation and speed. Digital signature can be particularly useful for sales proposals, purchase orders and health services. In addition, this chapter also focuses on the real time applications of digital signature algorithm and its implementations. This chapter deals with the Digital signature algorithm, Digital Signature types and the way of working.

Chapter 7

    Kannan Balasubramanian, Mepco Schlenk Engineering College, India
    M. Rajakani, Mepco Schlenk Engineering College, India

This chapter investigates the implementation attacks on cryptographic algorithms. The implementation attacks can be defined as invasive or non-invasive. The major attack types are Probing attacks, Fault Induction attacks, timing attacks, Power analysis attacks and Electromagnetic analysis attacks. The attacks target either the physical leakage of a device in which case they are considered physical attacks or try to observe some parameters of the algorithm which constitute logical attacks. The Various countermeasures for the attacks include physical protection against tampering of the device or use redundant computation in the algorithm to prevent observation of the parameters.

Chapter 8

    Kannan Balasubramanian, Mepco Schlenk Engineering College, India
    Jayanthi Mathanan, Mepco Schlenk Engineering College, India

Homomorphic encryption is a technique that enables mathematical operations to be performed on encrypted data. This type of encryption can be used to perform operations on encrypted data by a server without having to provide the key. An example application is searching or querying an encrypted database. The encryption schemes are classified as additive or multiplicative homomorphic if they support addition or multiplication on encrypted data. The Cryptosystems are classified as fully homomorphic, partially homomorphic or somewhat homomorphic based on the type and number of operations supported on the ciphertext.

Chapter 9

    Kannan Balasubramanian, Mepco Schlenk Engineering College, India
    Mala K., Mepco Schlenk Engineering College, India

Zero knowledge protocols provide a way of proving that a statement is true without revealing anything other than the correctness of the claim. Zero knowledge protocols have practical applications in cryptography and are used in many applications. While some applications only exist on a specification level, a direction of research has produced real-world applications. Zero knowledge protocols, also referred to as zero knowledge proofs, are a type of protocol in which one party, called the prover, tries to convince the other party, called the verifier, that a given statement is true. Sometimes the statement is that the prover possesses a particular piece of information. This is a special case of zero knowledge protocol called a zero-knowledge proof of knowledge. Formally, a zero-knowledge proof is a type of interactive proof.

Most of the voting protocols proposed so far can be categorized into two main types based on the approach taken: schemes using blind signatures and schemes using homomorphic encryption. In the schemes using blind signatures, the voter initially obtains a token – a blindly signed message unknown to anyone except himself. In the schemes using homomorphic encryption the voter cooperates with the authorities in order to construct an encryption of his vote. Due to the homomorphic property, an encryption of the sum of the votes is obtained by multiplying the encrypted votes of all voters. This chapter reviews schemes based on blind signatures and homomorphic encryption and proposes improvements to the existing schemes.

Chapter 11

To deal with active attacks in public key encryptions, the notion of security against an adaptive chosen ciphertext attack has been defined by Researchers. If an adversary can inject messages into a network, these messages may be ciphertexts, and the adversary may be able to extract partial information about the corresponding cleartexts through its interaction with parties in the network. The Security against chosen ciphertext attack is defined using an "decryption oracle." Given an encryption of a message the "ciphertext" we want to guarantee that the adversary cannot obtain any partial information about the message. A method of securing Public Key Cryptosystems using hash functions is described in this chapter.

The goal of secure two-party computation is to enable two parties to cooperatively evaluate a function that takes private data from both parties as input without exposing any of the private data. At the end of the computation, the participants learn nothing more than the output of the function. The two-party secure computation systems have three properties: (1) the application involves inputs from two independent parties; (2) each party wants to keep its own data secret; and (3) the participants agree to reveal the output of the computation. That is, the result itself does not imply too much information about either party's private input. Informally, the security requirements are that nothing is learned from the protocol other than the output (privacy), and that the output is distributed according to the prescribed functionality (correctness). The threat models in the two-party computation assume the presence of three different types of adversaries: 1) Semi honest, 2) Malicious and 3) Covert.

Kannan Balasubramanian, Mepco Schlenk Engineering College, India
M. Rajakani, Mepco Schlenk Engineering College, India

The Secure Multiparty computation is characterized by computation by a set of multiple parties each participating using the private input they have. There are different types of models for Secure Multiparty computation based on assumption about the type of adversaries each model is assumed to protect against including Malicious and Covert Adversaries. The model may also assume a trusted setup with either using a Public Key Infrastructure or a using a Common Reference String. Secure Multiparty Computation has a number of applications including Scientific Computation, Database Querying and Data Mining.

Kannan Balasubramanian, Mepco Schlenk Engineering College, India
Ahmed Mahmoud Abbas, The American University in Cairo, Egypt

The protection of Computer Hardware and Software using Cryptographic algorithms has assumed importance in the recent years. The Trusted Computing Group (TCG) has put forward certain conditions to be met by the computer hardware, software and firmware so that the devices may be considered trusted. The Trusted Platform Module is a hardware device that will authenticate the code modules contained in the Basic Input/Output System (BIOS) of a computer to ensure that the Computer System starts in a trustworthy state. This device can also protect against Memory Management attacks including Buffer Overflows and Memory Pointer attacks.

Kannan Balasubramanian, Mepco Schlenk Engineering College, India

Researchers have developed many different types of software for implementing Cryptography algorithms. One such software is Cryptool. This software can be used to demonstrate many Classical Cryptosystems and symmetric-Key Cryptosystems like DES and AES. This software can be used to demonstrate Public Key Cryptosystems like RSA and ECC as well as many hash algorithms like MD5, SHA-1, SHA-256, and SHA-512. The usage of the algorithms and sample input and outputs obtained from the software are included for the beginners and learners to the area of Cryptography.

Kannan Balasubramanian, Mepco Schlenk Engineering College, India
Ahmed Mahmoud Abbas, The American University in Cairo, Egypt

The most prevalent need for multiple precision arithmetic, often referred to as "bignum" math, is within the implementation of public key cryptography algorithms. Algorithms such as RSA and Diffie-Hellman require integers of significant magnitude to resist known cryptanalytic attacks. As of now, a typical RSA modulus would be at least greater than 10^{309}. However, modern programming languages such as ISO C and Java only provide intrinsic support for integers that are relatively small and single precision. This chapter describe the modules provided by one such library for the C Programming Language.

Most cryptographic systems are based on an underlying difficult problem. The RSA cryptosystem and many other cryptosystems rely on the fact that factoring a large composite number into two prime numbers is a hard problem. The are many algorithms for factoring integers. This chapter presents some of the basic algorithms for integer factorization like the Trial Division, Fermat's Algorithm. Pollard's Rho Method, Pollard's p-1 method and the Elliptic Curve Method. The Number Field Sieve algorithm along with Special Number field Sieve and the General Number Field Sieve are also used in factoring large numbers. Other factoring algorithms discussed in this chapter are the Continued Fractions Algorithms and the Quadratic Sieve Algorithm.

At the time when RSA was invented in 1977, factoring integers with as few as 80 decimal digits was intractable. The first major breakthrough was quadratic sieve, a relatively simple factoring algorithm invented by Carl Pomerance in 1981, which can factor numbers up to 100 digits and more. It's still the best-known method for numbers under 110 digits or so; for larger numbers, the general number field sieve (GNFS) is now used. However, the general number field sieve is extremely complicated, for even the most basic implementation. However, GNFS is based on the same fundamental ideas as quadratic sieve. The fundamentals of the Quadratic Sieve algorithm are discussed in this chapter.

Preface

We, the editors of this book titled *Algorithmic Strategies for Solving Complex Problems in Cryptography* would like to thank IGI-Global for agreeing to publish this book and for the cooperation extended during the development of this book. The final version of the book contains 18 chapters which are related to the current problems being studied in the field of Cryptography. The areas covered in this book relate to Public Key Cryptography, Key Exchange Protocols, Zero Knowledge Proofs, Homomorphic Encryption Schemes, Secure Two Party and Multiparty Computation, Cryptanalysis of Public Key Algorithms and Hash Functions and Digital Signature Algorithms.

One of the main problems faced by the Symmetric Encryption algorithms is the distribution of the shared private key to the parties involved in the encryption and decryption. The key distribution by a trusted third party solves the problem but still has to use the insecure channel. The invention of public key cryptography solved the problem of key distribution by allowing the parties to have two keys, one private and other public. The public key can be distributed over the insecure communication channels and can be used for encryption whereas the private key can be used for decryption. An example is the RSA public key algorithm invented by Rivest, Shamir and Adleman. This idea of private and public keys can also be used to establish shared session keys that can be used for encryption which avoids the problem of distributing keys over insecure channels. An example of this kind is the Diffie-Hellman Key Exchange protocol. The field of Cryptography has seen many proposals for the Public Key Encryption ever since the invention of RSA algorithm many of which have not been studied as extensively as the RSA algorithm. Some of the algorithms proposed for Public Key Encryption are examined in the chapters included in this book. The use of private key and Public keys can also be used to sign documents with the use of Hash functions. The chapters on Hash functions and Digital Signatures explore these ideas more deeply.

Besides Public Key Encryption, Key Exchange Protocols, Hash Functions and Digital signatures, other areas have also gained considerable attention in the field of Cryptography. The Zero Knowledge Proof is a protocol between two parties, a Prover and a Verifier. The Verifier verifies through a series of message exchanges that the prover knows a secret without the prover actually having to reveal the secret. The two party computation is similar to the Zero Knowledge Proof but the parties involved compute any arbitrary function instead of verifying a secret. The Multiparty Computation is a protocol run between multiple parties which allows certain number of corrupted parties. The corrupted parties may leak information they are not supposed to or may substitute some other values besides the ones they are supposed to use in the messages or simply may not follow the protocol specification. The investigation of the allowed numbers of corrupted parties is one of the problems of interest in the study of multiparty computation.

Another interesting area of development in Cryptography is Homomorphic Encryption which allows computation on encrypted data. This will allow Computer servers to perform search on encrypted data, to query encrypted databases and perform computation over encrypted data. The different types of Homomorphic Encryption Schemes identified include Partial Homomorphic Schemes, Somewhat Homomorphic Schemes and Fully Homomorphic Encryption Schemes. An example application for Homomorphic Schemes is in Cryptographic Voting Protocols. The chapter on Homomorphic Schemes surveys the various Homomorphic Schemes and their applications. Another chapter has been dedicated to Cryptographic Voting Protocols.

The Public Key Encryption Schemes that have been proposed are based on certain computationally difficult problems like integer Factoring, Discrete Logarithms and Elliptic Curve discrete Logarithms. The Cryptanalysis of these public key encryption schemes involve brute force computation of the decryption key given certain number of plaintext-ciphertext pairs encrypted using those public key algorithms. The study of security of public key encryption schemes have given rise to security notions like indistinguishability, non-malleability and security against adaptive chosen-ciphertext attacks. The chapters related to cryptanalysis of public key algorithms include integer factoring algorithms, the quadratic sieve algorithm for integer factoring and the strengthening of public key encryption schemes against adaptive chosen ciphertext attack.

This book also explored use of software tools in the study of cryptography which included the the LibTomMath that allows us to use arbitrarily long integers in the implementation of cryptographic operations and the CrypTool that provides demonstration of the basic Cryptographic algorithms. Both these tools have been explored in two different chapters in this book.

One of the problems in implementing Cryptography in hardware is the secure starting of services in a Computer System. The use of device called Trusted Platform Module is suggested for the secure booting up of a Computer System. A chapter examines the issues in the secure booting of services in the Computer System.

This book will prove to be a valuable resource for undergraduate and graduate students doing research in the area of cryptography. This book also will be valuable to researchers, developers of software related to Cryptography and Information Technology professionals.

The first chapter on 'Recent Developments in Cryptography: A Survey' presents a number of problems related to Cryptography that are currently being studied. This chapter introduces and explains topics in Cryptography such as Hash based Cryptography, Code based Cryptography, Lattice Based Cryptography, Multivariate Quadratic Equations Cryptography, Identity Based Cryptography, Group Based Cryptography and Chaos Based Cryptography. For those interested in furthering research in Cryptography, the introduction given in this chapter will prove to be useful.

Most of the Cryptographic algorithms used in practice are based on computationally difficult problems. The Second Chapter on 'Problems in Cryptography and Cryptanalysis' surveys the computationally difficult problems used in common Cryptographic algorithms like the RSA problem, The Quadratic Residuosity problem, The Square Root modulo *n* problem, the Subset-Sum problem, the Subset-Product problem, the Discrete Logarithm problem, the Diffie-Hellman Problem, the Elliptic Curve Discrete Logarithm Problem, The Syndrome Decoding Problem, The Shortest Vector Problem, the Closest Vector Problem, The Smallest Basis Problem, Matrix Decomposition Problem and the Discrete Optimization Problem. The problems in Cryptanalysis include the Exhaustive Key Search attack, Key Collision attack and Algebraic attacks. This chapter will prove to be useful for those who want to develop an understanding of the underlying problems in Cryptography and Cryptanalysis.

The Diffie-Hellman key exchange protocol is based on the difficulty of solving discrete logarithms. Since the introduction of the Diffie-Hellman Key Exchange protocol, many variations of the Diffie-Hellman problem have been invented all of which are equally difficult to solve. The third chapter on 'Variants of the Diffie-Hellman Problem' introduces many different variations of the Diffie-Hellman problem like the Computational Diffie-Hellman problem, Square Computational Diffie-Hellman problem, Inverse Computational Diffie-Hellman problem and the Divisible Computational Diffie-Hellman problem. It also introduces other variations of the Diffie-Hellman problem like the Twin Diffie-Hellman problem, the Elliptic Curve Discrete Logarithm problem and the Bilinear Diffie-Hellman problem.

The Group Key Agreement Protocol is meant to solve the problem of creating a shared symmetric key among a group of users. This leads to the generalization of the Diffie-Hellman problem to a group of users. The Group Diffie-Hellman problem and the Group Key Exchange protocols are introduced in the chapter on 'Secure Group Key Agreement Protocols'. This chapter also introduces toolkits for experimenting with Group Key Agreement protocol like Spread and Cliques.

The fifth chapter on 'Hash Functions and their Applications' introduces various types of hash functions like the One-Way hash Functions, Collision Resistant Hash Functions and the Universal One-Way Hash Functions. This chapter examines the construction of Hash functions, the attacks on them and the applications of the hash functions. It also introduces Message Authentication Codes which require a key to produce a message digest.

The Sixth Chapter on 'Efficient Implementation of Digital Signature Algorithms' explores the implementation of Digital Signature Algorithms like the Schnorr Signature and the Digital Signature Standard. The ease of implementation of the Signature algorithms may form a very important consideration in choosing the Digital Signature algorithms for signing documents.

The software and hardware implementation of Cryptographic Algorithms are vulnerable to physical attacks by attackers. The physical attacks considered in the chapter on 'Attacks on Implementation of Cryptographic Algorithms' examines attacks like Probing attacks, Fault induction attacks, Timing attacks, Power analysis attacks and Electromagnetic attacks. The countermeasures against these attacks are also discussed.

The eighth chapter on 'Homomorphic Encryption Schemes: A Survey' introduces the idea behind Homomorphic Encryption Schemes and discusses their applications in various cryptographic protocols. It also discusses the different types of Homomorphic Schemes like the Partial Homomorphic Encryption Schemes and Somewhat Homomorphic Encryption Schemes. This chapter provides a good introduction to this area of Cryptography.

The ninth chapter on 'Zero Knowledge Proofs: A Survey' introduces the concept of Zero Knowledge Proofs with examples. The applications of Zero Knowledge Proofs as well as the variations of Zero Knowledge Proofs like Non-interactive Zero Knowledge Proofs are examined. The examples given for Zero Knowledge Proofs are the Magical Cave, Hamiltonian Cycles, Graph 3-colorability, and Fiat-Shamir Identification Protocol. The relation between Commitment Schemes and Zero Knowledge Proofs is also examined.

The tenth chapter on 'Cryptographic Voting Protocols' introduces the electronic voting problem. Many schemes for electronic voting like Electronic Voting based on Homomorphic Encryption, Schemes based on Blind signatures and Anonymous channel and Chaum's Voting Scheme are discussed.

The eleventh Chapter on 'Securing Public Key Encryption Against Adaptive Chosen Ciphertext Attacks' introduces the notion of Semantic Security of Public Key Encryption Schemes. The RSA algorithm is shown to be semantically insecure and a general method of securing Public Key Encryption Schemes using hash functions is discussed.

The twelfth chapter on 'Secure Two Party Computation' introduces the security of a two party computation model. This chapter discusses the behavior of malicious and semi-honest adversaries and presents the Yao's Protocol and the Oblivious Transfer as examples.

The thirteenth chapter on 'Secure Multiparty Computation' introduces many problems in the area of privacy preserving scientific computation belonging to the Secure Multiparty computation model. This chapter discusses the ideal and real models for secure multiparty computation. It presents verifiable secret sharing as one of the examples of secure multiparty computation. This chapter also presents a classification of the security of multiparty computation based on the maliciousness of the adversaries, existence of a broadcast channel and composability of the protocols.

The fourteenth chapter on 'Secure Bootstrapping using the Trusted Platform Module' addresses the bootstrap process of the computer. The use of Digital Signatures to verify the integrity of each step in the bootstrap process is suggested for the secure booting of the computer operating system. A small hardware device called the Trusted Platform Module stores the hash values of code modules and verifies the hash values during the startup of the Computer System. This chapter also addresses the memory vulnerabilities and the Trusted Execution Technology. It examines the structure of the TPM and its role in Trusted Computing.

The fifteenth Chapter 'Experiments with the Cryptool Software' explores the various functions provided by the Cryptool software. It provides a demonstration of the classical Cryptographic algorithms as well as the more advanced symmetric and asymmetric algorithms like RSA and Diffie-Hellman. The symmetric Cryptographical algorithms explored include DES, TripleDES and AES. This chapter also explores the hash functions used in digital signatures and Cryptanalysis of ciphers. The capabilities of this tool in working with large numbers make this tool a valuable one for learners of Cryptography.

The sixteenth chapter on 'A Software Library for Multiprecision Arithmetic' discusses the design of a software library written in C for using arbitrarily long integers in Cryptographic algorithms. It looks at the basic data types used and the various primitives that can be used in the design and implementation of cryptographic protocols. This tool will prove to be useful for programmers and developers who design and implement cryptographic algorithms.

The seventeenth chapter on 'Integer Factoring Algorithms' discusses various algorithms used for factoring very large integers like Trial Division, Pollard's Rho method, Pollard's p-1 method, Elliptic Curve method, and the Fermat's method. It also discusses algorithms like the Special and Generalized Number Field Sieve algorithms, Continued Fractions Algorithm and the Quadratic Sieve algorithm. It also provides links to tools for integer factoring and some factoring challenges with varying number of decimal digits.

The eighteenth chapter on 'The Quadratic Sieve Algorithm for Integer Factoring' discusses the concepts behind the design of the Quadratic Sieve algorithm for integer factoring. This will be of interest to advanced level researchers in the field of cryptographic algorithms.

The book explores the current state of security in the implementation of Cryptography algorithms. It discusses the various issues in the design and use of Cryptographic algorithms and discusses how cryptanalysis of algorithms can improve the security of cryptographic implementations. With better understanding of the implementation issues surrounding the use of cryptographic algorithms, the security of computer systems can be improved.

Kannan Balasubramanian
Mepco Schlenk Engineering College, Sivakasi

M. Rajakani
Mepco Schlenk Engineering College, Sivakasi

Acknowledgment

The editors would like to thank the Management and Principal of Mepco Schlenk Engineering College, Sivakasi for providing the Resources needed to complete this book. The editors would also like to thank the faculty, staff and students of Mepco Schelenk Engineering College for directly or indirectly helping to bring this book into its final form.

Chapter 1
Recent Developments in Cryptography:
A Survey

Kannan Balasubramanian
Mepco Schlenk Engineering College, India

ABSTRACT

The field of cryptography has seen enormous changes ever since the invention of Public Key Cryptography by Diffie and Hellman. The algorithms for complex problems like integer factorization, Discrete Logarithms and Elliptic Curve Discrete Logarithms have improved tremendously making way for attackers to crack cryptosystems previously thought were unsolvable. Newer Methods have also been invented like Lattice based cryptography, Code based cryptography, Hash based cryptography and Multivariate cryptography. With the invention of newer public Key cryptosystems, the signature systems making use of public key signatures have enabled authentication of individuals based on public keys. The Key Distribution mechanisms including the Key Exchange protocols and Public Key infrastructure have contributed to the development of algorithms in this area. This chapter also surveys the developments in the area of identity Based Cryptography, Group Based Cryptography and Chaos Based Cryptography.

INTRODUCTION

The field of cryptography was characterized initially by the development of Classical Cryptosystems and later by the development of Symmetric Key Cryptosystems and Public Key Cryptosystems. The invention of Public Key Cryptosystems led to the development of number of Public Key algorithms with varying degrees of complexity and strength. While the Symmetric Key Cryptosystems and the Public Key Cryptosystems focussed on the security property of Confidentiality, the development of Hash algorithms focused on achieving Integrity of data. The invention of Public Key Cryptography also led to the use of Digital Signatures which provided a very important property of non-repudiation by combining the use of private keys and hash algorithms.

DOI: 10.4018/978-1-5225-2915-6.ch001

While there are a number of algorithms that exist that can perform encryption using public and private keys, it would be of interest to the researchers to develop algorithms based on different principles since they can provide a platform with which we can compare the performance of different algorithms and also we can choose from a variety of algorithms based on the nature of application in use. The public key encryption algorithms are usually based on a mathematically hard and computationally difficult problem. In this chapter, a survey of the developments that have taken place in Cryptography ever since the invention of public Key Cryptography by Diffie and Hellman (Diffie, et.al.,1976) is presented. There are many important classes of cryptographic systems beyond RSA (Diffie, 1988) and DSA (Kerry, et.al., 2013) and ECDSA (Hoffman, 2012). They are:

- **Hash Based Cryptography:** The classic example is Merkle's hash-tree public-key signature system (Merkle., 1989).
- **Code Based Cryptography:** The classic example is McEliece's hidden Goppa-code public-key encryption system (McEliece, 1978).
- **Lattice Based Cryptography:** The example that has attracted the most interest is the Hoffstein–Pipher–Silverman "NTRU" public-key-encryption system (Hoffstein et.al., 1988).
- **Multivariate Quadratic Equations Cryptography:** An example is the "Hidden Field Equations" by Patarin (1986).
- **Identity Based Cryptography:** A type of public-key cryptography in which a publicly known string representing an individual or organization is used as a public key. The public string could include an email address, domain name, or a physical IP address. An example is the scheme proposed by Adi Shamir (Shamir, A.,1984).
- **Group Based Cryptography:** Based on use of Groups for constructing cryptographic primitives. An example is the public key cryptography which is based on the hardness of the word problem (Magyarik et.al, 1985).
- **Chaos Based Cryptography:** The application of the mathematical chaos theory to the practice of cryptography.

Here we look at each of the above classes of Cryptography and how they affect research and developments in the area of cryptography.

HASH BASED CRYPTOGRAPHY

Hash-based digital signature schemes use a cryptographic hash function like any other digital signature schemes. Their security relies on the collision resistance of that hash function. The existence of collision resistant hash functions can be viewed as a minimum requirement for the existence of a digital signature scheme that can sign many documents with one private key. Each new cryptographic hash function yields a new hash-based signature scheme. Hence, the construction of secure signature schemes is independent of hard algorithmic problems in number theory or algebra. The hash based signature schemes depend only symmetric cryptography. Hash Based signature schemes were invented by Ralph Merkle (1989). Merkle started from one-time signature schemes, in particular that of Lamport and Diffie (Lamport, 1979).

One-time signature schemes are really the most fundamental type of digital signature schemes. However, they have a severe disadvantage. One key-pair consisting of a secret signature key and a public verification key can only be used to sign and verify a single document. This is inadequate for most applications. It was the idea of Merkle to use a hash tree that reduces the validity of many one-time verification keys (the leaves of the hash tree) to the validity of one public key (the root of the hash tree). The initial construction by Merkle was not very efficient, in particular in comparison to the RSA signature scheme. However in the meantime, many improvements have been found. Now hash-based signatures are the most promising alternative to RSA and elliptic curve signature schemes.

The most primitive hash based signature can be used only once, and only to sign a single-bit message. Alice picks two random values and publishes her public Key: $H(x)$ and $H(y)$. In order to sign a message, Alice publishes one of the two, original values depending on the value of the bit. Clearly, this works only for a single bit message. It is also a one-time signature because once one of the original values have been published, it is insecure for the same public key to be used again. The first extension to this scheme is to run many instances in parallel in order to sign larger messages. Assume that the hash function is fixed, say SHA-256. Now Alice picks 512 random values, x_0, x_1,..x_{255} and y_0,y_1,...y_{255} and publishes the hash of each of them as her public key. Now she can sign an arbitrary long message m by calculating $H(m)$ and then publishing either x_i or y_i based on the bits of $H(m)$.

This signing is still valid for only one-time. As soon as Alice signs a different message with the same public key then, for some values of i, both x_i and yi have been published. This lets an attacker forge signatures for messages that Alice hasn't signed. In order to allow signing multiple messages, we just generate multiple one-time signatures. This consumes a lot of memory and hence is not practical. The solution is to use a Merkle hash tree. In the Merkle binary hash tree, the leaves contain the hashes of the messages and each non-leaf node contains the hash of its children. Figure 1 shows a Merkle tree with four leaf nodes A,B,C and D.

If Bob believes that $H(H(AB)H(CD))$ is Alice's Public key, then anyone can convince him that A is part of Alice's pubic key by giving him A, B and $H(CD)$. Bob calculates $H(AB)$ from A and B and then $H(H(AB)H(CD))$ from $H(AB)$ and $H(CD)$. If the values match, then A must be part of Alice's public key. Now if A,B,C and D were one-time signature public keys then Alice's public key has been reduced to a single hash. Each signature now needs to include the one-time signature value, the rest of the public

Figure 1. A Merkle hash tree

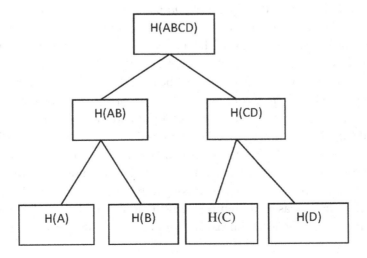

key, and also a proof that the public key is in the Alice's public key. In more detail, the signature contains either x_i or y_i depending on the bits of the hash of the message to be signed and also $H(x_i)$ and $H(y_i)$ for the bits that were not used. With that information, Bob can reconstruct the one-time signature public key. Then the signature contains the path up the tree, the values B and H(CD) in this example, which convince Bob that the one-time signature public key is part of Alice's overall public key. So now the public and private keys have been reduced to just 32 bytes (if we are using 256-bit hash). We can make the tree arbitrarily large, thus supporting arbitrarily many signatures.

The signatures still need a lot of storage. For 512 bits the total storage required is 512 x32=16KB. The Winternitz trick (Buchmann, J.,et.al., 2011a) involves iterating hashes. Winternitz started off by considering the one-time signature of a single bit and solved it by publishing $H(x)$ and $H(y)$ and then revealing one of the preimages. What if we generated a single value z and then published $H(H(z))$? We would reveal $H(z)$ if the bit was one, or z if the bit was zero. But an attacker could take our signature of zero(z) and calculate $H(z)$, thus creating a signature of one. So we need a checksum to make sure that, for any other message, the hash function needs to be broken. So we would need two of these structures and then we would sign 01 or 10. That way, one of the hash chains needs to be broken in order to calculate the signature of the different message. The second is the Winternitz's checksum.

The Winternitz's checksum becomes valuable when signing large messages. The Winternitz' hashes were 16 values long. That means one of them can cover 4 bits of the value that we are signing. If we were signing a 256-bit value, we only need 64 winternitz chains and three for the checksum. Also the Winternitz scheme makes it easy for the verifier to calculate the original public key. The signature size is 16 KB for 2,144 bytes. This signature scheme is stateful. This means when signing, the signer must absolutely record that a one-time key has been used so they never use it again. If the private key was copied into another computer and used there, then the whole system is broken.

To overcome the key management problem of one-time signature key pairs, Merkle proposed the use of hash trees. In the Merkel signature scheme (MSS), verification keys are hashed and they build the leaves of the tree. Neighbouring children are concatenated and then hashed to build the parent node. The root of the tree represents the public key of the scheme. A signature is generated by applying the private key of an one-time signature scheme. The corresponding verification key is handed on to the receiver of the message along with the signature. The verifier also has to be told about neighbouring nodes on the path to the root of the MSS tree, which is referred to as the authentication path. Using that information, the receiver can verify the signature and use the verification key to build the leaves and reach the root of the tree using the authentication path. The root is already known to the verifier as the public key, which he obtained earlier, for example via a certificate. For each new signature generated the next key pair must be used. As one can see, this scheme is stateful. For example, the index of the used key pair — respectively leaf — of the MSS tree must be stored. This is a whole new situation in the use of cryptographic schemes. Due to slow runtimes, as well as large key and signature sizes, this scheme was not used in practice since other schemes like RSA were known and easier to implement. But the interest in hash-based signatures led to renewed interest in those schemes and significant improvements occurred over the last years. Signature generation is much faster thanks to the use of pseudo-random number generators, the construction of large trees is easier thanks to multi-tree proposals and many more contributions have been made. In 2011, Andreas Hülsing introduced XMSS (Buchmann, J., et.al., 2011b), a hash-based signatures scheme based on minimal security assumptions. This scheme and its multi-tree variant XMSS^{MT} are the most advanced approaches for practical hash-based signatures.

To introduce hash-based signature schemes to today's cryptographic infrastructure, a few drawbacks must be overcome. Particularly statefulness has to be handled. Private keys of e.g. RSA are stateless. They can easily be used. It's possible to have several copies, no matter whether you allow access for several process for example talking about a TLS-server handling hundreds of connections or whether you want to make backups of your key. Due to the statefulness of hash-based schemes, private keys have become a critical resource. Also any kind of copy is a security threat as an attacker could get hold of an old key state and forge signatures. Another aspect are interfaces to cryptographic software like TLS libraries. Those are sometimes not prepared to deal with changing keys. Furthermore, issues emerging from the integration with a public key infrastructure (PKI) such as key distribution and revocation must be addressed.

CODE-BASED CRYPTOGRAPHY

The McEliece public key cryptosystem, introduced by McEliece in 1978, is similar to the Merkle-Hellman Knapsack cryptosystem in that it takes an easy case of an NP-problem and disguises it to look like the hard instance of the problem. In this cryptosystem, the problem that is used is drawn from the theory of error-correcting codes.

Syndrome decoding of linear codes (when considered as a decision problem) is an NP-complete problem if the number of errors is not bounded. However, there are classes of linear codes which have very fast decoding algorithms. The basic idea of the McEliece system is to take one of these linear codes and disguise it so that, the attacker when trying to decrypt a message, is forced to use syndrome decoding, while Bob, who set up the system, can remove the disguise and use the fast decoding algorithm. McEliece suggested using *Goppa Codes*, which are linear codes with a fast decoding algorithm, in the system, but any linear code with a good decoding algorithm can be used.

Let C be an (n,k)-linear code with a fast decoding algorithm that can correct t or fewer errors. Let G be a generator matrix for C. To create the disguise, let S be a $k \times k$ invertible matrix (the scrambler*)* and let P be an $n \times n$ permutation matrix (i.e., having a single 1 in each row and column and 0's everywhere else). The matrix,

$$G' = SGP$$

is made public while S, G and P are kept secret by Bob. For Alice to send a message to Bob, she blocks her message into binary vectors of length k. If x is one such block, she randomly constructs a binary n-vector of weight t (that is, she randomly places t 1's in a zero vector of length n), call it e and then sends to Bob the vector

$$y = xG' + e.$$

Oscar, upon intercepting this message, would have to find the nearest codeword to y of the code generated by G'. This would involve calculating the syndrome of y and comparing it to the syndromes of all the error vectors of weight t. As there are n choose t of these error vectors, good choices of n and t will make this computation infeasible. Bob, on the other hand, would calculate

$$yP^{-1} = (xG' + e)P^{-1} = xSG + eP^{-1} = xSG + e'$$

where e' is a vector of weight t (since P^{-1} is also a permutation matrix). Bob now applies the fast decoding algorithm to strip off the error vector e' and get the code word $(xS)G$. The vector xS can now be obtained by multiplying by G^{-1} on the right (however, if Bob had been smart, he would have written G in standard form $[I_k\ A]$, and then xS would just be the first k positions of xSG and this multiplication would not be needed). Finally, Bob gets x by multiplying xS on the right by S^{-1}.

For an example we will use the (7,4) Hamming code which corrects all single errors. A generator matrix for this code is given by:

$$G = \begin{matrix} 1000110 \\ 0100101 \\ 0010011 \\ 0001111 \end{matrix}$$

and Bob chooses the scrambler matrix

$$S = \begin{matrix} 1101 \\ 1001 \\ 0111 \\ 1100 \end{matrix}$$

and the permutation matrix

$$P = \begin{matrix} 0100000 \\ 0001000 \\ 0000001 \\ 1000000 \\ 0010000 \\ 0000010 \\ 0000100 \end{matrix}$$

Bob makes public the generator matrix

$$G' = SGP = \begin{matrix} 1111000 \\ 1100100 \\ 1001101 \\ 0101110 \end{matrix}$$

If Alice wishes to send the message $x = (1\ 1\ 0\ 1)$ to Bob, she first constructs a weight 1 error vector, say $e = (0\ 0\ 0\ 0\ 1\ 0\ 0)$ and computes

$$y = xG' + e$$

$$= (0\ 1\ 1\ 0\ 0\ 1\ 0) + (0\ 0\ 0\ 0\ 1\ 0\ 0)$$

$$= (0\ 1\ 1\ 0\ 1\ 1\ 0)$$

which she then sends to Bob.

Upon receiving y, Bob first computes $y' = yP^{-1}$, where

$$P^{-1} = \begin{matrix} 0001000 \\ 1000000 \\ 0000100 \\ 0100000 \\ 0000001 \\ 0000010 \\ 0010000 \end{matrix}$$

obtaining $y' = (1\ 0\ 0\ 0\ 1\ 1\ 1)$. Now Bob decodes y' by the fast decoding algorithm (Hamming decoding in this example). The syndrome of y' is $(1\ 1\ 1\ 0)^T$, so the error occurs in position 7 (details omitted). Bob now has the code word $y'' = (1\ 0\ 0\ 0\ 1\ 1\ 0)$. Because of the clever choice for G, Bob knows that $xS = (1\ 0\ 0\ 0)$, and he can now obtain x by multiplying by the matrix

$$S^{-1} = \begin{matrix} 1101 \\ 1100 \\ 0111 \\ 1001 \end{matrix}$$

obtaining $x = (1\ 0\ 0\ 0)S^{-1} = (1\ 1\ 0\ 1)$.

There are three major concerns with the McEliece cryptosystem.

1. The size of the public key (G') is quite large. Using the Goppa code with parameters suggested by McEliece, the public key would consist of 2^{19} bits. This will certainly cause implementation problems.
2. The encrypted message is much longer than the plaintext message. This increase of the bandwidth makes the system more prone to transmission errors.
3. The cryptosystem cannot be used for authentication or signature schemes because the encryption algorithm is not one-to-one and the total algorithm is truly asymmetric (encryption and decryption do not commute).

LATTICE-BASED CRYPTOGRAPHY

One of the examples of the Lattice-based Cryptosystem is the NTRU cryptosystem. The security of NTRU is based on the hardness of the shortest vector problem in high-dimensional Euclidean lattices (Hoffstein, J., 1998). The main operation is NTRU encryption involves arithmetic in a polynomial ring $R=Z[X]/(X^N-1)$. The addition in this ring is straightforward polynomial addition, while the multiplication is convolutional. All polynomials in the ring have integer coefficients (modulo some integers) and their degrees are at most N-1, so a typical element can be represented as $a = a_0 + a_1 X + \ldots a_{N-1} X^{N-1}$. The NTRU Encryption is parameterized by three parameters, N, P and Q, which satisfy the following conditions.

- N which is a prime number such that the maximal degree for all polynomials in the ring R is N-1.
- P and Q are two possible moduli for the coefficients of the polynomials in R, with P << Q with gcd(P,Q)=1

After arithmetic operations in R, the coefficients of the polynomials need to be reduced either modulo P or Q.

The NTRU encryption consists of three parts: key generation, encryption and decryption. Key generation does not happen frequently and hence is often done off-line.

1. **Key Generation:** A public key h and a private key (f_q, f_p) are generated as follows:
    ◦ Randomly choose a polynomial $f \in R$ with coefficients reduced modulo p.
    ◦ Randomly choose a polynomial $g \in R$ with coefficients reduced modulo p.
    ◦ Compute the private key f_p as the inverse polynomial f mod p
    ◦ Compute the private key f_q as the inverse polynomial f mod q
    ◦ Compute the public key $h = p f_q * g$ mod q

Here the '*' stands for multiplication in the NTRU Encrypt ring i.e. polynomial multiplication modulo x^n-1. If any of the polynomials are not invertible, then we start over and repeat until we succeed.

2. **Encryption:** The ciphertext is computed from the public key h, a random polynomial $r \in R$ mod P, and the message $m \in R$ mod p,

$e = P \times h * r + m$ mod q

3. **Decryption:** The decryption procedure has three steps.
    ◦ Compute $a = f * e$ mod q
    ◦ Shift the coefficients of a to the range $[-q/2, q/2]$ and then modulo p.
    ◦ Compute $d = a * f_p$ mod p.

As an example, take the parameters (n,p,q) as (7,3,41)

The polynomial f is chosen as $f(x)=x^6-x^4+x^3+x^2-1$ and the polynomial g is chosen as $g(x) =x^6+x^4-x^2-x$ The inverse f_q is computed as $8x^6+26x^5+31x^4+21x^3+40x^2+2x+37$ in the ring R_q and the inverse f_p $x^6+2x^5+x^3+x^2+x+1$ in the Ring R_p. The private key is (f_q, f_p) and the public key is computed as

$h(x) \equiv p f_q * g \bmod Q = 19x^6+38x^5+6x^4+32x^3+24x^2+37x+8$ in ring R_q

Using the above parameters the encryption and decryption can be performed as:

Let $m(x) = -x^5+x^3+x^2-x+1$. Using the ephemeral key $r(x) = x^6-x^5+x-1$, e(x) is computed as

$e(x) = 31x^6+19x^5+4x^4+2x^3+40x^2+3x+25 \pmod{41}$. Upon decryption $a \equiv f.e \pmod{Q}$

$a \equiv x^6+10x^5+33x^4+40x^3+40x^2+x+40 \pmod{41}$ and reducing modulo q

$a(x) \equiv x^6+10x^5-8x^4-x^3-x^2+x-1 \pmod{3}$ the message is obtained as $a * f_p \bmod P$ which is $-x^5+x^3+x^2+x+1$

MULTIVARIATE QUADRATIC EQUATIONS CRYPTOGRAPHY

Multivariate public key cryptography uses systems of multivariate quadratic equations as the public key and part of the private key. Thus, multivariate public key cryptosystems are in fact multivariate quadratic public key cryptosystems. These systems are studied because of two problems that are believed to be hard. The first is called the MQ problem, where the MQ stands for multivariate quadratic. The second is called the Isomorphism of Polynomials problem (IP problem). MQ-based encryption schemes are encryption schemes that rely on the difficulty of solving an apparently random instance of the MQ problem and the IP problem for their security.

The MQ Problem: The MQ problem over a finite fieeld F_q (where q is a prime power) is finding a solution $x \in 2 \ F_q^n$ to a given system of m quadratic polynomial equations $y = (p_1, ..., p_m)$ over F_q in n indeterminates. That is, we wish to solve

$$y_1 = p_1(x_1, ..., x_n)$$

$$y_2 = p_2(x_1, ..., x_n)$$

$$\ddots$$

$$y_m = p_m(x_1, ..., x_n)$$

for a given $y = (y_1, ..., y_m) \ 2 \ F_q^m$ and unknown $x = (x_1; x_2, ..., x_n) \in F_q^n$. True to the term quadratic, in the above system of equations, the polynomials p_i have the form $p_i(x_1, ...x_n) := \sum_{1 \leq j \leq k \leq n} \gamma_{i,j,k} x_j x_k + \sum_{j=1}^{n} \beta_{i,j} x_j + \alpha_i$

for $1 \leq i \leq m$; $1 \leq j \leq k \leq n$ and $\alpha_i, \beta_{i,j}, \gamma_{i,j,k} \in F_q$ (the constant, linear and quadratic coefficients, respectively). It has been shown that over a finite field, this problem is NP-hard (Patarin, J.,et.al., 1997).

The isomorphism of polynomials problem:Given a pair of (not necessarily quadratic) polynomial vectors, P and P⁰, where each vector is an m-tuple of polynomials over the same set of n indeterminates as in the previous section, the IP problem is to find a pair of affine transformations T and S such that

$$P = T \bigcirc P^0 \bigcirc S:$$

Thus, $T \in A \ (F_q^m)$ and $S \in 2A \ (F_q^n)$. They are therefore representable by the pairs of terms T_l and T_c, and S_l and S_c, respectively, where T_l and S_l are invertible $m \times m$ (resp. $n \times n$) matrices with elements from F_q. Similarly, T_c and S_c are column vectors over F_q of lengths m and n respectively. Thus, S(x), where $x = (x_1; x_2, ..., x_n)$ is given by $S(x) = S_1 x + S_c$, viewing x as a column vector, and using standard matrix multiplication for $S_1 x$ and standard matrix addition for the summation.

The difficulty of the IP problem is equivalent to solving for the unknowns of S and T using the entries of P and P^0 as constants. This is a problem quite similar to the MQ problem. Now, however, the unknown values are the values of T and S, while the values for P and P^0 are given. Solving such a problem reduces to solving a set of equations in the values of T and S of total degree one larger than the total degree of P^0. So, when solving problems in the situation of MQ-based encryption schemes, the total degree of these equations is 3, in the unknown entries of T and S, namely, the unknown entries of the matrices T_1, T_c, S_1, and S_c. It can be shown that this problem is NP-hard (Patarin, J., et. al.,1998).

Here is a simple example of an IP problem. Let $m = 1$ and let $n = 1$. Let $q = 3$, so we are working in F_3. Let $P^0 = x^2 + x$ and let $P = x^2 + x + 1$. Then we wish to find T and S such that

$$x^2 + x + 1 = (T \bigcirc P^0 \bigcirc S)(x):$$

Since we know that here $T(x) = t_1 x + t_2$, and $S(x) = s_1 x + s_2$, for indeterminates $t_1, t_2, s_1, s_2 \in F_2$, we have the following equation to solve:

$$x^2 + x + 1 = t_1 (s_1 x + s_2)^2 + s_1 x + s_2 + t_2:$$

The indeterminates can be determined by solving the following three equations, determined by setting the coe cients of x^2; x; 1 equal on each side of the previous equation:

$$1 = s_1^2 t_1$$

$$1 = 2 s_1 s_2 t_1 + s_1 t_1$$

$$1 = s_2^2 t_1 + s_2 t_1 + t_2:$$

Note that these equations are of degree 3, one higher than the total degree of P^0, as above. There are two solutions. The first equation gives us the fact $t_1 = 1$ and $s_1 \neq 0$. If we choose $s_1 = 1$, then $s_2 = 0$ and $t_2 = 1$. If we choose $s_1 = 2$, then $s_2 = 1$ and $t_2 = 1$.

A Generic MQ-Based Encryption Scheme

The private key of a generic MQ-based encryption scheme is an ordered set (T, P^0, S), following the same conventions as previous sections in this chapter. T and S are determined in the same way, so only the T case will be considered in detail. T is to be an invertible affine transformation on F_q^m. Thus, by finding T_1 and T_c, an invertible $m \times m$ matrix and a column vector of length m respectively, T is totally determined. So, using a cryptographically secure pseudorandom number generator over F_q, continue to determine random matrices in $F_q^{m \times m}$ until one is found with nonzero determinant. This is an expected constant-time operation, and its output will be T_1. Then choose a column vector of length m by choosing m elements from F_q with the random number generator. This determines T_c.

Determining P^0 is somewhat more difficult. P^0 is always a vector of quadratic polynomials. However, every MQ-based encryption scheme embeds some sort of trapdoor into the choice of P^0, so that for a known output y of the function P^0, the preimage of P^0 is easily computable. It is simplest to choose an invertible P^0. By building a small amount of redundancy into messages sent (usually by concatenating part or all of a message's hash to the message proper), it is possible for non-invertible P^0 functions to be used as well. Generally, P^0 is chosen uniformly at random from some appropriate space of quadratic functions.

The public key P is given by

$$P = T \bigcirc P^0 \bigcirc S$$

where one notes that as P^0 is quadratic and the functions T and S are affine, the total degree of P is also 2.

Encryption is accomplished by taking a message x and embedding it into F^n_q, possibly with the redundancy required by the choice of the key, and running it through the public key, forming $y = P(x)$. The decryption process varies slightly with the particular trapdoor built into P^0, but the general procedure is to take a given ciphertext y, and convert it to the plaintext by using the secret key (T, P^0, S) to invert P over the message space, recalling the possibility of message redundancy to ensure this is possible. T is known to be invertible, so as a first step, we get,

$$T^{-1}(y) = (P^0 \bigcirc S)(x):$$

Then we find the set of preimages of P^0,

$$(P^0)^{-1} (T^{-1}(y))$$

Then, each element $\tau \in (P^0)^{-1}(T^{-1}(y))$ is given as input to S^{-1}, which exists by definition of S. The exact redundancy specified by the encryption scheme will almost certainly occur in only one such preimage $S^{-1}(\tau)$. Remove the redundancy to retrieve the decrypted message in F^n_q. In the special case of invertible P^0, one simply applies the three inverses T^{-1}, $(P^0)^{-1}$, and S^{-1} to the ciphertext y in order, then by recovering the plaintext $x = S^{-1} \bigcirc P^{0-1} \bigcirc T^{-1} (y)$. Note that the only changing factor when encrypting or decrypting is the nature of the trapdoor built into P^0, which determines whether or not redundancy is required, and the exact technique used to find the preimage $S^{-1}(\tau)$.

A fundamental requirement for security is that the private key be difficult to obtain from the public key. Therefore, the IP problem must be difficult. There exist families of MQ-based schemes that have relatively few possible choices of private key value P^0 (for example, the Matsumoto and Imai C* scheme presented in (Matsumoto,T., et.al, 1988)). Therefore, if the IP problem is easy, simply solving it over and over again for the possible P^0 values will eventually return the remainder of the private key, breaking the system.

Similarly, the MQ problem must also be kept difficult for security reasons. If the MQ problem is easily solved, then for any ciphertext y, the associated plaintext x can be efficiently computed by solving an instance of the MQ problem.

IDENTITY BASED CRYPTOGRAPHY

Shamir (1984) proposed a concept of identity-based cryptography. In this new paradigm of cryptography, users' identifier information such as e-mail or IP addresses instead of digital certificates can be used as public key for encryption or signature verification. As a result, identity-based cryptography significantly reduces the system complexity and the cost for establishing and managing the public key authentication framework known as Public Key Infrastructure (PKI).

Although Shamir (1984) easily constructed an identity-based signature (IBS) scheme using the existing RSA (Rivest et.al., 1978) function, he was unable to construct an identity-based encryption (IBE) scheme, which became a long-lasting open problem. Only recently in 2001, Shamir's open problem was independently solved by Boneh and Franklin (Boneh, et.al, 2001) and Cocks (Cocks, 2001) .

The sender Alice can use the receiver's identifier information which is represented by any string, such as email or IP address, even a digital image (Sahai, A., et.al, 2004), to encrypt a message. The receiver Bob, having obtained a private key associated with his identifier information from the trusted third party called the "Private Key Generator (PKG)", can decrypt the ciphertext.

The steps of the Identity Based Encryption are as follows:

1. **Setup:** The PKG generates the Master (private) and Public key pair denoted as sk_{PKG} and pk_{PKG}.
2. **Private Key Extraction:** The receiver authenticates himself to the PKG and obtains his private key $sk_{ID_{Bob}}$ corresponding to his identity ID_{Bob}.
3. **Encryption:** Alice encrypts the plaintext using the identity of Bob ID_{Bob} and the public key of the PKG pk_{PKG}.
4. **Decryption:** Upon receiving the ciphertext C, Bob decrypts it by using his private key $sk_{ID_{Bob}}$ to get the plaintext M.

In an identical manner, the signature involves using the ID of Alice to sign a message using the public and private key pair of the PKG. The steps of the Identity Based Signatures are as follows:

1. **Setup**: The PKG generates the Master (private) and Public key pair denoted as sk_{PKG} and pk_{PKG}.
2. **Private Key Extraction:** The signer Alice authenticates herself to the PKG and obtains her private key $sk_{ID_{Alice}}$ corresponding to her identity ID_{Alice}.
3. **Signature Generation:** Using her private key $sk_{ID_{Alice}}$ Alice creates the signature σ on the message M.
4. **Signature Verification:** Having obtained the message M and signature σ, Bob verifies the signature using Alice's identity ID_{Alice} and the PKG's public key pk_{PKG}. If the verification succeeds, he returns 'Accept', otherwise he returns 'Reject'.

Public Key Infrastructures (PKIs) are currently the primary means of deploying asymmetric cryptography. PKIs refer to infrastructures that support the deployment of traditional asymmetric cryptographic algorithms, such as RSA (Rivest et. al, 1978). Because of the inherent public nature of the encryption or verification keys, the integrity of the public keys is usually protected with a certificate. The PKI is the infrastructure that supports the management of keys and certificates. In addition to the keys and certificates, the core components of a PKI are:

- **Certificate Authority (CA):** The CA is the entity that generates the certificates. It is responsible for ensuring the correct key is bound to the certificate, as well as ensuring the certificate content.
- **Registration Authority (RA):** The RA is responsible for ensuring that the user that receives the certificate is a legitimate user within the system. The functionality of the CA and RA is sometimes carried out by a single entity.
- **Certificate Storage:** In most systems certificates (as well as update information such as Certificate Revocation Lists) are stored in a CA managed database.
- **Software**: For the certificates to be of use, the software that is going to use the certificates need to be aware of what the certificate content represents within the scope of the system security policy.
- **Policies and Procedures:** Although the core of a PKI is mainly technical, there is, by necessity, a strong requirement for ensuring that the mechanisms are used correctly. The Certificate Policy (CP) and Certification Practice Statements (CPS) define the how the certificates are generated and managed. They also define the role of the certificates within the broader security architecture.

The core difference between an Identity based Cryptography and a traditional asymmetric algorithm in the means of generating the keys. The difference is identifiable in two ways:

- In both the signature and encryption variants, the public keys are generated from publicly identifiable information. This allows a client A to generate the public key of another client B without having to do a search in a directory or ask B for a copy of their key.
- Because of the theory that underpins the algorithms, the creation of the private key requires the knowledge of a master secret that is held by the Trusted Authority (TA), who is the analogue of the CA in a PKI.

Recently, it has been recognised that an identity need not be the only determinant of a client's public key. For example, information such as the client's position within an organisation, the validity period for the keys, etc. can be included in the data used to derive the key pair. This results in the broader concept of identifier-based public key cryptography.

Because the TA is directly responsible for the generation of the private key in an Identity

based Cryptography mechanism, there is an inherent escrow facility in the system. This may or may not be desirable. This forces a change in the role of the trusted third party within the system. In a PKI, the CA is concerned with validating the authenticity of the information present in the certificate, whereas, in an Identity based Cryptography, the TA is directly responsible for generating and distributing all keying material within the system.

There is also the requirement that the TA and the client are able to set up an independent secure channel for the distribution of private key material. This channel needs to protect both the authenticity and confidentiality of the private key.

Although the idea of using a client's identity as the base for their key pair is very appealing, it does not come without consequences. Two main issues are:

- Coping with the practicalities of implementation are not insignificant. If we take revocation as an example, because we cannot revoke a person's identity, there is a requirement for additional input to the key generation process. If we include validity dates, key usage, etc. then a push toward broader use of identifying information results, leading naturally to identifier-based cryptography.
- The authenticity of the information that is used as the identity or identifier is now crucial to the security of the system. In a PKI, the certificate is supposed to demonstrate the authenticity of identifying information. In Identity based Cryptography, because a private key may be generated after the public key, the TA may not have validated the authenticity of the information relating to the key pair prior to the public key's use. For example, *A* might use information it thinks is valid to generate a public key for *B*, but the information *A* uses could either relate to the wrong *B*, or may be completely invalid in the eyes of the TA.

As mentioned previously, because the TA is explicitly in charge of the generation of the private keys in an Identity Based Cryptography system, it can verify its security policy each time it hands out a new private key to a client. In the case of the CA in a PKI, the policy is verified at the time of certification, but it is generally left up to the client encrypting the information to verify the certificate content in the light of its own security policy.

While neither of these are design principles is strict – we could, for example, mimic the requirement to always fetch a new key from a TA within a PKI – the way in which the information flows through the system is an important consideration when deciding on which mechanism to use.

Expanding on the example given above, it would seem more natural to implement an Identity based Cryptography for short term keys where the policy at the TA might change regularly. Conversely, it would seem sensible to use a PKI in a widely distributed environment, or in one where the individual policy of each client took a significant role in the policy of the system as a whole.

Identity based Cryptography was introduced as a means of circumventing the difficulties associated with certificate management within PKIs. This has lead to a difference in the way the two proposed mechanisms are architected. We briefly look at the way in which this might affect the choices made when deciding between the two as a security architecture.

- On first inspection, there appears to be a potential for Identity Based Cryptography to develop more lightweight implementations at the client end. This is due to the lack of requirement for storing separate certification, identification and keying information. Provided the authenticity of such information could be verified, this could be useful for scenarios such as mobile systems, where *knowing* the identity of the other contact point in an interaction could be enough to generating keying information on the fly.
- It would appear that a PKI would be the implementation of choice in a widely distributed system. The ability for clients to generate their own key pairs to be certified by a CA which need not directly be in their security domains could provide benefits in some scenarios. For example, the use of third party CAs to certify SSL server keys would be difficult to replace using Idendity based Cryptography. The key escrow facility inherent in Identity Based Cryptography would probably not sit well with a corporation wishing to secure its Internet gateway using an SSL-enabled server.
- Within systems where the security is heavily centralized (i.e. where all users have to trust the CA/TA explicitly anyway) there doesn't seem to be a great deal of difference between PKI and Identity based Cryptography. The choice of which mechanism to implement is likely to come down to how

the protocols that use those mechanisms fit in the wider architecture of the system. This is similar to the situation where there is often little to choose between a symmetric and an asymmetric system in applications where non-repudiation is not a concern.

- In distributed systems where it's difficult to manage a revocation mechanism (e.g. mobile systems), one way which PKIs aim to deal with the problem is to use short lived certificates. This might be addressed more efficiently using Identity Based Cryptography, as the system would only require partial synchrony for the sender to generate a currently valid key for the recipient.

- One of the proposed benefits of PKIs is that they can be organised into hierarchies which reflect the internal structure of a large organisation or group of organisations. While this might seem provide an advantage for PKIs, recent work by Gentry and Silverberg (Gentry et al., 2002) develops mechanisms for implementing similar hierarchies in an Identity based cryptography context.

- An area where a PKI seems to have a distinct advantage over Identity Based Cryptography is in the consequences of the compromise of the CA/TA. While the compromise of a CA is disastrous to the future secure running of the system, if the system has been designed carefully, then all past encrypted traffic is still secure. If the TA within an Identity Based Cryptography system is compromised and the master secret revealed, by the very fact that the attacker now knows the secret from which all keys are derived, the attacker can now decrypt all previously encrypted information. The same would be true of signature keys. As a result, any signature on a document that had not been independently timestamped could be called into question.

In (Gentry, 2003), Gentry introduced the concept of Certificate-Based Encryption (CBE), with a view to simplifying revocation in traditional PKIs.

In Gentry's model, an entity B's private key consists of two components: a component which that entity chooses for itself and keeps private, and a component which is time-dependent and is issued to B on a regular basis by a CA. This second component can be transmitted over a public channel from the CA to B.

Matching the two private key components are two public key components. The first of these matches B's own private component and is assumed to be readily available to any entity A who wishes to encrypt a message to B. The second public component can be computed by A using only some public parameters of the scheme's CA together with the current time value and the assumed value of A's public key.

In encrypting a message to B, A makes use of both public components. Because of the structure of the CBE scheme, A is then assured that B can only decrypt messages encrypted by A if B is in possession of both private components. Thus the second private component acts as an *implicit certificate* for relying parties: one that a relying party can be assured is only available to B provided that B's certification has been issued for the current time period by the CA. The security of CBE depends critically on the CA binding the correct public key into B's implicit certificate in each time period. Thus (quite naturally), the initial registration of users and their public keys must take place over an authentic channel and be bootstrapped from some other basis for trust between B and the CA.

This approach can significantly simplify revocation in PKIs: notice that there is no need for A to make any status checks on B's public key before encrypting a message for B. So there are no CRLs and no requirement for OCSP. Nor are any certificates actually needed by A; rather A needs to be in possession of what it assumes is a copy of B's public key and an authentic version of the CA's public parameters. (Rather, an implicit certificate is needed by B in order to decrypt – for this reason, perhaps *Certificate-Based Decryption* would be a better name for the CBE concept.)

However, the basic CBE approach of (Gentry, 2003) does have a major drawback: the CA needs to issue new implicit certificates to every user in the scheme in every time period. A granularity of one hour per time period is suggested in (Gentry, 2003); this substantially adds to the computation and communication that takes place at the CA for a PKI with even a small user base. The basic CBE approach can be regarded as effectively trading simplified revocation for an increased workload at the CA. It can even be argued that CBE loses the one key feature enjoyed by a traditional PKI: that the certificates issued by the CA allow the CA to distribute trust in an almost off-line manner (the CA needs only to be on-line to perform a revocation function). A number of enhancements to the basic CBE approach are also presented in (Gentry, 2003). These reduce, but do not completely eliminate, the work that must be carried out by the CA.

The specific instantiation of CBE given in (Gentry, 2003) builds on ideas developed in Boneh and Franklin's identity-based public key encryption scheme (Boneh et.al, 2001).

Independently of Gentry's work, Al-Riyami and Paterson (Al-Riyami,S.,S., et.al., 2003) proposed another new model for supporting the use of public key cryptography. The key feature of this model is that it completely eliminates the need for certificates, hence the moniker *certificateless public key cryptography* (CL-PKC). The technical means by which it does so is actually rather closely related to that used in(Gentry, 2003): a user *A*'s private key is composed in two stages. In the first stage, an identity-dependent *partial private key* is received over a confidential and authentic channel from a trusted authority (called a key generation centre, KGC). In the second stage, the user produces his private key by combining the partial private key with some secret known only to the user.

The user also publishes a public key which matches the private key. However, this public key need not be supported by a certificate. Instead, an entity *A* who wishes to rely on *B*'s public key is assured that if the KGC has done its job properly, then only *B* who is in possession of the correct partial private key and user-generated secret could perform the decryption, generate the signature, etc.

In fact, CL-PKC allows *A* to use *B*'s public key but to choose an identifier for *B*. In order to decrypt *A*'s message, *B* must then fetch the correct partial private key from the KGC. Thus CL-PKC supports the temporal re-ordering of public and private key generation in the same way as Identity based Cryptography does.

CL-PKC combines elements from Identity Based Cryptography and traditional PKI. The schemes are no longer identity-based: they involve the use of *B*'s public key which is no longer simply derived from *B*'s identity. However, as we have already discussed, when using Identity based Cryptography in practice, it is rare that the public keys will depend on identities alone. On the other hand, CL-PKC avoids the key escrow inherent in Identity Based Cryptography by having user-specific private information involved in the key generation process. And CL-PKC does not need certificates to generate trust in public keys; instead this trust is produced in an implicit way. This would appear to make CL-PKC ideal for systems where escrow is unacceptable, but where the full weight of PKI is untenable. For example, it might be well suited to a mobile e-commerce application where signatures are needed to ensure non-repudiation of payments.

Perhaps not surprisingly, it is possible to convert a CL-PKC encryption (CL-PKE) scheme into a CBE scheme: if *B*'s identity in the CL-PKE scheme is extended to include a time period along with the public key, then the CL-PKE scheme effectively becomes a CBE scheme. On the other hand, if one omits certain fields from the certificates in a CBE scheme, one obtains an encryption scheme that is functionally similar to a CL-PKE scheme.

GROUP BASED CRYPTOGRAPHY

Algorithmic problems of group theory and Semi-group theory that we consider in this section are of two different kinds (Myasnikov,A., et.al., 2008):

1. *Decision problems* are problems of the following nature: given a property P and an object O, find out whether or not the object O has the property P.
2. *Search problems* are of the following nature: given a property P and the information that there are objects with the property P, find at least one particular object with the property P.

We discuss several particular algorithmic problems of group theory that have been used in cryptography.

The *word problem* (WP) is: given a recursive presentation of a group G and an element $g \in G$, find out whether or not $g = 1$ in G.

The *word search problem* (WSP) is: given a recursive presentation of a group G and an element $g = 1$ in G, find a presentation of g as a product of conjugates of defining relators and their inverses

The *conjugacy problem* (CP) is: given a recursive presentation of a group G and two elements $g, h \in G$, find out whether or not there is an element $x \in G$ such that $x^{-1}gx = h$.

The *conjugacy search problem* (CSP) is: given a recursive presentation of a group G and two conjugate elements $g, h \in G$, find a particular element $x \in G$ such that $x^{-1}gx = h$.

The *decomposition search problem*: given a recursive presentation of a group G, two recursively generated subgroups $A, B \leq G$, and two elements $g, h \in G$, find two elements $x \in A$ and $y \in B$ that would satisfy $x \cdot g \cdot y = h$, provided at least one such pair of elements exists.

The *factorization problem*: given an element w of a recursively presented group G and two subgroups $A, B \leq G$, find out whether or not there are two elements $a \in A$ and $b \in B$ such that $a \cdot b = w$.

The *factorization search problem*: given an element w of a recursively presented group G and two recursively generated subgroups $A, B \leq G$, find any two elements $a \in A$ and $b \in B$ that would satisfy $a \cdot b = w$, provided at least one such pair of elements exists.

The *membership problem*: given a recursively presented group G, a subgroup $H \leq G$ generated by $h_1, \ldots, h_k$, and an element $g \in G$, find out whether or not $g \in H$.

The *membership search problem*: given a recursively presented group G, a subgroup $H \leq G$ generated by $h_1, \ldots, h_k$, and an element $h \in H$, find an expression of h in terms of $h_1, \ldots, h_k$.

The *isomorphism problem* is: given two finitely presented groups G_1 and G_2, find out whether or not they are isomorphic.

A Public key cryptosystem based on the word problem: A finitely presented group G consists of generators $x_1, x_2, \ldots x_n$ and relators $r_1 = e, r_2 = e, \ldots, r_m = e$. Corresponding to each generator x_i, there is an inverse x_i^{-1}. The empty string e is also a word, the identity of the group. Each of the r_i above is a word. The group operation of combining words is concatenation. For each word w, the inverse word w^{-1} consists of all the symbols of w written in reverse order, where x_i is replaced by x_i^{-1} and x_i^{-1} is replaced by x_i. The group G consists of equivalence classes of all possible words. Two words w and v are equivalent in G if we can transform w to v by a finite sequence of replacement rules of the form

Rule 1: Changing $x_i x_i^{-1}$ or $x_i^{-1} x_i$ to e, that is eliminating $x_i x_i^{-1}$ or $x_i^{-1} x_i$.
Rule 2: Introducing $x_i x_i^{-1}$ or $x_i^{-1} x_i$ at any point,

Rule 3: Changing r_i or r_i^{-1} to e, that is eliminating r_i or r_i^{-1},

Rule 4: Introducing r_i or r_i^{-1} at any point.

The word problem for a group G is the decision problem that asks for each word w, whether w is equivalent to the identity of G. It turns out there exist specific groups for which the word problem is undecidable.

There is a similar and simpler word problem for semigroups. We start with generators and words in the generators as before but without the inverses. Instead of relators we have a list of equations of the form $a_1=b_1, a_2=b_2,\ldots a_m=b_m$. In defining equivalent words we can only replace any occurrence of a_i by b_i and vice versa. The discussion of groups can be regarded as a special case of semigroups since one could regard the group as a semigroup with extra symbols x_i^{-1} and extra equations $x_i x_i^{-1} = e$.

Now we can define a cryptosystem based on the *word* problem. To use the word problem to encrypt a single bit, start with a finitely presented group G and two special words w_1 and w_2 known to be inequivalent in G. Choose one of w_1 or w_2 and randomly apply Rule (i) to Rule (iv) to the word, resulting in a word v equivalent to either w_1 or w_2 (but not both). Thus the public key consists of the group G and the special words w_1 and w_2.

This is a randomized encryption procedure (Rivest, R. et.al., 1983) and there are infinitely many possible ciphertexts corresponding to each plaintext bit and the system has an arbitrarily large expansion factor. With good choices for the group and special words in the encryption method, it appears that decryption can be made very difficult.

CHAOS BASED CRYPTOGRAPHY

Chaotic systems are defined on real numbers. Any encryption algorithm which uses chaotic maps when implemented on a computer (finite-state machine) becomes a transformation from a finite set onto itself(Kocarev,L., 2001). An example is the public key cryptosystem based on the Finite State Chebyshev maps. A chebyshev polynomial map $T_p: R \rightarrow R$ of degree p is defined using the following recurrent relation:

$$T_{p+1}(x) = 2xT_p(x) + T_{p-1}(x)$$

With $T_0=1$ and $T_1=x$. This Chebyshev polynomial is restricted to the interval [-1.1] is a well-known chaotic map for all $p > 1$. The Finite-state Chebshev map $F_p: \{0,1,\ldots.N-1\} \rightarrow \{0,1,\ldots N-1\}$ is defined as:

$$y = T_p(_x) \ (\mathrm{mod}\ N)$$

where x and N are integers.

A public key cryptosystem based on the finite state chebyshev map: The algorithm consists of two steps: algorithm for key generation and algorithm for encryption.

Algorithm for key generation: Alice should do the following:

1. Generate two large random and distinct prime numbers p and q each roughly the same size.

2. Compute N=pq and $\varphi =(p^2-1)(q^2-1)$
3. Select a random integer e, $1 < e < \varphi$, such that gcd(e, φ)=1.
4. Compute the unique integer d, $1< d < \varphi$ such that $ed \equiv 1$ (mod φ)
5. Alice's public key is (N,e); Alice's private key is d.

Algorithm for Encryption:

1. **Encryption:** To encrypt a message m, Bob should do the following:
   a. Obtain Alice's authentic public key (N,e).
   b. Represent the message as an integer in the interval [1,N-1].
   c. Compute c=$T_e(m)$ (mod N) and send to Alice.
2. **Decryption:** To recover the message m from c, Alice should do the following:
   a. Use the private key d to recover m =$T_d(c)$(mod N)

The following property of the finite-state Chebyshev map holds:

$T_d(T_e(x)) \equiv x$(mod N).

Some examples of Chebyshev polynomials are:

$T_2(x) = 2x^2-1$

$T_3(x)=4x^3-8x^2+1$

$T4(x)=8x^4-8x^2+1$

SUMMARY

This chapter explored the development of Public Key Cryptography like Hash based Cryptography, Lattice based Cryptography,Group Based Cryptography and others. It remains to be studied to see how these public key cryptosystems compare with one another in terms of processing cost, difficulty in key generation and resistance against cryptographic attacks. The performance study of the implementations of these cryptosystems is very much required so the applications of these cryptosystems can be better understood.

REFERENCES

Al-Riyami, S. S., & Paterson, K. G. (2003). Certificateless public key cryptography. Proceedings of Asiacrypt 2003. doi:10.1007/978-3-540-40061-5_29

Bernstein, D.J., Buchmann, J., & Damen, E. (Eds.). (2009). *Post-Quantum Cryptography*. Springer-Verlag.

Boneh, D., & Franklin, M. (2001). Identity-Based Encryption from the Weil Pairing. *Proceedings of CRYPTO 2001*, 213-229. doi:10.1007/3-540-44647-8_13

Buchman, J., Dahmen, E., Ereth, S., Hulsing, A., & Ruckert, M. (2011a). On the Security of the Winternitz One-Time Signature Scheme. *AFRICACRYPT'11 Proceedings of the 4th International Conference on Progrewss in Cryptology in Africa.* Retrieved from: https://eprint.iacr.org/2011/191.pdf

Buchmann, J., & Hülsing, A. (2011b). XMSS — A Practical Forward Secure Signature Scheme based on Minimal Security Assumptions. In B.-Y. Yang (Ed.), *Post-Quantum Cryptography* (Vol. 7071). Springer. doi:10.1007/978-3-642-25405-5_8

Cocks, C. (2001). An Identity Based Encryption Scheme Based on Quadratic Residues. *Cryptography and Coding - Institute of Mathematics and Its Applications International Conference on Cryp-tography and Coding, Proceedings of IMA 2001*, 360-363.

Diffie, W., & Hellman, M. E. (1976). New Directions in Cryptography. *IEEE Transactions on Information Theory*, *22*(6), 644–654. doi:10.1109/TIT.1976.1055638

Diffie, W. (1988). The first ten years of Public-Key Cryptography. *Proceedings of the IEEE*, *76*(5), 560–577. doi:10.1109/5.4442

Gentry, C., & Silverberg, A. (2002). Hierarchical ID-based cryptography. Advances in Cryptology – ASIACRYPT 2002, 548-566.

Gentry, C. (2003). Certificate-based encryption and the certificate revocation problem. Advances in Cryptology – EUROCRYPT 2003, 272-293. doi:10.1007/3-540-39200-9_17

Hoffstein, J., Pipher, J., & Silverman, J. H. (1998). NTRU: a ring based public key cryptosystem. *Proceedings of ANTS-III*, 267–288. doi:10.1007/BFb0054868

Kerry, C. F., & Gallagher, P. D. (2013). *FIPS PUB 186-4, Digital Signature Standard*. National Institute of Standards and Technology.

Koblitz, N., & Menezes, A. (2010). *Intractable Problems in Cryptography*. International Association for Cryptological Research. Retrieved from: http://eprint.iacr.org/2010/290.pdf

Kocarev, L. (2001). Chaos-Based Cryptography: A Brief Overview, (Invited paper). *IEEE Circuits and Magazine*, *1*(3), 6–21. doi:10.1109/7384.963463

Kocarev, L., & Lian, S. (Eds.). (2011). *Chaos-Based Cryptography Theory Algorithms and Applications*. Springer.

Hoffman, P. (2012). *Elliptic Curve Digital Signature Algorithm (DSA) for DNSSEC*. RFC6605. doi:10.1007/978-3-642-20542-2

Lamport, L. (1979). *Constructing digital signatures from a one way function*. Technical Report SRI-CSL-98, SRI International Computer Science Laboratory. Retrieved from http://research.microsoft.com/en-us/um/people/lamport/pubs/dig-sig.pdf

Magyarik, M. R., & Wagner, N. R. (1985). Lecture Notes in Computer Science: Vol. 196. *A Public Key Cryptosystem Based on the Word Problem*. Berlin: Springer.

Matsumoto, T., & Imai, H. (1988). Public quadratic polynomial-tuples for efficient signature verification and message-encryption. Advances in Cryptology, 419-453.

McEliece, R.J., (1978). A Public-Key Cryptosystem based Algebraic Coding Theory. *DSN Progress Report*, 42-44.

Merkle, R. C. (1989). A Certified Digital Signature. *Advances in Cryptology, CRYPTO '89 Proceedings,* 218-238.

Mollin, R. (2003). *RSA and Public-Key Cryptography*. Chapman & Hall/CRC.

Myasnikov, A., Shpilrain, V., & Ushakov, A. (2008). *Group-based Cryptography*. Birkauser.

Patarin, J. (1986). *Hidden Fields Equations (HFE) and Isomorphisms of Polynomials(IP): Two new families of Asymmetric Algorithms*. Springer-Verlag.

Patarin, J., & Goubin, L. (1997). Trapdoor one-way permutations and multivariate polynomials. *International Conference on Information Security and Cryptology,* 356-368. Retrieved from http:// citeseer. nj.nec.com/patarin97trapdoor.html

Patarin, J., Goubin, L., & Courtois, N. T. (1998). Improved algorithms for isomoprhisms of polynomials, *Advances in Cryptology,* 184-200. Retrieved from http://www.minrank.org/ip6long.ps

Rivest, R. L., Shamir, A., & Adleman, L. (1978). A Method for Obtaining Digital Signatures and Public-Key Cryptosystems. *Communications of the ACM, 21*(2).

Sahai, A., & Waters, B. (2004). *Fuzzy Identity Based Encryption*. IACR ePrint Archive, Report 2004/086. Retrieved from http://eprint.iacr.org/

Shamir, A. (1984). Identity-Based Cryptosystems and Signature Schemes. *Advances in Cryptology: Proceedings of CRYPTO 84, Lecture Notes in Computer Science, 7,* 47—53.

KEY TERMS AND DEFINITIONS

Ciphertext: The output of an encryption function using a particular key and a plaintext. If the key is available and the algorithm is known, the plaintext can be obtained from the ciphertext.

Codes: Codes are representation of objects. An example is representation of integers using the binary digits 0 and 1.

Confidentiality: This term refers to protection against eavesdropping or snooping which is usually achieved by means of encrypting messages.

Groups: Groups are mathematical objects which satisfy certain properties like closure, associativity, identity and invertibility.

Hash Functions: A hash function is a function that converts its input message into a fixed size hash. The hash values of messages can be used to create signatures of a given message.

Integrity: This term refers to protection against modification of a message which is usually achieved by creating a hash of a message and verifying the hash at the receiver.

Lattice: Lattice is an abstract structure in mathematics that consists of a partially ordered set in which every two elements have a unique supremum (a least upper bound) or a unique infimum (a greatest lower bound). An example is the set of natural numbers partially ordered by divisibility for which the unique supremum is the least common multiple and the unique infimum is the greatest common divisor.

Non-Repudiation: A property by which the sender or receiver of a message cannot deny having sent or received a message. This is usually achieved by encrypting the hash of a message by the private key of the sender.

Plaintext: This term refers to the input of an encryption function. Although traditionally it referred to the English text, it is now used to describe binary input to an encryption function.

Public Key Cryptography: An encryption system which uses a pair of keys private and public. The public key is used for encryption and the private key is used for decryption.

Public Key Infrastructure: A system to sign, distribute and validate public keys. The user's public keys are signed by the Certificate Authority which can be used to verify the validity of public keys.

Quadratic Equations: A polynomial of degree two expressed as $ax^2+bx+c=0$ where a,b,c are constants and x is a variable.

Signature: This term signature refers to encrypted hash of a message. The signature associates a signer and a message using the signer's private key.

Symmetric Key Cryptography: An encryption system which uses a single private key for encryption and decryption. The sender and the receiver must have the same key.

Chapter 2
Problems in Cryptography and Cryptanalysis

Kannan Balasubramanian
Mepco Schlenk Engineering College, India

Rajakani M.
Mepco Schlenk Engineering College, India

ABSTRACT

The integer factorization problem used in the RSA cryptosystem, the discrete logarithm problem used in Diffie-Hellman Key Exchange protocol and the Elliptic Curve Discrete Logarithm problem used in Elliptic Curve Cryptography are traditionally considered the difficult problems and used extensively in the design of cryptographic algorithms. We provide a number of other computationally difficult problems in the areas of Cryptography and Cryptanalysis. A class of problems called the Search problems, Group membership problems, and the Discrete Optimization problems are examples of such problems. A number of computationally difficult problems in Cryptanalysis have also been identified including the Cryptanalysis of Block ciphers, Pseudo-Random Number Generators and Hash functions.

INTRODUCTION

Cryptography is the science of 'hidden writing' meaning ability to transform the original text into a form that is not intelligible to other parties. Cryptanalysis is the science of uncovering the plaintext from the ciphertext or guessing the key given sufficient plaintext-ciphertext pairs. The problems in distributing the key in symmetric Key Cryptosystems led to the invention of Public Key Cryptosystems which are usually based on a mathematically and computationally difficult problem. This chapter surveys the mathematical basis on which most of the cryptography algorithms are based on. This chapter also surveys the different types of attacks on cryptosystems and the threat models which cryptanalysts in analyzing the strength of the cryptographic algorithms. The fields of Cryptography and Cryptanalysis present a number of problems that are both computational and information-theoretic in nature. Those problems are discussed in the following paragraphs.

DOI: 10.4018/978-1-5225-2915-6.ch002

PROBLEMS IN CRYPTOGRAPHY

In search for more efficient and/or secure alternatives to established cryptographic protocols (such as RSA which is based on the factorization problem), there have been proposals for public key establishment protocols as well as with public key cryptosystems based on hard search problems from combinatorial (semi) group theory. These problems include the conjugacy search problem (Anshel et al.,1999; Ko, 2000), the homomorphism search problem (Grigoriev et al., 2006; Shpilrain, 2006a), the decomposition search problem (Cha et.al, 2001; Ko, 2000; Shpilrain, 2005) and the subgroup membership search problem (Shpilrain, 2006b). All these are problems of the following nature: given a property P and the information that there are objects with the property *P*, find at least one particular object with the property *P* from a pool *S* of objects.

The following problems have been considered difficult problems and used in cryptography.

The RSA Problem: Given a positive integer *n* that is a product of two distinct odd primes *p* and *q* and a positive integer *e* such that $\gcd(e,(p\text{-}1)(q\text{-}1)) = 1$ and an integer *c*, find an integer *m* such that $m^e \equiv c \pmod{n}$.

The RSA Problem is that of finding the eth roots modulo a composite integer *n*. The underlying one-way function $f(x) = x^e \pmod{n}$ (f: $Z_n \rightarrow Z_n$) is called the RSA function. Z_n is the set of integers modulo *n* i.e., $Z_n = \{0, 1, 2, \ldots n\text{-}1\}$. Addition, Subtraction and Multiplication are performed modulo *n*. The inverse is $f(x)^{-1} = x^d \pmod{n}$, where $d \equiv e^{-1} \pmod{\varphi(n)}$

The Quadratic Residuosity Problem: Given an odd composite integer *n* and integer having Jacobi symbol $\left(\dfrac{a}{n}\right) = 1$, decide whether or not *a* is a quadratic residue modulo *n*. The integer *a* is said to be a quadratic residue if there exists an *x* such that $x^2 \equiv a \pmod{n}$.

If the prime factorization is $n = p_1^{e_1} p_2^{e_2} \ldots p_m^{e_m}$. then the Jacobi symbol is evaluated as

$$\left(\frac{a}{n}\right) = \left(\frac{a}{p_1}\right)^{e_1} \left(\frac{a}{p_2}\right)^{e_2} \ldots \left(\frac{a}{p_m}\right)^{e_m}$$

where $\left(\dfrac{a}{p_i}\right)$ evaluates to 0, 1, or -1 if *a* divides p_i or *a* is a quadratic residue or if *a* is a quadratic non-residue of p_i.

The Square Root Modulo n Problem: Given a composite integer *n* and $a \in Q_n$ (the set of quadratic residues modulo *n*), find a square root of *a* modulo *n*.

If the factors *p* an *q* of are known, then the square root problem can be efficiently by first finding square roots of *a* modulo *p* and *a* modulo *q* and then combining them using Chinese Remainder Theorem (Zhu, 2001).

The subset-sum problem: Given positive integers (or weights) $s_1, s_2, \ldots s_n$, and T, determine whether there is a subset of the s_i's that sums to T. This is equivalent to determining a (0-1) vector $x = (x_1, x_2, \ldots x_n)$ such that

$$\sum_{i=1}^{n} x_i s_i = T$$

If one thinks of T as the capacity of the knapsack and the s_i as the sizes of the various items, then the question is whether the knapsack can be filled by some collection of the items. The subset sum problem is known to be a hard problem. However, it can be solved easily for some special cases such as having a "hidden structure" or "low density" where density is defined as $n/\log$ T. If s is chosen as the superincreasing sequence where

$$s_j > \sum_{i=0}^{j-1} s_i$$

where $2 \leq j \leq n$, then the resulting knapsack is easy to solve.

The Merkle-Hellman Cryptosystem (Merkle, 1978) uses a superincreasing sequence as an easy knapsack and disguises it using modular multiplication. The original set serves as the private key while the transformed set can serve as the public key. In the setup, the receiver first chooses a prime p exceeding the sum of all p_i's as well as a multiplier a. Then he disguises his superincreasing sequence into a seemingly arbitrarily one by a modular transformation,

$$t_i = as_i \bmod p$$

Any solution $(x_1, x_2, \ldots, x_n)$ to the knapsack problem $\sum_{i=1}^{n} x_i t_i = y$ is also a solution to the knapsack

problem $\sum_{i=1}^{n} x_i s_i = z$ where z = a^{-1}y mod p. The public key is t. The private key is (p,a,s).

Despite the transformation, the knapsack systems have been to be insecure against attacks (Shamir, 1984).

The Subset-Product Problem: The subset-product problem is to determine, given positive integers (or weights) $s_1, s_2, \ldots s_n$ whether there is a subset of the s_i's such that the product (i.e., the result of multiplying together all in the subset) is equal to K.

Okamoto (Okamoto et al., 2000) proposed a quantum public-key scheme based on the subset-product problem. The security of the quantum public-key cryptosystem is based on the hardness of the subset-product problem.

The Discrete Logarithm Problem: Given a prime p, a generator α of Z_p^* and an element $\beta \in Z_p^*$, find the integer x, such that $0 \; 0 \leq x \leq p-2$, such that $\alpha^x \equiv \beta(\bmod p)$. The Z_n^* is the multiplicative group of Z_n defined as $Z_n^* = \left\{ a \in Z_n \mid \gcd(a,n) = 1 \right\}$.

The Generalized Discrete Logarithm Problem: Given a finite cyclic group G of order n, a generator α of G, and an element $\beta \in G$, find the integer x, $0 \leq x \leq n-1$ such that $\alpha^x \equiv \beta$.

The groups of most interest in Cryptography are the multiplicative group F_q^* of the finite field F_q including the particular case of the multiplicative group Z_p^* of the integers modulo a prime p, and the multiplicative group $F_{2^m}^*$ of the finite field F_{2^m} of characteristic two. Also of interest are the group Z_n^*

where n is a composite integer, the group of points defined over an elliptic field, and the Jacobian of a hyperelliptic curve defined over a finite field (Menezes, 1996).

The discrete logarithm problem is a well-studied problem. The best discrete logarithms have expected running times similar to those of the factoring algorithms. Currently the best algorithms to solve the discrete logarithm problem are broken into two classes: Index-calculus methods and collision search methods. Index calculus methods are very similar to the fastest current methods for integer factoring and they run in superpolynomial time. Collision search algorithms run in exponential time. Index Calculus problems require certain properties to be present whereas collision search algorithms can be applied much more generally. Collision search methods are the best known methods for attacking the general elliptic curve Discrete Logarithm problem. Closely related to the Discrete Logarithm problem is the Diffie-Hellman problem.

The Diffie-Hellman Problem: Given a prime p, a generator α of Z_p^*, and elements $\alpha^a \bmod p$, and $\alpha^b \bmod p$, find $\alpha^{ab} \bmod p$.

The Generalized Diffie-Hellman Problem: Given a finite cyclic group G, a generator α of G, and group elements α^a and α^b, find α^{ab}.

The Elgamal encryption is based on the Diffie-Hellman problem (El gamal, 1985). The Elgmal encryption is probabilistic as there will be many ciphertexts that are encryptions of the same plaintext. The problem of breaking the Elgamal encryption is equivalent to breaking the Diffie-Hellman problem. Analysis based on the best algorithms for both factoring and discrete logarithms shows that RSA and Elgamal have similar security for equivalent key lengths. The main disadvantage of Elgamal is the need for randomness and its slower speed. Another potential disadvantage of the Elgamal system is that message expansion by a factor takes place during encryption. However, such message expansion can be tolerated if the cryptosystem is used only for exchange of secret keys.

The Elliptic Curve Discrete Logarithm Problem: Given an elliptic curve E_p, a point $P \in E_p$ of order n and a point $Q \in E_p$ find $a \in Z_n$ such that Q= aP, provided that such an a exists. An elliptic curve consists of elements (x,y) satisfying the equation $y^2 \equiv x^3+ax+b \pmod{p}$ where $a,b \equiv Z_p$ are constants such that $4a^3+27b^2 \neq 0 \pmod{p}$ together with a special element Θ called the point at infinity.

Elliptic Curve Cryptosystems are analogs of public key cryptosystems (such as RSA and Elgamal) in which modular multiplication is replaced by Elliptic Curve addition operation (Koblitz, 1987; Miller, 1985). One can easily construct Elliptic Curve encryption, signature, and key agreement schemes by making analogs of Elgamal, DSA and Diffie-Hellman. Elliptic Key Cryptosystems have emerged as a promising new area in public-key cryptography in recent years due to their potential for offering similar security to established public-key cryptosystems with reduced key sizes.

The Syndrome Decoding Problem: Given a linear code (n, k, d) and a syndrome of a vector, find the nearest codeword to the vector.

An (n, k) linear code is a k-dimensional subspace of $(Z_2)^n$, the vector space of all binary n-tuples. The distance d between two n-tuples is the number of coordinates in which the two n-tuples differ. The minimal distance of a (n, k) code is the minimum of distances between any two n-tuples. A code with a minimal distance is denoted as (n, k, d) code.

The purpose of an error correcting code is to correct random errors in the transmission of (binary) data through a noisy channel. Let G be a generating matrix for an (n, k, d) code. Suppose Alice wants to transmit a binary k-tuple x. She encodes x as $y = x$G and sends y through the channel. Suppose Bob receives the n-tuple r, which may or may not be the same as y. He will decode r using the strategy of nearest neighbor decoding. That is, to find the codeword y' that has minimum distance to r. Then he decodes r to y' and finally, determines the k-tuple x' such that $y' = x'G$. If $y' = y$ then $x' = x$ and the transmission errors have been corrected. If at most $(d-1)/2$ errors occurred, then nearest neighbor decoding can correct all errors.

An efficient approach for nearest neighbor decoding is through the use of parity check matrices. A parity-check matrix for (n, k, d) linear code is an $(n-k)$ x n binary matrix with the property that for each vector of the code the product (mod 2) of the matrix by the vector is zero. This product can be computed for any vector and is called the syndrome. A syndrome is a column vector with $(n-k)$ components. A vector is a codeword only if its syndrome is zero.

The syndrome decoding problem is a hard problem meaning that there is no polynomial time algorithm for solving the problem in the worst case. However, for some special classes of codes, polynomial-time algorithms are known to exist. One such class of codes, the Goppa codes are used as the basis of the McEliece cryptosystem.

The McEliece cryptosystem (McEliece, 1978) is based on the intractability of the syndrome decoding problem. The idea is to select a code for which an efficient decoding algorithm is known and then disguise it as a general-looking linear code. A description of the original code can serve the private key while the description of the transformed code serves as the public key. Goppa Codes are used in the McEliece cryptosystem.

Compared with other public-key cryptosystems which involve modular exponentiation, the McEliece scheme has the advantage of high-speed encryption and decryption. An implementation of this scheme would be two to three orders magnitude faster than RSA. In addition, the McEliece scheme employs probabilistic encryption, which is better than other types of deterministic encryption in preventing the elimination of any information leaked through public-key cryptography. The McEliece scheme suffers from the drawback that the public key is very large. Another drawback is that there is message expansion by a factor of n/k. For the parameters n=1024, t=38 and k $\geq$ 644, the public key is about 2^{19} bits in size, while the message expansion factor is 1.6.

The Shortest Vector Problem: Given a basis of a lattice L, find the shortest nonzero vector $v \in L$.

The Closest Vector Problem: Given a basis of a lattice L and a vector $v \in R^n$, find a lattice vector which minimizes the distance to v.

The Smallest Basis Problem: Find a lattice basis that minimizes the length of the longest vector.

Let B = $\{b_1, b_2, ..., b_m\}$ be a set of linearly independent vectors in R^n (so that $m \leq n$). The set L of all integer linear combinations of $b_1, b_2, ..., b_m$ is called a lattice of dimension m. The set B is called a basis for the lattice L.

Lattices are regular arrangements of points in n-dimensional space. A lattice can have infinitely many bases when $m \geq 2$. Since a lattice is discrete, it has a shortest nonzero vector. The goal of lattice reduction is to find interesting lattice bases, such as bases consisting of reasonably short and almost orthogonal vectors.

Two lattice-based public key cryptosystems have been proposed so far: the Ajtai-Dwork (AD)Cryptosystem and Goldwasser-Goldreich-Halevi (GGH) Cryptosystem. The AD cryptosystem is based on a variant of the shortest vector problem whereas the GGH Cryptosystem is based on the Closest vector problem. The drawback of the AD cryptosystem is the huge public-key size and message expansion.

Matrix Decomposition Problem: Many cryptographic schemes have been based on the matrix decomposition problem (Meletiou et al., 2015). The LU factorization (also called LU decomposition) has been used in many cryptographic schemes. Factorizing a matrix A = L.U is computationally feasible, but however reconstructing the matrix knowing only U or only L is a difficult problem (Choi et al., 2004). The matrix A can be used for the representation of an image, a diagram or a data table. The main idea is to factorize A in order to achieve availability, persistence, integrity and confidentiality of the information. The LU decomposition has been used in key-predistribution schemes (Choi et al., 2005). Users are represented as nodes where each node corresponds to i-th row and i-th column of a symmetric matrix $A = \left(A_{ij} \right)_{1 \leq i \leq j \leq n}$ and the entry $A_{ij} = A_{ji}$ is the symmetric key between the i-th and j-th user. The matrix A is decomposed as A= L.U. The i-th row of L is kept secret by the user as the private key, while the i-th column of U is the public key. Users i and j exchange their columns and compute A_{ij} and A_{ji} respectively which coincide since A is symmetric.

User Authentication Schemes also have been proposed based on LU decomposition. A user is authenticated from a central server. A central authority generates a symmetric square matrix A and assigns an entry of the form $A_{ij} = A_{ji}$ for each user and matrix A is factorized as A = L.U and a smart card is issued to each user. The information which is contained on the card includes the i-th column of U, key A_{ij}, j in encrypted form and the identity of the user. The main idea is to derive authentication by comparing A_{ij} and A_{ji} since A is symmetric.

Problems in Cryptography as Discrete Optimization Tasks: In (Laskari et al., 2005), a number of problems originating from the integer factorization problem are formulated as discrete optimization tasks. Tow evolutionary computation algorithms, namely the particle swarm optimization method and the differential evolution method are proposed to tackle several instances of the optimization problems.

The first problem under consideration is defined as follows: Given a composite integer N, find pairs of integers $x,y \in Z_N^*$ such that $x^2 \equiv y^2 \pmod{N}$ with $x \neq \pm y \pmod{N}$. This problem is equivalent to finding non-trivial factors of N, as N divides $(x^2-y^2) = (x-y)(x+y)$, but N does not divide either $(x-y)$ or $(x+y)$. Hence the gcd$(x-y, N)$ is a non-trivial factor of N. This problem can be formulated as a discrete optimization task by defining the minimization function f: $\{1, 2, ...N-1\} \times \{1, 2, ...N-1\} \rightarrow \{0, 1, ...N-1\}$ with

$$f(x,y) = x^2 - y^2 \pmod{N}$$

subjected to the constraints $x \neq \pm y \pmod{N}$. The constraint $x= -y$ can be incorporated to the problem by changing the domain of the function. Thus the problem reduces to minimizing the function g: $\{2,3... (N-1)/2\} \times \{2, 3, ...(N-1)/2\} \rightarrow \{0, 1, ...N-1\}$ with

$$g(x,y) = x^2 - y^2 \pmod{N}$$

subjected to the constraint $x \neq y \pmod{N}$. The minimization problem is two-dimensional and the global minimum of the function g is zero. Similar problems that can be studied are:

Minimize the following: $h := \{1, ...N-1\} \rightarrow \{0,...N-1\}$ with

$$h(x) = (x-a)(x-b) \pmod{N}$$

where a, b are non-zero integers and $x \neq a \pmod{N}$ and $x \neq b \pmod{N}$. In a more general form we can consider the minimization of the function

$w(x) = (x\text{-}a)(x\text{-}b)\ldots(x\text{-}m) \pmod{N}$

where $x \in \{0,, .,,N\text{-}1\}$ and $x \neq \{a,b,\ldots m\} \bmod N$.

PROBLEMS IN CRYPTANALYSIS

Similar to the problems in the design of cryptosystems, we can think of computationally difficult problems in Cryptanalysis. We describe the attack models and the problems in cryptanalysis. The concept of attack against a block cipher includes several notions: its outcome, the threat model in which it can be realized, its type, and its complexity (Junod, 2005).

Outcome of an Attack

According to the type of information recovered during an attack, (Knudsen, 1998) classified the possible outcomes of an attack in a hierarchical way.

- **Total Break:** An adversary recovers (or reconstructs) the secret key k.
- **Global Deduction:** An adversary finds an algorithm functionally equivalent to $e_k(.)$ or $d_k(.)$ without knowing the actual value of the key k where $e_k(.)$ and $d_k(.)$ refer to encryption and decryption using key k. A global deduction is possible when a block cipher contains "block structures", i.e. if certain subsets of the ciphertext are independent of certain subsets of the plaintext; in this case, independent of the key length, such a block cipher is vulnerable to a global deduction in a known-plaintext attack. Another possibility of global deduction is that an attack is able to recover the round subkeys but not the key, in the case where the key-schedule algorithm is designed to be a (secure) one-way function, for instance.
- **Instance (Local) Deduction:** An adversary finds the plaintext (or ciphertext) of an intercepted ciphertext (or plaintext) which (s)he did not obtain from the legitimate sender. An instance deduction may be as dangerous as a total break if the number of likely plaintexts (or ciphertexts) is small.
- **Distinguishing Attack:** An adversary is able to tell whether the attacked block cipher is a permutation chosen uniformly at random from the set of all permutations or one of the 2^l permutations specified by the secret key. Distinguishing attacks are often considered as the least serious threat in practice; however, they often can be transformed into a key-recovery attack which may lead to a total break (or a global deduction).

In addition to these four outcomes, (Knudsen, 1998) defines an "information deduction attack": an adversary gains some information about the secret key, the plaintexts or the ciphertexts (s)he did not have a priori. For instance, an adversary, after an attack, may learn that some plaintexts are distributed according to ASCII English text or that the key comes from a subset of the set of all possible keys. In practice, an information deduction may be a serious problem if the plaintext (or ciphertext) possesses low entropy.

Threat Model

A usual model of threats classification consists in building a hierarchy of attacks according to the adversary's potential (or assumed) capabilities, ranked from the least powerful attacks to the most powerful ones:

- **Ciphertext-Only Attack:** In this kind of passive attack, an adversary tries to deduce some information about the key (or about the plaintext) by only observing a certain amount of ciphertexts. Usually, one assumes some known property about the plaintext or the key; for instance, the adversary may know that the plaintext consists of ASCII characters. Block ciphers vulnerable to ciphertext only attacks are considered to be completely broken.
- **Known-Plaintext Attack:** In this case, one assumes that an adversary knows a certain amount of plaintext-ciphertext pairs; the goal of this kind of passive attack consists in finding the key. Typically, one encounters known-plaintext attacks in scenarios where an adversary can observe encrypted version of well-known data, like the data exchanged during the setup phase of a protocol, for instance. A typical example of known-plaintext attack is the linear cryptanalysis.
- **Non-Adaptive Chosen-Plaintext Attack:** When performing this kind of active attack, the adversary is able to choose plaintexts and obtains the corresponding ciphertexts; the plaintext must not depend on the obtained ciphertexts. Subsequently, the adversary uses any information deduced in order to recover either the key, or plaintext(s) corresponding to previously unseen ciphertext(s). One may encounter such a scenario for instance when a tamper-proof module implementing a block cipher with a fixed key falls in the hands of an adversary and where it is not possible to recover directly the key (e.g. with physical means). A typical example of a non-adaptive chosen-plaintext attack is the differential cryptanalysis.
- **Adaptive Chosen-Plaintext Attack:** Such an attack is a chosen-plaintext attack wherein the choice of the plaintext may depend on the ciphertext received from previous requests.
- **(Non-) Adaptive Chosen-Ciphertext Attack:** One assumes that the adversary is able to decrypt arbitrary ciphertexts (in an adaptive way or not) and obtain the corresponding plaintext with the objective of re-covering the key or to encrypt a (not previously observed) plaintext. In the context of block ciphers, this kind of attack is very similar to chosen-plaintext attacks.
- **Combined Chosen-Plaintext and Chosen-Ciphertext Attack:** This extremely powerful type of adaptive attacks assumes that the adversary can encrypt and decrypt arbitrary texts as desired. A typical example of such an attack is Wagner's boomerang attack (Wagner, 1999).
- **Related-Key Attack:** This model of attack assumes that the adversary knows (or can choose) additionally some mathematical relation between the keys used for encryption and decryption, but not their values. This kind of attack may be practical when a block cipher is used as a primitive for a hash function, for instance.

Types of Attacks

Depending on the knowledge of the internal details of a block cipher, and depending on the information gathered when analyzing implementation de-tails, one can classify attacks in an alternative way as follows:

- **Black-Box Attacks:** These are generic attacks which treat the block cipher as a black box taking plaintexts and a key as input and outputs a ciphertext; as such attacks do not depend on any internal details of the algorithm, one can apply them against every block cipher, and their complexity depends only on parameters like the key length ` and the block length n of the block ciphers under consideration. Examples of black-box attacks are exhaustive key search or generic time-memory tradeoffs.

- **Shortcut Attacks:** On contrary to black-box attacks, shortcut attacks are based on a mathematical analysis of the internal details of the block ciphers under consideration. The most powerful known attacks are of course shortcut attacks.
- **Side-Channel Attacks:** Side-channel attacks exploit various physical phenomenon generated by the software and hardware implementations. For instance, timing attacks can be applied when the execution time of an algorithm is dependent of the data and/or the key value. Another way to exploit weaknesses of physical implementations of block ciphers is to measure the power consumption of tamper-proof hardware and infer some information about the key from these measures. Finally, fault analysis exploits the idea that one can induce faults during the execution of a block cipher by using any physical mean (like power glitches) and can study the effects of these faults on the algorithm behavior resulting in extraction of some information about the key.

Parameters of an Attack

Attacks against block ciphers, besides the threat model under consideration, depend on several parameters:

- The time complexity of an attack is the amount of computational processing required to perform this attack successfully. The computational unit is often chosen such that one can compare the attack to an exhaustive key search. Furthermore, we divide this time complexity in two parts, namely the pre-computation and post-computation times, if the attack needs to perform computations off-line.
- By data complexity, one means the number of data (like ciphertexts, known-plaintext, chosen-plaintext, etc.) required to perform an attack in the threat model under consideration. Since these data must be obtained from the key holder, this has a direct in influence on the communication complexity.
- The success probability of an attack measures the frequency at which the attack is successful when repeated a certain number of times in a (statistically) independent way.
- The memory complexity measures the amount of memory units necessary to store either pre-computed data necessary to perform the attack, or (possibly parts of) the data obtained in the threat model under consideration.

Black-Box Attacks

Some of the known attacks against block ciphers can be applied in a "black-box" fashion, i.e. without attacking the internal structure of the block cipher. These attacks include the exhaustive key search, attacks dedicated to multiple encryption, key-collision attacks, and time-memory tradeoffs.

- **Exhaustive Key Search:** One of the simplest way to attack a block cipher consists in trying one key after the other until the right one is found. Typically, for a block cipher e having a key size l

and a block size n, and provided that a very small number of known plaintext-ciphertext pairs (slightly more than $\left\lceil \frac{n}{l} \right\rceil$).

We can recover this key k by exhaustive search; this operation has a worst case time complexity equal to 2^l evaluations of e and an average time complexity of 2^{l-1}. If the underlying plaintext space is known to contain some redundancy (for instance, it is ASCII text), then one can even consider a ciphertext-only exhaustive search. One of the interesting properties of an exhaustive key search is that it is an attack which can be executed in parallel on many processors or dedicated machines, each one testing disjoint subsets of the key space. The success probability of an exhaustive key search is equal to the fraction of the key space searched. if one searches one tenth of the key space, then one has roughly a 10% probability to succeed. In other terms, a fixed key size l defines an upper bound on the security of a block cipher. Thus, for any secure block cipher, l should be large enough to thwart exhaustive key search attacks. A minimal key length of 75 bits is recommended for providing adequate protection against the most serious threats For protecting information in a secure way during the next 20 years, they estimate that a minimal key length of 90 bits should be sufficient (Blaze, 1996). Modern block ciphers usually allow keys of 128, 192, 256 bits or even more which a thwarts an exhaustive search of the key space.

- **Key-Collision Attack:** The key collision attack described in (based on the birthday paradox. Assuming that we are attacking a block cipher with a key length l and a block length $n < l$, a known plaintext p is encrypted under many distinct keys. We can build a table of p encrypted under $2^{\frac{l}{2}}$ random distinct keys and, by the birthday paradox, we expect that, after observing about ciphertexts, the probability to recover at least one key becomes non-negligible. Table 1 gives the relation between the number of precomputed encryptions and the expected number of keys found in the case of a key-collision attack against DES.
- **Multiple Encryption:** An example of this type of attack is the meet-in-the-middle attack on double DES.
- **Time-Memory Tradeoffs:** Hellman (Hellman, 1980) proposed a time-memory tradeoff which can be applied to an exhaustive key search. The idea here consists in precomputing some information and to use it in order to speed up key searches. This attack is able to recover an l-bit secret key after $O\left(2^{\frac{2l}{3}}\right)$ encryption operations by using $O\left(2^{\frac{2l}{3}}\right)$ words of memory, whose content is initialialized in a unique precomputation step needing 2^l encryptions.

Algebraic Attacks

In his work (Shannon, 1949), Shannon stated that breaking a block cipher should require as much work as solving a system of equations in a large number of unknowns of a complex type.

Table 1. Complexity of a key-collision attack against DES

Number of precomputed Ciphertexts	2^{28}	2^{32}	2^{40}	2^{48}	2^{56}
Expected number of keys found	1	2^8	2^{24}	2^{40}	2^{56}

- **Interpolation Attack:** A purely algebraic way to break a block cipher is the interpolation attack proposed by Jacobsen and Knudsen (1997). It is based on the well-known Lagrange's formula. If F is a field, the unique polynomial p(x) ∈ F[x] of degree at most n-1, such that p(x_i) = y_i for n pairs is (x_i, y_i) ∈ F² is equal to

$$p(x) = \sum_{i=1}^{n} y_i \prod_{\substack{1 \le j \le n \\ j \ne i}} \frac{x - x_j}{x_i - x_j}$$

In an interpolation attack, one is interested in constructing polynomials using inputs and outputs of the block cipher. The attack's idea is that if the constructed polynomials have a small degree, only few plaintexts and the corresponding ciphertexts are necessary to solve for the key-dependent coefficients of the polynomial.

- **Courtois-Pieprzyk Attack:** Under a purely algebraic approach, the first step is to express a given block cipher in a system of equations; actually, every component of a block cipher can be described with help of a set of algebraic equations. If one collects these descriptions, one gets a large system which mathematically defines the complete block cipher. If it is possible to solve this system faster than an exhaustive key search, then the cipher may be considered to be broken. Surprisingly, Ferguson, Schroeppel and Whiting (Ferguson et.al, 2001) have managed to do in the case of Rijndael. Actually, they express Rijndael as a single equation made of 2^{50} terms. Undoubtedly, such a huge equation is extremely difficult to work with, but it demonstrates that the cipher can be formulated using a system of equations.

Logical Cryptanalysis

An interesting method is to do cryptanalysis using logical reasoning as proposed in (Massacci et al, 2000). The cryptanalytic procedure encodes the abstract, functional properties of a cryptographic algorithm in a suitable logic so that, for instance, finding a model of the corresponding formulae is equivalent to recovering a key in a cryptanalytic attack. Once the properties of the algorithm are represented as (propositional) formulae, we can use efficient and effective automatic reasoning tools such as the ones for the Satisfiability (SAT) problem for the analysis and the verification of the algorithm. This approach is referred to as logical cryptanalysis.

The main intuition behind logical cryptanalysis is that we should view each bit sequence P, C, K as a sequence of propositional variables P, C, K, in which every variable is true when the corresponding bit is 1 and false when it is 0. Then we simply need to encode the properties of the cryptographic algorithm with a logical formula E(P, C, K) which is true if and only if for the corresponding sequences of bits we have that C = E_K(P) holds. Propositional logic is the straightforward choice, but other logics (such as temporal logic) might give a more compact encoding. The intuition behind logical cryptanalysis is that, once we have the formula describing the cipher, the cryptanalysis problems can be easily formalized.

As an example, consider the encoding the Data Encryption Standard(DES). An algorithm that formulates the cryptanalysis problem as a satisfiability problem can be described as follows:

1. Fix the number of rounds of DES we are interested in;
2. Generate randomly a key K (the solution of the SAT problem)
3. Generate randomly 400 blocks of plaintext P (a block is 64 bits).
4. Encrypt the plaintext with the key using DES limited to the requested number of rounds and generate the ciphertext $C = E_K(P)$.
5. Encode the limited version of DES as a formula E(P, K, C) and substitute the values of the plaintext v_P and v_C.

The key search problem is modeled as the Boolean satisfiability problem which can be solved using SAT-solvers or automated reasoning tools.

Attacks on Cryptographic Functions

In this section, various attacks that can be launched on Cryptographic functions are discussed.

- **Random Number Generators:** The need for random and pseudo random numbers arises in many cryptographic applications. For instance, common cryptosystems employ keys that must be generated in a random fashion. In addition, many cryptographic protocols require random or pseudo random inputs at various points such as, auxiliary quantities used in generating digital signatures, or for generating challenges in authentication protocols. Different methods have been proposed for the generation of random numbers. In (Geetha et al., 2015) an algorithm for random number generation using an Artificial Bee Colony algorithm. Physical sources of randomness are often too costly and therefore most systems use a pseudo-random number generator (Dorrendorf et al., 2007). The generator is modeled as a function whose input is a short random seed, and whose output is a long stream which is indistinguishable from truly random bits. Implementations of pseudo-random generators often use a state whose initial value is the random seed. The state is updated by an algorithm which changes the state and outputs pseudo-random bits, and implements a deterministic function of the state of the generator. The theoretical analysis of pseudo-random generators assumes that the state is initialized with a truly random seed. Implementations of pseudo-random generators initialize the state with random bits ("entropy") which are gathered from physical sources, such as timing of disk operations, of system events, or of a human interface. Many implementations also refresh ("rekey") the state periodically, by replacing the existing state with one which is a function of the existing state and of entropy similar to that used in the initialization. The most basic security requirements that must be provided by pseudo-random generators are:
    - **Pseudo-Randomness:** The generators output looks random to an outside observer.
    - **Forward Security**: An adversary which learns the internal state of the generator at a specific time cannot learn anything about previous outputs of the generator. Forward security, on the other hand, is concerned with ensuring that the state of the generator does not leak information about previous states and outputs. If a generator does not provide forward security then an attacker who learns the state at a certain time can learn previous outputs of the generator, and consequently, past transactions of the user of the system. Forward security can be easily guaranteed by ensuring that the function which advances the state is one-way.

○ **Backward Security (also known as Break-In Recovery):** An adversary which learns the state of the generator at a specific time does not learn anything about future outputs of the generator, provided that sufficient entropy is used to refresh the generator's state. The generator operates as a deterministic process and therefore knowledge of the state of the generator at a specific time can be used to compute all future outputs of the generator (by simply simulating the operation of the algorithm run by the generator). Consequently, backward security can only be provided if the state of the generator is periodically refreshed with data ("entropy") which is sufficiently random.

Constructing a constructing an actual implementation of a pseudo-random number generator is quite complex. The following are some reasons.

- **Performance:** Provably secure generators might incur high computation overhead.
- **Real World Attacks:** Actual implementations are prone to many attacks which do not exist in the cryptographic formulation used to design and analyze pseudo-random generators (consider, for example, timing attacks and other side-channel attacks).
- **Seeding and Reseeding the Generator:** Generators are secure as long as they are initialized with a truly random seed. Finding such a seed is not simple. Furthermore, the state of the generator must be periodically refreshed with a fresh random seed in order to prevent backward security attacks. The developer of a generator must therefore identify and use random sources with sufficient randomness.

Hash Functions: A hash function is simply a mapping.

$$h: \{0, 1\}^* \rightarrow \{0, 1\}^m$$

from the set of all binary strings to the set of binary strings of a fixed size. Every good hash function has the property that two different inputs are very unlikely to be mapped to the same value. Only cryptographic hash functions that fulfill certain security properties may be used in cryptographic applications such as digital signatures and pseudo-random number generators. Cryptographic hash functions must not only have good statistical properties. They must also withstand serious attack by malicious and powerful attackers who are trying to invade our privacy. The design of such cryptographic hash functions is an important but extremely difficult task. Many have been proposed, but most of them soon turned out to be too weak to resist attacks. Only two families of hash functions came to be widely used (namely the MD and SHA families, the most well-known members of which are MD5 and SHA-1, respectively). Unfortunately, their security relies on heuristic arguments rather than mathematical proofs (Massierer, 2006). As might be expected, weaknesses have recently been found in both of them and as a result, there currently exist no secure and practical cryptographic hash functions. Hence there is little basis for trust in the applications that use them, and a great need for research into good cryptographic hash functions.

Cryptographic hash functions are created as one-way functions meaning that it is easy to compute the hash for a given message, but it is hard to find the original message given the hash. Cryptographic hash functions are expected to produce no collisions even when a malicious attacker deliberately tries to create them using all his/her mathematical knowledge, computational power and any other resources available to him/her. This would be called a collision attack. Similarly, an attack that tries to produce a preimage of a hash value (under a certain hash function) is called a preimage attack on that hash function, and an attack that attempts to create a second preimage is called a second preimage attack. These are the three properties of hash functions which may be attacked (and therefore it is desirable to somehow prove that such attacks are hard).

The Brute Force attack on hash functions tries to find a preimage for a given digest d would try many different messages, hash them, and compare the results to d until it finds a match. If a hash function has 2^m possible output values (for an m-bit hash), then one would have to try on the average 2^{m-1} messages to on average to find a preimage. We can say that the hash function has m-1 bits of security.

The birthday attack on hash functions (Massierer, 2006) reduces the security of hash functions even further. The security of hash function is only $2^{m/2}$ under birthday attack.

A brute force attack is possible on any hash function, regardless of its structure. Hence one needs to make sure that the hash value is big enough, so that brute force attacks become too complex for even the fastest computers available. The MD-5 hash function is 128-bits in size, the SHA-1 is 160 bits in size and NIST (National Institute of Standards and Technology) recommends at least 256 bits to resist birthday attacks.

SUMMARY

The public key cryptosystems are based on a computationally difficult problem. The problems that form the basis for the public key cryptosystems like the RSA problem, the Diffie-Hellman problem, the Syndrome-decoding problem, the Shortest Vector problem in Lattices, the Matrix Decomposition problem and the Discrete Optimization problem are discussed in this chapter. The important problems in Crypanalysis include Exhaustive Key Search attack, Key Collision attack, Algebraic attacks, Logical Cryptanalysis, attacks on Pseudo Random Generators and Hash functions. The analysis of these attacks can provide insight into the functioning of Cryptographic algorithms and functions.

REFERENCES

Anshel, I., Anshel, M., & Goldfeld, D. (1999). An algebraic method for public-key cryptography. *Math. Res. Lett*, *6*(3), 287–291. doi:10.4310/MRL.1999.v6.n3.a3

Biham, E. (1996), How to forge DES-encrypted messages in 2^{28} steps (technical Report CS-0884). Computer Science Department, Technion, Haifa, Israel.

Blaze, M., Diffie, W., Rivest, R., Schneier, B., Shimomura, T., Thompson, E., & Wiener, M. (1996). Minimal key lengths for symmetric ciphers to provide adequate commercial security. Retrieved from http://www.schneier.com/paper-keylength.html

Cha, J. C., Ko, K. H., Lee, S. J., Han, J. W., & Cheon, J. H. (2001). An efficient Implementation of Braid Groups. *Proceedings of ASIACRYPT '01*, LNCS (Vol. *2248*, pp. 144–156). doi:10.1007/3-540-45682-1_9

Choi, S. J., & Youn, H. Y. (2004). A novel data encryption and distribution approach for high security and availability using LU decomposition. In Computational Science and Its Applications, *LNCS* (Vol. *3046*, pp. 637–646).

Choi, S. J., & Youn, H. Y. (2005). An Efficient Key Pre-Distribution Scheme for Secure Distributed Sensor Networks. In *EUC Workshops, LNCS* (Vol. *3823*, pp. 1088–1097).

Dorrendorf, L., Gutterman, Z., & Pinkas, B. (2007). Cryptanalysis of the Random Number Generator of the Windows Operating System. Retrieved from http://eprint.iacr.org/419.pdf

Elgamal, T. (1985). A public-key cryptosystem and a signature scheme based on discrete logarithms. *IEEE Transactions on Information Theory*, *31*(4), 469–472. doi:10.1109/TIT.1985.1057074

Ferguson, N., Schroeppel, R., & Whiting, D. (2001, August 16-17). A simple algebraic representation of Rijndael. In S. Vaudenay & A. Youssef (Eds.), *Selected Areas in Cryptography: 8th Annual International Workshop SAC '01*, Toronto, Ontario, Canada, LNCS (Vol. 2259, pp. 103-111). Springer-Verlag. doi:10.1007/3-540-45537-X_8

Geetha, J. S., & Amalarethinam, D. I. (2015). ABC-RNG For Public Key Cryptography for Random Number Generation. *International Journal of Fuzzy Mathematical Archive*, *6*(2), 177–186.

Grigoriev, D., & Ponomarenko, I. (2006). Homomorphic public-key cryptosystems and encrypting boolean circuits. *Appl. Algebra Engrg. Comm. Comput*, *17*(3-4), 239–255. doi:10.1007/s00200-006-0005-x

Hellman, M. E. (1980). A cryptanalytic time-memory tradeoff. *IEEE Transactions on Information Theory*, *26*(4), 401–406. doi:10.1109/TIT.1980.1056220

Jacobsen, T., & Knudsen, L. (1997). The The interpolation attack against block ciphers. In E. Biham(Ed), *Fast Software Encryption: 4th International Workshop FSE'97, LNCS* (Vol. 1267, pp. 28-40). Springer-Verlag.

Junod, P. (2005). Statistical Cryptanalysis of Block Ciphers, *Doctoral dissertation*, Lusanne, EPFL.

Knudsen, L. (1998). Contemporary block ciphers. In I. Damgard, (Ed.), Lectures on Data Security Modern Cryptology in Theory and Practice, LNCS (Vol. 1561, pp. 105-126). Springer-Verlag.

Ko, K. H., Lee, S. J., Cheon, J. H., Han, J. W., Kang, J., & Park, C. (2000). New public-key cryptosystem using braid groups. In *Advances in cryptology, LNCS* (Vol. 1880, pp. 166-183). Springer.

Koblitz, N. (1987). Elliptic Curve Cryptosystems. *Mathematics of Computation*, *48*(177), 203–209. doi:10.1090/S0025-5718-1987-0866109-5

Laskari, E. C., Meletiou, G. C., & Vrahatis, M. N. (2005). Problems of Cryptography as Discrete Optimization Tasks. *Nonlinear Analysis*, *63*(5-7), 831–837. doi:10.1016/j.na.2005.03.003

Massacci, F., & Marraro, L. (2000). Logical Analysis as a SAT Problem, Encoding and Analysis of the U.S. Data Encryption Standard. *Journal of Automated Reasoning*, *24*(1/2), 165–203. doi:10.1023/A:1006326723002

Massierer, M. (2006). Provable Secure Cryptographic Hash Functions [B.S. thesis]. University of New South Wales.

McEliece, R. J. (1978). A Public-Key System based on Algebraic Coding Theory, *Jet Propulsion Lab. DSN Progress Report*, *44*, 114–116.

Meletiou, G. C., Triantafllou, D. S., & Vrahatis, M. N. (2015). Handling problems in cryptography with matrix factorization. *Journal of Applied Mathematics and Bioinformatics*, *5*(3), 37–48.

Menezes, A., Van Oorshoot, P. C., & Vanstone, A. (1996). *Handbook of Applied Cryptography*. CRC Press. doi:10.1201/9781439821916

Merkle, R., & Hellman, M. (1978). Hiding Information and signatures in trapdoor knapsacks. *IEEE Transactions on Information Theory*, *IT-24*(5), 525–530. doi:10.1109/TIT.1978.1055927

Miller, S. V. (1985). Use of Elliptic Curves in Cryptography. In *Advances in cryptology: CRYPTO'85* (pp. 417–426).

Okamoto, T., Tanaka, K., & Uchiyama, S. (2000). Quantum Public-Key Cryptosystems. In *Advances in Cryptology: CRYPTO 00* (pp. 147–165).

Pathan, A. S. K., Hong, C. S., & Suda, T. (2007), A novel and efficient bilateral remote user authentication scheme using smart cards. *Proceedings of the IEEE International Conference on Consumer Electronics* (pp. 1-2). doi:10.1109/ICCE.2007.341503

Shamir, A. (1984). A polynomial time algorithm for breaking the basic Merkle-Hellman Cryptosystem. *IEEE Transactions on Information Theory*, *IT-30*(5), 699–704. doi:10.1109/TIT.1984.1056964

Shannon, C. (1949), Communication Theory of secrecy systems. *Bell System Technical Journal*, *2894*, 656-719.

Shpilrain, V., & Ushakov, A. (2005) Thompson's group and public key cryptography. In ACNS '05, LNCS (Vol. 3531, pp. 151-164). doi:10.1007/11496137_11

Shpilrain, V., & Zapata, G. (2006a). Combinatorial group theory and public key cryptography. *Appl. Algebra Engrg. Comm. Comput.*, *17*(3-4), 291–302. doi:10.1007/s00200-006-0006-9

Shpilrain, V., & Zapata, G. (2006b). Using the subgroup membership search problem in public key cryptography, *Con-temp. Math., Amer. Math. Soc.*, *418*, 169-179.

Wagner, D. (1999). The boomerang attack. In L. Knudsen (Ed.), *Fast Soft-ware Encryption: 6th International Workshop FSE'99*, Rome, Italy, *LNCS* (Vol. 1636, pp. 156-170). Springer-Verlag. doi:10.1007/3-540-48519-8_12

Zhu, H. (2001). *Survey of Computational Assumptions Used in Cryptography Broken or Not by Shor's Algorithm* [Master's Thesis]. McGill University, Canada.

KEY TERMS AND DEFINITIONS

Brute-Force Attack: The brute-force attack tests all possible values exhaustively for the correct solution. In Symmetric and Public Key Cryptography, the brute force attack attempts to find the symmetric or private key given a few plaintext-ciphertext pairs.

Closest Vector Problem: Given a Lattice and a vector, find a vector which is as close to the given vector as possible.

Differential Evolution Method: Differential Evolution Method optimizes a problem by maintaining a population of candidate solutions and creating new candidate solutions by combining existing ones according to its simple formulae, and then keeping whichever candidate solution has the best score or fitness on the optimization problem at hand.

Diffie-Hellman Problem: The Diffie-hellman problem is related to the discrete logarithm problem. This is stated as "Given a generator g and g^x and g^y, what is the value of g^{xy}?".

Logical Cryptanalysis: The cryptanalytic procedure encodes the abstract, functional properties of a cryptographic algorithm in a suitable logic so that, for instance, finding a model of the corresponding formulae is equivalent to recovering a key in a cryptanalytic attack.

Matrix Decomposition Problem: The matrix decomposition problem is reconstructing matrix A=L.U knowing only L or U.

Particle Swarm Optimization: Is a computational method that optimizes a problem by iteratively trying to improve a candidate solution with regard to a given measure of quality. It solves a problem by having a population of candidate solutions, called particles, and moving these particles around in the search-space according to simple mathematical formulae over the particle's position and velocity. Each particle's movement is influenced by its local best known position, but is also guided toward the best known positions in the search-space.

Pseudo Random Generator(PRNG): The PRNG generates a long sequence of Pseudo random sequence starting with a given seed number.

RSA Problem: The RSA problem is related to the integer factorization problem. The RSA problem is to efficiently compute the plaintext m given the public key e, the modulus n and the ciphertext c.

Satisfiability Problem: The satisfiability problem is determining if there exists an assignment for the Boolean variables that satisfies a given Boolean equation.

Shortest Vector Problem: Lattices are points in n-dimensional space. A basis for a vector is set of m vectors in the n-dimensional space. Given a basis for a Lattice, finding the shortest nonzero vector is a difficult problem.

Side-Channel Attacks: The side-channel attacks exploit various physical phenomena generated by the software/hardware implementations.

Smallest Basis Problem: The smallest Basis problem is to find a basis whose length of the longest vector is as short as possible.

Syndrome Decoding Problem: The syndrome identifies errors in a codeword. The value of the syndrome is the position of the code where the error is. With a binary code, this also implies that the error can be easily corrected. The syndrome tells us the symbol of the code which is erroneous. With a binary code, if the current erroneous symbol is 0, we simply switch it to a 1, and vice versa. Then what is left is the sent codeword which is easy to decode. This is the syndrome decoding problem.

Chapter 3
Variants of the Diffie–Hellman Problem

Kannan Balasubramanian
Mepco Schlenk Engineering College, India

ABSTRACT

Many variations of the Diffie-Hellman problem exist that can be shown to be equivalent to one another. We consider following variations of Diffie-Hellman problem: square computational and Square decisional Diffie-Hellman problem, inverse computational and inverse computational decisional Diffie-Hellman problem and divisible computational and divisible decisional Diffie-Hellman problem. It can be shown that all variations of computational Diffie-Hellman problem are equivalent to the classic computational Diffie-Hellman problem if the order of a underlying cyclic group is a large prime. We also describe other variations of the Diffie-Hellman problems like the Group Diffie-Hellman problem, bilinear Diffie-Hellman problem and the Elliptic Curve Diffie-Hellman problem in this chapter.

INTRODUCTION

The Diffie-Hellman problem is to compute g^{xy} given g^x and g^y using a generator in a cyclic group. This is a difficult problem and is used in the Diffie-Hellman Exchange protocol. Many other problems can be shown to be equivalent to this protocol by reducing one problem to another. The Diffie-Hellman problems can be either computational or decisional. Both the computational and the decisional variants of the square Diffie-Hellman problem, Inverse Diffie-Hellman problem and the divisible Diffie-Hellman problems are considered in this chapter and shown to be equivalent if the order of the underlying cyclic group is large prime.

The basic tools for relating the complexities of various problems are polynomial reductions and transformations. We say that a problem A reduces in polynomial time to another problem B, denoted by A if and only if there is an algorithm for A which uses a subroutine for B, and each call to the subroutine for B counts as a single step, and the algorithm for A runs in polynomial-time. The latter implies that the subroutine for B can be called at most a polynomially bounded number of times. The practical implication comes from the following proposition: If A polynomially reduces to B and there is a polynomial time algorithm for B, then there is a polynomial time algorithm for A also.

DOI: 10.4018/978-1-5225-2915-6.ch003

DIFFIE-HELLMAN PROBLEM

In this chapter, we are considering useful variations of Diffie-Hellman problem: square Computational (and decisional) Diffie-Hellman problem, inverse computational (and decisional) Diffie-Hellman problem and divisible computational (and decisional) Diffie-Hellman problem. We are able to show that all variations of computational Diffie-Hellman problem are equivalent to the classic computational Diffie-Hellman problem if the order of an underlying cyclic group is a large prime (Bao et al., 2003).

Let p be a large prime number such that the discrete logarithm problem defined in Z_p^* is hard. Let $G \in Z_p^*$ be a cyclic group of prime order q and g is assumed to be a generator of G. It is assumed that G is prime order, and security parameters p; q are defined as the fixed form $p = 2q + 1$ and $ord(g) = q$. A remarkable computational problem has been defined on this kind of set by Diffie and Hellman (Diffie, 1976). The Diffie-Hellman assumption (CDH assumption) is stated as follows:

- **Computational Diffie-Hellman Problem (CDH):** On input g, g^x, g^y, computing g^{xy}. An algorithm that solves the computational Diffie-Hellman problem is a probabilistic polynomial time Turing machine, on input g, g^x, g^y, outputs g^{xy} with non-negligible probability. The Computational Diffie-Hellman assumption means that such a probabilistic polynomial time Turing Machine does not exist. This assumption is believed to be true for many cyclic groups, such as the prime sub-group of the multiplicative group of finite fields.
- **Square Computational Diffie-Hellman Assumption:** The square computational Diffie-Hellman problem, introduced in (Maurer et al., 1998) is defined as follows:
- **Square Computational Diffie-Hellman Problem (SCDH):** On input g, g^x, computing g^{x^2}. An algorithm that solves the square computational Diffie-Hellman problem is a probabilistic polynomial time Turing machine, on input g, g^x, outputs g^{x2} with non-negligible probability. The square computational Diffie- Hellman assumption means that there no such a probabilistic polynomial time Turing machine does not exist.

It can be argued that the SCDH assumption and the CDH assumption are equivalent.

- **Inverse Computational Diffie-Hellman Assumption:** A variation of computational Diffie-Hellman problem, called inverse computational Diffie-Hellman assumption (In-vCDH assumption) is discussed next.
- **Inverse Computational Diffie-Hellman Problem(invCDH):** On input g, g^x, outputs $\left(g^x\right)^{-1}$. An algorithm that solves the inverse computational Diffie-Hellman problem is a probabilistic polynomial time Turing machine, on input g, g^x, outputs $\left(g^x\right)^{-1}$ with non-negligible probability. Inverse computational Diffie-Hellman assumption means that such a probabilistic polynomial time Turing machine does not exist. It can be shown that that the SCDH assumption and InvCDH assumption are equivalent.
- **Divisible Computational Diffie-Hellman Assumption:** The divisible Computational Diffie-Hellman Assumption is defined as follows:
- **Divisible Computational Diffie-Hellman Problem (DCDH):** On random input g, g^x, g^y, computing $g^{y/x}$. An algorithm that solves the divisible computational Diffie-Hellman problem is a proba-

bilistic polynomial time Turing machine, on input g, g^x, g^y, outputs $g^{y/x}$ with non-negligible probability. The Divisible computation Diffie-Hellman assumption means that there is no such a probabilistic polynomial time Turing machine. It can be shown that divisible computational Diffie-Hellman assumption is equivalent to the computational Diffie- Hellman assumption. It can also be shown that all the variations of the Diffie-Hellman are equivalent.

VARIATIONS OF THE DECISIONAL DIFFIE-HELLMAN PROBLEM

The variations of the decisional Diffie-Helman problem have been known for many years (Sadehi et al., 2001).

- **Decisional Diffie-Hellman Assumption-DDH:** Let G be a large cyclic group of prime order q defined above. Consider the following two distributions:
   - Given a Diffie-Hellman quadruple g, g^x, g^y and g^{xy}, where $x, y \in Z_q$, are random strings chosen uniformly at random;
   - Given a random quadruple g, g^x, g^y and g^r, where $x, y, r \in Z_q$, are random strings chosen uniformly at random.

An algorithm that solves the Decisional Diffie-Hellman problem is a statistical test that can efficiently distinguish these two distributions. Decisional Diffie-Hellman assumption means that there is no such polynomial statistical test. This assumption is believed to be true for many cyclic groups, such as the prime sub-group of the multiplicative group of finite fields.

- **Square Decisional Diffie-Hellman Assumption-SDDH:** Let G be a large cyclic group of prime order q defined above. We consider the following two distributions:
   - Given a square Diffie-Hellman triple g, g^x and g^{x^2}, where $x \in Z_q$, is a random string chosen uniformly at random;
   - Given a random triple g, g^x and g^r, where $x, r \in Z_q$, are two random strings chosen uniformly at random.

An algorithm that solves the square decisional Diffie-Hellman problem (SDDH for short) is a statistical test that can *efficiently* distinguish these two distributions. Square decisional Diffie-Hellman assumption means that there is no such a polynomial statistical test.

- **Inverse Decisional Diffie-Hellman Assumption -InvDDH:** Let G be a large cyclic group of prime order q defined above. We consider the following two distributions:
   - Given am inverse Diffie-Hellman triple g, g^x and $g^{x^{-1}}$, where $x \in Z_q$, is a random string chosen uniformly at random.;
   - Given a random triple g, g^x and g^r, where $x; r \in Z_q$, are random strings chosen uniformly at random.

An algorithm that solves the Inverse decisional Diffie-Hellman problem (In-vDDH for short) is a statistical test that can efficiently distinguish these two distributions. Inverse decisional Diffie-Hellman assumption means that there is no such polynomial statistical test.

- **Divisible Decision Diffie-Hellman Assumption-DDDH:** Let G be a large cyclic group of prime order q defined above. We consider the following two distributions:
  - Given a divisible Diffie-Hellman quadruple g, g^x, g^y and $g^{x/y}$, where x, $y \in Z_q$, are random strings chosen uniformly at random;
  - Given a random quadruple g, g^x and g^y and g^r, where x, y, $r \in Z_q$, are random strings chosen uniformly at random.

An algorithm that solves the divisible decision Diffie-Hellman problem (DDDH for short) is a statistical test that can efficiently distinguish these two distributions. Divisive decision Diffie-Hellman assumption means that there is no such polynomial statistical test.

It can be shown that the variations of the Decisional Diffie-Hellman assumptions are equivalent.

GENERALIZED VARIATIONS OF THE DIFFIE-HELLMAN PROBLEM

The Generalized Decisional Diffie-Hellman assumption is discussed next.

- **Generalized Decisional Diffie-Hellman Assumption:** For any k, the following distributions are indistinguishable.
  - The distribution R^{2k} of any random tuple $(g_1, \ldots, g_k; u_1, \ldots, u_k)$ 2 G^{2k}, where $g_1, \ldots, g_k$, and $u_1, \ldots, u_k$ are uniformly distributed in G^{2k}
  - The distribution D^{2k} of tuples $(g_1, \ldots, g_k, u_1, \ldots, u_k) \in G^{2k}$, where $g_1, \ldots, g_k$ are uniformly distributed in G^k, and $u_1 = g_1^r$, $u_k = g_k^r$ for random $r \in Z_q$ chosen at random.

An algorithm that solves the generalized decisional Diffie-Hellman problem is a statistical test that can efficiently distinguish these two distributions. Generalized decisional Diffie-Hellman assumption means that there is no such polynomial statistical test.

- **Generalized Square Decisional Diffie-Hellman Assumption (GSDDH):** Let G be a large cyclic group of prime order q defined above. Consider the following two distributions:
  - The distribution R^{3k} of any random tuple $(g_1, \ldots, g_k g_1^{x1}, \ldots, g_k^{xk}; u_1, \ldots, u_k) \in G^{3k}$, where $g_1, \ldots, g_k, x_1, \ldots, x_k$ and $u_1, \ldots, u_k$ are uniformly distributed in G^{3k};
  - The distribution D^{3k} of tuples $(g_1, \ldots, g_k, g_1^{x1}, \ldots, g_k^{xk} u_1, \ldots, u_k) \in G^{3k}$, where $g_1, \ldots, g_k, g_1^{x1}, \ldots, g_k^{xk}$ are uniformly distributed in G^k while $u_1 = g_1^{x_1^2}, \ldots, u_k = g_k^{x_k^2}$ for each x_i uniformly distributed in Z_q.

An algorithm that solves the generalized square decisional Diffie-Hellman problem is a statistical test that can efficiently distinguish these two distributions. Square decisional Diffie-Hellman assumption means that there is no such a polynomial statistical test.

- **Generalized Inverse Decisional Diffie-Hellman Assumption (GInvDDH):** Let G be a large cyclic group of prime order q defined above. Consider the following two distributions:
  - The distribution R^{3k} of any random tuple $(g_1, ..., g_k \, g_1^{x1}, ..., g_k^{xk}; u_1, ..., u_k) \in G^{3k}$, where g_1, ..., g_k, x_1, ..., x_k and u_1, ..., u_k are uniformly distributed in G^{3k};
  - The distribution D^{3k} of tuples $(g_1, ..., g_k g_1^{x1}, ..., g_k^{xk} u_1, ..., u_k) \in G^{3k}$, where $g_1, ..., g_k, g_1^{x1}, ..., g_k^{xk}$ are uniformly distributed in G^k while $u_1 = g_1^{x_1^{-1}}, ..., u_k = g_k^{x_k^{-1}}$ for each x_i uniformly distributed in Z_q.

An algorithm that solves the generalized inverse decisional Diffie-Hellman problem (GInvDDH for short) is a statistical test that can efficiently distinguish these two distributions. Generalized inverse decisional Diffie-Hellman assumption means that there is no such a polynomial statistical test.

THE ELGAMAL ENCRYPTION SCHEME

Let G be a finite cyclic group, say $G = Z_p^*$, the multiplicative group of integers modulo a (large) prime p. The group operation of G is denoted multiplicatively, so that repeated multiplication is represented by exponentiation. Let g be a generator for G; that is, the elements of G are $\left\{ g^1, g^2, ..., g^{|G|} \right\}$

Diffie and Hellman (Diffie et. al., 1976) suggested that two parties communicating over a channel subject to (passive) eaves- dropping could come to share a secret key using the following procedure. The first party chooses a random number $u \in \{1, 2, ..., |G|\}$ and sends g^u to the second party. The second party chooses a random number v $v \in \left\{1, 2, ..., |G|\right\}$ and sends g^v to the first party. The shared key is declared to be g^{uv}, which the first party can calculate as $(g^v)^u$ and the second party can calculate as $(g^u)^v$. Roughly said, the *Diffie-Hellman assumption* for asserts that an adversary who sees g^u and g^v (for a random u and v) cannot compute g^{uv}.

ElGamal (1985) explained how to adapt the above to give a public key encryption method. The intended receiver of an encrypted message has a public key which specifies g^v (where was chosen randomly from $\left\{1, 2, ..., |G|\right\}$). The sender wants to send to that receiver a ciphertext C which is the encryption of a message M $\in$ G. The sender computes C by choosing a random u (again in $\left\{1, 2, ..., |G|\right\}$) and transmitting C= $(g^u, M. g^{uv})$. Knowing v, the receiver can compute $g^{uv} = (g^u)$ from C and then multiply M. g^{uv} by the inverse of g^{uv} to recover M.

THE TWIN DIFFIE-HELLMAN PROBLEM

In some situations, basing security proofs on the hardness of the Diffie-Hellman problem is hindered by the fact that recognizing correct solutions is also apparently hard. There are a number of ways for circumventing these technical difficulties. One way is to simply make a stronger assumption, namely, that the Diffie-Hellman problem remains hard, even given access to a corresponding decision oracle. Another way is to work with groups that are equipped with efficient pairings, so that such a decision oracle is immediately available. To avoid making stronger assumptions, or working with specialized groups, a variation of the Diffie-Hellman problem is introduced in (Cash et al., 2009).

The Twin Diffie-Hellman problem has the following interesting properties:

- The twin Diffie-Hellman problem can easily be employed in many cryptographic constructions where one would usually use the ordinary Diffie-Hellman problem, without imposing a terrible efficiency penalty;
- The twin Diffie-Hellman problem is hard, even given access to a corresponding decision oracle, assuming the ordinary Die-Hellman problem (without access to any oracles) is hard.

Using the twin Diffie-Hellman problem, a new variant of El Gamal encryption is constructed that is secure against chosen ciphertext attack in the random oracle model, under the assumption that the ordinary Diffie-Hellman problem is hard. Compared to other El Gamal variants with similar security properties, our scheme is attractive in that it has very short ciphertexts and a very simple and tight security proof.

HASHED ELGAMAL ENCRYPTION

This public-key encryption scheme (Abdalla et al., 2001) makes use of a group G of prime order q with generator $g \in G$, a hash function H, and a symmetric cipher (E, D). A public key for this scheme is a random group element X, with corresponding secret key x, where $X = g^x$.

To encrypt a message m, one chooses a random $y \in Z_q$, computes

$$Y := g^y, Z := X^y, k := H(Y, Z), c := E_k(m),$$

and the ciphertext is (Y, c). Decryption works in the obvious way: given the ciphertext (Y, c), and secret key x, one computes

$$Z := Y^x, k := H(Y, Z), m := D_k(c)$$

Clearly, the hashed El Gamal encryption scheme is secure only if it is hard to compute Z, given the values X and Y. Let

$$dh(X, Y) := Z, \text{ where } X = g^x, Y = g^y, \text{ and } Z = g^{xy}.$$

The problem of computing dh(X, Y) given random X, Y $\in$ G is the D-H problem. The DH assumption asserts that this problem is hard. However, this assumption is not sufficient to establish the security of hashed El Gamal against a chosen ciphertext attack, regardless of what security properties the hash function H may enjoy.

To illustrate this problem, suppose that an adversary selects group elements Y' and Z' in some arbitrary way and computes $k' = H(Y', Z')$ and $c' = E_k(m')$ for some arbitrary message m'. Further suppose that the adversary gives the ciphertext (Y', c') to a decryption oracle obtaining the decryption m. Now it is very likely that $m'=m$ if and only if $Z'=dh(X, Y')$. Thus, the decryption oracle can be used by the adversary as an oracle to answer questions of the form "is dh (X, Y') = Z'?" for group elements Y' and

Z' of the adversary's choosing. In general, the adversary would not be able to efficiently answer such questions on his own, and so the decryption oracle is leaking some information about that secret key x which could conceivably be used to break the encryption scheme.

The Strong DH Assumption: Therefore, to establish the security of hashed ElGamal against chosen ciphertext attack, we need a stronger assumption. For X', Y', Z' $\in$ G let us define the predicate

$$\text{dhp}(X, Y', Z') := \text{dh}(X, Y') \overset{?}{=} Z'$$

At a bare minimum, we need to assume that it is hard to compute dh(X, Y) given random X,Y $\in$ G. along with access to a decision oracle for the predicate dhp(X,.,.) which on input (Y',Z') returns dhp(X,Y',Z'). Moreover, it is not hard to prove, if H is modeled as a random oracle, that hashed ElGamal is secure against chosen ciphertext attack under the strong DH assumption, and under the assumption that the underlying symmetric cipher is itself secure against chosen ciphertext attack (Abdalla et al., 2001).

Note that the strong DH assumption is different (and weaker) than the so-called gap DH assumption discussed in (Okamoto, 2001) where an adversary gets access to a full decision oracle the predicate dhp(., ., .), which on input (X', Y', Z'), returns dhp(X', Y', Z').

THE TWIN DIFFIE HELLMAN ASSUMPTIONS

For general groups, the strong DH assumption may be strictly stronger than the DH assumption. Here a slightly modified version of the DH problem is presented that is just as useful as the (ordinary) DH problem, and which is just as hard as the (ordinary) DH problem, even given access to a corresponding decision oracle. Using this, we obtain a modified version of hashed ElGamal encryption which can be proved secure under the (ordinary) DH assumption, in the random oracle model. This modified system is just a bit less efficient than the original system.

Again, let G be a cyclic group with generator g, and of prime order q. The function dh is defined as

$$\text{dh}(X, Y) := Z, \text{ where } X = g^x, Y = g^y, \text{ and } Z = g^{xy}.$$

Define the function

$$2\text{dh}: G^3 \to G^2$$

$$(X_1, X_2, Y) \mapsto \text{dh}(X_1, Y), \text{dh}(X_2, Y)).$$

We call this the twin DH function. One can also define a corresponding twin DH predicate:

$$2\text{dhp}(X_1, X_2, Y', z_1', z_2^1) := 2\text{dh}(X_1, X_2, Y') \overset{?}{=} (z_1', z_2^1)$$

The twin DH assumption states it is hard to compute $2dh(X_1, X_2, Y)$, given random $X_1, X_2, Y \in G$. It is clear that the DH assumption implies the twin DH assumption. The strong twin DH assumption states that it is hard to compute $2dh(X_1, X_2, Y)$, given random $X_1, X_2, Y \in G$, along with access to a decision oracle for the predicate $(X_1, X_2, ., ., .)$ which on input (Y', z_1', z_2^1) returns $2dhp(X_1, X_2, Y', z_1', z_2^1)$.

It can be shown that the ordinary DH assumption holds if only if the strong twin DH assumption holds.

THE TWIN ELGAMAL ENCRYPTION SCHEME

This scheme makes use of a hash function H and a symmetric cipher (E, D). A public key for this scheme is a pair of random group elements (X_1, X_2), with corresponding secret key (x_1, x_2), where $x_i = g^{x_i}$ for i = 1, 2. To encrypt a message m, one chooses a random $y \in Z_q$ and computes

$$Y := g^y, Z_1 := X_1^y, Z_2 := X_2^y, k := H(Y, Z_1, Z_2), c := E_k(m).$$

The ciphertext is (Y, c). Decryption works in the obvious way: given the ciphertext (Y, c), and secret key (x_1, x_2), one computes

$$Z_1 := Y^{x_1}, Z_2 := Y^{x_2}, k := H(Y, Z_1, Z_2), m := D_k(c).$$

One can easily show that the twin El Gamal encryption scheme is secure against chosen ciphertext attack, under the strong twin DH assumption, and under the assumption that (E, D) is secure against chosen ciphertext attack, if H is modeled as a random oracle.

THE TWIN DH KEY-EXCHANGE PROTOCOL

In Diffie et al (1976), Diffie and Hellman propose a simple non-interactive key exchange protocol. Alice chooses a random $x \in Z_q$, computes $X := g^x \in G$, and publishes the pair (Alice, X) in a public directory. Similarly, Bob chooses a random $y \in Z_q$, computes $Y := g^y \in G$, and publishes the pair (Bob, Y) in a public directory. Alice and Bob may compute the shared value $Z := g^{xy} \in G$ as follows: Alice retrieves Bob's entry from the directory and computes Z as Y^x, while Bob retrieves Alice's key X, and computes Z as X^y. Before using the value Z, it is generally a good idea to hash it, together with Alice's and Bob's identities, using a cryptographic hash function H. Thus, the key that Alice and Bob actually use to encrypt data using a symmetric cipher is $k := H(Alice, Bob, Z)$.

Unfortunately, the status of the security of this scheme is essentially the same as that of the security of hashed El Gamal against chosen ciphertext attack, if we allow an adversary to place arbitrary public keys in the public directory (without requiring some sort of "proof of possession" of a secret key). The issue is very similar to the problem inherent in El Gamal, where an adversary can inject a key Y' of its choosing and then request and then request a symmetric key *k* with Y' and and some other user's key X. The adversary can test dhp(X, Y', Z') for any Z' by checking if k = H(Alice, Bob, Z').

To avoid this problem, we define the twin DH protocol, as follows: Alice's public key is (X_1, X_2), and her secret key is (x_1, x_2), where $X_i = g^{x_i}$ for $i = 1, 2$; similarly, Bob's public key is (Y_1, Y_2), and his secret key is (y_1, y_2), where $Y_i = g^{y_i}$ for $i = 1, 2$; their shared key is

k:= H(Alice, Bob, dh(X_1, Y_1), dh(X_1, Y_2), dh(X_2, Y_1), dh(X_2, Y_2)),

where H is a hash function. Of course, Alice computes the 4-tuple of group elements in the hash as

$$\left(Y_1^{x_1}, Y_2^{x_1}, Y_1^{x_2}, Y_2^{x_2} \right)$$

and Bob computes them as

$$\left(X_1^{y_1}, X_1^{y_2}, X_2^{y_1}, X_2^{y_2} \right)$$

Using the "trapdoor test," it is a simple matter to show that the twin DH protocol satisfies a natural and strong definition of security, under the (ordinary) DH assumption, if H is modeled as a random oracle.

The trapdoor test can be defined as follows: given a random group element X_1, we can efficiently construct a random group element X_2, together with a secret "trapdoor" τ, such that

- X_1 and X_2 are independent (as random variables)
- If we are given group elements (Y', z_1', z_2^1) computed as functions of X_1 and X_2 (but not τ), then using τ, we can efficiently evaluate the predicate 2dhp($X_1, X_2, Y', z_1', z_2^1$) making a mistake with only negligible probability

OTHER VARIANTS OF THE DIFFIE-HELLMAN PROBLEM

- **The l-Weak Diffie-Hellman (l-wDH) Problem:** Given g and g^{α_i} in G for $i = 1, 2, \ldots, \grave{}$, compute $g^{1/\alpha}$. This problem was introduced by Mitsunari, Sakai, and Kasahara (Mitsunari et al., 2002) for a traitor tracing scheme.
- **The l-Strong Diffie-Hellman (l-SDH) Problem:** Given g and g^{α_i} in G for $i = 1, 2, \ldots, \grave{}$, compute $g^{\alpha^{l+1}}$. This problem is considered as a weaker version of l-SDH problem. It was first introduced by Boneh and Boyen to construct a short signature scheme, that is provably secure in the standard model (without random oracles), and later a short group signature scheme (Boneh et al., 2004a, 2004b).

The SDH problem is generalized into a group with bilinear maps. We further assume that e: $G \times G \rightarrow G'$ is an admissible bilinear map between two abelian groups G and G' with prime order p.

- **The l-Bilinear Diffie-Hellman Inversion (l-BDHI) Problem:** Given g and g^{α_i} in G for $i = 1, 2, \ldots, \grave{}$, compute $e(g, g)^{1/\alpha} \in G'$. This problem was introduced by Boneh and Boyen to construct an identity-based encryption that is secure in the standard model (Boneh et al., 2004c) . It is also used to construct verifiable random functions (Dodis, 2005).

- **The l-Bilinear Diffie-Hellman Exponent (l-BDHE) Problem:** Given g, h, and g^{α_i} (i = 1, 2, . . ., $l-1, l+1, \ldots, 2l$) in G, compute $e(g, h)^{\alpha^l} \in G$. This problem was introduced by Boneh, Boyen and Goh (2005a) to construct a hierarchical identity-based encryption scheme with constant size ciphertext, and later used for a public key broadcast encryption scheme with constant size transmission overhead (Boneh et al., 2005b).

THE GROUP DIFFIE-HELLMAN PROBLEM

The Diffie Hellman problem can be extended to allow more than one party to agree on a key (Steiner et al., 1996). In case of each three parties, each party picks a random value $x_i \in \{1, \ldots, |G|\}$ and they exchange the set of values g^{x_i}, $g^{x_i x_j}$ for $1 \leq i < j \leq 3$ to compute the common group Diffie-Hellman secret $g^{x_1 x_2 x_3}$.

- **Group Computational Diffie-Hellman Assumption:** The group computational Diffie Hellman assumption (GCDH) states that given the values $g^{\prod x_i}$ for some choice of proper subsets of $\{1, \ldots, n\}$, a computationally bounded adversary cannot recover the group Diffie Hellman secret (Bellare et al., 1993; Bresson et al., 2001a, 2001b, 2002). This assumption has also found application in the context of pseudo-random functions (Naor et al., 1997).
- **Group Decisional Diffie-Hellman Assumption:** The group Decisional Diffie Hellman assumption (GDDH) states that given the values $g^{\prod x_i}$ for some choice of proper subsets of $\{1, \ldots, n\}$, a computationally bounded adversary cannot distinguish the secret from a random element in the group (Bresson et al., 2002b).
- **Generalized Group Decisional Diffie-Hellman Assumption:** The Generalized group Decisional Diffie Hellman assumption (Generalized -GDDH) states that given the values $g^{\prod x_i}$ formed from all the proper subsets of $\{1, \ldots, n\}$, a computationally bounded adversary cannot distinguish the secret from a random element in the group (Steiner et al., 1996). It was shown that the DDH assumption and the Generalized-GDDH assumption are equivalent using an asymptotic reduction.

BILINEAR DIFFIE-HELLMAN ASSUMPTION

The variant of the Bilinear Diffie-Hellman discussed above and the bilinear Diffie-Hellman problem are based on the concept of bilinear pairings. A symmetric bilinear pairing on (G_1, G_2) is a map

$$e: G_1 \times G_1 \rightarrow G_2$$

satisfying the following conditions:

1. e is bilinear: $\forall R, S, T \in G_1, e(R + S, T) = e(R, T) \cdot e(S, T)$ and

$e(R, S + T) = e(R, S) \cdot e(R, T)$.

2. e is non-degenerate: If $\forall \, R \in G_1$, $e(R, S) = 1$, then $S = O$.

The Key exchange in the bilinear pairing is computed as follows:

Alice randomly selects a secret integer a modulo the order of G_1 and broadcasts the value aP to the other parties. Similarly and simultaneously, Bob and Charlie select their one secret integer b and c and broadcast bP and cP. Alice (and Bob and Charlie respectively) can now compute the shared secret key:

$K = e(bP, cP)^a = e(P, P)^{abc}$

We know that the security of DH-based protocols often relies on the hardness of the CDH and DDH problems. Likewise, the security of pairing-based protocols depends on the problem of computing $e(P, P)^{abc}$ given P, aP, bP and cP, which is known as the computational bilinear Diffie-Hellman problem (CBDH or simply BDH). This problem also exists in its decision form (DBDH).

DISCRETE LOGARITHM PROBLEM

Many popular public key cryptosystems are based on discrete exponentiation. If G is a multiplicative group, such as the group of invertible elements in a finite field or the group of points on an elliptic curve, and g is an element of G, then g^x is the discrete exponentiation of base g to the power x. This operation shares basic properties with ordinary exponentiation, for example $g^{x+y} = g^x \, g^y$. The inverse operation is, given h in G, to determine a value of x, if it exists, such that $h = g^x$. Such a number x is called a discrete logarithm of h to the base g, since it shares many properties with the ordinary logarithm. If, in addition, some normalization of x is required. To limit the possible answers to single valid value we can then speak of *the* discrete logarithm of h. Indeed, without such a normalization, x is not unique and is only determined modulo the order of the element g (Joux et al., 2014).

We say that we solve the discrete logarithm problem (DLP) in G if, given any element g^x in G we are able to recover x. To normalize the result, we usually ask for x to be taken in the range $0 \leq x < |G|$. The main impetus to intensive study of discrete logarithms came from the invention of the Diffie-Hellman method in 1976 (Diffie et al., 1976). Much later, the introduction of pairing in cryptography in 2000 (Joux, 2004; Boneh, 2003) increased the level of attention on some atypical finite fields, with composite extension degrees and/or medium-sized characteristic.

In fact, given an algorithm that solves the computational Diffie-Hellman problem, it is possible to effectively compute discrete logarithms, but it requires to find previously an auxiliary object that makes this computation feasible. More precisely, assuming that $|G|$ is prime, we need to consider an elliptic curve defined over $F_{|G|}$ such that its order has small prime factors only.

In order to describe the exact level of hardness of a computational problem, the main approach is to describe the complexity classes the problem belongs to. To this end, the traditional approach is to work with decision problems, i.e., problems with a yes/no answer. Since the discrete logarithm problem itself is not a decision problem, the first step is to introduce a related decision problem whose hardness is essentially equivalent to computing discrete logarithms. This can be done in many ways, for example, let us consider the following problem.

- **Log Range Decision:** Given a cyclic group G and a triple (g, h, B):
  ○ Output YES if there exists $x \in [0 \cdots B]$ such that $h = g^x$.
  ○ Otherwise output NO.

An algorithm or oracle that solves this problem can be used to compute discrete logarithms using a binary search. This requires a logarithmic number of calls to *Log Range Decision*. As a consequence, the hardness of *Log Range Decision* is essentially the same as the hardness of the Discrete Logarithm Problem itself.

ELLIPTIC CURVE DISCRETE LOGARITHM PROBLEM

Given an elliptic curve E and a field F_q, we consider the rational points $E(F_q)$ of the form (x,y) where both x and y belong to F_q. We choose the point at infinity to be σ.

- Define the operation "+" on the set of rational points of E as follows. If P and Q are two rational points on E, then P+Q is given by the following rule:
- Draw the line joining P and Q, take the third point of intersection of this line with the Curve as R.
- Draw the line through σ and R, and take the third point of intersection of this line with E. This point is the point P+Q. Note the operation "+" is commutative. In particular we have, $\sigma + \sigma = \sigma$ and $P+(-P) = \sigma$.
- Define the operation "*" as follows $*: Z \times E(F_q) \rightarrow E(F_q)$ and if P is some point in $E(F_q)$, then we define n*P as P+P+P+...+P, n times. Note that for integers j and k, $j*(k*P) = (j*k)*P = k*(j*P)$.
- The set of rational points on E form an abelian group under the operation "+" with identity σ. *Elliptic Curve Discrete Logarithm Problem* (ECDLP): is to determine the integer k, given rational points P and Q on E, and given that k*P=Q.

The ECDLP problem can be used to construct a key exchange protocol as described below:

1. A particular rational base point P is published in a public domain for use with a particular elliptic curve $E(F_q)$ also published in a public domain.
2. Alice and Bob choose random integers k_A and k_B respectively, which they use as private keys.
3. Alice computes k_A*P, Bob computes k_B*P and they exchange these values over an insecure network.
4. Using the information they received from each other and their private keys, both Alice and Bob compute $(k_A*k_B)*P = k_A*(k_B*P) = k_B*(k_A*P)$. This value is then the shared secret that only Alice and Bob possess. Note that the difficulty of the ECDLP ensures that the private keys k_A and k_B and the shared secretly $(k_A*k_B)*P$ are difficult to compute given k_A*P and k_B*P. Thus, Alice and Bob do not compromise their private keys or their shared secret in the exchange.

SUMMARY

A number of variations of the Diffie-Hellman exist all of which can be shown to be computationally equivalent. The computational and the decisional variants of the square, inverse and divisible Diffie-

Hellman problems as well the twin Diffie-Hellman problem, the Group Diffie-Hellman problem and the Bilinear Diffie-Hellman problem can all be shown equivalent to each other. This chapter also discussed Elgamal Encryption and the twin D-H based Key Exchange protocol.

REFERENCES

Abdalla, M., Bellare, M., & Rogaway, P. (2001). The oracle Diffie-Hellman assumptions and an analysis of DHIES. In Topics in Cryptology, LNCS (Vol. *2020*, pp. 143–158). doi:10.1007/3-540-45353-9_12

Bao, F., Deng, R. H., & Zhu, H. (2003). Variations of Diffie-Hellman problem. In Information and Communications Security, LNCS (Vol. *2836*, pp. 301–312). doi:10.1007/978-3-540-39927-8_28

Bellare, M., & Rogaway, P. (1993). Random Oracles are practical: a paradigm for designing efficient protocols. *Proc. of ACM CCS* '93 (pp. 62-73). doi:10.1145/168588.168596

Boneh, D., & Boyen, X. (2004a). Short Signatures Without Random Oracles. In *Eurocrypt 2004, LNCS* (Vol. 3027, pp. 56-73). Springer-Verlag.

Boneh, D., & Boyen, X. (2004c). Efficient Selective-ID Secure Identity-Based Encryption Without Random Oracles. In *Eurocrypt 2004, LNCS* (Vol. 3027, pp. 223-238). Springer-Verlag.

Boneh, D., Boyen, X., & Goh, E. (2005a). Hierarchical Identity Based Encryption with Constant Size Ciphertext. In *Eurocrypt 2005, LNCS* (Vol. 3494, pp. 440-456). Springer-Verlag.

Boneh, D., Boyen, X., & Shacham, H. (2004b). Short Group Signatures. In *Crypto 2004, LNCS* (Vol. 3152, pp. 41-55). Springer-Verlag.

Boneh, D., & Franklin, M. K. (2003). Identity-based encryption from the Weil pairing. *SIAM Journal on Computing*, *32*(3), 586–615. doi:10.1137/S0097539701398521

Boneh, D., Gentry, C., & Waters, B. (2005b). Collution Resistant Broadcast Encryption with Short Ciphertexts and Private Keys. In *Crypto 2005, LNCS* (Vol. 3621, pp. 258-275). Springer-Verlag.

Bresson, E., Chevassut, O., & Pointcheval, D. (2002a). Group Diffie-Hellman secure against dictionary attacks. In Zheng (Ed.), Proc. of Asiacrypt '02. Springer.

Bresson, E., Chevassut, O., & Pointcheval, D. (2002b). Dynamic Group Diffie-Hellman key exchange under standard assumptions. In L.R. Knudsen (Ed.), Proceedings of Eurocrypt '02, LNCS (Vol. 2332, pp. 321-326).

Bresson, E., Chevassut, O., Pointcheval, D., & Quisquater, J.-J. (2001a). Provably authenticated group Diffie-Hellman Exchange. In P. Samarati (Ed.), *Proc. of ACM CCS* '01 (pp. 255-264).

Bresson, E., Chevassut, O., Pointcheval, D., & Quisquater, J.-J. (2001b). Provably authenticated group Diffie-Hellman Exchange-The dynamic case. In C. Boyd (Ed.), Proc. of Asiacrypt '01, LNCS (Vol. 2248, pp. 290-309).

Cash, D., Kiltz, E., & Shoup, V. (2009). The Twin Diffie-Hellman problem and its applications. Retrieved from https://eprint.iacr.org/2008/067

Diffie, W., & Hellman, M. (1976). New Directions in Cryptography. *IEEE Transactions on Information Theory, 2*(6), 644–654.

Dodis, Y., & Yampolskiy, A. (2005). A Verifiable Random Function with Short Proofs and Keys. In *Public Key Cryptography 2005, LNCS* (Vol. *3386*, pp. 416–431).

Elgamal, T. (1985). A Public Key Cryptosystem and signature scheme based on Discrete Logarithms. *IEEE Transactions on Information Theory, 31*(4), 469–472. doi:10.1109/TIT.1985.1057074

Joux, A. (2004). A one round protocol for tripartite Diffie-Hellman. *Journal of Cryptology, 17*(4), 263–276. doi:10.1007/s00145-004-0312-y

Joux, A., Odlyzko, A., & Pierrot, C. (2014). The Past, Evolving Present and future of Discrete Logarithm, In Ç.K. Koç (Ed.), Open Problems in Mathematics and Computational Science (pp. 5-36). Springer.

Maurer, U. M., & Wolf, S. (1998). Diffie-Hellman, Decision Diffie-Hellman, and discrete logarithms. *Proceedings of the IEEE Symposium on Information Theory*, Cambridge, USA.

Mitsunari, S., Sakai, R., & Kasahara, M. (2002). A New Traitor Tracing. IEICE Trans. Fundamentals, E85-A(2), 481-484.

Naor, M., & Reingold, O. (1997). Number Theoretic constructions of efficient Pseudo-random functions. *Proceedings of FOCS'97* (pp. 458-467). IEEE Computer Society Press. doi:10.1109/SFCS.1997.646134

Okamoto, T., & Pointcheval, D. (2001). The gap-problems: A new class of problems for the security of cryptographic schemes. In Public Key Cryptography, LNCS (Vol. *1992*, pp. 104–118). doi:10.1007/3-540-44586-2_8

Sadehi, A.-R., & Steiner, M. (2001). *Assumptions related to Discrete Logarithms; Why Subtleties Make a Real Difference. In Eurocrypt 2001, LNCS* (Vol. *2045*, pp. 243–260). Springer-Verlag.

Steiner, M., Tsudik, G., & Waidner, M. (1996). Diffie Hellman key distribution extended to group communication. *Proceedings of ACM CCS '96* (pp. 31-37). doi:10.1145/238168.238182

KEY TERMS AND DEFINITIONS

Chosen-Ciphertext Attack: An attack on encryption algorithms where the attacker can choose ciphertext and obtain the corresponding plaintext.

Decisional Diffie-Hellman Assumption: A variant of the Computational Diffie-Hellman Assumption that requires a YES or NO answer.

Diffie-Hellman Assumption: An assumption about the hardness of computing using exponentiation in cyclic groups.

Discrete Logarithm: An intractable problem used in the construction of key exchange protocol.

Encryption: A Cryptographic algorithm that provides confidentiality by producing a ciphertext from plaintext.

Group Diffie-Hellman Assumption: The two party Diffie-Hellman problem extended to multiple parties.

Hash Functions: The hash functions are easy to compute but difficult to invert.

Key Exchange: An algorithm to establish secret keys over an insecure channel.

Public Key Encryption: An encryption algorithm that uses two different keys - a public key and a private key for encryption and decryption.

Chapter 4
Secure Group Key Agreement Protocols

Kannan Balasubramanian
Mepco Schlenk Engineering College, India

Mala K.
Mepco Schlenk Engineering College, India

ABSTRACT

This chapter focusses on Secure Key Exchange protocols executed among a group of parties, called group key exchange (GKE) protocols. Authentication and Key Establishment are very important in any secure communication. Authentication is generally based on long-term keys which can be associated with identities. To associate identities with long-term keys, we can assume the existence of a public-key infrastructure (PKI) which provides parties with some mechanisms for secure key registration and secure access to long-term keys of prospective peers. In most cases, there is also a need for some temporary keys. The Group Key Exchange protocols can be classified as Centralized, Distributed or Contributory. A few toolkits such as Spread and Cliques for the implementation of Group Key Exchange Protocols are also discussed.

INTRODUCTION

Key exchange is an important problem in cryptographic protocols since algorithms that use symmetric keys need the keys to be distributed to the sending and receiving parties in a secure fashion. Two party key exchange algorithms like the Diffie-Hellman key exchange protocol provide a method of establishing the key between two parties in a secure way. The Group key exchange protocols generalize this key exchange mechanism to a group of more than two parties. This chapter focuses on key exchange protocols executed among a group of parties, called group key exchange (GKE) protocols. GKE protocols will have applications such as satellite TV, Internet video broadcasting, collaborative systems and video/audio conferencing.

DOI: 10.4018/978-1-5225-2915-6.ch004

KEY AGREEMENT IN SECURE COMMUNICATION

Authentication and Key Establishment are very important in any secure communication. Authentication is generally based on long-term keys which can be associated with identities. The term "long-term key" is usually very broad and covers all forms of information which can be linked to identities. For example, it not only includes cryptographic keys such as DES or RSA keys but also encompasses passwords and biometric information. However, passwords and biometric information rarely used in Group Key establishment since passwords exhibit low entropy and the biometric information cannot be easily used for remote authentication.

To associate identities with long-term keys, we can assume the existence of a public-key infrastructure (PKI) which provides parties with some mechanisms for secure key registration and secure access to long-term keys of prospective peers. We can assume that the PKI, or, more precisely, the involved registration and certification authorities, is unconditionally trusted to securely and reliably associate the correct identities and keys of entities. We can assume that the PKI, or, more precisely, the involved registration and certification authorities, is unconditionally trusted to securely and reliably associate the correct identities and keys of entities. It is not required that the certification authorities verify on registration to ensure a public key pair is unique nor is it required that the party registering a public key also knows the corresponding secret key. For example, an adversary will be able to register a public key of some-body else under his name.

Security properties — such as authenticity, integrity and confidentiality — are normally only meaningful when guaranteed during a complete session of closely related interactions over a communication channel whether it is a single transfer of e-mail between two parties or a long-standing connection between two servers. In most of these cases, there is a need for some temporary keys, e.g., an encryption key for a shared-key encryption scheme in the e-mail scenario or a key for a message authentication code in the second example. The goal of using temporary keys instead of using the long-term keys directly is three-fold: (1) to limit the amount of cryptographic material available to cryptanalytic attacks; (2) to limit the exposure when keys are lost; and (3) to create independence between different and unrelated sessions.

Furthermore, if our long-term keys are based on asymmetric cryptography, using session keys based on (faster) symmetric cryptography can bring a considerable gain in efficiency. The establishment of such temporary keys, usually called session keys, often involves interactive cryptographic protocols. These protocols should ensure that all the required security properties, such as the authenticity and freshness of the resulting session key, are guaranteed. Such protocols are called key establishment protocols.

Authentication is central to security. However, the term is very broad and can mean anything from access control, authentication of entities, data origin or keys to non-repudiation. A protocol providing entity authentication (often also referred to as identification) informally means that a party successfully engaging another party in such a protocol can be assured of the other party's identity and its active presence during the protocol.

KEY AGREEMENT APPROACHES

Several group key management approaches have been proposed in the last decade. These approaches fall into three categories: 1) Centralized, 2) Distributed and 3) Contributory. Centralized group key management is conceptually simple as it involves a single entity (or a small set of entities) that generates and distributes keys to group members. The Centralized group key management is not appropriate for peer group communication since the central key server must be, at the same time, continuously available and present in every possible subset of a group in order to support continued operation in the event of arbitrary network partitions. Continuous availability can be addressed with fault-tolerance and replication techniques.

Distributed group key management is more suitable to peer group communication, especially over unreliable networks. It involves dynamically selecting a group member that acts as a key server. Although robust, this approach has a notable drawback in that it requires the key server to maintain long-term pairwise secure channels with all current group members in order to distribute group keys. Consequently, each time a new key server comes into play, significant costs must be incurred to set up these channels.

In contrast, contributory group key agreement requires each group member to contribute an equal share to the common group key (computed as a function of all members' contributions). This approach avoids the problems with the single points of trust and failure. Moreover, some contributory methods do not require the establishment of pairwise secret channels among group members.

Many of the centralized and distributed key management protocols such as the Logical Key Hierarchy Protocol (LKH) (Wallner et al., 1999; Wong et al. 2000), LKH+ (Caronni et al., 1999), One-Way Function Tree (OWFT) protocol (Sherman et al., 2003), and Centralized Flat Table (CFT) (Caronni et al., 1999) rely on symmetric encryption to distribute group keys, as opposed to contributory protocols which rely on modular exponentiations. Therefore, they do not provide PFS. However, such protocols scale to large groups and have a lighter overhead than contributory ones.

As can be expected, the cost of group key management protocols is largely determined by two dominating factors: communication and computation. Typically, efficiency in one comes at the expense of the other. Protocols that distribute computation usually require more communication rounds or messages, whereas, protocols minimizing communication require more computational effort.

TOOLKITS FOR GROUP KEY MANAGEMENT

Here we survey the toolkits for group key management systems. The toolkits surveyed are: *Spread*, *Cliques* and SEAL. Spread (Amir et al., 1998) is a group communication system for wide and local area networks. It provides reliability and ordering of messages (FIFO, causal, total ordering) and a membership service. The toolkit supports two different semantics: Extended Virtual Synchrony and View Synchrony. The system consists of a daemon and a library linked with the application. This architecture has many benefits, the most important being the ability to pay the minimum possible price for different causes of group membership changes for wide-area settings. A simple join or leave of a process translates into a single message, while a daemon disconnection or connection requires a full membership change. The process and daemon memberships correspond to the model of light-weight and heavy-weight groups (Floyd et al., 1997).

Spread operates in a many-to-many communication paradigm, each member of the group can be both a sender and a receiver. It is designed to support small to medium groups, but can accommodate a large number of different collaboration sessions, each of which spans the Internet. This is achieved by using unicast messages over the wide-area network and routing them between Spread nodes on the overlay network. Spread scales well with the number of groups used by the application without imposing any overhead on network routers. Group naming and addressing is not a shared resource (as in IP multicast addressing), but rather a large space of strings which is unique to a collaboration session.

The Spread toolkit is publicly available (www.spread.org) and is being used by several organizations in both research and practical settings. The toolkit supports cross-platform applications and has been ported to several Unix platforms as well as to Windows and Java environments.

Cliques (Steiner et al., 1998) is a cryptographic toolkit that implements a number of key agreement protocols for dynamic peer groups. The toolkit assumes the existence of a reliable communication platform that transports protocol messages and provides ordering of messages, deals with group membership management, and performs all computations required to achieve a shared key in a group. The current implementation is built atop the popular OpenSSL library. Currently, Cliques includes five group key agreement protocols: GDH, CKD, TGDH, STR and BD:

1. GDH (Group Diffie-Hellman) is a protocol based on group extensions of the two-party Diffie-Hellman key exchange (Diffie et al., 1976; Steiner et al., 2000) and provides fully contributory authenticated key agreement. GDH is fairly computation-intensive requiring $O(n)$ cryptographic operations upon each key change. It is, however, bandwidth-efficient.

2. CKD is a centralized key distribution with the key server dynamically chosen from among the group members. The key server uses pairwise Diffie-Hellman key exchange to distribute keys. CKD is comparable to GDH in terms of both computation and bandwidth costs.

3. TGDH combines a binary key tree structure with the group Diffie-Hellman technique (Kim, 2000). TGDH seems to be efficient in terms of computation as most membership changes require $O(\log n)$ cryptographic operations.

4. STR (Kim, 2001) is a form of TGDH with a so-called "skinny" or imbalanced tree. It is based on the protocol by Steer et al. STR is more efficient than the above protocols in terms of communication; whereas, its computation costs for subtractive group events are comparable to those of GDH and CKD.

5. BD is a protocol proposed by Burmester-Desmedt (1994), another variation of group Diffie-Hellman. BD is computation-efficient requiring a constant number of exponentiations upon any membership (group key) change. However, communication costs are significant.

All the protocols in the Cliques library provide key independence and perfect forward secrecy (PFS). Informally, key independence means that a passive adversary who knows any proper subset of group keys cannot discover any other (future or previous) group key. PFS means that a compromise of a member's long-term key cannot lead to the compromise of any short-term group keys. Only outside intruders (both passive and active) are considered in Cliques. In this model, any entity who is not a current group member is considered an outsider. Attacks coming from the inside of the group are not considered, as our focus is on the secrecy of group keys and the integrity of the group membership. Consequently, insider attacks are not relevant in this context since a malicious insider can always reveal the group key and/or its own private key(s) thus allowing for fraudulent membership authentication. All the above protocols were proven secure with respect to passive outside (eavesdropping) attacks. Active outsider attacks consist of injecting, deleting, delaying and modifying protocol messages. Some of these attacks aim to cause denial of service and we do not address them. Attacks with the goal of impersonating a group member are prevented by the use of public key signatures, since every protocol message is signed by its sender and verified by all receivers. Other, more subtle, active attacks aim to introduce a known (to the attacker) or old key. These are prevented by the combined use of: timestamps, unique protocol message identifiers and sequence numbers which identify the particular protocol run.

Secure Spread (Amir et al., 2004) is a library that, along with the same reliable and ordered message dissemination and membership services as the Spread client library, provides security services such as data confidentiality and integrity. The main added functionality in Secure Spread is as follows: Whenever the group membership changes, Secure Spread detects it and initiates the execution of a group key agreement protocol. It then detects the termination of the key agreement protocol and notifies the application about the membership change and the new key. In addition, Secure Spread encrypts and decrypts user data using the group key once a group is operational. One major consideration in designing the library was modularity and flexibility. Secure Spread currently supports five key agreement protocols: BD, CKD, GDH, STR, TGDH (all described in detail below). The architecture of Secure Spread allows it to handle different key agreement algorithms for different groups. A client can be a member of different groups, each group with its own key agreement protocol.

SEAL (Secure Communication Library) is a Linux-based C language application programming interface (API) library that implements secure group key agreement algorithms that allow a communication group to periodically renew a common secret group key for secure and private communication (Lee et al., 2007). The group key agreement protocols satisfy several important characteristics: distributed property (i.e., no centralized key server is needed), collaborative property (i.e., every group member contributes to the group key), and dynamic property (i.e., group members can join or leave the group without impairing the efficiency of the group key generation). To offer data privacy, an effective approach is to require all group members to establish a common secret group key, which is held only by group members, but not outsiders, for encrypting the transmitted data. In particular, rekeying, or renewing the group key, is necessary whenever there is any change in the group membership (e.g., a new member joins the group or an existing member leaves the group) in order to guarantee both backward confidentiality (i.e., no joining member can read the previous data) and forward confidentiality (i.e., no leaving member can access the future data).

One simple way for a communication group to perform rekeying is to set up a centralized key server that is responsible for renewing the group key and distributing it to all group members. However, relying on a centralized key server introduces the single-point-of-failure problem since if the key server is compromised, the whole key establishment process fails. Moreover, centralized management is not adequate for decentralized network settings such as peer-to-peer or mobile ad hoc networks. A secure group key agreement scheme should allow the group members to agree upon the group key without relying on a centralized key server. The group key scheme should satisfy the distributed, collaborative and dynamic properties. Both distributed and collaborative properties seek to eliminate the single-point-of-failure problem such that when one member is compromised, the group can still continue with its secure communication by excluding the compromised member.

The design of SEAL includes the following steps to perform rekeying operation:

1. When a new member joins a communication group, it connects to a Spread daemon, a group communication service that guarantees the reliable and ordered message delivery under the same membership view.
2. Among the existing group members, the communication group selects a leader, a single member that is responsible for synchronizing the rekeying operations carried out by all group members.

    At regular rekeying intervals, the leader notifies all other group members to start a new rekeying operation via the broadcast of a rekeying message

3.   Each group member updates its own key tree based on the agreed-upon interval-based algorithm (i.e., Rebuild, Batch, or Queue-batch) and checks whether it is a sponsor. Any member that becomes the sponsor will broadcast the updated blinded keys.

4.   Each member carries out the key confirmation process to assure that every other member has actually obtained the same group key. If this key confirmation process succeeds, then the rekeying operation is finished.

5.   If there are some members leaving the communication group in the middle of a rekeying operation (i.e., after the leader initiates the rekeying operation but before the group key is confirmed), the communication group either continues with its existing rekeying operation, or starts a rekeying operation reflecting the departures of those members.

    The implementation of SEAL is built upon the Spread toolkit, which implements the view synchrony property for reliable group communication. When a new member joins a communication group, it connects to a Spread daemon, a group communication service which maintains an active TCP connection to all other Spread daemons and keeps track of the current membership status of the communication group. Each Spread daemon can be associated with more than one member, so the group communication model forms a two-level hierarchy consisting of the Spread daemons and the group members. When a member joins or leaves the group, every member will receive the latest membership view from its associated Spread daemon. Also, the Spread daemon associated with the joining or leaving member notifies other daemons to flush the remaining messages to the original membership view and to block the transmission of new messages until all Spread daemons and existing group members install the updated membership view. Similarly, if a Spread daemon fails, the associated members are removed from the membership view by the remaining Spread daemons. Therefore, every existing group member always holds the latest membership view. Also, all messages are originated from the sender and delivered to all members under the same membership view, or equivalently between two consecutive membership events. To ensure the ordered delivery, the Spread daemons append a timestamp to every transmitted message.

    The leader is the single member that is responsible for periodically notifying all group members to start a rekeying operation synchronously at regular rekeying intervals. We select the member that stays in the communication group for the longest time to be the leader. When a group member joins the group as a new participant or is notified that the leader has left the group, it decides which member should be the current leader based on the agreed-upon member ship view provided by its associated Spread daemon.

    Since each member holds the identical membership view, any member that falsely claims to be the leader will be detected by other group members and excluded from the communication group. We point out that the leader is not a centralized key server that generates the group key, so the contributory requirement of our proposed algorithms still holds. When a member is selected to be the leader of a communication group, it immediately broadcasts a rekeying message to the group and repeats the broadcast periodically at regular rekeying intervals. Since new members do not know the rekeying information including the present join and leave events as well as the existing key tree when they join the group, each rekeying message should contain the existing key tree as well as the join and leave requests in the last rekeying interval. It is possible that a newly selected leader does not know the current key tree structure. This occurs when it has just joined the group and has not started any rekeying operation. In this case, the leader should include only an empty tree and the join events in the first rekeying message. The leave events, however, are not required as they do not take effect in an empty tree.

Sponsors, refer to the group members that need to broadcast the blinded keys associated with the nodes in a key tree during a rekeying operation. Since each member holds the blinded keys along its own co-path, which is a list of nodes whose siblings belong to its key path, the sponsors have to broadcast the blinded keys of the non-renewed nodes, which are the children of the renewed nodes so that members can compute the secret keys of the renewed nodes. Broadcasting non-renewed blinded keys is essential for the new members which know nothing about the group before they join, as well as for the existing members whose co-path does not include the nonrenewed nodes prior to the rekeying operation.

TWO PARTY KEY EXCHANGE

Key exchange or key establishment is defined to be any process whereby a shared secret key becomes available to two or more parties, for subsequent cryptographic use (Menezes et al., 2001). It can be divided into key transport and key agreement based on how the shared key is generated by the parties. In a key transport protocol one party generates a secret key and securely transmits it to the other participating entities. A simple example of key transport is a party encrypting the generated secret key with the receiver's public key and sending it over an insecure channel. The disadvantage of a key transport protocol is that the secret key is always completely generated by the sending party and it may not be desirable for some applications used by the recipients, for example, due to difference in key size. On the other hand, key agreement is a process in which a shared secret is derived by two or more entities such that no single entity can predetermine the resulting value.

The two-party Diffie-Hellman protocol between two parties A and B. The parties agree on common domain parameters (G, g, p), where g is a generator of the group G of prime order p. In the protocol, A and B pick private keys x and y respectively and exchange the corresponding public keys X and Y. The parties A and B then compute the shared secrets KAB and KBA respectively using the knowledge of their own private key and the incoming public key. Finally, the session key is derived by applying a key derivation function on the shared secret. A key derivation function (Chevassut et al., 2005) ensures that the session key is uniformly distributed in the desired session key space i.e., a set containing all the session keys of desired length. In the security proofs of key exchange protocols, the key derivation function is usually either modelled as a random oracle or instantiated using PRFs.

The fundamental goals of a two-party key exchange protocol that provides security against active adversaries are identified as follows:

- **Implicit Key Authentication:** A key exchange protocol is said to provide implicit key authentication if each party in the protocol is assured that no party aside from the other protocol participants can possibly learn the value of the session key. A key exchange protocol which provides implicit key authentication to all the parties is called an authenticated key exchange (AKE) protocol.
- **Key Confirmation:** A key exchange protocol is said to provide key confirmation if each party is assured that all the other participating entities actually have the possession of the session key.
- **Explicit Key Authentication:** If both implicit key authentication and key confirmation are provided, then the key exchange protocol is said to provide explicit key authentication. A basic goal on the secrecy of the session key is that it should be computationally infeasible for a passive

adversary to compute the established session key. The desired security goals of a key exchange protocol are:

- **Known Key Security:** The knowledge of a session key should not enable an adversary to learn the session keys established in the other sessions. Known key security ensures that the session key established in each session is fresh and does not depend on the other session keys.

- **(Perfect) Forward Secrecy:** A protocol is said to have forward secrecy if the leakage of the long-term key of a party does not compromise the security of the session keys established by that party in the past sessions. A general technique to achieve forward secrecy for key exchange protocols is to ensure that the shared secret contains a component formed by the ephemeral contributions of both the parties.

- **Unknown-Key Share:** A protocol resists unknown-key share attacks, if an entity A cannot be coerced into sharing a key with an entity B without A's knowledge, i.e., when A believes the key is shared with some entity C which is not the same as B. Unknown-key share attacks are also called identity misbinding attacks and can generally be avoided by making sure that the public keys of the parties are certified and that the identities of the parties are included as input to the key derivation function.

- **Key Compromise Impersonation Resistance:** A protocol is resilient to key compromise impersonation (KCI) attacks, if revealing an entity A's long-term private key does not enable the adversary to impersonate other honest entities to A. KCI attacks can generally be thwarted using signature-based authentication.

- **(No) Key Control:** In a key exchange protocol, it is desired that no party is able to predetermine or influence the final value of the session key. Key control is an undesirable property which may enable a malicious party to bias the distribution of the session key or force it to be a key established in the earlier sessions.

A key exchange protocol is said to be insecure or attacked if any of its desired goals are violated. The attacks can broadly be divided into passive or active depending on the type of the adversary (passive or active) that has carried out the attacks. The only passive attack that an adversary can perform is eavesdropping wherein the protocol transcripts are recorded by the adversary but not altered in any way. The basic active attacks include an adversary modifying or deleting the protocol messages in transit, inserting completely new messages and replaying older messages.

GROUP KEY EXCHANGE

A group key exchange (GKE) protocol allows a group of parties to agree upon a common secret session key over a public network. Since we generally consider the group to contain more than two parties, the number of messages exchanged in a GKE protocol will be more than those in a two-party key exchange protocol. The communication efficiency of a GKE protocol is measured by the number of rounds it takes to complete the protocol and the number and size of the messages exchanged. A round includes all the messages that can be sent simultaneously by the parties during the protocol execution. This implies that in any given round, the parties do not have to wait for the messages from the other parties before sending out their messages in that particular round. It is desirable that a GKE protocol is scalable i.e., the number of rounds should not depend on the number of parties.

All the security goals that we have discussed in the previous section for 2PKE protocols apply equally to GKE protocols. Usually it can be assumed that the adversary is an outsider, i.e., a party who does not participate in the protocol. However, we also have to take into account the possible existence of malicious insider parties who may try to disrupt the protocol goals. Note that it is impossible to keep the session key secret from malicious insiders since they are very much part of the protocol execution like other honest parties. However, there are still potential security risks in the presence of insider adversaries. The adversarial actions by the insiders may result in the insiders recovering the long-term private keys of the honest parties or fixing the session key to a predetermined value.

Group DH Protocol

Biswas (2008) proposed an efficient contributory multi-party key-exchanging technique for a large static group. In this protocol, which is based on Diffie Hellman technique, a member who acts as a group controller configures two-party groups with other participants and creates a DH-style shared key for each group; then combines these generated shared keys into a single multi-party key and behaves as a normal group member. It is assumed that two parties are agreed about two large positive integers; q and α. The parameter q is a prime number and α is a generator of finite cyclic group G of order q.

Step 1: An arbitrary member acts as a group controller, for example P_c, and exchanges public keys with other members. Each group individually generates a DH-style key using DH technique. Obviously, the public Key X_c for group controller P_c s generated using the DH formula as below.

$$X_c = \alpha^{e_c} \bmod q \ (e_c \text{ is the private key of the controller})$$

The public Key X_i for node P_i is generated using the formula: $X_i = \alpha^{e_i} \bmod q$ (e_i a private key of the node). Each member generates a unique shared key, K_i with group controller as

$$K = \alpha^{e_i e_c} \bmod q$$

Step 2: The group controller actually calculates n-1 shared keys for n-1 groups. Then it combines these generated keys to make a single Group key Y_i to send it to the node P_i

$$Y_i = \alpha^{\prod_{j=1}^{j=n} K_{j\neq i}} \bmod q$$

Upon receiving Y_i, each node produces the group key K as $K = Y_i^{K_i}$ while the group controller generates the group key as $K = \alpha^{K_1 K_2 \dots K_n} \bmod q$.

SUMMARY

This chapter discussed the extension of two-party to a multi-party setting or a group of parties. The attacks on the two-party key exchange model as discussed in the context of group as well security notions to be supported when members join or leave the group. The security notion of Perfect Forward Secrecy when new members join the group is introduced and discussed. A generalization of the two-party Diffie-Hellman key exchange protocol is discussed in this chapter. This chapter also discussed the practical implementations of the Group Key Exchange Protocols called the *Spread* toolkit and *Cliques*.

REFERENCES

Amir, Y., Kim, Y., Nita-Rotaru, C., Schultz, J. L., Stanton, J., & Tsudik, G. (2004). Secure group communication using robust contributory key agreement. *IEEE Transactions on Parallel and Distributed Systems*, *15*(5), 468–480. doi:10.1109/TPDS.2004.1278104

Amir, Y., & Stanton, J. (1998). The Spread wide area group communication system (Tech. Rep. 98-4). Johns Hopkins University, Center of Networking and Distributed Systems.

Biswas, G. P. (2008). Diffie-Hellman Technique: Extended to multiple two-party keys and one multi-party key. *IET Information Security*, *2*(1), 12–18. doi:10.1049/iet-ifs:20060142

Burmester, M., & Desmedt, Y. (1994, May). A secure and efficient conference key distribution system. In *Advances in Cryptology EUROCRYPT'94*.

Caronni, G., Waldvogel, M., Sun, D., Weiler, N., & Plattner, B. (1999). The VersaKey framework: Versatile group key management. *IEEE Journal on Selected Areas in Communications*, *17*, 9.

Chevassut, O., Fouque, P.-A., Gaudry, P., & Pointcheval, D. (2005). Key derivation and randomness extraction. Retrieved from http://eprint.iacr.org/2005/061

Diffie, W., & Hellman, M. E. (1976). New directions in cryptography. *IEEE Transactions on Information Theory*, *IT-22*(6), 644–654. doi:10.1109/TIT.1976.1055638

Floyd, S., Jacobson, V., Liu, C., McCanne, S., & Zhang, L. (1997). A reliable multicast framework for light-weight sessions and application level framing. *IEEE/ACM Transactions on Networking*, *5*(6), 784–803. doi:10.1109/90.650139

Kim, Y., Perrig, A., & Tsudik, G. (2000). Simple and fault-tolerant key agreement for dynamic collaborative groups. *Proceedings of 7th ACM Conference on Computer and Communications Security* (pp. 235–244). ACM Press. doi:10.1145/352600.352638

Kim, Y., Perrig, A., & Tsudik, G. (2001). Communication-efficient group key agreement. *Proceedings of IFIP SEC '01*.

Lee, P. P. C., Lui, J. C. S., & Yau, D. K. Y. (2007). SEAL: A secure communication library for building dynamic group key agreement applications. *Journal of Systems and Software*, *80*(3), 356–370. doi:10.1016/j.jss.2006.04.016

Menezes, A., Oorschot, P. C. V., & Vanstone, S. A. (2001). *Handbook of Applied Cryptography.* CRC Press.

Sherman, A. T., & McGrew, D. A. (2003). Key establishment in large dynamic groups using one-way function trees. *IEEE Transactions on Software Engineering, 29*(5), 444–458. doi:10.1109/TSE.2003.1199073

Steiner, M., Tsudik, G., & Waidner, M. (1998). CLIQUES: A New Approach to Group Key Agreement. Retrieved from http://www.isi.edu/div7/publication_files/cliques_a_new.pdf

Steiner, M., Tsudik, G., & Waidner, M. (2000). Key agreement in dynamic peer groups. *IEEE Transactions on Parallel and Distributed Systems, 11*(8), 769–780. doi:10.1109/71.877936

Wallner, D., Harder, E., & Agee, R. (1999). Key management for multicast: Issues and architectures.

Wong, C. K., Gouda, M. G., & Lam, S. S. (2000). Secure group communications using key graphs. *IEEE/ACM Transactions on Networking, 8*(1), 16–30. doi:10.1109/90.836475

KEY TERMS AND DEFINITIONS

Group Controller: The group controller in a group is responsible for computing the group key and distributing it to the members in a secure way.

Group Diffie-Hellman Key Exchange: The Diffie-Hellman Key exchange protocol is extended to a group of parties.

Group Keys: When there are more than three parties involved in the communication, a common group keys is used for communication by the parties. The Group Keys are established by a Group Key Exchange protocol.

Perfect Forward Secrecy or Perfect Backward Secrecy: When group members join a group, the rekeying procedure should remain secure achieving perfect secrecy.

Rekeying: When members leave or join the group, the Group Key needs to be recalculated by all the parties involved. This procedure is called rekeying.

Session Keys: Session keys are used by parties involved in the communication for a particular session only. They are usually established by using public key encryption or by using a key exchange protocol like Diffie-Hellman Key Exchange protocol.

Chapter 5
Hash Functions and Their Applications

Kannan Balasubramanian
Mepco Schlenk Engineering College, India

ABSTRACT

Cryptographic Hash Functions are used to achieve a number of Security goals like Message Authentication, Message Integrity, and are also used to implement Digital Signatures (Non-repudiation), and Entity Authentication. This chapter discusses the construction of hash functions and the various attacks on the Hash functions. The Message Authentication Codes are similar to the Hash functions except that they require a key for producing the message digest or hash. Authenticated Encryption is a scheme that combines hashing and Encryption. The Various types of hash functions like one-way hash function, Collision Resistant hash function and Universal hash functions are also discussed in this chapter.

INTRODUCTION

Cryptographic Hash functions are used to achieve a number of security objectives. In this chapter, we bring out the importance of hash functions and their variations, the design techniques and the attacks on them. Throughout the development of Cryptography and Cryptanalysis, confidentiality has taken the primary position and it was believed that if privacy is maintained (using symmetric encryption and secret key) then the authentication will automatically be achieved. Cryptographic Hash Functions are used to achieve a number of Security Goals like Message Authentication, Message Integrity, and are also used to implement Digital Signatures (Non-repudiation), Entity Authentication and steganography. Considerable research has undergone in the field of Cryptographic Hash Functions. Hash Functions can be generated from existing primitives like the Block ciphers (Baretto et al., 2003). as well as being explicitly and specially constructed from scratch as in the MD-4 and MD-5 hash functions (Rivest, 1992a, 1992b) and the family of SHA hash functions. (FIPS 180, FIPS 180-1, FIPS 180-2 and FIPS 180-3 standard of NIST).

DOI: 10.4018/978-1-5225-2915-6.ch005

CRYPTOGRAPHIC HASH FUNCTIONS

Cryptographic Hash functions are one of the most important tool in the field of cryptography and are used to achieve a number of security goals like authenticity, digital signatures, pseudo number generation, digital steganography, digital time stamping and other security goals. The following definition of hash functions is due to Rompay (2004).

- **Hash Function:** A hash function is a function h: D $\rightarrow$ R, where the domain D = {0,1}* and R = {0,1}^{n} for some n > = 1.

Cryptographic Hash Functions are broadly of two types i.e. Keyed Hash functions; the ones that use a secret key, and Unkeyed Hash Functions; the other ones which do not use a secret key. The keyed Hash functions are referred to as Message Authentication codes (MAC). Generally, the term hash functions refer to unkeyed hash functions only. Unkeyed or simply Hash functions (some time also known as MDC – Manipulation Detection Codes) can further be classified into OWHF (One Way Hash Functions), CRHF (Collision Resistant Hash Functions) and UOWHF (Universal One Way Hash Functions) depending on the additional properties they satisfy.

- **One Way Hash Functions (OWHF):** One Way Hash Function as defined by Merkle (1979) is a hash function H that satisfies the following requirements:
    1. H can be applied to block of data of any length. (In practice, 'any length' may be actually be bounded by some huge constant, larger than any message we ever would want to hash).
    2. H produces a fixed-length output.
    3. Given H and x (any given input), it is easy to computer message digest H(x).
    4. Given H and H(x), it is computationally infeasible to find x.
    5. Given H and H(x), it is computationally infeasible to find x and x' such that H(x) = H(x').

The first three requirements are a must for practical applications of a hash function to message authentication and digital signatures. The fourth requirement also known as pre-image resistance or one way property, states that it is easy generate a message code given a message but hard (virtually impossible) to generate a message given a code (Sobti et al., 2012). The fifth requirement also known as Second pre-image resistance guarantees that an alternative message hashing to the same code as a given message cannot be found.

- **Collision Resistant Hash Functions (CRHF):** A Collision Resistant Hash Function (Merkle, 1979). may be defined as a Hash function H, that satisfies all the requirements 1 through 5 of OWHF and in addition satisfy the following collision resistance property:

Given H, it is computationally infeasible to find a pair (x, y) such that H(x) = H(y)

- **Universal One Way Hash Functions (UOWHF):** The Security property of a Universal One Way Hash Functions as described in Naor et al (1989) is defined as follows:

Let U contain a finite number of hash functions with each having the same probability of being used. The probabilistic polynomial time algorithm A (A is a collision adversary) that operates in two phases: Initially, A receives input k and outputs a value x known as initial value, then a hash function H is chosen from the family U. A then receives H and must output y such that $H(x) = H(y)$. In other words, after getting a hash function from the family of hash functions it tries to find a collision with the initial value. Now U is called as a family of Universal One Way Hash Functions if for all polynomial-time A the probability that A succeeds is negligible. The problem of constructing higher orders UOWHFs efficiently is a difficult problem in cryptography.

- **Random Oracles:** A fixed-size random oracle is a function f: $\{0, 1\}^a \rightarrow \{0, 1\}^b$, chosen uniformly at random from the set of all such functions. For interesting sizes a and b, it is infeasible to implement such a function, or to store its truth table. Thus, we assume a public oracle which, given $x \in \{0, 1\}^a$, computes $y = f(x) \in \{0, 1\}^b$.

A variably-sized random oracle is a random function g: $\{0, 1\}^* \rightarrow \{0, 1\}^b$, accessible by a public oracle. Equivalently, it can be viewed as an infinite set of fixed-size random oracles, one oracle g_a: $f\{0, 1\}^a \rightarrow \{0, 1\}^b$ for each a.

- **Shannon Cipher (or an Ideal Block Cipher):** A Shannon cipher is the invertible counterpart of a random oracle. Consider a function E: $\{0, 1\}^n$ x $\{0,1\}^m \rightarrow \{0, 1\}^n$, such that for each M $\in \{0, 1\}^m$, the function $E(., M) = E_M(.)$ is a permutation, i.e., an inverse function $E^{-1}(., M)$ exists. A Shannon (block) cipher E is uniformly chosen at random from all such functions. Again, we cannot implement a Shannon cipher, but we can assume a "Shannon oracle": Given x and M, one can ask the oracle for $y = E(x, M)$, and, given y and M, one can ask the oracle for $x = E^{-1}(y, M)$.

USES OF HASH FUNCTIONS

- **Hash Functions as Pseudo Random Number Generators:** Hash functions as one way functions can be used to implement PRNGs (Pseudo random number generator). A very simple technique can be to start from an initial value s known as seed and compute $H(s)$ and then $H(s+1)$, $H(s+2)$ and so on. Some other ways of given some other ways of constructing Pseudo random strings from Hash functions are described in Bellare et al. (1996a) and Hiatner (2006).
- **Deriving Session Keys:** Hash functions as one way functions can be used to generate sequence of session keys that are used for the protection of successive communication sessions. Starting from a master key K_0, the first session key can be $K_1 = H(K_0)$ and second session key can be $K_2 = H(K_1)$ and so on. A key management scheme based on control vectors which makes use of hash functions and Encryption functions for generating session keys is described in (Matyas et al., 1991).
- **Construction of Block Ciphers:** Block ciphers can be used to construct cryptographic hash functions however the inverse is also true and there have been a few block ciphers designed using Hash functions. In Handschuh et al (2000). Handschuh and Naccache proposed to use the compression function of cryptographic hash function SHA-1 in encryption mode. SHACAL-1 (originally named SHACAL) and SHACAL-2 are block ciphers based on SHA-1 and SHA-256 respectively. SHACAL-1 (originally named SHACAL) is 160-bit clock cipher and SHACAL -2 is 256-bit

block cipher. Both were selected for the second phase of NESSIE project. In 2003 SHACAL- 1 was not recommended for NESSIE portfolio because of concerns about its key schedule, while SHACAL-2 was finally selected as one of the 17 NESSIE finalists.

- **Achieving Integrity and Authentication:** Message Integrity & Authentication may be implemented in multiple ways. Symmetric Encryption based mechanisms may be used but they have their own drawbacks. In order to implement message authentication and integrity, the alternative techniques (other than the methods mentioned in last paragraph) are *MAC* or *hash functions*. MACs may be constructed out of block ciphers like DES. More recently, however, there has been a lot of interest in the idea of constructing MACs from cryptographic Hash Functions (Bellare et al., 1996b). In addition to using Hash Functions for implementing MAC, Hash functions can be used to achieve message authentication and integrity goals without the use of symmetric encryption (Tsudik, 1992; Rompay, 2004). The usage of Hash Functions for Message Authentication to ensure message integrity has increased because majority of hash functions are faster than block ciphers in software implementation and the software implementations for hash functions are freely available.

- **Digital Signatures:** Hash functions are used to simplify the digital signature schemes. Without the use of Hash, the signature will be of same size as message. The fundamental concept here is instead of generating the signature for the whole message which is to be authenticated; the sender of the message only signs the digest of the message using a signature generation algorithm. The sender then transmits the message and the signature to the intended receiver. The receiver verifies the signature of the sender by computing the digest of the message using the same hash function as the sender and comparing it with the output of the signature verification algorithm. This approach saves a lot of computational overhead involved in signing and verifying the messages in which would have been the case without the use of hash functions.

ATTACKS ON HASH FUNCTIONS

The various attacks on hash functions are discussed below (Lucks., 2004):

- **Collision Attack**: Find two messages $M \neq M'$ such that $H(M) = H(M')$.
- **Preimage Attack**: Given a random value $Y \in \{0,1\}^n$, find a message M with $H(M) = Y$.
- **Second Preimage Attack**: Given a message M, find a message $M' \neq M$ with $H(M) = H(M')$.
- **K-Collision Attack (k> = 2):** Find K different messages $M^1, M^2...M^K$, such that $H(M^1) = H(M^2) = ...H(M^K)$.
- **K-Way (2nd) Preimage Attack:** For $K \geq 1$: Given Y (or M with $H(M) = Y$), find K different messages $M^1, M^2...M^K$, such that $H(M^1) = H(M^2) = ...H(M^K) = Y$.
- **Second Collision Attack:** If we have $H(M) = H(N)$ while $M \neq N$ and the length of M and N are the same, then a second collision can be obtained by extending M and N with an arbitrary string S, $H(M \parallel S) = H(N \parallel S)$.
- **Related Message Attack:** By knowing the length of message M that is, L and $H(M)$, one can easily compute a related or extended message M' for an unknown message M. $H(M \parallel L \parallel x)$ is hash of extended message M using the suffix $L \parallel x$. If attacker knows length of message L, he may trace out how M has been padded before being hashed.

- **Length Extension Attack:** An attacker can take advantage of the padding scheme for the messages in Merkle-Damgård construction by applying length extension attack (also called an extension attack). Length extension attack can be used to break the secret prefix MAC scheme where the attacker computes the authentication tags without the knowledge of the secret key (Al-Ahmad et al., 2013).

- **Joux Multi Collison Attack:** Joux attack or Joux multi-collision attack is an attack on Merkle-Damgård hash function, where Antoine Joux shown that finding multiple collisions (more than two messages hashing to the same digest) in a Merkle-Damgård hash function is not much harder than finding single collisions. In his multi-collision attack, Joux assumed access to a machine C that given an initial state, returns two colliding messages (Joux, 2004). Also, Joux used his multi-collision in Merkle-Damgård hash function to produce a collision attack in a concatenation of two independent hash functions.

- **Long Message Second Preimage Attack:** In the second preimage attacks, the attacker finds a second preimage S for a given message M, where $M \neq S$ and $H(M) = H(S)$ with an effort less than 2^t computation of H. In the long message second preimage attack, the attacker tries to find a second preimage for a long target message M of 2^q+1 message blocks. The attacker does this by finding a linking message block M_{link}. Where, the digest of f_{IV} of the linking message block M_{link} matches one of the intermediate states H_i obtained in the hashing of M. The computation cost of this attack is about 2^{t-q} calls to the compression function f.

- **Herding Attack:** This attack is due to Kelsey and Kohno (Kelsey et al., 2006) and is closely related to the multi-collision and second preimage attacks is when an adversary commits to a hash value D (which is not random) that he makes public and claims (falsely) that he possesses knowledge of unknown events (events in the future) and that D is the hash of that knowledge. Later, when the corresponding events occur, the adversary tries to herd the (now publicly known) knowledge of those events to hash to D as he previously claimed).

- **Specific Attacks (Attacks on Specific Hash Functions):** Specific attacks on hash functions are due to the hash functions themselves. For example, attacks on MD5, SHA-0 and SHA-1 are called multi-block collision attacks. Multi Block Collision Attack (MCBA) technique on iterated hash function (i.e Merkle-Damgård construction) finds two colliding messages each at least two blocks on length. In such attack, collisions are found by processing more than one message block.

CONSTRUCTION OF HASH FUNCTIONS

The commonly used designs for the construction of hash functions are discussed below:

Merkle-Damguard Construction: The Merkle-Damgård construction (Damguard, 1989; Merkle, 1989) splits the input message into r-equal sized m-bit blocks $\left(m_0, m_1, \ldots m_{r-1} \right)$ after padding the last block as necessary and appending the message length. Then the construction iterates through each message block applying a compression function

$$C:\{0,1\}^n \times \{0,1\}^m \rightarrow \{0,1\}^n$$

The input to the compression function is the previous compression function output CV_{i-1} and the current message block m_i. The compression function output CV_i is called the Chaining Value and the initial chaining value CV_0 is the called the initialization vector or *IV*. Unfortunately, due to the iterative nature of classic Merkle-Damgård (MD) construction certain generic attacks such as multicollision attack (Joux, 2004) and lengthextension attacks exist that differentiate an MD hash function from a random oracle (Bellare et al., 1993).

The most distinctive and special part of Merkle-Damgård construction is that the problem of designing a collision-resistant hash function reduced to designing a collision-resistant compression function. This means, if the compression function is collision resistant, then, the hash function is collision resistant. So the properties of the compression function will be transformed to the hash function. The Merkle-Damgård construction used in designing popular hash functions such as MD5, SHA-1 and SHA-2. Two different Merkle-Damgård construction versions were developed: wide pipe hash construction and fast wide pipe construction. In the wide pipe hash construction, the internal state size is made larger than the final hash size.

In the fast wide pipe construction, the input to each compression function is divided into half and one half is input to the compression function and the other half is XORed with the output of the compression function.

The Sponge Construction: The sponge construction (Lucks, S., 2004) maps a variable length input to a variable length output. By using a fixed length transformation (or a permutation) that operates on a fixed number of $b = r+c$ number of bits where r is called the bitrate and c is the capacity. The b bits of the state are initialized to zero. The sponge construction operates in two phases:

1. **Absorbing Phase:** The r-bit message blocks are XORed with the first r bits of the state of the function F. After processing all the message blocks, the squeezing phase starts.
2. **Squeezing Phase:** The first r bits of the state are returned as output blocks of the function F. The number of output blocks is chosen by the user.

MESSAGE AUTHENTICATION CODES

A MAC is a function which takes the secret key k (shared between the parties) and the message m to return a tag $MAC_k(m)$. The adversary sees a sequence $(m_1, a_1), (m_2, a_2), ..., (m_q, a_q)$ of pairs of messages and their corresponding tags (that is, $a_i = MAC_k(m_i)$) transmitted between the parties. The adversary breaks the MAC if she can ¯find a message m, not included among $m_1, ..., m_q$, together with its corresponding valid authentication tag $a = MAC_k(m)$. The success probability of the adversary is the probability that she breaks the MAC. (It should be noted that an adversary who finds the key certainly breaks the scheme, but the scheme can also be broken by somehow combining a few messages and corresponding checksums into a new message and its valid checksum.)

To build secure message authentication functions from cryptographic hash functions (in particular, from iterated hash functions), a first clear obstacle is that while secret keys are an essential ingredient in a message authentication function, most cryptographic hash functions, and specifically functions like MD5 or SHA-1, do not use keys at all. Therefore, we first need to define a way to use cryptographic hash functions in conjunction with a key (Bellare et al., 1996).

The most common approach to key a hash function is to input the key as part of the data hashed by the function, e.g., hashing data x using key k is performed by applying the hash function F to the concatenation of k and x. Another approach is to key the function's IV. Namely, instead of using a fixed and known IV as defined by the original function, we replace it by a random and secret value known only to the parties.

AUTHENTICATED ENCRYPTION

One of methods for combining message encryption and authentication are authenticated encryption(AE) modes of operation, which clearly specify how to achieve both privacy and authenticity simultaneously. The authentication component of AE mode is the focus of this section and algorithms designed for the specific purpose of message authentication i.e.: Message Authentication Codes (MACs) based on CBC mode, MACs based on cryptographic hash functions and MACs based on universal hashing are discussed.

The following definition for Message Authentication Code was given by Preneel in . A MAC is a function h satisfying the following conditions:

1. The description of h must be publicly known and the only secret information lies in the key.
2. The argument M can be of arbitrary length and the result $h_K(M)$ has a fixed length of n bits.
3. Given h, M and K, the computation of $h_K(M)$ must be "easy".
4. Given h and M, it is "hard" to determine $h_K(M)$ with a probability of success "significantly higher" than $1/2^n$. Even when a large set of pairs $\{M_i, h_K(M_i)\}$ is known, where the M_i have been selected by the opponent, it is "hard" to determine the key K or to compute $h_K(M')$ for any $M' \neq M_i$.

There are a few constructions that are designed for the specific purpose of message authentication. One of the first approaches for designing a MAC was to build it on the top of an existing block cipher E and then proceed with a common mode of operation. Such MAC is the CBC-MAC, which is a well-studied method to generate a message authentication code based on the Cipher Block Chaining mode (NIST, 2001).

The MAC key is used as cipher key in each step of the iteration, and the message block to be processed in the current step serves as plaintext input to the cipher, after being added bit by bit to the ciphertext output from the previous step:

$$H_1 = E_K(X_1);$$

$$H_i = E_K(X_i \oplus H_{i-1}), (2 \leq i \leq n).$$

Here we assume that the message X (after padding) is divided into blocks $X_1, ..., X_n$ of lengths appropriate for the block cipher used. E_K denotes encryption with secret key K and H_n forms the output of the MAC algorithm. The inherited CBC chaining dependency leads to a general disability of the CBC-MAC to process messages in parallel. There is also no possibility for preprocessing, because it is necessary to know the result of processing the previous block of message in order to process the next block. Furthermore, CBC-MAC is insecure for arbitrary long messages (Bellare et al., 1994). Several more secure variations of the scheme exist however e.g. EMAC, XCBC (Black et al., 2000), OMAC (Iwata et al., 2003), RIPE-MAC (Bosselears et al., 1992). Eventually, one of CBC-MAC like construction was adapted to the AES block cipher and NIST published CMAC (NIST, 2005) as the recommended block cipher mode for message authentication.

An alternative type of MAC construction are message authentication codes based on a cryptographic hash function. This is a common approach because these MACs are usually faster than MACs based on a block cipher. HMAC (Bellare et al., 1996b) is a nested construction that computes a MAC for an underlying hash function h, message X and secret key K, as follows (*opad* and *ipad* are constant values):

$$HMAC(K, X) = h((K \oplus opad) \parallel h((K \oplus ipad) \parallel X)) .$$

The objective of HMAC is to use, with no modification, hash function for its MAC construction. The security of HMAC is based entirely on the underlying hash function, meaning that a weakness in the MAC would only appear if the hash function has not enough cryptographic strength. HMAC is generally much faster than CBC-MAC construction and the reason behind it is that cryptographic hash functions are significantly faster than the multiple block cipher operations used in the latter.

Message Authentication Codes given above use a single cryptographic primitive for their constructions, either block cipher or cryptographic hash function. Carter and Wegman suggested different approach for designing a MAC, namely how to design a MAC using Universal Hash Function Families (Carter et al., 1979, 1981).

- **Universal Hash Functions:** Fix a domain D and range R. A finite multiset of hash functions $H = \{h: D \rightarrow R\}$ is said to be Universal if for every $x, y \in D$, *where* $x \neq y$, $Pr_{h \in H}[h(x) = h(y)] \leq 1/|R|$.

Instead of applying some cryptographic primitive to the message X to be MACed, X was hashed down to a smaller size using a hash function drawn from a Universal Hash Function Family, which had only a combinatorial property (rather than a cryptographic one). Then a cryptographic primitive one-time pad encryption to the smaller resulting string was applied to the resulting string.

Where:

$$Tag_K \left(X, N \right) = h_{K_1} \left(X \right) \oplus f_{K_2} \left(N \right)$$

Tag- authentication tag

X- message to be authenticated

N- nonce (number used once)

K- keys space, $K1, K2 \in K$

h_{K_1} - function drawn from a Universal Hash Function Family

f_{K_2} - block cipher encryption

Universal hash function families based MACs include, but are not limited to UMAC (Black et al., 1999) cryptographic CRC (Krawczyk et al., 1994), bucket hashing (Nevelsteen et al., 1999) or MMH (Halevi et al., 1997). An extensive study for the performance of several universal hash functions for MACs is given by Nevelsteen and Preneel (1999).

Recently, lots of efforts are put into area of authenticated encryption (AE), i.e. into providing both privacy and authenticity of the message simultaneously. AE scheme combines encryption component with authentication component in a secure way. The most straightforward option is to calculate the MAC, append it to the information and subsequently encrypt the new message. An alternative is to omit the encryption of the MAC. The third solution is to calculate the MAC on the encrypted message, then the advantage is that the authenticity can be verified by a receiver without knowing the plaintext (with no need to decrypt if a message is not valid).

SUMMARY

This chapter discussed the various types of hash functions, the various types of attacks on them and methods of construction of hash functions. Hash functions have been used in a number of applications like authenticated Encryption which was briefly discussed in the above chapter.

REFERENCES

Al-Ahmad, M.A., & Alshaikhli, I.F. (2013). Broad view of Cryptographic Hash Functions. *International Journal of Computer Science Issues*, *10*(4).

Baretto, P. S. L. M., & Rijmen, V. (2003). *The Whirlpool Hash Function.*

Bellare, M., Canetti, R., & Krawczyk, H. (1996a). Pseudorandom Functions Revisited: The Cascade Construction and Its Concrete Security. Proceedings of FOCS (pp. 514-523).

Bellare, M., Canetti, R., & Krawczyk, H. (1996b). Keying Hash Functions for Message Authentication. *Proceedings of CRYPTO '96* (pp. 1-15).

Bellare, M., Kilian, J., & Rogaway, P. (1994). *The security of Cipher Block Chaining. Proc. of Crypto'94, LNCS (Vol. 839).* Springer-Verlag.

Bellare, M., & Rogaway, P. (1993). Random oracles are practical: a paradigm for designing efficient protocols. *Proceedings of the 1st ACM conference on Computer and Communications Security* (pp. 62-73). doi:10.1145/168588.168596

Black, J., Halevi, S., Krawczyk, H., Krovetz, T., & Rogaway, P. (1999). *UMAC: Fast and Secure Message Authentication. Proc. Crypto '99, LNCS (Vol. 1666).* Springer-Verlag.

Black, J., & Rogaway, P. (2000). *CBC MACs for Arbitrary-Length Messages: The Three-Key Constructions. Proc. Crypto '00, LNCS (Vol. 1880).* Springer-Verlag.

Bosselaers, A. (1992). Integrity Primitives for Secure Information Systems, Final Report of RACE Integrity Primitives Evaluation.

Carter, L., & Wegman, M. N. (1979). Universal Classes of Hash Functions. *Journal of CSS, 18*(20), 143–154.

Damguard, I. (1989) A Design Principal for Hash Functions. *Proceedings of CRYPTO '89, LNCS* (Vol. 435, pp. 416-427). doi:10.1007/0-387-34805-0_39

Gauravram, P. (2003). Cryptographic Hash Functions: Cryptanalysis, design and Applications [Ph.D. thesis]. Queensland University of Technology, Brisbane, Australia.

Haitner, I., Harnik, D., & Reingold, O. (2006). Efficient Pseudorandom Generators from Exponentially Hard One-Way Functions. Proceedings of ICALP (Vol. 2, pp. 228-239). doi:10.1007/11787006_20

Halevi, S., & Krawczyk, H. (1997). MMH: Software Message Authentication in the Gbit/Second Rates. *Proceedings of Fast Software Encryption FSE'97, LNCS* (Vol. 1267).

Handschuh, H., & Naccache, D. (2000). SHACAL (Submissions to NESSIE). *Proceedings of the First Open NESSIE Workshop.*

Iwata, T., & Kurosawa, K. (2003). OMAC: One-Key CBC MAC. *Proc. of FSE'03, LNCS* (Vol. 2887).

Joux, A. (2004). Multicollisions in Iterated Hash Functions. Application to Cascaded Constructions. *Proceedings of CRYPTO'04 (Vol. 3152,* pp. 306-316).

Kelsey, J., & Kohno, T. (2006). Herding hash functions and the nostradamus attack. In S. Vaudenay (Ed.), *Advances in Cryptology, LNCS* (Vol. 4004, pp. 183–200). doi:10.1007/11761679_12

Krawczyk, H. (1994). LFSR-based Hashing and Authentication. *Proc. of CRYPTO'94, LNCS* (Vol. 839). Springer-Verlag.

Lucks, S. (2004). Design Principles for Iterated Hash Functions. Retrieved from http://eprint.iacr.org/2003/253

Matyas, S. M., Le, A. V., & Abraham, D. G. (1991). A Key-Management Scheme Based on Control Vectors. *IBM Systems Journal, 30*(2), 175–191. doi:10.1147/sj.302.0175

Merkle, R. C. (1989). One Way Hash Functions and DES. *Proceedings of CRYPTO'89, LNCS* (Vol. 435, pp. 428-446).

Merkle, R. C. (1979). Secrecy, Authentication and Public Key Systems [Ph.D. thesis]. Stanford University, Stanford, USA.

Naor, M., & Yung, M. (1989). *Universal One-Way Hash Functions and their Cryptographic Applications* (pp. 33–43). STOC. doi:10.1145/73007.73011

Nevelsteen, W., & Preneel, B. (1999). Software Performance of Universal Hash Functions. *Proc. of Eurocrypt '99, LNCS* (Vol. 1592).

Wegman, M. N., & Carter, J. L. (1991). New hash functions and their use in authentication and set equality. *Journal of Computer and System Sciences*, 22(3), 265-279.

NIST. (2001). NIST Special Publication 800-38A, Recommendation for Block Cipher Modes of Operation - Methods and Techniques.

NIST. (2005). NIST Special Publication 800-38B, Recommendation for Block Cipher Modes of Operation: The CMAC Mode for Authentication.

Preneel, B. (2003). Analysis and design of cryptographic hash functions [PhD thesis]. Katholieke Universiteit Leuven, Belgium.

Purohit, R., Mishra, U., & Bansal, A. (2013). A survey on Recent Cryptographic Hash Function Designs. *International Journal of Emerging Trends and Technology in Computer Science*, 1(1), 117–122.

Rivest, R. (1992a). The MD4 Message Digest Algorithm, IETF RFC 1320.

Rivest, R. (1992b). The MD5 Message Digest Algorithm, IETF RFC 1321.

Rompay, B. V. (2004). Analysis and Design of Cryptographic Hash functions, MAC algorithms and Block Ciphers [Ph.D. thesis]. Electrical Engineering Department, Katholieke Universiteit, Leuven, Belgium.

Sobti, R., & Geetha, G. (2012). Cryptographic Hash Functions: A Review. *International Journal of Computer Science Issues*, 9(2), 461-479.

Tsudik, G. (1992). Message Authentication with One-Way Hash Functions. In INFOCOM (pp. 2055-2059).

KEY TERMS AND DEFINITIONS

Authentication: Message authentication refers to the authentication of messages whereas user authentication refers to the user who has sent the message. In authentication protocols, authentication is achieved by symmetric or public key encryption.

Collision Resistance: The property of collision resistance refers to the property that it is infeasible to produce two different messages that produce the same hash value. A weak collision resistance refers to the property that given a message that it is infeasible to produce another message that produces the same hash value.

Compression Function: A compression function is used in the design of hash functions. It converts a large block input and the output from the previous stage and produces an output that can be sent to the next stage.

Digital Signature: A digital signature authenticates both the user sending the message and the message being sent. A digital signature is produced by encryption the hash of a message with the private key of the user.

Hash Functions: A hash function converts an input message into a fixed size output which can be used to provide message integrity.

Message Authentication Codes(MACs): The message authentication Codes are similar to hash function in that they convert an input message into a fixed size message digest but they also require a key to produce the message digest.

Message Integrity: Message Integrity provides protection against alteration or modification of messages.

Pseudo Random Number Generator(PRNG): A PRNG is a function that produces random values using a seed value. Since the random values may repeat after a certain range, they are called Pseudo random values.

Random Oracle: A random oracle is a black-box that responds to every unique query with a random response chosen uniformly form its output domain. If a query is repeated, it responds the same way every time the query is submitted.

Chapter 6
Efficient Implementation of Digital Signature Algorithms

Sumathi Doraikannan
Malla Reddy Engineering College, India

ABSTRACT

Digital Signature is considered as an authentication tool of electronic records. The main benefits of the digital signature are cost, security, time stamping, non-repudiation and speed. Digital signature can be particularly useful for sales proposals, purchase orders and health services. In addition, this chapter also focuses on the real time applications of digital signature algorithm and its implementations. This chapter deals with the Digital signature algorithm, Digital Signature types and the way of working.

INTRODUCTION

This chapter deals with the Digital signature algorithm. Digital Signature is considered as an authentication tool of electronic records. Many situations might arise where there is no trust between the sender and receiver, and something more than authentication is needed. A digital signature has the same function as the hand-written signature. Digital signatures are used to detect whether any modifications are made in the document. It enables the recipient of the information to verify the sender's authentication and also it checks whether the information is unflawed. In addition, digital signature provides non-repudiation. Non-repudiation refers to the ability of ensuring that the sender will not deny the authenticity of their signature on a document. Thus, digital signature provides data integrity, non-repudiation and authentication. Suppose, if a branch office of any bank is in need of changing the balance of an account, the message will be sent to the head office. The head office person has to check for the authenticity of the message. If it is not proved, then the information is treated as it emerges from the unreliable source. First, this chapter presents the issues related to the digital signatures. The authors have discussed about the types of digital signatures, and its applications. Digital Signatures are an application of asymmetric cryptography.

Conventional HAND-WRITTEN signature is used to authorize a document and it is included in the document as a part of it. Digital Signatures is used to automate the signatures in a reliable way. Using

DOI: 10.4018/978-1-5225-2915-6.ch006

digital signatures eliminates the cost reduction and improves the speed of production processes. Digital signature can be particularly useful for sales proposals, purchase orders and health services etc. The properties of digital signature are

1. Digital signatures could be relatively easy produced.
2. Verifying and recognizing digital signature algorithm is easy.
3. Information used by the digital signature will be unique to the sender in order to prevent forgery and denial of service.

Advantages and disadvantages of digital signature are as follows:

The main benefits of the digital signature are cost, security, time stamping, non-repudiation and speed etc.

Disadvantages of digital signature are

1. Senders and receivers must buy digital certificates from trusted certification authorities.
2. Compatibility of the digital signatures plays an important role and it leads in the complication of sharing the digitally signed documents.

Digital Signature algorithm works in three steps

1. Key generation algorithm is used to generate the keys which are used to sign the document.
2. Signature generation algorithm is used for generating the signatures.
3. Verification algorithm which produces the output as accepts or rejects the signature.

The digital signature is classified based on the usage of key system. There are two key systems used for signing. 1) Private key system 2) Public key system. RSA named after Rivest, Shamir and Aldeman and Digital Signature Algorithm (DSA) use the public key system. Public key system based digital signatures have more advantages than the private-key system based digital signatures.

HISTORY OF DIGITAL SIGNATURE

Nowadays transactions and activities that take place over the Internet needs a lot of protection against various malicious activities. Out of various concerns, security plays a vital role during information transmission. Various schemes like cryptographic systems, digital Signatures were implemented in order to secure the information transmission system. A system has to be deployed for binding the documents electronically since the financial activities, business transactions grow in number nowadays. Digital signatures play the vital role in such bindings. Let us see some of the Milestones in the history of digital signature as show in Figure 1.

Figure 1. Milestones of digital signature

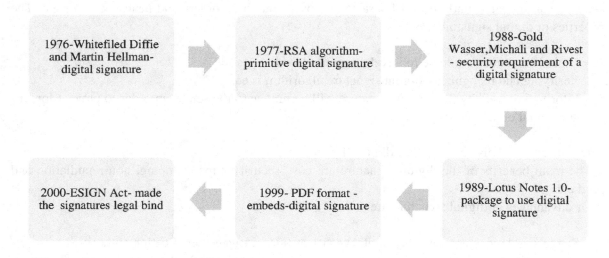

DIGITAL SIGNATURES

Signatures can be either hand-written form or in digital form. The main objective of applying the digital signature is to provide security. The security services provided by the digital signatures are as follows:

- **Authentication:** It ensures that the information has been received from the purported sender. It merely checks who the system or person is. Normally, the authentication process is done by the server and it is usually done by verifying the username and password. Beyond passwords, various other ways of authentication are voice recognition, finger prints, retina scans and OTP etc.
- **Data Integrity:** This security service is used to verify the integrity of the information that has been received by the user. It also checks whether the identity of the sender is valid or not. The objective of data integrity is to ensure the correctness, completeness, wholeness and compliance of data. For example, when a batch of transactions is done, one could make sure that all the information is present and accurately accounted for.
- **Non-Repudiation:** It is used to ensure that both the sender and receiver cannot deny the sending and receiving messages respectively. For example, when Alice sends message to Bob, Alice could generate a proof and show that to Bob to convince. In addition, Bob could get the assurance from Alice in order to show the same proof to the third party.
- **Categories of Digital Signature:** A variety of methods has been proposed for digital signature function could be categorized into two methods namely direct digital signature and arbitrated digital signature.

Direct Digital Signature

- This is the simplest type of digital signature.
- Communication is done between the sender and receiver. (Stallings, 2016)

In this method, the receiver knows the public key of the sender. Digital signature is formed by encrypting the entire information or the hash code of the message with the sender's private key. Encrypting the message assures that the message is kept confidential. In addition to the encryption, signature is created with the receiver's public key or shared secret key as illustrated in the Figure 2. It is important to perform the signature function first and then an outer confidentiality function. If any disputes arise due to any situation, a third party must view the message and its signature. If the signature is generated based on the encrypted message, then the third-party needs decryption key in order to access the original message. On the other hand, if signature function is carried over first as the inner operation, then the receiver can store the original message and the signature could be used for later usage in resolving the disputes.

Shortcomings of Direct Digital Signature

The important factor is that there is a need for trust between the sender and receiver because the verification process takes place independently.

Sender's private key is used for encryption. If the sender likes to deny the process of sending messages, then the sender might claim that the private key is lost or stolen and someone might forge the signature. This type of stealing or forging is treated as a potential security threat. One method to overcome this threat is to include a timestamp with every message and an authority should be appointed to monitor the reports, notifications of loss of keys.

Arbitrated Digital Signature

Arbiter, the trusted third party addresses the problems associated with the direct digital signature. Every signed message that is originated from the sender is tested by the arbiter 'T' in order to check its origin and content before it reaches the receiver. After testing, the message bears the date of testing and it is done by the arbiter 'T'. This mainly resolves the disputes that arise during the denial of sending the message by the sender in direct digital signature. It is very sensitive and crucial for the arbiter to play the role in this scheme. Arbiters might have the chance of accessing the messages whereas in few schemes they don't have the permission.

Shortcomings of Arbitrated Signature

1. Arbiter must have a complete trust from both the sender and receiver that the data is not altered.
2. Arbiter might be bias towards sender or the receiver.

Schnorr Digital Signature

This signature is similar to Elgamal Digital Signature. It uses exponentiation in a finite field. Schnorr's security is based on the discrete logarithm problem. Using this signature, the message dependent computation time is minimized. Signature generation work can be done during the idle time of the processor. This scheme is based on prime modulus 'p' with p-1 having a prime factor q, p-1$\equiv$ (mod q). Here p is of 1024-bit number and q is of 160-bit number which is the length of the SHA-1 hash value.

The generation of a private/public key pair is shown below in the following steps.

Step 1: The prime number p and q is chosen.

Step 2: $a^q = 1$ mod p is computed.

Step 3: Key is generated by every user.

Step 4: A random number 'x' is selected between 0 and q. Here 'x' is private key.

Step 5: Compute the public key of the user as $P_k = a^{-x}$ mod q.

The global parameters are (a, p, q) since all the users have access to these parameters.
Signature Generation Steps:

Step 1: A random number 'n' is chosen and it is used for computation $u = a^n$ mod p.

Step 2: The message is concatenated with u and hashing algorithm is applied as e = H (M || u).

Step 3: Computes s = (n+ x.e) mod q.

Step 4: Now the signature pair is (e, s).

Signature Verification Steps:

Step 1: Compute $U^1 = a^s P_k^e$ mod P.

Step 2: Verifying e = H(M || U^1).

Step 3: $U^1 = a^s P_k^e$ mod P.

$\quad = a^s a^{-x e}$ mod P.

$\quad = a^{s-xe}$ mod P.

$\quad = a^n$ mod P.

Therefore $U^1 = U$. Hence H(M || u) = H(M || U^1).

Digital Signature Standard

Federal Information Processing Standards Publications (FIPS PUBS) are issued by the National Institute of Standards and Technology (NIST).FIPS 186 is known as the Digital Signature Standard (DSS). This standard uses the Secure Hash Algorithm (SHA) and a new digital signature technique called the Digital Signature Algorithm (DSA) has been presented. This standard approved three techniques for generation of digital signature that is used for the data protection and for verification and validation of those digital signatures. The three techniques proposed are

1. The Digital Signature Algorithm (DSA) specification in this standard includes criteria for the generation of private and public key pairs.
2. The RSA Algorithm is mentioned in American National Standard (ANS) X9.31 and Public Key Cryptography Standard (PKCS) #1. Both these standards and its implementations were approved by FIPS 186-4.
3. FIPS 186-4 also approves the use of Elliptic Curve Digital Signature Algorithm (ECDSA) which has been specified in ANS X9.62.

ORIGINAL DSS ALGORITHM

The algorithm focuses only on digital signature function. RSA provides encryption, digital signature and key exchange whereas the DSS does not provide encryption and key exchange. In DSS approach as shown in the below Figure 2, the message is given as input to the hash function and hash code is produced as output. The hash code is combined with the random number 'r' and given as the input to the signature function. In addition, the sender's private key and global public key is given as input to the function. Then, the output is combined with the message and it is sent to the receiver. The receiver generates the hash function. The verifier on the other side receives the signature for verification process. The signature is compared with the signature that has been concatenated with the incoming message that is been given by the sender. If there is a match, then it is proved that the authentication of the message is a successful process.

In the RSA approach, the hash function takes the message as the input and produces a hash code of fixed length. This code is encrypted with the sender's private key and the signature is generated. Then, the signature and the message is transmitted to the receiver. At the receiver side, the receiver receives

Figure 2. DSS approach

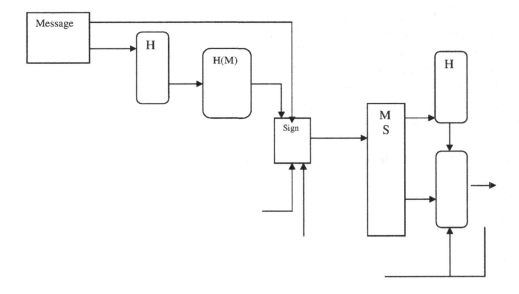

Table 1. Notations used in the DSS

M	Message
H	Hash Function
S	Signature
V	Verifier
R	Random Number

the message and hash function is applied to the message to produce the hash code. The global public key is used for decrypting the signature. If the signature is matched with the hash code that has been generated, then the signature is a valid signature. RSA approach is shown in figure 3.

APPLICATIONS OF DSS

It is mainly used for verifying the integrity of the message, non-repudiation and for authentication verification. Main areas that use DSS are electronic fund transfer, data storage, software distribution and to check for integrity of the database.

Digital Signature Algorithm

Let us have a brief discussion on Digital Signature Algorithm.

It is computed using the parameters such as private key P_k, a secret number 'k', message to be transmitted and a hash function. The digital signature is verified with the help of public key 'P_{uk}' that has been associated with the private key and the hash function used during the generation of signature.

The global parameters used in this algorithm are

1.   P - Prime number where $2^{L-1} < P < 2^L$. Here L is the bit length of P.
2.   q - Prime divisor of (P-1) where $2^{N-1} < P < 2^N$. Here N is the bit length of q.
3.   g - It is in the multiplicative group of GF(P) such that $1< g< P$.
4.   P - Sender's private key. Range is [1,q-1].
5. P_{uk} - Public key. $= g^{Pk}$ mod P.
6.   r - A random number is generated for each message and its range is $1 < r < q-1$. This random number is unique for each message.

This DSS specifies the bit lengths of p and q respectively for L and N.

1.   L = 1024, N =160
2.   L = 2048, N =224

Figure 3. RSA approach

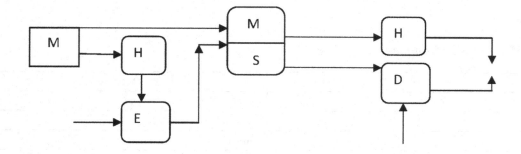

3.   L = 2048, N = 256
4.   L = 3072, N = 256

SIGNATURE GENERATION

1.   The signature consists of two components namely α and β.
2.   compute $\alpha = (g^r \bmod p) \bmod q$.
3.   compute $\beta = (r^{-1} (Z + P_k.\alpha)) \bmod q$. Here Z refers to the leftmost bits of hash value of the message.
4.   Now the signature is (α, β).

SIGNATURE VERIFICATION

This signature verification process could be done either by any third party or the corresponding receiver. Verification process requires the public key. The verifier's identity has to be proved in an authenticated manner before the verification process. Here, in this process, a Certification Authority (CA) delivers the public key that is in the form of a certificate.

1.   Compute $S = (\beta)^{-1} \bmod q$.
2. $u = (H(M).S) \bmod q$. AND $v = (\alpha).S \bmod q$.
3. $T = [(g^{u1} . P_{uk}{}^{v}) \bmod p] \bmod q$.
4.   Check if $T = \alpha$.

In the signature generation process a signature component (α, β), the user's private key, the hash value of the message and a random integer 'r' unique for each signing are used. At the receiving end, the receiver generates a part of the signature component 'T' with the help of parameters such as public key and the hash code of the message. If this component matches the α component of the signature, then the signature is validated.

APPLICATIONS OF DIGITAL SIGNATURE

Digital Signatures are used in secure e-mail and credit card transactions over the Internet. Pretty Good Privacy and Secure/Multipurpose Internet Mail Extension uses digital signatures. Implementation is based on RSA as well as the DSS-based signatures. Secure Electronic Transaction (SET) is used for credit card transactions over the Internet.

REFERENCES

Digital Signature Standard. (n. d.) Retrieved from http://www-2.cs.cmu.edu/afs/cs/academic/class/15827-f98/www/Slides/lecture2/base.024.html

Federal Information Processing Standards Publication 186. (n. d.). Retrieved from http://jbr.org/articles.html

Microsoft. (n. d.) Applications of Digital Signature. Retrieved from https://technet.microsoft.com/en-us/library/cc962021.aspx

Digital Signature Standard. (n. d.). *Digital Signature Algorithm.* Retrieved from http://home.pacbell.net/tpanero/crypto/dsa.html

Stallings, W. (2013). *Cryptography and Network Security Principles and Practice* (7th ed.). Prentice Hall.

NIST. (n. d.) Digital Signature Standard. Retrieved from http://www.itl.nist.gov/fipspubs/fip186.htm

Chapter 7
Attacks on Implementation of Cryptographic Algorithms

Kannan Balasubramanian
Mepco Schlenk Engineering College, India

M. Rajakani
Mepco Schlenk Engineering College, India

ABSTRACT

This chapter investigates the implementation attacks on cryptographic algorithms. The implementation attacks can be defined as invasive or non-invasive. The major attack types are Probing attacks, Fault Induction attacks, timing attacks, Power analysis attacks and Electromagnetic analysis attacks. The attacks target either the physical leakage of a device in which case they are considered physical attacks or try to observe some parameters of the algorithm which constitute logical attacks. The Various countermeasures for the attacks include physical protection against tampering of the device or use redundant computation in the algorithm to prevent observation of the parameters.

INTRODUCTION

This chapter examines the implementation attacks on cryptographic algorithms. Physical attacks on cryptographic algorithms exploit properties of an implementation such as leakage through physically observable parameters (side-channel analysis) or susceptibility to errors (fault analysis) to recover secret cryptographic keys. In the absence of adequate countermeasures, such attacks are often much more efficient than classical cryptanalytic attacks. Embedded devices that implement cryptography in a variety of security-demanding applications are particularly vulnerable to physical attacks.

Modern electronic devices that implement cryptography are more advanced than previous electro-mechanical machines, but they are still vulnerable to physical eavesdropping and tampering. Physical cryptanalytic attacks pose a particular threat to embedded devices that implement cryptography, since embedded devices are almost always exposed to the environment that is out of the owner's control and is therefore considered untrusted. For example, a payment terminal accepting bank cards in a shop can be modified in a malicious way to extract information from the card, and this can be later used for steal-

DOI: 10.4018/978-1-5225-2915-6.ch007

ing money from the owner's account. Traditional computers such as desktops and servers are also at risk: they are exposed to the network, and this situation makes it possible to remotely observe execution timing and protocol messages which can be used in a more general class of implementation attacks.

CONVENTIONAL AND PHYSICAL CRYPTANALYTIC ATTACKS

Cryptographic algorithms are designed to withstand cryptanalysis following the keystone rule formulated in the end of the19-th century known as (second) Kerckhoffs' principle, which states that a cryptosystem should be secure even if everything about the system, except the key, is public knowledge. A cryptographic key is a piece of information which in the case of a cipher is used to uniquely encrypt a plaintext to obtain the ciphertext, and perform the inverse action. Among the keyed algorithms, there are symmetric cryptographic algorithms where encryption and decryption are performed with the same secret key, and public key cryptographic algorithms that use a pair of a public and a private key. Secret keys and private keys are targets of key recovery attacks, with which this work deals. There are unkeyed cryptographic algorithms, e.g. hash functions, but we do not consider them in this work, though physical attacks on some of them, for instance on physical random number generators, are possible.

A brute force attack tries every key against a plaintext-ciphertext pair is always possible against cryptographic algorithms. An attack is said to happen when the complexity expressed in some basic operations such as encryption algorithm executions or processor clock ticks is below the brute force complexity. With the modern computational resources, attacks are practical only up to about 2^{64} basic operations. Typical key sizes for symmetric algorithms range today from 80 to 256 bits.

In the classical cryptanalytic scenario an attacker tries to recover the secret key knowing the algorithm description and having (depending on the concrete scenario) some inputs to the algorithm, the corresponding outputs, or both. A physical implementation of an algorithm is considered to be a black box in the sense that only inputs and outputs are observed, but not the internal variables or any other information about what happens during the execution. In contrary to the classical scenario, in the physical cryptanalysis scenario an adversary observes or manipulates some physical parameters of the device running the algorithm. For instance, one can observe power consumption, electromagnetic radiation, execution duration, or tamper with the supply voltage or the clock signal.

TARGETS FOR PHYSICAL ATTACKS

Here we look at two different types of targets for physical attacks: the Smart Card and the FPGA.

- **Smart Card:** One of the most typical targets of side-channel attacks (and one often chosen in the literature) is the smart card. They are also easy to get hold on: usually carried around in many places, small-sized, and an easy target for a pickpocket. In addition, smart cards are pretty easy to scrutinize: as a smart card depends on the reader it is inserted in in many ways (see below), running time, current, etc., are easy to monitor. Finally, they are quite simple devices, typically running one process at a time, and with a much simpler processor than a desktop PC or mainframe. Basically, a smart card is a computer embedded in a safe. It consists of a (typically, 8-bit or

32-bit) processor, together with ROM, EEPROM, and a small amount of RAM, which is therefore capable of performing computations. The main goal of a smart card is to allow the execution of cryptographic operations, involving some secret parameter (the key), while not revealing this parameter to the outside world. This processor is embedded in a chip and connected to the outside world through eight wires. Following components of the Smart Card are of interest to us.

- **Power Supply:** Smart cards do not have an internal battery. The current they need is provided by the smart card reader. This will make the smart card's power consumption pretty easy to measure for an attacker with a rogue reader.

- **Clock:** Similarly, smart cards do not dispose of an internal clock either. The clock ticks must also be provided from the outside world. As a consequence, this will allow the attacker to measure the card's running time with very good precision.

Smart cards are usually equipped with protection mechanisms composed of a shield (the passivation layer), whose goal is to hide the internal behavior of the chip, and possibly sensors that react when the shield is removed, by destroying all sensitive data and preventing the card from functioning properly.

The following Reference provides additional material on Smart Cards (Rankl et al, 1997).

- **FPGA (Field Programmable Gate Array):** While, smart cards that are typical standardized general purpose circuits, FPGAs are a good example of circuits allowing application specific implementations. Fundamentally, both smart cards and FPGAs (and most processors and Application Specific Integrated Circuits (ASICs)) share the same leakage sources and are consequently similar in terms of susceptibility against physical attacks. However, the following differences are to be noted.
  - They are generally used for completely different applications: smart cards have limited computational power while FPGAs and ASICs are usually required for their ability to deal with high throughput.
  - FPGAs and ASICs allow parallel computing and have a more flexible architecture (as it is under control of the designer). This may affect their resistance against certain attacks.
  - FPGAs usually contain an array of computational elements whose functionality is determined through multiple programmable configuration bits. These elements, sometimes known as logic blocks, are connected using a set of routing resources that are also programmable. They can be used to implement a variety of digital processing tasks. FPGAs allow the designer to determine the allocation and scheduling of the tasks in the circuit (e.g. to trade surface for speed), which is typically out of control of the smart card programmer.

Differences between platforms may affect the physical security at two distinct levels. Firstly, the devices may be based on different technologies and consequently have different physical behaviors. For example, certain side-channel attacks require to make predictions of the leakage. The prediction model may be different for different devices. Similarly, fault insertion techniques may have different effects on different technologies. Second, as already mentioned, different platforms may have different architectures, leading to different computational paradigms. For example, smart cards are small processors where the data is managed sequentially. FPGA designs (i.e. the hardware counterpart of smart card programs) have a more flexible architecture and allow parallel computation.

IMPLEMENTATION ATTACKS

All implementation attacks fall into two large groups depending on whether an adversary just observes some parameters of the implementation or influences its execution. Passive implementation attacks exploit results of observing an implementation while it works (largely) as intended. The adversary can feed inputs but does not interfere with the execution of an algorithm or a protocol. The attacks in this group includes side-channel attacks, where physical leakage of a device during an algorithm execution is observed, and higher-level logical attacks, where some parameters of a protocol execution, for instance error messages, are observed.

Active implementation attacks exploit results of influencing an implementation, or manipulating with it, such that it behaves abnormally. They comprise fault attacks where errors are introduced into an execution of a cryptographic algorithm or a protocol, and other attacks that do not directly exploit the properties of a cryptographic algorithm or a protocol, such as dumping the device's memory that contains the secret key.

Another dimension of classification concerns the level of intrusion into an implementation. They are: (i) non-invasive attacks where a device remains intact and only the environmental parameters are observed or changed, (ii) semi-invasive attacks where device's case or package is removed, for instance a microchip is decapsulated, to get better access to the internals, and(iii) invasive attacks where a direct contact to device internals is established.

These two dimensions of classification are not independent in practice, and the classification is not complete. Side-channel attacks are mainly non-invasive, whereas semi-invasive and invasive attacks are mainly active, but there are special cases. For instance, attacks exploiting electromagnetic radiation of a device often benefit from partially removing the package of an integrated circuit that enables to register stronger fields close to the silicon chip surface (Kizhvatov, 2011).

Probing attacks are made when the adversary physically connects to wires of an integrated circuit (decapsulating the device and cutting into the silicon chip) to read the transferred bits, can hardly be categorized as either side-channel (since this is a direct connection) or fault attacks (no errors are introduced). Attacks exploiting data remanence (residual representation of digital data that remains even after attempts have been made to remove or erase the data.) are another special category of implementation attacks. Bug attacks that exploit production-or design-stage defects of a device are similar to fault attacks but are passive. Furthermore, active and passive techniques can also be combined.

A large subset of implementation attacks are physical attacks that are characterized by a physical contact with a device. Since this mainly means proximity to the device, side-channel attacks observing timing variations of the implementation remotely over the network can be viewed as a special case.

The following is a summary of the classification of attacks on implementation:

- **Invasive vs. Non-Invasive:** Invasive attacks require depackaging the chip to get direct access to its inside components; a typical example of this is the connection of a wire on a data bus to see the data transfers. A non-invasive attack only exploits externally available information (the emission of which is however often unintentional) such as running time, power consumption, etc.,) One can go further along this axis by distinguishing local and distant attacks: a local attack requires close – but external, i.e. non-invasive – proximity to the device under concern, for example by a direct connection to its power supply. As opposed, a distant attack can operate at a larger distance, for example by measuring electromagnetic field several meters (or hundreds of meters) away, or by interacting with the device through an internet connection.

- **Active vs. Passive:** Active attacks try to tamper with the device's proper functioning; for example, fault-induction attacks will try to induce errors in the computation. In contrast, passive attacks will simply observe the device's behavior during its processing, without disturbing it. Note that these two axes are very much orthogonal: an invasive attack may completely avoid disturbing the device's behavior, and a passive attack may require a preliminary depackaging for the required information to be observable. These attacks are of course not mutually exclusive: an invasive attack may for example serve as a preliminary step for a non-invasive one, by giving a detailed description of the chip's architecture that helps to find out where to put external probes.

The following five major attack groups are usually considered.

1. Probing attacks consist in opening a device in order to directly observe its internal parameters. These are thus invasive, passive attacks.
2. Fault induction attacks try to influence a device's behavior, in a way that will leak its secrets. The difficulty lies not so much in inducing a fault than in being able to recover secret parameters from the faulty result, and this is the question that will retain most of our attention. These attacks are by essence active, and can be either invasive or non-invasive
3. Timing attacks exploit the device's running time.
4. Power analysis attacks focus on the device's electric consumption.
5. Electromagnetic analysis attacks measure the electromagnetic field surround- surrounding the device during its processing.

The three last groups are usually denoted as side-channel attacks. Their basic idea is to passively observe some physical characteristic during the device's processing, and to use this "side-channel" to derive more information about the processed secret. They are thus passive, and typically non-invasive, although some exceptions exist.

In some sense, timing, power and electromagnetic analysis attacks can be viewed as an evolution in the dimension of the leakage space. Timing attacks exploit a single, scalar information (the running time) for each run. Power attacks provide a one-dimensional view of the device's behavior, namely instant power consumption at each time unit. With the possibility to move the sensor around the attacked device (or to use several sensors), electromagnetic analysis provide a 4-dimensional view: spatial position and time. This allows for example to separate the contributions of various components of the chip, and therefore to study them separately.

Timing attacks and Simple Power Analysis provide an indirect access to the data processed, via the observation of the operations performed whereas power or electromagnetic analysis offer direct access to the data processed.

PROBING ATTACKS

One natural idea when trying to attack a security device is to attempt to depackage it and observe its behavior by branching wires to data buses or observing memory cells with a microscope. These attacks are called probing attacks. The most difficult part of probing attacks lies in managing to penetrate the device and access its internals. An useful tool for this purpose is a probing station. Probing stations consist of microscopes with micromanipulators attached for landing fine probes on the surface of the chip. They are widely used in the semi-conductor manufacturing industry for manual testing of production-line samples. To make observation easier, the attacker may try to slow down the clock provided to the chip, so that successive states are easily observable. An introduction on probing attacks can be found in (Anderson, 2001), and a good overview about ways to depackage a card and probe its content is given in (Kommerling et al, 1999).

Smart cards are usually protected by a passivation layer, which is basically a shield covering the chip, in order to prevent them from observing their behavior. In addition, some smart cards are equipped with detectors, for example in the form of additional metallization layers that form a sensor mesh above the actual circuit and that do not carry any critical signals. All paths of this mesh need to be continuously monitored for interruptions and short-circuits, and the smart card has to refuse processing and destroy sensitive data when an alarm occurs. Better protection techniques, such as stronger passivation layers, that will make it difficult for the attacker to remove them without damaging the chip itself, are also developed.

The most obvious target is of course the part of memory where secret keys are stored; similarly, in a software-based device, the attacker can also tape the data buses connecting memory to processor, as he knows that the secret key will of course be processed during the signature (or decryption), and hence transit through that wire.

FAULT INDUCTION ATTACKS

A powerful cryptanalysis technique consists of tampering with a device in order to have it perform some erroneous operations, hoping that the result of that erroneous behavior will leak information about the secret parameters involved. The faults may be characterized from several aspects:

- **Permanent vs. Transient:** A permanent fault damages the cryptographic device in a permanent way, so that it will behave incorrectly in all future computations; such damage includes freezing a memory cell to a constant value, cutting a data bus wire, etc., In contrast, with a transient fault, the device is disturbed during its processing, so that it will only perform fault(s) during that specific computation. Some examples of such disturbances are radioactive bombing, abnormally high or low clock frequency and abnormal voltage in power supply.
- **Error Location:** Some attacks require the ability to induce the fault in a very specific location (memory cell); others allow much more flexibility;
- **Time of Occurrence:** Similarly, some attacks require to be able to induce the fault at a specific time during the computation, while others do not.
- **Error Type:** Many types of error may be considered:
  - Flip the value of some bit or some byte,
  - Permanently freeze a memory cell to 0 or 1,
  - Induce (with some probability) flips in memory, but only in one direction (e.g. a bit can be flipped from 1 to 0, but not the opposite),
  - Prevent a jump from being executed,
  - Disable instruction decoder.

- **Fault Induction Techniques:** Faults are induced by acting on the device's environment and putting it in abnormal conditions. Many channels are available to the attacker:
- **Voltage:** Unappropriate voltage might of course affect a device's behavior. For example, smart card voltages are defined by ISO standards: a smart card must be able to tolerate on the contact VCC a supply voltage between 4, 5V and 5, 5V, where the standard voltage is specified at 5V. Within this range the smart card must be able to work properly. However, a deviation of the external power supply, called spike, of much more than the specified 10% tolerance might cause problems for a proper functionality of the smart card. Indeed, it will most probably lead to a wrong computation result, provided that the smart card is still able to finish its computation completely.
- **Clock:** Similarly, standards define a reference clock frequency and a tolerance around which a smart card must keep working correctly. Applying an abnormally high or low frequency may of course induce errors in the processing.
- **Temperature:** Having the device process in extreme temperature conditions is also a potential way to induce faults, although it does not seem to be a frequent choice in nowadays attacks.
- **Radiations:** Correctly focused radiations can harm the device's behavior.
- **Light:** Recently, Skorobogatov and Anderson (Skorobogatov,S.,et.al., 2002) observed that illumination of a transistor causes it to conduct, thereby inducing a transient fault. By applying an intense light source (produced using a photoflash lamp magnified with a microscope), they were able to change individual bit values in an SRAM. By the same technique, they could also interfere with jump instructions, causing conditional branches to be taken wrongly.
- **Eddy Current:** Quisquater and Samyde (QuisQuater et al, 2002) showed that eddy currents induced by the magnetic field produced by an alternating current in a coil could induce various effects inside a chip as for example inducing a fault in a memory cell, being RAM, EPROM, EEPROM or Flash (they could for example change the value of a pin code in a mobile phone card).
- **Cryptanalyses Based on Fault:** Attack on RSA with CRT (Boneh et al, 1997; Joye et al, 1999) is probably the most exemplary instance of fault induction attack. Biham and Shamir (Biham, 1997) showed that such attacks could be applied against block ciphers as well, by introducing the concept of differential fault analysis (DFA).

Other fault models have also been considered, which allow some trivial attacks. Some authors, for example, consider a model in which memory cells can be flipped from one to zero (or from zero to one), but not the opposite. An obvious way to exploit this is to repeatedly induce faults on the key, until all its bits have been forced to zero (and producing some ciphertexts between each fault induction). The chain is then explored backwards, starting from the known (null) key, and guessing at each step which bits have been flipped; correct guesses are identified by comparison with the ciphertexts. An even simpler attack is given in Blomer et al (2002), that additionally assumes that it is possible to choose the location of the flipped bit. In this case, the attack simply consists in forcing a key bit to zero and checking if the result is different from the one obtained without fault induction. If this is the case, conclude the key bit was 1, otherwise conclude 0.

Finally, several obvious ways to exploit very specific faults can easily be devised: for example, a fault that would affect a loop counter so that only two or three rounds of DES are executed would of course allow to break the scheme. Similarly, disabling the instruction decoder could have the effect that all instructions act as a NOP so the program counter cycles through the whole memory.

TIMING ATTACKS

Usually the running time of a program is merely considered as a constraint paramaeter that must be reduced as much as possible by the programmer. More surprising is the fact that the running time of a cryptographic device can also constitute an information channel, providing the attacker with invaluable information on the secret parameters involved. This is the idea of timing attack. This idea was first introduced by Kocher (1996).

In a timing attack, the information at the disposal of the attacker is a set of messages that have been processed by the cryptographic device and, for each of them, the corresponding running time. The attacker's goal is to recover the secret parameters.

Power Analysis Attacks

In addition to its running time, the power consumption of a cryptographic device may provide much information about the operations that take place and the involved parameters (Kocher et al, 1999).

Different power analysis attacks have been considered: Simple Power Analysis, Differential Power Analysis, and Correlation Attacks.

Electromagnetic Attacks

Any movement of electric charges is accompanied by an electromagnetic field. Electromagnetic attacks, first introduced by Quisquater and Samyde (Quisquater et al, 2002) exploit this side channel by placing coils in the neighborhood of the chip and studying the measured electromagnetic field. The information measured can be analyzed in the same way as power consumption (simple and differential electromagnetic analysis –SEMA and DEMA – or more advanced correlation attacks), but may also provide much more information and are therefore very useful, even when power consumption is available.

Countermeasures Against Physical Attacks

The most direct way to prevent physical opponents is obviously to act at the physical/hardware level. A typical example related to probing is the addition of shields, conforming glues, or any process that makes the physical tempering of a device more complex. Detectors that react to any abnormal circuit behaviors (light detectors, supply voltage detectors, ...) may also be used to prevent probing and fault attacks. With respect to side-channel attacks, simple examples of hardware protection are noise addition, or the use of detachable power supplies. Technological solutions can also be considered. There exist circuit technologies that offer inherently better resistance against fault attacks. Finally, most of the proposed techniques aim to counteract fault and side-channel attacks at the algorithmic level. Certain solutions, such as the randomization of the clock cycles, use of random process interrupts or bus and memory encryption, may be used to increase the difficulty of successfully attacking a device, whatever physical attack is concerned. Most solutions however relate to one particular attack. With respect to faults, they mainly include different kinds of error detection/correction methods based on the addition of space or time redundancies. Regarding side-channel attacks, a lot of countermeasures intend to hide (or mask) the leakage or to make it unpredictable. One could for example think about performing a "square and multiply always" algorithm (i.e. always perform a multiplication and discard the result if the operation was not necessary) for exponentiation, and using a similar "reduce always" method for Montgomery multiplication in order to counter timing attack (Koeune et al, 2005).

SUMMARY

This chapter examined various physical attacks on cryptographic devices. Various attacks like the probing attacks, fault induction attacks, timing attacks, power analysis attacks and electromagnetic attacks are discussed. The countermeasures these attacks are also discussed.

REFERENCES

Anderson, R. J. (2001). *Security Engineering*. New York: Wiley &sons.

Biham, E., & Shamir, A. (1997) Differential fault analysis of secret key cryptosystems. In B. Kaliski (Ed.), Proc. of Advances in Cryptology – Crypto '97, LNCS (Vol. 1294, pp. 513–525). doi:10.1007/BFb0052259

Blomer,J., and Seifert,J.P. (2002) Fault based cryptanalysis of the advanced encryption standard (AES).

Boneh, D., DeMillo, R. A., & Lipton, R. J. (1997). On the importance of checking crypto-graphic protocols for faults. In W. Fumy (Ed.), Advances in Cryptology - EUROCRYPT '97, Konstanz, Germany LNCS (Vol. 1233, pp. 37–51). Springer.

Joye, M., Lenstra, A. K., & Quisquater, J.-J. (1999). Chinese remaindering based cryptosystems in the presence of faults. *Journal of Cryptology*, *12*(4), 241–245. doi:10.1007/s001459900055

Kizhvatov, I. (2011). Physical Security of Cryptographic Algorithm Implementations [Ph.D Dissertation]. University of Luxemborg.

Kocher, P. (1996) Timing attacks on implementations of Diffie-Hellman, RSA, DSS, and other systems. In N. Koblitz (Ed.), Advances in Cryptology - CRYPTO '96, Santa Barbara, California, LNCS (Vol. 1109, pp. 104–113). Springer.

Kocher, P., Jaffe, J., & Jub, B. Differential power analysis. In M. Wiener (Ed.), Proc. of Advances in Cryptology – CRYPTO '99, LNCS (Vol. 1666, pp. 388–397). Springer-Verlag.

Koeune, F., & Standaert, F.-X. (2005). A Tutorial on Physical Security and Side-Channel Attacks. In Foundations of Security Analysis and Design III, *LNCS* (Vol. *3655*, pp. 78–108). doi:10.1007/11554578_3

Kommerling, O., & Kuhn, M. G. (1999). Design principles for tamper-resistant smartcard processors. *Proc. of USENIX Workshop on Smartcard Technology (Smartcard '99)*.

Quisquater, J-J., & Samyde, D. (2002). Eddy current for magnetic analysis with active sensor. *Proc. of Esmart '02*.

Rankl, W., & Effing, W. (1997). *Smart Card Handbook*. John Wiley & Sons.

Skorobogatov, S., & Anderson, R. (2002). Optical fault induction attacks. In B. S. Kaliski et al. (Eds.), *CHES-2002, LNCS* (Vol. 2523). Springer-Verlag.

Smart, N., (Ed.) (2010). ECRYPT II yearly report on algorithms and keysizes. *ECRYPT II deliverable, Revision* 1.0. Retrieved from http://www.ecrypt.eu.org/documents/D.SPA.13.pdf

KEY TERMS AND DEFINITIONS

Electro-Magnetic Attacks: The electromagnetic attacks study the electromagnetic field surrounding the device to gather information about the secret parameters.

Fault-Induction Attacks: A techniques where errors are introduced into the device to learn about the secret parameters of the algorithm.

Invasive Attacks: An attack which exploits a direct contact with the device performing the computation.

Non-Invasive Attacks: An attack where only the environmental parameters are changed are observed.

Power Analysis Attacks: Attacks that try to decipher information about the computation based on the power being consumed.

Probing Attacks: Probing attacks make use of a probing station to penetrate the internals of a device and learn about the device and the computation being performed.

Side Channel Attacks: Side channel attacks on cryptographic implementation make use of information regarding time taken, power consumption and the like to decipher the bits being used.

Timing Attacks: Attacks that observe the time taken to decipher information.

Chapter 8
Homomorphic Encryption Schemes:
A Survey

Kannan Balasubramanian
Mepco Schlenk Engineering College, India

Jayanthi Mathanan
Mepco Schlenk Engineering College, India

ABSTRACT

Homomorphic encryption is a technique that enables mathematical operations to be performed on encrypted data. This type of encryption can be used to perform operations on encrypted data by a server without having to provide the key. An example application is searching or querying an encrypted database. The encryption schemes are classified as additive or multiplicative homomorphic if they support addition or multiplication on encrypted data. The Cryptosystems are classified as fully homomorphic, partially homomorphic or somewhat homomorphic based on the type and number of operations supported on the ciphertext.

INTRODUCTION

Homomorphic encryption is a technique that enables mathematical operations to be performed on encrypted data. Homomorphic encryption is a form of encryption which allows specific types of computations to be carried out on ciphertext and generate an encrypted result which, when decrypted, matches the result of operations performed on the plaintext. With most encryption schemes, the encrypted data has to be decrypted entirely before any significant work (e.g., math or programming operations) can be done on it. Homomorphic Encryption, on the other hand, lets you perform mathematical operations directly on the encrypted data *and* have the results of that mathematical operations show in the underlying data.

An encryption scheme that allows meaningful computation on encrypted data, namely a homomorphic encryption scheme. Fix a particular plaintext space P which is a ring (e.g., $P = F2$). Let C be a class of

DOI: 10.4018/978-1-5225-2915-6.ch008

arithmetic circuits over the plaintext space P. A somewhat homomorphic (public-key) encryption relative to C is specified by the procedures KeyGen, Enc, Dec (for key generation, encryption, and decryption, respectively) and the additional procedure Eval that takes a circuit from C and one ciphertext per input to that circuit, and returns one ciphertext per output of that circuit.

Homomorphic encryption schemes are malleable by design. Homomorphic encryption is the conversion of data into ciphertext that can be analyzed and worked with as if it were still in its original form. Homomorphic encryptions allow complex mathematical operations to be performed on encrypted data without compromising the encryption. In mathematics, homomorphic describes the transformation of one data set into another while preserving relationships between elements in both sets. Because the data in a homomorphic encryption scheme retains the same structure, identical mathematical operations, whether they are performed on encrypted or decrypted data, will yield equivalent results.

Suppose you want to add two numbers that are stored in an encrypted file. Traditionally the only way to do it was to decrypt the file, add the two numbers and then re-encrypt the file. Of course, to do the addition you had to have access to the entire contents. This also meant that ther people could access it while it was stored as plain text. There are lots of of situations where it would be good if the data could be stored in encrypted form, say in the cloud, and still operated on without having to decrypt it. This is the goal of fully homomorphic encryption.

It is a crypto system that allows another party to perform operations on your ciphertext without having knowledge of your secret key. For example, it would allow a service to add two encrypted numbers and return the result without ever decrypting the two numbers. So if $E(x)$ represents the encryption of the number x with my secret key, another party would be able to compute $E(x_1 + x_2)$ if one were to pass them $E(x_1)$ and $E(x_2)$ using a homomorphic cryptosystem.

HOMOMORPHIC OPERATIONS

Addition: Given two ciphertexts C_1, C_2 that decrypt to $B_1; B_2$, respectively [2], it is easy to see that the matrix $C = C_1 + C_2$ mod q would be decrypted to $B_1 + B_2$ mod 2, as long as there is no overflow in any entry. Specifically, if we have $C_1 = AS_1 + 2X_1 + B_1$ and $C_1 = AS_2 + 2X_2 + B_2$ then

$$C = C_1 + C_2 = A(S_1 + S_2) + 2(X_1 + X_2) + (B_1 + B_2)$$

which would be decrypted as $B_1 + B_2$ as long as all the entries in $T(2(X_1 + X_2) + B_1 + B_2)T^t$ are smaller than q/2.

Multiplication: Given two ciphertexts C_1, C_2 that encrypt B_1, B_2, respectively, we compute the product ciphertext as $C = C_1.C_2^t$ mod q. If we have $C_1 = AS_1 + 2X_1 + B_1$ and $C_2 = AS_2 + 2X_2 + B_2$ then

$$C = C_1.C_2^t = \left(AS_1 + 2X_1 + B_1\right)\left(AS_2 + 2X_2 + B_2\right)^t$$
$$= A.\underbrace{\left(S_1 C_2^t\right)}_{S} + 2\underbrace{\left(X_1\left(2X_2 + B_2\right) + B_1 X_2^t\right)}_{x} + \underbrace{B_1 B_2^t}_{B} + \underbrace{\left(2X_1 + B_1\right)S_2^t}_{s'}.A^t \left(\text{mod } q\right)$$

Hence the product ciphertext has the form $AS + 2X + B + S'A^t$.

PARTIALLY HOMOMORPHIC CRYPTOSYSTEMS

In the following examples, the notation $\epsilon(x)$ is used to denote the encryption of the message x.

Unpadded RSA

If the RSA public key is modulus m and exponent e, then the encryption of a message x is given by $\epsilon(x) = x^e \bmod m$. The homomorphic property is then

$$\epsilon(x_1).\ \epsilon(x_2) = x_1^e\, x_2^e \bmod m = (x_1\, x_2)^e \bmod m = \epsilon\, (x_1.\, x_2)$$

ElGamal

In the ElGamal cryptosystem, in a group G, if the public key is (G, q, g, h), where, $h = g^x$ and x is the secret key, then the encryption of a message m is $\epsilon(m) = (g^r, m.h^r)$, for some random $r \in \{ 0, ..., q\text{-}1 \}$. The homomorphic property is then

$$\epsilon(b1) = (g^r,\ b1.h^r)$$

$$\epsilon(b2) = (g^r,\ b2.h^r)$$

$$\epsilon(b1).\ \epsilon(b2) = x^{b1}r_1^2 x^{b2}r_2^2 = x^{b1+b2}(r_1 r_2)^2 = \epsilon(b1 \oplus b2)$$

where $\oplus$ denotes addition modulo 2, (i.e. exclusive-or).

One of its main advantage is that it is simple, natural and efficient, Its security is clearly understood. Its disadvantage is that this scheme requires the encoding of messages into group elements, in order to be semantically secure.

Paillier

In the Paillier cryptosystem, if the public key is the modulus m and the base g, then the encryption of a message x is $\epsilon(x) = (g^x r^m \bmod m^2)$, for some random $r \in \{0, ..., m\text{-}1\}$. The homomorphic property is then

$$\epsilon(x_1) = (g^{x1} r^m \bmod m^2)$$

$$\epsilon(x_2) = (g^{x2} r^m \bmod m^2)$$

$$\epsilon(x_1).\ \epsilon(x_2) = (g^{x1} r_1^m)(g^{x2} r_2^m) = g^{x1+x2}(r_1 r_2)^m = \epsilon(x_{1+}x_2 \bmod c)$$

Okamoto–Uchiyama Cryptosystem

The system works in the group $(Z / nZ)^*$, where n is of the form $p^2 q$ and p and q are large primes. Like many public key cryptosystems, this scheme works in the group $(Z / nZ)^*$. A fundamental difference of this cryptosystem is that here n is a of the form p^2q, where p and q are large primes. This scheme is homomorphic and hence malleable.

Key Generation

A public/private key pair is generated as follows:

- Generate large primes p and q and set $n = p^2q$.
- Choose $g \in (Z / nZ)^*$ such that $g^P \neq 1 \bmod p^2$.
- Let $h = g^n \bmod n$.

The public key is then (n, g, h) and the private key is the factors (p, q).

Message Encryption

To encrypt a message m, where m is taken to be an element in Z / nZ

- Select $r \in Z / nZ$ at random. Set
- $C = (g^m h^r \bmod n)$

Message Decryption

If we define $L(x) = \dfrac{x-1}{p}$, then decryption becomes

$m = L(C^{p-1} \bmod p^2)/ L(g^{p-1} \bmod p^2) \bmod p$

Naccache–Stern Cryptosystem

Like many public key cryptosystems, this scheme works in the group $*(Z / nZ)^*$ where n is a product of two large primes. This scheme is homomorphic and hence malleable.

Key Generation

- Pick a family of k small distinct primes $p_1, ..., p_k$.
- Divide the set in half and set $u = \displaystyle\prod_{i=1}^{k/2} p_i$ and $v = \displaystyle\prod_{k/2+1}^{k} p_i$.
- Set $\sigma = uv = \displaystyle\prod_{i=1}^{k} p_i$
- Choose large primes a and b such that both $p = 2au+1$ and $q=2bv+1$ are prime.
- Set $n = pq$.
- Choose a random $g \bmod n$ such that g has order $\varphi(n)/4$.

The public key is the numbers σ, n, g and the private key is the pair p, q.

When $k=1$ this is essentially the Benaloh cryptosystem.

Message Encryption

This system allows encryption of a message m in the group $Z/\sigma Z$.

- Pick a random $x \in Z/nZ$
- Calculate $E(m) = x\sigma\, g^m \bmod n$

Then $E(m)$ is an encryption of the message m.

Message Decryption

To decrypt, we first find $m \bmod p_i$ for each i, and then we apply the Chinese remainder theorem to calculate $m \bmod \sigma$.

Given a ciphertext c, to decrypt, we calculate

$Ci \equiv C\varphi^{(n)/Pi} \bmod n$. Thus

$$C\varphi^{(n)/Pi} \equiv X\sigma\, \varphi^{(n)/Pi} g^m \varphi^{(n)/Pi} \bmod n$$

$$\equiv g^{(mi+yiPi)} \varphi^{(n)/Pi} \bmod n$$

$$\equiv g^{(mi} \varphi^{(n)/Pi} \bmod n$$

where $m_i \equiv m \bmod p_i$.

- Since p_i is chosen to be small, m_i can be recovered by exhaustive search, i.e. by comparing Ci to $g^j \varphi^{(n)/Pi}$ for j from 1 to p_i-1.
- Once m_i is known for each i, m can be recovered by a direct application of the Chinese remainder theorem.

Damgård–Jurik Cryptosystem

It is a generalization of the Paillier cryptosystem.

Key generation

1. Choose two large prime numbers p and q randomly and independently of each other.
2. Compute $n = pq$ and $\lambda = \text{lcm}(p-1,q-1)$.
3. Choose an element $g \in Z^*_{n^{s+1}}$ such that $g=(1+n)^j x \bmod n^{s+1}$ for a known j relative prime to n and $x \in H$.

4. Using the Chinese Remainder Theorem, choose d such that d mod $n \in Z^*{}_n$ and $d = 0$ mod λ. For instance d could be λ as in Paillier's original scheme.

   ○ The public (encryption) key is (n, g).
   ○ The private (decryption) key is d

Encryption

1. Let m be a message to be encrypted where $m \in Z^*{}_n$.
2. Select random r where $r \in Z^*{}_n s+1$.
3. Compute ciphertext as: $c = g^m.r^{ns}$ mod n^{s+1}.

Decryption

1. Ciphertext $v \in Z^*{}_n s+1$
2. Compute C^d mod n^{s+1}c. If C is a valid ciphertext then
   $C^d = (g^{m}r^{ns})^d = ((1+n)^{jm}x^m r^{ns})^d = (1+n)^{jmd \bmod ns}(x^m r^{ns})^{d \bmod \lambda} = (1+n)^{jmd \bmod ns}$
3. Apply a recursive version of the Paillier decryption mechanism to obtain *jmd*. As *jd* is known, it is possible to compute $m = (jmd).(jd)^{-1} \bmod n^s$

Castagnos scheme: Castagnos explored the possibility of improving the performance of homomorphic encryption schemes using quadratic fields quotations. This scheme achieves an expansion value of 3 and the ratio of encryption/decryption cost with s=1 over Paillier's scheme can be estimated to be about 2.

Galbraith scheme: This is an adaptation of the existing homomorphic encryption schemes in the context of elliptic curves. The most important advantage of this scheme is that the cost of encryption and decryption can be decreased using larger values of s. In addition, the security of the scheme increases with the increase in the value of s as it is the case in Damgard-Jurik's scheme. Its expansion is equal to 3. For s = 1 the ratio of the encryption cost for this scheme over that of Paillier's scheme can be estimated to be about 7, while the same ratio for the cost of decryption cost is about 14 for the same value of s.

SOMEWHAT HOMOMORPHIC ENCRYPTION SCHEMES

Somewhat-homomorphic encryption (SWHE) is using an encryption system that supports only limited computations on encrypted data. Somewhat homomorphic encryption schemes, which support a limited number of homomorphic operations, can be much faster, and more compact. Somewhat homomorphic encryption" (SHE) scheme allows a fixed number of multiplications of ciphertexts.

Functions:

Functions with a somewhat homomorphic encryption scheme are:

- Average of n terms{Ci}: as a pair $\left(\sum\limits_{i=1,...n} C_i, n \right)$ where $m = \dfrac{\sum\limits_{i=1,...n} C_i}{n}$

- Standard deviation: $\sqrt{\dfrac{\sum_{i=1,...n}(Ci-m)2}{n}}$, returned as a pair which is the numerator and denominator of the expression, before taking the square root.

- Logistical regression: $x = \left(\sum_{i=1,...n}\alpha i, xi\right)$, where α_i is the weighting constant or *regression coefficient for the variable x_i and the prediction is $f(x) = e^x/1 + e^x$*

The somewhat homomorphic encryption scheme SHE = (SH.Keygen, SH.Enc, SH.Add, SH.Mult, SH.Dec) is associated with a number of parameters:

- The dimension n, which is a power of 2,
- The cyclotomic polynomial $f(x) = x^n + 1$,
- The modulus $q \equiv 1 \pmod{2n}$
- The error parameter σ which defines a discrete Gaussian error distribution $X = DZ^n$, σ with standard deviation σ
- A prime t < q which defines the message space of the scheme as $R_t = Z_t[x]/\langle f(x)\rangle$
- A number D>0, which defines a bound on the maximum number of multiplications that can be performed correctly using the scheme.

SH.Keygen(1^k): Sample a ring element $s \xleftarrow{\;\varepsilon\;} X$ and define the secret key sk $\triangleq$ s. Sample a uniformly random ring element $a_1 \leftarrow R_q$ and an error e$\leftarrow$X and compute the public key

pk $\triangleq$ (a_0=-(a_1s + te), a_1). Publish *pk* and keep *sk* secret.

SH.Enc(*pk*, m): Given the public key *pk*=(a_0,a_1) and a message m ϵ R_q the algorithm samples u$\leftarrow$X and f, g$\leftarrow$X and compute the ciphertext

ct = (c_0,c_1) $\triangleq$ (a_0 u + tg + m,, a_1u + tf)

SH.Dec(*sk,* ct = (c0,c1,...,cδ): To decrypt compute

$\tilde{m} = \sum_{i=0}^{\delta} c_i s^i \epsilon Rq$ and output the message as $\tilde{m} \pmod t$

SH.Add(*pk*,ct$_0$, ct$_1$): Let ct = (c_0,$c_{1,...,}$ cδ) and ct' = ($c_{0'}, c_{1'}, ..., c\lambda'$) be the two ciphertexts. Assume $\lambda = \delta$, Otherwise pad the shorter ciphertext with zeroes.

ct$_{add}$ = (c_0 + co', c_1 + c$1'$, ..., $c_{\max(\delta,\lambda)}$, c'$_{\max(\delta,\lambda)}$) ϵ Rq$^{\max(\delta,\lambda)}$

SH.Mult(*pk*,ct$_0$,ct$_1$): Let ct = (c_0,$c_{1,...,}$ cδ) and ct'= ($c_{0'}, c_{1'}, ..., c\lambda'$) be the two ciphertexts. Here we do not pad either of the ciphertexts with zero. v be the symbolic variable.

$$(\sum_{i=0}^{\delta} C_i v^i) \cdot (\sum_{i=0}^{\lambda\delta} C'_i v^i) = (\sum_{i}^{\delta+\gamma} \hat{Ci}_i v^i)$$

The output cipher is $ct_{mlt} = (\hat{C}_0, \ldots, \hat{C}_{\delta+\gamma})$

THE BGN CRYPTOSYSTEM

The cryptosystem devised by Boneh, Goh, and Nissim was the first to allow both additions and multiplications with a constant-size ciphertext. The additive property is the same as for the ElGamal variant, only one multiplication is permitted. The system is thus called somewhat homomorphic.

Boneh, Goh, and Nissim described a cryptosystem that permitted arbitrary number of additions and one multiplication, without growing the ciphertext size.

Gen(): Choose large primes q, r and set n = qr. Find a super singular elliptic curve E/Fp with a point P of order n and let G = <P>.

Choose $Q' \xleftarrow{R} G \setminus \{\infty\}$

And set Q = [r]Q'; then Q has order q. Let ê: G X G → $\mu_n \subset Fp^2$ be the modified Weil pairing (constructed from the Weil pairing using a distortion map). Output the public key pk = (*E, ê, n, P,Q*) and the secret key sk = q.

Enc(pk,*m*): Choose $t \xleftarrow{R} [1, n]$ and output C = [*m*]P + [*t*]Q.

Dec(sk,*C*): Compute $P = \lceil \overline{q} \rceil P$ and $C = \lceil \overline{q} \rceil C$ and output *m'* = $\log_p$C.

Decryption is correct since if C = [m]P +[t]Q, then $C = \lceil \overline{mq} \rceil P + \lceil \overline{qt} \rceil Q = \lceil \overline{mq} \rceil P = \lceil m \rceil$ C = [mq] P +[qt]Q = [mq]P = [m] P. For efficient decryption we require the message space to be small as in the ElGamal variant. for efficient decryption we require the message space to be small as in the ElGamal variant.

To add encrypted messages and perform one multiplication

Add(pk, C_1, C_2): Choose $t' \xleftarrow{R} [1, n]$ and output C' = C_1 + C_2 + [t']Q ∈ G.

Mult(pk, C_1, C_2): Choose $u \xleftarrow{R} [1, n]$ and output D = $\hat{e}$ (C_1,C_2) . e(Q,Q)^u ∈ μ_n .

In conclusion, using the BGN system we can encrypt messages $m_1, \ldots, m_l$ in the group G and use the Add, Mult, and Add0 algorithms to evaluate any *l*-variable quadratic polynomial in the m_i.

Efficient Encoding of Integers for Arithmetic Operations:

Given a list of integers $(m_1, \ldots, m_l) \in Z^l$. To compute their sum or product over the integers homomorphically, the choice is to encrypt them directly. For every m in the list, compute

$$Enc(pk,m) = (c_0,c_1) = (a_0 u + tg + m, a_1 u + tf)$$

Obtain $\sum_i m_i$ over the integers. Break each m into bits $(m^{(0)}, \ldots, m^{(n-1)})$, create a degree (n-1) polynomial $pm(x) = \sum_j m_i^{(j)} x^j$ and encrypt m as $Enc(pk,m) = (C_0,C_1) = (a_0 u + tg + pm, a_1 u + tf)$. The result is simply $pm_{add}(x) = \sum_i pm_i(x)$

Homomorphic cryptography offers a similar pair of pathways. We can do arithmetic directly on the plaintext inputs x and y. Or we can encrypt x and y, apply a series of operations to the ciphertext values, then decrypt the result to arrive at the same final answer. The two routes pass through parallel universes: plainspace and cipherspace.

A number is conveniently represented as a sequence of bits (binary digits 0 and 1) and algorithms act on the bits according to rules of logic and arithmetic.

Among the many operations on numbers addition and multiplication is used. Doing mathematics in cipherspace is much stranger. Encryption is a process that thoroughly scrambles the bits of a number, whereas algorithms for arithmetic are extremely finicky and give correct results only if all the bits are in the right places.

Homomorphic addition takes milliseconds, multiplication generally less than a second. These timings are a vast improvement over earlier efforts,

The operations on the objects are addition and multiplication. Plaintext integers are encrypted by doubling; then any sequence of additions and multiplications can be carried out; finally, the result is decrypted by halving.

APPLICATIONS OF HOMOMORPHIC ENCRYPTION

Homomorphic encryption is one of the most exciting new research topics in cryptography, which promises to make cloud computing perfectly secure. With it, a Web user would send encrypted data to a server in the cloud, which would process it without decrypting it and send back a still-encrypted result. a user can store encrypted data on a server, and allow the server to process the encrypted data without revealing the data to the server.

The homomorphic property of various cryptosystems can be used to create secure voting systems, collision-resistant hash functions, private information retrieval schemes and enable widespread use of cloud computing by ensuring the confidentiality of processed data.

- **Protection of Mobile Agents:** One of the most interesting applications of homomorphic encryption is its use in protection of mobile agents. Since all conventional computer architectures are based on binary strings and only require multiplication and addition, such homomorphic cryptosystems would offer the possibility to encrypt a whole program so that it is still executable.

Hence, it could be used to protect mobile agents against malicious hosts by encrypting them. The protection of mobile agents by homomorphic encryption can be used in two ways: (i) computing with encrypted functions and (ii) computing with encrypted data. Computation with encrypted functions is a special case of protection of mobile agents. In such scenarios, a secret function is publicly evaluated in such a way that the function remains secret. Using homomorphic cryptosystems the encrypted function can be evaluated which guarantees its privacy. Homomorphic schemes also work on encrypted data to compute publicly while maintaining the privacy of the secret data. This can be done encrypting the data in advance and then exploiting the homomorphic property to compute with encrypted data

- **Multiparty Computation:** In multiparty computation schemes, several parties are interested in computing a common, public function on their inputs while keeping their individual inputs private. This problem belongs to the area of computing with encrypted data. Usually in multiparty computation protocols, we have a set of $n \geq 2$ players whereas in computing with encrypted data scenarios n=2. Furthermore, in multi-party computation protocols, the function that should be computed is publicly known, whereas in the area of computing with encrypted data it is a private input of one party.

- **Secret Sharing Scheme:** In secret sharing schemes, parties share a secret so that no individual party can reconstruct the secret form the information available to it. However, if some parties cooperate with each other, they may be able to reconstruct the secret. In this scenario, the homomorphic property implies that the composition of the shares of the secret is equivalent to the shares of the composition of the secrets.

- **Threshold Schemes**: Both secret sharing schemes and the multiparty computation schemes are examples of threshold schemes. Threshold schemes can be implemented using homomorphic encryption techniques.

- **Zero-Knowledge Proofs**: This is a fundamental primitive of cryptographic protocols and serves as an example of a theoretical application of homomorphic cryptosystems. Zeroknowledge proofs are used to prove knowledge of some private information. For instance, consider the case where a user has to prove his identity to a host by logging in with her account and private password. The user wants her private information (i.e., her password) to stay private and not to be leaked during the protocol operation. Zero-knowledge proofs guarantee that the protocol communicates exactly the knowledge that was intended, and no (zero) extra knowledge.

- **Election Schemes:** In election schemes, the homomorphic property provides a tool to obtain the tally given the encrypted votes without decrypting the individual votes. Watermarking and fingerprinting schemes: Digital watermarking and fingerprinting schemes embed additional information into digital data. The homomorphic property is used to add a mark to previously encrypted data. In general, watermarks are used to identify the owner/seller of digital goods to ensure the copyright. In fingerprinting schemes, the person who buys the data should be identifiable by the merchant to ensure that data is not illegally redistributed.

- **Oblivious Transfer:** It is an interesting cryptographic primitive. Usually in a two-party 1-out-of-2 oblivious transfer protocol, the first party sends a bit to the second party in such a way that the second party receives it with probability ½, without the first party knowing whether or not the second party received the bit.

- **Commitment Schemes**: Commitment schemes are some fundamental cryptographic primitives. In a commitment scheme, a player makes a commitment. She is able to choose a value from some set and commit to her choice such that she can no longer change her mind. She does not have to reveal her choice although she may do so at some point later. Some commitment schemes can be efficiently implemented using homomorphic property.

- **Lottery Protocols**: Usually in a cryptographic lottery, a number pointing to the winning ticket has to be jointly and randomly chosen by all participants. Using a homomorphic encryption scheme this can be realized as follows: Each player chooses a random number which she encrypts. Then using the homomorphic property, the encryption of the sum of the random values can be efficiently computed. The combination of this and a threshold decryption scheme leads to the desired functionality.

- **Mix-Nets:** Mix-nets are protocols that provide anonymity for senders by collecting encrypted messages from several users. For instance, one can consider mix-nets that collect ciphertexts and output the corresponding plaintexts in a randomly permuted order. In such a scenario, privacy is achieved by requiring that the permutation that matches inputs to outputs is kept secret to anyone except the mix-net. In particular, determining a correct input/output pair, i.e., a ciphertext with corresponding plaintext, should not be more effective then guessing one at random. A desirable property to build such mix-nets is reencryption which is achieved by using homomorphic encryption.

- **Data Aggregation in Wireless Sensor Networks:** In-network data aggregation in WSNs is a technique that combines partial results at the intermediate nodes en route to the base station, thereby reducing the communication overhead and optimizing the bandwidth utilization in the wireless links. In applications such as healthcare and military surveillance where the sensitivity of private data of the sensor is very high, the aggregation has to be carried out in a privacy-preserving way, so that the sensitive data are not revealed to the aggregator. Homomorphic encryption schemes can be applied to protect privacy of input data while computing an arbitrary aggregation function in a wireless sensor network.

APPLICATIONS BASED ON CLOUD SERVICE

Clouds are a large pool of easily usable and accessible virtualized resources (such as hardware, development platforms and/or services). These resources can be dynamically reconfigured to adjust to a variable load (scale), allowing also for an optimum resource utilization (Nakkala et al., 2014).

Medical Applications: Private Data and Public Functions (Patient Controlled Encryption)

All data for a patient's medical record is encrypted by the healthcare providers before being uploaded to the patient's record in the cloud storage system. The patient controls sharing and access to the record by sharing secret keys with specific providers. With FHE, the cloud can compute functions on the encrypted data and send the patient updates, alerts, or recommendations based on the received data.

Encrypted input to the functions could include blood pressure or heart monitor or blood sugar readings, for example, along with information about the patient such as age, weight, gender, and other risk factors. The functions computed may not need to be private in this case since they may be a matter of public health and thus public (Nakkala et al., 2014).

Financial Applications: Private Data and Private Functions

In the financial industry there is a potential application scenario in which both the data and the function to be computed on the data is private and proprietary. As an example, data about corporations, their stock price or their performance or inventory is often relevant to making investment decisions. Data may even be streamed on a continuous basis reacting the most up-to-date information necessary for making decisions for trading purposes.

The cloud service evaluates the private function by applying the encrypted description of the program to the encrypted inputs it receives. After processing, the cloud returns the encrypted output to the customer.

Advertising and Pricing

The consumer uses a mobile phone as a computing device, and the device constantly uploads contextual information about the consumer, including location, the time of day, information from email or browsing activity such as keywords from email or browser searches.

In the future, imagine that information is uploaded potentially constantly from video devices: either pictures of objects of interest such as brands or faces which are automatically identified, or from a video stream from a camera on the body which is identifying context in the room (objects, people, workplace vs. home vs. store). When contextual information is uploaded to the cloud server and made accessible to the cosmetics company, the company computes some function of the contextual data and determine which targeted advertisement to send back to the consumer's phone.

SOME PROPERTIES OF HOMOMORPHIC ENCRYPTION SCHEMES

Homomorphic encryption schemes have some interesting mathematical properties. In the following, we mention some of these properties.

- **Re-Randomizable Encryption/Re-Encryption:** Re-randomizable cryptosystems (Groth, 2004) are probabilistic cryptosystems with the additional property that given the public key K_e and an encryption $E_{K_e}(m,r)$ of a message $m \in M$ under the public key K_e and a random number $r \in Z$. It is possible to efficiently convert $E_{K_e}(m, r)$ into another encryption $E_{K_e}(m, r')$ that is perfectly indistinguishable from a fresh encryption of m under the public key K_e. This property is also called re-encryption.

$$\text{Add}\,(\,E_{K_e}(m,r),\ E_{K_e}(m,r'))\, =\, E_{K_e}(m+0,r')\, =\, E_{K_e}(m,r')$$

where r' is an appropriate random number.

- **Random Self-Reducibility:** Along with the possibility of re-encryption comes the property of random self-reducibility concerning the problem of computing the plaintext from the ciphertext. A cryptosystem is called random self-reducible if any algorithm that can break a non-trivial fraction of ciphertexts can also break a random instance with significant probability.
- **Verifiable Encryptions / Fair Encryptions:** If an encryption is verifiable, it provides a mechanism to check the correctness of encrypted data without compromising on the secrecy of the data. For instance, this is useful in voting schemes to convince any observer that the encrypted name of a candidate, i.e., the encrypted vote is indeed in the list of candidates. Verifiable encryptions are also called fair encryptions.

SUMMARY

A homomorphic cryptosystem is a cryptosystem with the additional property that there exists an efficient algorithm to compute an encryption of the sum or the product, of two messages given the public key and the encryptions of the messages but not the messages themselves. It can be used whenever the need of doing computations on pieces of un-owned information appears.

Instead of encrypting each plaintext bit separately, multiple bits can be packed together, thereby "amortizing" the encryption effort and reducing overhead. Homomorphic addition takes milliseconds, multiplication generally less than a second. These timings are a vast improvement over earlier efforts. Common cryptography can't directly calculate on encrypted data, but homomorphic encryption can, meanwhile, the operation results of homomorphic encryption will be automatically encrypted.

REFERENCES

Ahila, S., & Shunmuganathan, K.L. (2014). State Of Art in Homomorphic Encryption Schemes. *Int. Journal of Engineering Research and Applications, 4*(2), 37-43.

Bhargav, Y., & Moorthy, P. S. (2013). Homomorphic Recommendations for Data Packing- A Survey. *International Journal of Computer Science and Mobile Applications, 1*(5), 18-37.

Boneh, D., Gentry, C., Halevi, S., Wang, F., & Wu, D. J. (2013). Private Database Queries Using Somewhat Homomorphic Encryption. Proceedings of *ACNS '13* (pp. 102–118).

Castagnos, G. (2007). An Efficient Probabilistic Public-Key Cryptosystem over Quadratic Fields Quotients. *Finite Fields and Their Applications, 13*(3), 563–576. doi:10.1016/j.ffa.2006.05.004

Coron, J.-S., Lepoint, T., & Tibouchi, M. (2014): Scale-Invariant Fully Homomorphic Encryption over the Integers. Proceedings of IACR Cryptology '14 (pp. 311-328).

Erkin, Z., Beye, M., Veugen, T., & Lagendijk, R. L. , (2012). Privacy-Preserving Content-Based Recommendations through Homomorphic Encryption. *Proceedings of the 33rd WIC Symposium on Information Theory in the Benelux and The 2nd Joint WIC/IEEE Symposium on Information Theory and Signal Processing in the Benelux* (pp. 71-77).

Galbraith, S. D. (2002). Elliptic Curve Paillier Schemes. *Journal of Cryptology*, *15*(2), 129–138. doi:10.1007/s00145-001-0015-6

Gentry, C., Sahai, A., & Waters, B. (2013). Homomorphic Encryption from Learning with Errors: Conceptually-Simpler, Asymptotically-Faster, Attribute-Based.

Lauter, K., Naehrig, M., & Vaikuntanathan, V. (2011) Can Homomorphic Encryption be Practical? *Proceedings of the ACM Cloud Computing Security Workshop CCSW '11*, Chicago, IL, USA (pp. 113-124).

Maimu, D., Patrascu, A., & Simion, E. (2012). Homomorphic Encryption Schemes and Applications for a Secure Digital World. *Journal of Mobile, Embedded and Distributed Systems*, *4*(4).

Nakkala, N.K., Ram Mohan, C., & Rao, N.V. (2014). Generating Private Recommendations Efficiently Using GAE Datastore and Data Packing. *International Journal of Advanced Research in Computer and Communication Engineering, 3*(2).

KEY TERMS AND DEFINITIONS

Commitment Schemes: The commitment schemes are a type of cryptographic primitive where the send commits to one of several choices. The sender may be asked to reveal the choice at a later point.

Encryption: An algorithm that converts plaintext into ciphertext.

Homomorphic Encryption: An encryption schemes that allows computing over encrypted data.

Key Generation: The key generation procedure generates the keys needed for encryption.

Oblivious Transfer: An oblivious transfer is a type of cryptographic primitive where a sender sends one out of many pieces of information and remains oblivious to which information was sent. A 1-out-of-2 oblivious transfer a sender sends a message with a certain probability but remains oblivious whether the message was transferred or not.

Secret Sharing Systems: The secret sharing systems are a type of cryptographic systems where a particular secret is split among a number of parties, say n, and to reconstruct the secret, a minimum number of parties t have to be present.

Zero Knowledge Proofs: A Zero-Knowledge Proof system is a proof between a prover and a verifier, where the prover does not reveal any information beyond what is required for the proof. As an example, the prover can prove that he knows the password to a system by logging into the system and not actually revealing the password to the verifier.

Chapter 9
Zero Knowledge Proofs:
A Survey

Kannan Balasubramanian
Mepco Schlenk Engineering College, India

Mala K.
Mepco Schlenk Engineering College, India

ABSTRACT

Zero knowledge protocols provide a way of proving that a statement is true without revealing anything other than the correctness of the claim. Zero knowledge protocols have practical applications in cryptography and are used in many applications. While some applications only exist on a specification level, a direction of research has produced real-world applications. Zero knowledge protocols, also referred to as zero knowledge proofs, are a type of protocol in which one party, called the prover, tries to convince the other party, called the verifier, that a given statement is true. Sometimes the statement is that the prover possesses a particular piece of information. This is a special case of zero knowledge protocol called a zero-knowledge proof of knowledge. Formally, a zero-knowledge proof is a type of interactive proof.

INTRODUCTION

A Zero-Knowledge Proof system is an example of a two-party computation where a prover tries to prove something to a verifier without revealing anything more than what is being proved. For example, the prover can prove to the verifier that that he knows a password without actually revealing the password. The Zero Knowledge Proofs are a special case of type of Proof systems called Interactive Proof. In this chapter, we provide a number of examples to show how zero knowledge proofs can be constructed. We also discuss the variations of the zero knowledge proofs and their applications.

This chapter is about proof schemes, protocols with which Peggy "the Prover" can try and prove something to Veronica "the Verifier" who can either accept or reject Peggy's claim. Suppose that Peggy wishes to prove to Veronica that she knows the code to a safe. Peggy could simply tell Veronica the code. This is a perfectly good proof scheme but Veronica ends up knowing not just that Peggy knows the code, but the code itself too. Peggy could also just state that she knows the code. This protects Peggy's secret

DOI: 10.4018/978-1-5225-2915-6.ch009

knowledge, but might not convince Veronica. However, Peggy could also let Veronica observe the closed safe, ask her to look away then enter the code and open the safe, allowing Veronica to deduce that Peggy knows the code without Veronica gaining the ability to open the safe herself. This is what cryptographic proof schemes aim to achieve, security guarantees for both Peggy's secret and Veronica's trust.

ZERO-KNOWLEDGE PROTOCOLS

Peggy's knowledge is protected by properties such as zero-knowledge, which informally says that Veronica gains no extra knowledge from Peggy by following a proof scheme with her, beyond whatever Peggy wanted to prove in the first place. The security properties for Veronica can include a protocol being sound, i.e. Peggy cannot convince Veronica of a false claim. The scheme can also be a "proof of knowledge" which informally means that Peggy cannot convince Veronica unless she actually knows what she claims to know.

Zero knowledge protocols provide a way of proving that a statement is true without revealing anything other than the correctness of the claim. Zero knowledge protocols have practical applications in cryptography and are used in many applications. While some applications only exist on a specification level, a direction of research has produced real-world applications.

Zero knowledge protocols, also referred to as zero knowledge proofs, are a type of protocol in which one party, called the prover, tries to convince the other party, called the verifier, that a given statement is true. Sometimes the statement is that the prover possesses a particular piece of information.

This is a special case of zero knowledge protocol called a zero-knowledge proof of knowledge. Formally, a zero-knowledge proof is a type of interactive proof.

An interactive proof system is an interaction between a verifier and a prover satisfying the following properties:

- **Completeness**: If the statement being proven is true, an honest verifier, a verifier correctly following the protocol, will be convinced after interacting with an honest prover.
- **Soundness**: If the statement is false, no prover, either honest or dishonest, will be able to convince an honest verifier, except with some small probability.

For an interactive proof to be a zero-knowledge proof it must also satisfy the condition of zero knowledge. A proof is zero knowledge if any knowledge known by the prover or the verifier before performing the proof is the same as the knowledge known by either party after performing the proof. In other words, no additional knowledge is gained by either party because of the proof. Another way of thinking about this is that the proof reveals zero knowledge (Mohr, 2007).

THE MAGICAL CAVE

The classic example for zero knowledge protocols is the cave example.

Peggy has stumbled across a magical cave. Upon entering the cave there are two paths, one leading to the right and one leading to the left. Both paths eventually lead to a dead end. However, Peggy has discovered a secret word that opens up a hidden door in the dead end, connecting both paths.

Victor hears about this, and offers to buy the secret from Peggy. Before giving Peggy the money Victor wants to be certain that Peggy actually knows this secret word. How can Peggy (the prover) convince Victor (the verifier) that she knows the word, without revealing what it is?

The two of them come up with the following plan. First, Victor will wait outside the cave while Peggy goes in. She will randomly pick either the right or the left path and go down it. Since Victor was outside he should have no knowledge of which path Peggy took. Then Victor will enter the cave. He will wait by the fork and shout to Peggy which path to return from.

Assuming that Peggy knows the word, she should be able to return down the correct path, regardless of which one she started on. If Victor says to return down the path she started on, she simply walks back. If Victor says to return down the other path, she whispers the magic word, goes through the door, and returns down the other path.

If Peggy does not know the word, there is a 50% chance that Victor will choose the path she did not start down. If this happens there is no way that she can return down the correct path. The experiment should be repeated until Victor either discovers Peggy is a liar because she returned down the wrong path, or until he is sufficiently satisfied that she does indeed know the word.

This is a zero-knowledge protocol because it satisfies each of the three requirements. It satisfies completeness because if Peggy knows the word she will be able to convince Vic-tor. It is sound because if Peggy does not know the word, she will not be able to convince Victor unless she was very lucky. Finally, it is zero knowledge because if Victor follows the protocol he will not be able to learn anything besides whether or not Peggy knows the word.

HAMILTONIAN CYCLES

A more practical example is proving that one knows a Hamiltonian cycle for a graph, without revealing what the cycle is. Before going into the example, we first need some graph theory background. A cycle is a sequence of vertices, two consecutive vertices in the sequence are adjacent (connected) to each other in the graph, which starts and ends at the same vertex. A Hamiltonian path, is a sequence of vertices in which each vertex in the graph is listed exactly once and includes all vertices of the graph. Finally, a Hamiltonian cycle is a Hamiltonian path which is also a cycle. In other words, it is a sequence of vertices which begins and ends with the same vertex, and each vertex in the graph is listed exactly once (https://en.wikipedia.org/wiki/Hamiltonian_path).

For a large enough graph, finding a Hamiltonian cycle is computationally infeasible. A Zero Knowledge protocol for the Hamiltonian Cycle problem is described below. The proof uses the idea of graph isomorphism. An isomorphism, f: V (G) $\rightarrow$ V (H), of graphs G and H is a bijection between the vertex sets of G and H such that any two vertices u and v of G are adjacent in G if and only if f(u) and f(v) are adjacent in H. Here the prover, P, knows a Hamiltonian Cycle for a graph, G. The verifier, V, has knowledge of G but not the cycle. For P to show V that she knows the cycle, they must perform several rounds of the following protocol:

At the beginning of each round, P constructs H, graph which is isomorphic to G. It is simple to translate a Hamiltonian cycle between two isomorphic graphs, so since P knows a Hamiltonian cycle for G they must know one for H as well.

P commits to H, using a one-way function. The benefit of using a one-way function is that when given an input, the output is easy to compute. The opposite is not true. When given the output it should be infeasible to compute the input. Finding two inputs which result in the same output should also be a difficult task. A hash function is an example of a one-way function. Since P used a one-way function, V will have no knowledge of the input, but will still be able to check if P changed it by comparing the outputs.

Doing this means that P cannot change H without V finding out.

V then randomly asks P to do one of two things. Either show the isomorphism between H and G, or show a Hamiltonian cycle in H.

If P was asked to show that the two graphs are isomorphic, they start by revealing H to V. They also provide the vertex translations which map G to H. V can then verify that the two graphs are isomorphic.

If P was asked to show a Hamiltonian cycle in H, she first translates the cycle from G onto H. She then reveals to V the edges of H which are a part of the Hamiltonian cycle. This is enough for V to verify that H contains a Hamiltonian cycle.

In both cases V must also verify that H is the same graph that P committed to by using the same one-way function and comparing the outputs.

This protocol is complete because if P is an honest prover, she can easily answer either question asked by V by either providing the isomorphism which she has, or by applying the isomorphism to the cycle in G to demonstrate a Hamiltonian cycle. This protocol is sound because if P does not know the cycle, she can either generate a graph isomorphic to G or find the Hamiltonian cycle for another graph, but she cannot do both since she does not know a Hamiltonian cycle for G. With a reasonable number of rounds, it is unrealistic for P to fool V in this manner. This protocol is zero knowledge because in each round V will only learn either the isomorphism of H to G or a Hamiltonian cycle in H. V would need both pieces of information in order to reconstruct the Hamiltonian cycle in G. Therefore, as long as P can generate a distinct H each round, V will never discover the cycle in G.

GRAPH 3-COLORABILITY

Another problem for which zero-knowledge problems are usually discussed is the graph coloring problem. A graph G(V, E) is said to be 3-colorable if there exists a mapping $\varphi: V \rightarrow \{1, 2, 3\}$ (called a proper coloring) such that every two adjacent vertices are assigned different colors. Such 3-coloring induces a partition of the vertex set of the graph to three independent sets. The language graph 3-colorability, denoted G3C, consists of the set of undirected graphs that are 3-colorable.

Zero Knowledge Proof for Graph 3-Colorability

Input: A graph $G=(V,E)$, $|V|=n$, $|E|=m$

The following four steps are executed m^2 times each time using independent coin tosses

(P1) The prover chooses at random an assignment of three colors to the three independent sets induced by (the proper 3-coloring) φ, colors the graph using this 3-coloring, and places these colors in n locked boxes each bearing the number of the corresponding vertex. More specifically, the prover chooses a permutation $\pi \in_R S_3$ (the symmetric group of 3 elements), places $\pi(\varphi(i))$ in a box marked i ($\forall i \in V$), locks all boxes and sends them (without the keys) to the verifier.

(V1) The verifier chooses at random an edge $e \in_R E$ and sends it to the prover. (Intuitively, the verifier asks to examine the colors of the endpoints of $e \in E$.)

(P2) If $e = (u, v) \in E$, then the prover reveals the colors of u and v (to the verifier) by sending the keys to boxes u and v. Otherwise, the prover does nothing.

(V2) The verifier opens boxes u and v using the keys received and checks whether they contain two different elements of $\{1, 2, 3\}$. If the keys do not match the boxes, or the contents violates the condition, then the verifier rejects and stops. Otherwise, the verifier continues to the next iteration.

If the verifier has completed all m^2 iterations, then it accepts.

FIAT-SHAMIR IDENTIFICATION PROTOCOL

In cryptography, ZKPs are primarily used as a means of entity authentication. That is, Peggy possesses some secret S that only she can know. She proves to Victor that she is indeed Peggy (and not an impostor) by proving that she possesses S. Of course, she wants to do so without revealing S to Victor (or any potential eavesdroppers). The Fiat-Shamir identification protocol, while itself not usually implemented in modern systems, is the basis of zero-knowledge identification protocols currently in use, such as Feige-Fiat-Shamir and Guillou-Quisquater. As such, it serves to illustrate the properties which are important in more sophisticated schemes.

Fiat-Shamir Identification Protocol

Initialization

1. A trusted center T selects and publishes an RSA-like modulus $n = pq$ but keeps the primes p and q secret.
2. The prover selects a secret s coprime to n, $1 \leq s \leq n - 1$, computes $v = s^2 \mod n$, and registers v with T as her public key.

Identification Protocol

The following steps are executed t times, each time using independent ran-dom coin tosses.

(P1) The prover choses a random r, $1 \leq r \leq n - 1$ and sends $x = r^2 \mod n$ to the verifier.

(V1) The verifier randomly selects a bit $e \in \{0, 1\}$ and sends e to the prover.

(P2) The prover computes and sends to the verifier y, where $y = r$ (if e = 0) or $y = rs \mod n$ (if e = 1).

(V2) The verifier rejects if y=0 or if $y^2 \neq x.r^2 \mod n$ to the verifier. (Depending on e, $y^2 = x$ or $y^2 = xv \mod n$ since $v = s^2 \mod n$. Checking for $y=0$ precludes the case $r=0$.)

If the verifier has completed all t iterations of the above steps, then he accepts.

It can be shown that the Fiat Shamir Identification protocol constitutes a zero knowledge entity authentication protocol. It upholds the properties of completeness, soundness, and zero-knowledge.

- **Completeness**: Suppose the prover possesses the secret s. Then she can always correctly provide the verifier with $y = r$ or $y = rs$ upon request. Therefore, an honest verifier will complete all t iterations and accept with probability 1.
- **Soundness**: Suppose the prover does not possess the secret s. Then, during any given round, she can provide only one of $y = r$ or $y = rs$ (see remark). Therefore, an honest verifier will reject with probability 1/2 in each round (which implies an overall probability of 2^{-t} that a cheating prover will not be caught).
- **Zero-Knowledge:** The only information revealed in each round is $x = r^2 \bmod n$ (in step P1) and either $y = r$ or $y = rs$ (in step P2). Such pairs (x, y) could be simulated by choosing y randomly, then defining $x = y^2$ or $x = y^2/v$. Such pairs, while not generated in the same way as in the protocol, are computationally indistinguishable from them.

An example for the Fiat-Shamir Identification protocol is given below:
Initialization:

1. Let $p = 5$ and $q = 7$. Then, $n = pq = 35$. n is published to a trusted center.
2. Peggy secretly chooses s = 16, which is coprime to n. She publishes v = s^2 mod n = 11 to the trusted center.

Identification protocol:
Suppose Victor is very easy to convince, and hence requires only 2 successful iterations of the protocol in order to accept.

(P1$_1$) Peggy randomly selects r = 10. She sends x = r^2 mod n = 10^2 mod 35 = 30 to Victor.
(V1$_1$) Victor randomly selects e = 0 and sends it to Peggy.
(P2$_1$) Since $e = 0$, Peggy computes $y = r = 10$ and sends it to Victor. (V2$_1$) Victor verifies that $y^2 = 10^2 \equiv 30 \pmod{35}$.
(P1$_2$) Peggy randomly selects $r = 20$. She sends $x = r^2 \bmod n = 20^2 \bmod 35 = 15$ to Victor.
(V1$_2$) Victor randomly selects $e = 1$ and sends it to Peggy.
(P2$_2$) Since $e = 1$, Peggy computes $y = sr \bmod n = 16 \cdot 20 \bmod 35 = 5$ and sends it to Victor.
(V2$_2$) Victor verifies that $y^2 = 25 \equiv 15 \cdot 11 \pmod{35}$.

Peggy has successfully completed $t = 2$ rounds, so Victor accepts.

COMMITMENT SCHEMES AND ZERO KNOWLEDGE PROTOCOLS

In this section, the connection between commitment schemes and Zero knowledge protocols is examined. In the context of cryptography, making a commitment simply means that a player in a protocol is able to choose a value from some (finite) set and commit to his choice such that he can no longer change his mind. He does not however, have to reveal his choice - although he may choose to do so at some later time.

As an informal example, consider the following game between two players P and V:

1. P wants to commit to a bit b. To do so, he writes down b on a piece of paper, puts it in a box, and locks it using a padlock.
2. P gives the box to V.
3. If P wants to, he can later open the commitment by giving V the key to the padlock.

There are two basic properties of this game, which are essential to any commitment scheme:

- Having given away the box, P cannot anymore change what is inside. Hence, when the box is opened, we know that what is revealed really was the choice that P committed to originally. This is usually called the binding property.
- When V receives the box, he cannot tell what is inside before P decides to give him the key. This is usually called the hiding property
  - As an example of this kind of commitments, consider the case where P has a pair of RSA keys, where V (like anyone else) knows the public key with modulus n and public exponent e. To commit to a bit b, P can build a number x_b, which is randomly chosen modulo n, such that its least significant bit is b. Then he sends the encryption $C = x_b^e \bmod n$ to V. But it should be intuitively clear that P is stuck with his choice of b since the encryption C determines all of x_b uniquely, and that V will have a hard time figuring out what b is, if he cannot break RSA. Thus, at least intuitively, the binding and hiding requirements are satisfied.

A formal definition for a commitment scheme is that it is a probabilistic polynomial time algorithm G called a generator. It takes as input 1^l where l is a security parameter and corresponds to e.g. the length of RSA modulus we want. It outputs a string *pk*, the public key of the commitment scheme. The scheme defines for every public key *pk* a function commit$_{pk}$: $\{0, 1\}^l \times \{0, 1\} \rightarrow \{0, 1\}^l$.

To use the scheme in practice, one first executes a set-up phase (once and for all) where either P or V runs G, and sends the public key *pk* to the other party. In some schemes it is necessary in addition to convince the other party that *pk* was correctly chosen, in case this is not easy to verify directly. Thus, one of the parties may reject in the set-up phase, meaning that it refuses to use the public key it received.

Assuming that the public key was accepted, to commit to a bit b, P chooses r at random from $\{0,1\}^l$ and computes the commitment $C \leftarrow$ commit$_{pk}$ (r,b). To open a commitment, r and b are revealed and V checks that indeed $C =$ commit$_{pk}(r,b)$

In the description of the following protocol, the user, who is wanting to convince the other about the truth of some claim will be called the Prover (P), and the host, who is interested in checking that the claim is true, will be called the verifier (V).

1. If the prover claims to be A, the verifier chooses a random message M, and sends the ciphertext C $= P_A(M)$ to the prover.
2. The prover decrypts C using S_A and sends the result M^0 to the verifier.
3. The verifier accepts the identity of the prover if and only if $M^0 = M$.

Let us look at this protocol from the point of view of both parties. Should the verifier be happy about this protocol? the answer is yes if the public key system used is secure: while the owner of S_A can always conduct the protocol successfully, an adversary who knows only the public key and a ciphertext should not be able to find the plaintext essentially better than by guessing at random.

Now what about security from the (honest) prover's point of view - is any unnecessary knowledge being communicated to the verifier here? At first sight, it may seem that everything seems to be fine: if we consider the situation of the verifier just after sending C, then we might argue that since the verifier has just chosen the message M himself, he already knows what the prover will say; therefore he learns no information it didn't know before, and so the protocol is zero-knowledge.

But this reasoning is incorrect. It assumes that the verifier follows the protocol, in particular that C is generated as prescribed. This is of course unreasonable because nothing in the protocol allows the prover to check that the verifier is behaving honestly. Assume that an adversary takes control of the verifier, and sends instead of a correctly generated C some ciphertext C^0 intended for the correct prover, that the adversary has eavesdropped elsewhere. And now, following the protocol, the unsuspecting prover will kindly decrypt C^0 for the adversary.

This is certainly not the kind of knowledge we wanted to communicate, and hence this protocol is definitely not zero-knowledge. The basic problem we is that when the verifier sends C, we are not sure if it really knows the corresponding plaintext M. If it did, we would be fine. However, the verifier will of course not be willing to reveal M immediately, since from its point of view, the purpose of the protocol is to test if the prover can compute M based only on C. And for the reasons we saw above, the prover will not be willing to go first in revealing M either. This can be solved by using commitment.

Assume we have a commitment scheme that lets the prover commit to any message that can be encrypted by the public key system. Let $commit_{pk}(r, M)$ denote a commitment to message M. Then consider the following protocol:

1. If the prover claims to be A, the verifier chooses a random message M, and sends the ciphertext $C = P_A(M)$ to the prover.
2. The prover decrypts C using S_A and sends a commitment to the result $commit_{pk}(r, M^0)$ to the verifier.
3. The verifier sends M to the prover.
4. The prover checks if $M = M^0$. If not, he stops the protocol. Otherwise he opens the commitment, i.e. he sends r, M^0 to the verifier.
5. The verifier accepts the identity of the prover if and only if $M^0 = M$ and the pair r, M^0 correctly opens the commitment.

The protocol demonstrates that the prover can decrypt C based on C alone, since when the verifier finds the right plaintext inside the commitment, this shows that the prover knew it already in step 2, by the binding property of the commitment scheme. As for zero-knowledge, either the verifier knows M or not. If yes, then it can send the correct M in step 3, but then it already knows what it will find inside the commitment in step 5 and so learns nothing new. If not, then it cannot send the right value in step 3, the prover will stop the protocol, and the verifier will be left with an unopened commitment which by the hiding property is a useless piece of information that might represent any value whatsoever.

VARIATIONS OF ZERO KNOWLEDGE PROOFS

The idea of zero knowledge proof is formalized by requiring the existence of a simulator that can efficiently generate a transcript which is indistinguishable from the view of the verifier in a real execution with the prover. This, in particular, implies that anything a verifier can learn after having communicated with a prover, he could have efficiently generated by himself without the help of the prover.

As opposed to the single execution of the zero knowledge proofs, concurrent execution of the protocol by many parties is also possible (Dwork et al., 1998; Feige, 1990; Pass, 2004). The concurrent setting presents the new risk of a coordinated attack in which an adversary controls many parties, interleaving the executions of the protocols while trying to extract knowledge based on the existence of multiple concurrent executions. In particular, the adversary may use messages received in one of the executions in order to cheat in a different execution.

It would be desirable to have cryptographic protocols that retain their security properties even when executed concurrently. The different ways of composing the zero knowledge protocols is discussed next.

- **Self-Composition:** The simplest form of concurrent composition is that of concurrent self-composition. Roughly speaking, we say that a protocol is secure under concurrent self-composition (or just concurrent composition) if the protocol remains secure even if many simultaneous executions of that protocol are taking place. Zero-knowledge proofs that have this property are called concurrent zero-knowledge proofs.
- **General Composition:** A more general form of concurrent composition is that of concurrent general composition. Whereas the notion of concurrent self-composition only considers the security of a protocol when concurrently executed with many instances of the same protocol, the notion of general composition considers the security of a protocol that is concurrently executed with many other, possibly different, protocols. One important framework for addressing these security demands is the framework for Universal Composability (Canetti, 2002).

LIMITATIONS OF ZERO KNOWLEDGE PROOFS

It was shown that two communication rounds (i.e., one message sent from the verifier to the prover, followed by one message from the prover to the verifier) are not sufficient in order to implement zero-knowledge proofs (Goldreich et al., 1994). Furthermore, it was shown that a certain type of zero-knowledge proofs called black-box zero-knowledge proofs necessitate four communication rounds. Even though there exist non-black-box zero-knowledge protocols (which all use more than four communication rounds) all currently known practical protocols are black-box zero knowledge. The notion of black-box zero-knowledge requires the existence of a simulator which only uses the verifier V as a black-box in order to perform the simulation.

NONINTERACTIVE ZERO KNOWLEDGE PROOF SYSTEMS

Noninteractive zero knowledge proof system contains only a message sent by a prover to verifier, which can be better used in the construction of cryptographic protocols. To define the both ZKP and NIZKP systems, let $\{0,1\}^n$ denote the set n-bit strings and let $\{0,1\}*$ denote the set of all strings. Two probability ensembles are said to be computationally indistinguishable (denoted by $\approx_c$), if no probabilistic polynomial time Turing machine (we can think of Turing Machine as Prover or Verifier) can distinguish them with nonnegligible probability. Two probability ensembles are said to be statistically indistinguishable or statistically close (denoted by $\approx_s$), if their statistical distance is negligible (Wu et al, 2014).

Formal Definition of Zero Knowledge Interactive Proof System

For a Language $L \subseteq \{0,1\}*$ and a pair of interactive Turing machines (P,V) in which P Possesses unlimited computation power and V is probabilistic polynomial time, (P,V) is said to be zero knowledge interactive proof system of Language L is the following three conditions are true.

1. **Completeness**: For any common input $x \in L$ and polynomial $p(.)$,

$$\Pr\left[\left(P,V\right)\left(x\right) = 1\right] \geq 1 - \frac{1}{p\left(|x|\right)}$$

2. **Soundness**: For any common input $x \notin L$ and any interactive Turing machine P', and polynomial $p(.)$,

$$\Pr\left[\left(P',V\right)\left(x\right) = 1\right] < 1 - \frac{1}{p\left(|x|\right)}$$

3. **Zero Knowledge**: For each probabilistic polynomial time Turing machine V*, there is a probabilistic polynomial time algorithm M*, such that for any $x \in L$,

(P,V*) $(x) \approx_c$ M*(x)

P is called the prover and V is called the verifier.

The completeness reflects correctness of the system, which means for valid input $x \in L$, a prover can always complete the proof successfully such that the verifier accepts. Soundness is defined against the malicious prover which means, for invalid input $x \notin L$, no prover can construct a valid proof system such that the verifier accepts. While for the verifier, zero knowledge means no malicious verifier is able to derive extra knowledge from the process of interaction.

In addition, according to different computational capabilities of the prover and verifier, the above properties (2) and (3) can also be modified, respectively. If the indistinguishability of the two probability ensembles in property (3) is statistically indistinguishable or identically distributed, zero knowledge will be correspondingly defined as statistical zero knowledge and perfect zero knowledge. On the other hand, if soundness holds for any probabilistic polynomial time prover, that is, computational soundness, then the interactive proof system is called the zero-knowledge argument system.

Formal Definition of Non-Interactive Zero Knowledge Proof System

For a pair of probabilistic Turing machines (P, V), in which P is probabilistic polynomial time and V is deterministic polynomial time, (P, V) is called the noninteractive zero-knowledge proof system for language L if the following conditions are met.

1. **Completeness**: For any common input $x \in$ L and polynomial $p(.)$,

$$\Pr\left[V\left(x, R, P\left(x, R\right)\right) = 1\right] \geq 1 - \frac{1}{p\left(|x|\right)}$$

where R is string in {0, 1}* bounded in length

2. **Soundness**: For any common input $x \notin$ L and any interactive Turing machine P', and polynomial $p(.)$,

$$\Pr\left[V\left(x, R, P'\left(x, R\right)\right) = 1\right] < \frac{1}{p\left(|x|\right)}$$

3. **Zero Knowledge**: For any $x \in$ L, there is a probabilistic polynomial time algorithm M such that

$$V\left(x\right) = \left(x, R \in \left\{0,1\right\}^{c(|x|)}, P\left(x, R\right)\right) \approx_{c} M\left(x\right)_{x \in L}$$

It can be shown that only languages in BPP (Bounded Probabilistic Polynomial) have NIZKP systems. The class of problems in BPP are the decision problems solvable by probabilistic polynomial time Turing machine with an error probability bounded away from 1/3 of all instances. The definition of NIZKP systems usually contain an initial-set up assumption. At present, it is generally acceptable to construct NIZKP in the Common Reference String(CRS) model. In cryptography, the common reference string (CRS) model captures the assumption that a trusted setup in which all involved parties get access to the same string *crs* taken from some distribution *D* exists. Schemes proven secure in the CRS model are secure given that the setup was performed correctly.

SUMMARY

Zero-knowledge Proofs are an important construct in cryptography in which a prover tries to prove to the verifier something without revealing anything other than the claim. They are a special type of proof called the Interactive Proof. In this chapter, various examples are given to construct Zero-Knowledge Proofs including the Magical Cave, Hamiltonian Cycles, Graph 3-colorability and the Fiat-Shamir Identification Protocol. This chapter also introduced a type of proof system called the Non-interactive Zero-knowledge Proofs.

REFERENCES

Aronsson, H. (1995). *Zero Knowledge Protocols and Small Systems*. Retrieved from Http://www.tml. tkk.fi/Opinnot/Tik-110.501/1995/zeroknowledge.html

Bernhard, D. (2014). *Zero Knowledge Proofs in Theory and Practice* [Ph.D. dissertation]. University of Bristol.

Canetti, R. (2000). Security and Composition of Multiparty Cryptography Protocols. *Journal of Cryptology*, *13*(1), 143–202. doi:10.1007/s001459910006

Canetti, R. (2002). Universally composable Security: A New paradigm for cryptographic protocols, Proceedings of the 34th STOC (pp. 494-503).

Desmedt, Y., & Wang, Y. (n. d.). Efficient Zero Knowledge Proofs for Some Practical Graph Problems. Retrieved from webpages.uncc.edu/yonwang/papers/zkip.pdf

Dwork, C., Naor, M., & Sahai, A. (1998). *Concurrent Zero Knowledge. Proceedings of the 30th STOC* (pp. 409–418).

Feige, U. (1990) *Alternative Models of Zero Knowledge Proofs*. [Ph.D. Dissertation]. Weismann Institute of Science.

Goldreich, O., & Oren, Y. (1994). Definitions and Properties of Zero Knowledge Systems. *Journal of Cryptology*, *7*(1). doi:10.1007/BF00195207

Malka, L. (2008). *A study of Perfect Zero Knowledge Proofs* [Ph.D. dissertation]. University of Victoria.

Mohr, A. (2007). A survey of Zero Knowledge Proofs with applications to Cryptography. Retrieved from austinmohr.com/work/files/zkp.pdf

Pass, R. (2004). Alternative variants of Zero Knowledge Proofs. Retrieved from http://www.cs.cornell. edu/~rafael/papers/raf-lic.pdf

Wu, H., & Wang, F. (2014). A Survey of Noninteractive Zero knowledge Proof system and its applications. *TheScientificWorldJournal*. doi:10.1155/2014/560484 PMID:24883407

KEY TERMS AND DEFINITIONS

Bit Commitment: A proof system where the prover commits to a bit which cannot be later changed.

Graph 3-Colorability: In this problem, we try to color the vertices of a graph such that no two adjacent vertices share the same color. The graph 3-coloring problem tries to color the vertices of a graph with only 3-colors.

Hamiltonian Cycle: The Hamiltonian Cycle problem in Graphs is determining whether a Hamiltonian Cycle exists in a given Graph. A Hamiltonian Cycle is a Hamitonian Path which is a cycle. A Hamiltonian path is a path in a graph which visits each vertex exactly once.

Interactive Proof: An interactive Proof system is a type of proof system which satisfies the Completeness and the soundness properties.

Non-Deterministic Polynomial Problem: The class of NP problems describes a collection problems Whose solution can be verified in polynomial time.

Proof System: Proof systems describe a sequence of message exchanges between a prover and a verifier

Protocol Composition: Composition of protocols means running many instances of the protocol simultaneously.

Zero Knowledge Proof: A proof system where the prover does not reveal anything beyond the assertion being proved.

Chapter 10
Cryptographic Voting Protocols

Kannan Balasubramanian
Mepco Schlenk Engineering College, India

Jayanthi Mathanan
Mepco Schlenk Engineering College, India

ABSTRACT

Most of the voting protocols proposed so far can be categorized into two main types based on the approach taken: schemes using blind signatures and schemes using homomorphic encryption. In the schemes using blind signatures, the voter initially obtains a token – a blindly signed message unknown to anyone except himself. In the schemes using homomorphic encryption the voter cooperates with the authorities in order to construct an encryption of his vote. Due to the homomorphic property, an encryption of the sum of the votes is obtained by multiplying the encrypted votes of all voters. This chapter reviews schemes based on blind signatures and homomorphic encryption and proposes improvements to the existing schemes.

INTRODUCTION

With the advent of the digital era, Electronic Voting has become common. Many issues remain to be solved in electronic voting schemes. This chapter explores the use of cryptographic protocols in electronic voting especially the application of homomorphic encryption to electronic voting. Most of the existing voting protocols can be categorized into two main types based on the approach taken: schemes using blind signatures and schemes using homomorphic encryption. In the schemes using blind signatures, the voter initially obtains a token – a blindly signed message unknown to anyone except himself. Next, the voter sends his token together with his vote anonymously. These schemes require voter's participation in many rounds. In the schemes using homomorphic encryption, the voter cooperates with the authorities in order to construct an encryption of his vote. Due to the homomorphic property, an encryption of the sum of the votes is obtained by multiplying the encrypted votes of all voters. Finally, the result of the election is computed from the sum of the votes which is jointly decrypted by the authorities. This chapter reviews schemes based on blind signatures and homomorphic encryption and proposes improvements to the existing schemes.

DOI: 10.4018/978-1-5225-2915-6.ch010

FORMULATION OF THE VOTING PROBLEM

A voting scheme must ensure not only that the voter *can* keep his vote private, but also that he *must* keep it private. In other words, the voter should not be able to prove to the third party that he has cast a particular vote. He must not be able to construct a receipt proving the content of his vote. This property is referred to as receipt-freeness.

Only a few schemes guaranteeing receipt-freeness have been proposed. Known receipt-free scheme using blind signatures (Okamoto, 1997), assumes the existence of a special anonymous untappable channel. Achieving both secure and anonymous communication would, however, be extremely difficult. As for the schemes using homomorphic encryption, some efficient receipt-free schemes have already been proposed. Only the scheme proposed by Hirt and Sako (Hirt et al., 2000).

The Voting committee takes count of the voters: It allows only eligible voters to vote, and it ensures that every voter votes at most once. After the elections, the voting committee counts the votes and publishes the result. The votes remain secret. No one should not be able to say how anyone has voted. Even if the person says how he has voted, we cannot believe him, since he can lie. On the other hand, a person casting his vote cannot be absolutely sure that his vote was really counted. Everyone has to believe that the voting committee is honest and it would not disrupt the elections.

Basic Model

The participants in our schemes are voters and authorities. Let the number of Voters be M and the number of authorities be N. M is usually much greater than N. In general, the voters need not concern themselves with the voting process-they simply need to cast their votes. A voter can abstain from voting if he wishes to. Further we can assume, that he can store some amount of data in some secret place inaccessible to anyone except himself.

The authorities manage the elections. They have large computing power and they can store large amount of data in secret. Authorities can also act as voters. Of course, some number of authorities will be faulty. The maximum of faulty authorities will be assumed to be t. We assume that the remaining N-t authorities will do their prescribed work correctly and honestly.

The structure of Votes depends on the election (Rjaskova, 2002). The following types of elections are usually considered.

- **Yes/No Voting**: Voter's answer is yes or no. Vote is one bit: 1 for yes, 0 for no.
- **1-out-of-L Voting**: Here, the voter has L possibilities and the voter chooses one of them. The vote is a number in the range $1...L$.
- **K-Out-of-L Voting**: Voter selects K different elements from the set of L possibilities. The order of the selected elements is not important. The Vote is a K-tuple $(v_1 \cdots v_K)$.
- **K-Out-of-L Ordered Voting**: The Voter select K different elements in order from the set of L possibilities. Vote is an ordered K-tuple $(v_1 \cdots v_K)$.
- **1-L-K Voting**: Voter picks out one of the L sets of possibilities, and from the selected set he chooses K elements. Vote is a K +1-tuple $(i, a_1 \cdots a_K)$; $a_1 \cdots a_K$ are elements of the ith set.
- **Structured Voting**: Voting is done from sets of possibilities in n levels.
- **Write-In Voting**: Voter formulates his own answer and writes it down. Vote is a string with a specified maximum length.

In addition, weights may be assigned to vote i.e., vote V_i is assigned a weight w_i.

Trust

Each participant (voter as well as authority) has to believe that at least $N - t$ authorities are honest. This trust can be a sort of "general suspicion", when (from the participant's point of view) every authority is dishonest with the same probability, but the participant believes that the actual number of the dishonest authorities will not exceed t. Authorities do not trust voter at all.

Communication Channels

Any participant can send a message to any other participant through the public channel. An example is the Bulletin board. Any participant can write in (only in his own section), but nobody can delete or change anything in the bulletin board. Bulletin board can be considered as public channels with memory.

Untappable channel is a secret channel between two participants. Communication through the untappable channel is physically secure: no one else can see or change the sent message, and even the participant cannot later demonstrate to anyone what was sent. The existence of the untappable channel is assumed in some schemes between the voter and the authority.

Untraceable anonymous channel, or anonymous channel for short, is a channel guaranteeing the anonymity of the sender. Recipient of the message that has been sent through the anonymous channel does not know the identity of the sender. No one is able to trace the message back to the sender. The anonymous channel need not to be untappable.

Untappable anonymous channel is a channel guaranteeing both the anonymity of the sender and the physical security of the transmission: the sender / receiver cannot later demonstrate what was sent / received. No one can intercept the transmission of the message. Implementation of the untappable anonymous channel is hard in practice.

Electronic Voting Schemes

The aim is to design the voting scheme in such a way that malicious or improper behavior of the voter will be detected, and invalid or double-votes will not be taken into account.

An Electronic voting scheme consists of three main stages: initialization stage, voting stage, and counting stage. The stage can consist of more phases: During the Initialization stage. the authorities set up the system. They announce the elections, formulate the question and possibilities for an answer, create a list of eligible voters, and so on. They generate their public and secret keys, and publish the public values.

During the Voting stage, Voters cast their votes. The voter communicates with authorities through the channels he can use, forming a ballot containing his vote. Finally, the voter sends his ballot to its destination. During the Counting stage. Authorities use their public and secret information to open the ballots and count the votes. They publish the result of elections.

Security Requirements

The following are the security requirements of the voting scheme.

1. **Eligibility:** Only eligible voters cast the votes. Every voter cast only one vote.
2. **Privacy:** No coalition of participants (of reasonable composition) not containing voter himself can gain any information about the voter's vote. By reasonable composition we mean coalition of at most t authorities and any number of voters.
3. **Individual Verifiability:** Each eligible voter can verify that his vote was really counted.
4. **Universal Verifiability:** Any participant or passive observer can check that the election is fair: the published final tally is really the sum of the votes.
5. **Fairness:** No participant can gain any knowledge about the (partial) tally before the counting stage (the knowledge of the partial tally could affect the intentions of the voters who has not yet voted).
6. **Robustness:** Faulty behavior of any reasonably sized coalition of participants can be tolerated. No coalition of voters can disrupt the election and any cheating voter will be detected.
7. **Receipt-Freeness, Incoercibility:** The scheme is incoercible if the voter cannot convince any observer how he has voted. This requirement prevents vote-buying and coercion. Before the election, someone can bribe or coerce the voter to vote in a particular way. The coercer can order the voter how he should behave during the voting process (e.g. generates for him random bits). During the election, the coercer can observe the public communication between the voter and the authorities.

After the election, he will want to see a proof that the voter really voted this way. In the scheme achieving privacy, the coercer alone or with reasonable coalition of participants cannot open the voter's vote. Thus, the coercer will force the voter to show him his secret information. Using this information, he is capable of opening the ballot and seeing the vote. Incoercible scheme provides the voter with the ability to modify his secrets and to open his ballot in any desired way. Thus, the voter can vote on his own will and he can feed the coercer with a false proof.

APPROACHES TO THE ELECTRONIC VOTING SCHEME PROBLEM

The most difficult part in designing a voting scheme is achieving privacy. Privacy means that the link between the voter and his vote is disposed or inaccessible to everyone (including authority), even if all of the public communication is monitored. This can be accomplished in three ways:

*   It is easy to see the vote, but it is impossible to trace it back to the voter.
*   It is impossible or computationally infeasible to see the actual vote, but it is easy to see the identity of the voter.
*   Both seeing the actual vote and obtaining the identity of the voter is impossible or computationally infeasible.

Schemes of the first and the third type have to use some special kind of channel for casting the votes (usually untraceable anonymous channel). In the first approach, the actual votes are published and anybody can count them, but nobody knows who sent which vote. However, a special care is required to achieve eligibility, to ensure that the voter cannot cast more votes and to prevent improper voters from voting. On the other hand, in the schemes of the second type there is a problem of the vote counting. Besides, anybody can see which voters have voted and which have not.

Schemes Based on Anonymous Channel

The voting stage is a composition of the registration phase and the voting phase. The voter obtains a token in the registration phase, which gives him the right to vote in the voting phase. The voter is not able to create the token by himself, but only after interacting with the authority. The authority helps the eligible voter to construct the token only once, so the voter gets only one token. The authority has no idea how the voter's token looks like. Moreover, the validity of the token is verifiable to anyone. This concept is realized via blind signatures.

In the voting phase, the voter sends a ballot containing the token and his vote through the anonymous channel to the authority. The authority will not accept the ballot with invalid token or with the token that has already been used. This ensures that only eligible voters can vote (only eligible voters have been allowed to construct tokens), and that they can vote at most once (they can obtain at most one token). As no one (even the authority) can make any connection between the voter and the token or trace the cast ballot back to the voter, no one can deduce anything about how the voter voted. Hence, privacy is achieved.

In general, token may consist of whatever you want: hidden voter's identity (a hash value for instance), random numbers, encrypted vote, voting tag (unique for each election), etc. The only restriction is that it should be hard or impossible to extract the voter's identity from the token and that each voter gets a unique token. Structure of the token is specified in the voting scheme. The token is sometimes called a pseudonym. The term "pseudonym" emphasizes the fact that the voter's identity and the token (pseudonym) cannot be linked.

Schemes Based on Homomorphic Encryption

In this kind of schemes, the voter sends encrypted vote through the public channel (usually to the bulletin board). The vote can be decrypted by any set of at least $t + 1$ authorities, and any set of t authorities can tell nothing about the vote. This can be accomplished in two ways:

- The Threshold public-key cryptosystem is used for encrypting the votes (A key to decrypt the vote is shared between any set of t + 1 authorities say for example using the El Gamal Cryptosystem)
- Each authority has its own instance of the cryptosystem. The voter shares the secret (his vote) among the N authorities using $(t+1, N)$ secret sharing scheme (for example, using Shamir's secret sharing scheme). The voter sends its encrypted share to each authority.

This prevents a small coalition of malicious authorities from abusing their role and from violating a voter's privacy. Problem arises only in counting the votes. Encryption method used for encrypting votes is homomorphic: multiplication of the encrypted votes is an encrypted sum of the votes.

In the first case, encrypted votes are multiplied and authorities decrypt only the sum of the votes. In the second case, each authority multiplies its encrypted shares, decrypts the sum of its shares, and the final sum of the votes can be computed by anyone from the $t + 1$ partial sums. In a yes/no voting, where 1 expresses a yes-vote and 0 expresses a no-vote, the sum of the votes is the number of yes-votes. As the whole number of votes is known, the number of no-votes is easily computed.

The authorities should be able to distinguish between the valid and the invalid encrypted votes (for example, the voter can encrypt 2 instead of 1 so that his vote will counted twice). Invalid votes should be rejected. Usually, the voter is required to prove that his vote is of the correct form (either 1 or 0) with-out disclosing any other information about his vote (the proof should be zero knowledge).

Usually, schemes based on homomorphic encryption are not receipt-free: let the voter's favorite vote be V, and encryption of the V be C. Voter sends C to the bulletin board, so C is publicly known. Further, suppose that the coercer's favorite vote is W, and that W ≠ V. The Coercer can later force the voter to reveal how W is encrypted to C. Of course, C is the encryption of V, and the only chance for the voter is to show the coercer that C looks like the encryption of W. This is possible only if the deniable encryption is used. However, a deniable encryption with homomorphic property and suitable to threshold cryptographic techniques is not yet known.

Schemes Based on Mixing the Votes

Consider the simple case of 1-out-of-L voting. The authorities take the list of the L possible votes (original list), and mix it to produce the final list. The first authority takes the list of L possible votes (original list), permutes it in a random order, and re-encrypts each possible vote. It unveils the permutation only to the voter and no one else. To increase the security, the authority sends the permutation to the voter through untappable channel. The created list containing re-encrypted and permuted possible votes is published and handled to the next authority. Seeing just the original and created list, no one is able to say anything about the permutation mapping each item from the original list to its re-encryption in the created list, unless this permutation is revealed to him by the authority. The next authority takes the handled list, and shuffles it in the same way as the first authority shuffed the original list: permute the list in a random order, re-encrypt each item, unveil the permutation to the voter through the untappable channel and publish the produced list. Successively, each authority takes the list handled by the previous authority, shuffles it in the manner described above, and handles the produced list to the next authority. The list produced by the last authority is called the final list. Only the voter can keep track of the permutations that have been sequentially applied to the original list by the authorities. Therefore, only he knows the permutation mapping each item from the original list to its re-encryption in the final list. The voter just selects one item from the final list as his vote.

In the case that the used encryption is homomorphic, the voter writes his selected item to the bulletin board. The votes are counted as in the schemes based on homomorphic property: all encrypted votes are multiplied, and the authorities cooperate to decrypt the sum of the votes.

The coercer cannot tap on the secure channel, so the voter can adjust the permutations he received from the authorities as it comes useful. Therefore, the voter is not able to prove how he has voted and these schemes are receipt-free. Schemes of this type are presented in (Sako et al., 1995; Hirt, 2000).

ELECTRONIC VOTING SCHEMES

Here we review the electronic voting schemes that have been proposed till now.

Chaum's Voting Scheme

The anonymous channel and the first voting scheme was proposed by Chaum (Chaum, D.L.,1981). The authorities are N mix-servers with their public keys $E_1, \ldots E_N$. The voter V_i generates his public key K_i

and writes $E_1(E_2(\cdots E_N(K_i))\cdots)$ to his section in the bulletin board. Mix-servers shuffles these messages (sequential permutation and decryption), and produce a list of keys K_i. Here, the voter may complain when his K_i is not on the list. In that case, the elections are restarted. If no complaint is raised, the voter writes $E_1(\cdots E_N(K_i k K_i^{-1}(v_i))\cdots)$ in the bulletin board. Again, the mix-servers shuffes these messages, and the list of $K_i k K_i^{-1}(v_i)$ is combined with the previous list to obtain the votes v_i.

This scheme has many drawbacks. For example, failure of the single voter will disrupt the election and the election has to be restarted. Moreover, if the election has to be restarted after the second phase, when some votes have already been published, it can affect the re-election.

Schemes Based on Blind Signatures and Anonymous Channel

The voter first obtains a token which is a message blindly signed by the authority. The voter is able to obtain only one token, since the authority blindly signs only one message for the voter. Next, the voter sends the token with his vote through the anonymous channel back to the authority. The authority collects the votes and publishes them together with the tokens.

The authority issuing the tokens is called an administrator, and the authority collecting the votes a collector. The terms administrator and collector may refer to two different authorities, or to the same authority acting both as the administrator and as a collector depending on the scheme. This approach brings about some problems and security drawbacks. The most important ones are:

- There is no fairness – some participant (the collector) knows the intermediate result (partial sum) before the counting stage
- The scheme is not collision-free – there is a chance that two voters will gain the same token at the registration, hence the vote of one of the voters will be excluded as double-vote
- A dishonest authority (administrator) may impersonate the voters abstaining from the voting and add its own votes, or secretly provide some voters with more than one token
- In the case that the voter's vote has not been counted, the voter cannot complain about this without revealing his vote

To enhance the fairness, we can prevent the collector from seeing the actual votes with a simple trick. Allow the collector collect the encryptions of the votes. The actual votes will be decrypted later at the counting stage. The decryption key can be sent anonymously by the voter (who has encrypted the vote), or the decryption key can be reconstructed by some set of authorities.

Collision-freeness can be achieved by inserting the voter's identification into the token in such a way that it is infeasible to extract it. The dishonest behavior of the authority may be avoided by distributing the power of the single authority to several authorities.

The Schemes proposed in Chaum (1988), Boyd (1988), Fujioka et al. (1992), Radwin (1995), Juang et al. (1997), and Juang et al. (1998) are of this type.

Schemes Using Homomorphic Encryption

An example of this type of scheme is the Benaloh's scheme (Benaloh, 1987). In this scheme, two primitives are used: secret sharing scheme and probabilistic public-key encryption with homomorphic property

$$E(m_1, k_1)E(m_2, k_2) = E(m_1 + m_2, k_1 k_2)$$

where $(k_1, k_2$ are random parameters used in encrypting messages m_1, m_2 Bulletin board is implicitly used for collecting votes. Other schemes of this type are (Shoenmaker, 1999; Cramer et al., 1997; Hirt et al., 2000).

IMPLEMENTATION OF THE UNTAPPABLE CHANNEL

Existence of the untappable channel is sometimes assumed between the voter and the authority. Untappable channel can be realized by providing multiple channels between the sender and the receiver under the assumption that the coercer cannot tap on all channels simultaneously. The sender sends the message through one of the channels randomly selected. If the coercer can tap merely on a few channels, he can intercept the message only with small probability. If this approach is not applicable, we have to assume that tapping on the channel between the voter and the authority is likely. Nevertheless, intercepting the communication between the voter and the authority should be useless for the coercer; the voter should be able to mislead him by interpreting the intercepted communication in the coercer's desired way. The coercer should not obtain any information about the transmitted message, except for its length.

Standard cryptographic implementations of the secure channel are not suitable. If the adversary intercepts the transmission of the encrypted message and later forces the sender to reveal the secret keys and the random choices generated during the encryption, the cleartext is exposed.

Using traditional encryption methods, the sender is bound to the clear text. For an intercepted ciphertext, the sender cannot generate fake secret keys and fake random choices will persuade the adversary that the given ciphertext corresponds to a different cleartext.

An encryption scheme allowing the sender generating his fake random choices and his fake secret keys that will make the ciphertext looks like the encryption of a different cleartext is called sender-deniable encryption. An encryption scheme satisfying analogous requirements for the receiver is called receiver-deniable encryption. The concept of deniable encryption was introduced in (Canetti, 1996). One-time pad is an example of the deniable encryption.

SUMMARY

This chapter examined the problem of electronic voting and proposed the use of cryptographic protocols for the electronic voting problem. This chapter reviewed the various electronic voting schemes in existence and proposed schemes based on cryptographic constructs.

REFERENCES

Benaloh, J. C. (1987). *Verifiable Secret Ballot Elections* [PhD thesis]. Yale University.

Boyd, C. (1988). A new multiple key cipher and an improved voting scheme. *Lecture Notes in Computer Science, 434,* 617–625. doi:10.1007/3-540-46885-4_58

Canetti, R., Dwork, C., Naor, M., & Ostrovsky, R. (1996). Deniable Encryption. Retrieved from https://eprint.iacr.org/1996/002.ps

Chaum, D. L. (1981). Untraceable electronic mail, return address, and digital pseudonym. *Communications of the ACM, 24*(2), 84–90.

Chaum, D. L. (1988). Elections with unconditionally-secret ballots and disruption equivalent to breaking RSA. *Proceedings of EUROCRYPT '88.*

Cramer, R., Gennaro, R., & Schoenmakers, B. (1997). A secure and optimally efficient multi-authority election scheme. In Advances in Cryptology EUROCRYPT '97.

Fujioka, A., Okamoto, T., & Ohta, K. (1992). A practical secret voting scheme for large scale elections. In *Advances in Cryptology AUSCRYPT'92.*

Hirt, M., & Sako, K. (2000). Efficient Receipt-free voting based Homomorphic Encryption. In *EUROCRYPT '00.*

Juang, W., & Lei, C. (1997). A secure and practical electronic voting scheme for real world environment. *IEICE Trans. On Fundamentals, E80-A*(1).

Juang, W., Lei, C., & Yu, P. (1998). A verifiable multi-authorities secret elections allowing abstaining from voting. *Proceedings of the International Computer Symposium*, Taiwan.

Okamoto, T. (1997). Receipt-free electronic voting scheme for large-scale election. *In Security Protocols (pp. 25-35).*

Radwin, M. J. (1995). An untraceable, universally verifiable voting scheme. Retrieved from http://citeseerx.ist.psu.edu/viewdoc/download?doi=10.1.1.9.1758&rep=rep1&type=pdf

Rujaskova, Z. (2002). Electronic Voting Schemes [Diplomova Praca dissertation]. Comenius University, Bratislava.

Sako, K., & Kilian, J. (1995). Receipt-free Mix type voting scheme- a practical solution to the implementation of a voting booth. In *Advances in Cryptology EUROCRYPT '95.*

Shoenmakers, B. (1999). A simple publicly verifiable secret sharing scheme and its application to electronic voting. In Crypto 1999, LNCS (Vol. *1666*, pp. 148–164). doi:10.1007/3-540-48405-1_10

KEY TERMS AND DEFINITIONS

Anonymous Channel: An anonymous channel guarantees the anonymity of the sender.
Authorities: Officials administering the initialization, voting and vote-counting phases.
Blind Signatures: Each signature is uniquely signed using a random value.
Deniable Encryption: Deniable encryption is used in the implementation of the untappable channel. An example of deniable encryption is the one-time pad.

Electronic Voting: A voting scheme where users cast their votes with the assurance of increased security. Since the voting is carried out electronically, counting of votes is easier and protection from untrusted authorities can be provided.

Homomorphic Encryption: An encryption scheme satisfying the homomorphic property. An example is the RSA algorithm which exhibits multiplicative homomorphism.

Untappable Channel: An untappable channel secures the message exchange and prevents eavesdropping of messages.

Chapter 11
Securing Public Key Encryption Against Adaptive Chosen Ciphertext Attacks

Kannan Balasubramanian
Mepco Schlenk Engineering College, India

ABSTRACT

To deal with active attacks in public key encryptions, the notion of security against an adaptive chosen ciphertext attack has been defined by Researchers. If an adversary can inject messages into a network, these messages may be ciphertexts, and the adversary may be able to extract partial information about the corresponding cleartexts through its interaction with parties in the network. The Security against chosen ciphertext attack is defined using an "decryption oracle." Given an encryption of a message the "ciphertext" we want to guarantee that the adversary cannot obtain any partial information about the message. A method of securing Public Key Cryptosystems using hash functions is described in this chapter.

INTRODUCTION

In this chapter, we define the notion of security against adaptive chosen ciphertext attack for a public key encryption scheme. This security is defined using a decryption oracle. This chapter proposes a method using hash functions to secure public key encryption schemes. This chapter introduces the notion of Semantic Security and discusses modifications to the RSA algorithm to achieve semantic Security.

SECURITY OF PUBLIC KEY ENCRYPTION SCHEMES

Semantic security as defined by Goldwasser and Micali, (1984) captures the intuition that an adversary should not be able to obtain any partial information about a message given its encryption. However, this guarantee of secrecy is only valid when the adversary is completely passive, i.e., can only eavesdrop. Indeed, semantic security offers no guarantee of secrecy at all if an adversary can mount an active attack, i.e., inject messages into a network or otherwise influence the behavior of parties in the network.

DOI: 10.4018/978-1-5225-2915-6.ch011

To deal with active attacks, Racko and Simon (1991) defined the notion of security against an *adaptive chosen ciphertext attack*. If an adversary can inject messages into a network, these Messages may be ciphertexts, and the adversary may be able to extract partial information about the corresponding cleartexts through its interactions with the parties in the network. Racko and Simon's definition models this type of attack by simply allowing an adversary to obtain decryptions of its choice, i.e., the adversary has access to a "decryption oracle." now, given an encryption of a message the "ciphertext" we want to guarantee that the adversary cannot obtain any partial information about the message. To achieve this, we have to restrict the adversary's behavior in some way, otherwise the adversary could simply submit the target ciphertext itself to the decryption oracle. The restriction proposed by Racko and Simon is the weakest possible: the adversary is not allowed to submit the target ciphertext itself to the oracle; however, it may submit any other ciphertext, including ciphertexts that are related to the target ciphertext.

A different notion of security against active attacks, called Non-Malleability, was proposed by Dolev, Dwork, and Naor (1991). Here, the adversary also has access to a decryption Oracle, but his goal is not to obtain partial information about the target ciphertext, but rather, to create another encryption of a different message that is related in some interesting way to the original, encrypted message. For example, for a non-malleable encryption scheme, given an encryption of n, it should be infeasible to create an encryption of $n + 1$. It turns out that non-malleability and security against adaptive chosen ciphertext attack are equivalent (Bellare et al., 1998; Dolev et al., 2000).

An encryption scheme secure against adaptive chosen ciphertext attack is a very powerful cryptographic primitive. It is essential in designing protocols that are secure against active adversaries. For example, this primitive is used in protocols for authentication and key exchange (Dwork et al., 1996; Dolev et al., 2000; Shoup, 1999) and in protocols for escrow, certified e-mail, and more general fair exchange (Asokan et al., 2000). It is by now generally recognized in the cryptographic research community that security against adaptive chosen ciphertext attack is the right notion of security for a general-purpose public-key encryption scheme. This is exemplified by the adoption of Bellare and Rogaway's OAEP scheme (Bellare, M (a practical but only heuristically secure scheme) as the internet encryption standard rsa pkcs#1 version 2, and for use in the set protocol for electronic commerce.

Another motivation for security against adaptive chosen ciphertext attack is Bleichenbacher's attack (Bleichenbacher, 1998) on the widely-used SSL key establishment protocol, which is based on RSA pkcs#1 version Bleichenbacher showed how to break this protocol by mounting a specific chosen ciphertext attack (SSL still uses RSA pkcs#1 version 1, but the protocol has been patched so as to avoid bleichenbacher's attack).

There are also intermediate notions of security, between semantic security and adaptive Chosen Ciphertext security. Naor and Yung (1990) propose an attack model where the adversary has access to the decryption oracle only prior to obtaining the target ciphertext, and the goal of the adversary is to obtain partial information about the encrypted message.

Naor and Yung called this type of attack a *chosen ciphertext attack*; it has also been called a "lunchtime" or "midnight" attack, and also an indifferent chosen ciphertext attack.

SECURITY AGAINST ADAPTIVE CHOSEN CIPHERTEXT ATTACK

Security is defined via the following game played by the adversary: First, the encryption scheme's key generation algorithm is run, with a security parameter as input. Next, the adversary makes arbitrary queries to a "decryption oracle," decrypting ciphertexts of his choice. Next the adversary chooses two messages, m_0 and m_1, and sends these to an "encryption oracle." The encryption oracle chooses a bit b $\in \{0, 1\}$ at random, and encrypts m_b. The corresponding ciphertext is given to the adversary (the internal coin tosses of the encryption oracle, in particular b, are not in the adversary's view).

After receiving the ciphertext from the encryption oracle, the adversary continues to query the decryption oracle, subject only to the restriction that the query must be different from the output of the encryption oracle.

At the end of the game, the adversary outputs $b' \in \{0, 1\}$, which is supposed to be the adversary's guess of the value b. If the probability that $b' = b$ is $1/2 + \varepsilon$, then the adversary's advantage is defined to be ε.

The cryptosystem is said to be secure against adaptive chosen ciphertext attack if the advantage of any polynomial-time adversary is negligible (as a function of the security parameter).

A PUBLIC KEY ENCRYPTION SECURE AGAINST CHOSEN CIPHERTEXT ATTACK

Here we present the public key encryption presented by Cramer and Shoup. (https://www.zurich.ibm.com/security/ace/cs.pdf). We assume that we have a group G of prime order q, where q is large. We also assume that cleartext messages are (or can be encoded as) elements of G. We also use a universal one-way family of hash functions that map long bit strings to elements of Z_q. The key generation algorithm runs as follows. Random elements $g_1, g_2 \in$ G are chosen, and random elements

$$x_1, x_2, y_1, y_2, z \in Z_q$$

are also chosen.

Next, the group elements

$$c = g_1^{x_1} g_2^{x_2}, d = g_1^{y_1} g_2^{y_2}; h = g_1^z$$

are computed. Next, a hash function H is chosen from the family of universal one-way hash function. The public key is (g_1, g_2, c, d, h, H), and the private key is (x_1, x_2, y_1, y_2, z).

Encryption: Given a message $m \in$ G, the encryption algorithm runs as follows. First, it chooses $r \in Z_q$ at random. Then it computes

$$u_1 = g_1^r, u_2 = g_2^r, e = h^r m \quad \alpha = H(u_1, u_2, e), v = c^r d^{r\alpha}$$

The ciphertext is

$$(u_1, u_2, e, v)$$

Decryption: Decryption. Given a ciphertext (u_1, u_2, e, v), the decryption algorithm runs as follows. It first computes $\alpha = H(u_1, u_2, e)$, and tests if

$$u_1^{x_1 + y_1\alpha} u_2^{x_2 + y_2\alpha} = v$$

If this condition does not hold, the decryption algorithm outputs "reject"; otherwise, it outputs

$$m = e / u_1^z$$

We can verify that this is an encryption scheme, in the sense that the decryption of an encryption of a message yields the message. Since $u_1 = g_1^r$ and $u_2 = g_2^r$, we have

$$u_1^{x_1} u_2^{x_2} = g_1^{rx_1} g_2^{rx_2} = c^r$$

Likewise, $u_1^{y_1} u_2^{y_2} = d^r$, and $u_1^z = h^r$. Therefore, the test performed by the decryption algorithm will pass, and the output will be $e / h^r = m$.

SECURING PUBLIC KEY ENCRYPTION SYSTEMS

Let P be a cryptographic problem. An access (possibly with certain restrictions on entries) to an oracle solving a problem Q may be a way to find more easily a solution to problem P. More precisely, the oracle solving Q is an *interactive* resource that is given to the adversary. For a pair (P, Q), the problem consisting in solving P with an access to a Q-solver oracle is called the (P, Q) *assisted problem*. Even if the problem Q is expected to be computationally hard (and thus, even if the Q-solver oracle gives a lot of extra power to the attacker), the (P, Q) assisted problem may remain hard. These problems are considered in (Pailier, 2006; Paillier et al., 2007). The assumption that solving the $(P; Q)$ assisted problem is only negligibly easier than solving the P problem is called the $(P; Q)$ *instance-independence assumption* (Abdalla et al., 2001).

The first example is *assisted factorization*: with an oracle solving factorization of $n \neq n_0$ (with the restriction that $n \neq 0 \bmod n_0$ for obvious reasons), it should remain hard to factor modulus n_0. Another example is the *assisted e-th root computation*: with an oracle returning e-th roots modulo n (for (e, n) $\neq (e_0, n_0)$) | where $(e; n)$ is a possible output of some RSA key generator), it should remain hard to compute an e_0-th root modulo n_0.

We stress that instance-independence assumptions should not be con-fused with *one-more assumptions*. In a one-more-P problem, one is given access to two oracles, O_{Gen} and O_{Solve}, and needs to solve $(n + 1)$ independent instances of the P challenge (these challenges being given by O_{Gen}), using at most n accesses to O_{Solve}, which is an oracle that solves any chosen instance of problem P. Examples of one-more problems include the one-more RSA, the one-more DL and the one-more CDH (Bellare et al., 2003).

The assisted (P, Q)-problems, which are supposedly as hard as their primitive problem P under instance-independence assumptions, are of different nature. Indeed, they consist in solving only *one* instance of the *P*-problem, using a possibly very large number of queries to an oracle solving the *Q*-problem. What makes these assisted problems non-trivial is the fact that, in contrast with one-more problems, the entries of the *Q*-problem solver are supposed to be "not too related" to the *P*-challenge (hence the name of *instance-independence*). As a consequence, assisted problems and one-more problems can hardly be linked or compared together.

Public Key Encryption

A *public-key encryption scheme*, $E = $ (Gen, Enc, Dec), can be described as a tuple of probabilistic polynomial-time algorithms. By default, the message space is $\{0,1\}^*$.

- **Key Generation**: Given a security parameter k, Gen(1^k) produces a pair (pk, sk) of matching public and private keys.
- **Encryption**: Given a message m in message space M and public key pk, $\text{Enc}_{pk}(m)$ produces a ciphertext $c \leftarrow \text{Enc}_{pk}(m)$. If x denotes the random coins used by Enc, we equivalently write $c = \text{Enc}_{pk}(m, x)$.
- **Decryption**: Given a ciphertext c and private key sk, $\text{Dec}_{sk}(c)$ returns a plain-text m or a special symbol *?* denoting that the ciphertext is invalid.

We require that if $c \leftarrow \text{Enc}_{pk}(m)$, then $\text{Dec}_{sk}(c)$ returns m for all $(pk, sk) \leftarrow \text{GEN}(1^k)$ and messages drawn in the message space.

Semantic Security

The notion of *semantic security* (IND) (Goldwasser et al., 1984), also known as *indistinguishability of encryptions*, captures a strong notion of privacy: The attacker should not learn any information whatsoever about a plaintext given its encryption. The adversary $A = (A_1, A_2)$ is said to (k, ε, τ)-break IND when

$$Adv_\varepsilon^{IND}(A) = 2 \times \Pr_{b,x} \left[\begin{array}{l} (pk, sk) \leftarrow GEN(1^k), (m_0, m_1, s) \leftarrow A_1(pk), \\ c \leftarrow ENC_{pk}(m_b) : A_2(m_0, m_1, s, c) = b \end{array} \right] - 1 \geq \varepsilon$$

where the probability is taken over the random coins of the experiment according to the distribution induced by GEN(1^k) as well as the ones the adversary, where $b \in \{0, 1\}$ and $m_0, m_1 \in M$. A must run in at most τ steps and it is imposed that $|m_0| = |m_1|$. An encryption scheme is said to be *semantically secure* (or IND secure) if no probabilistic algorithm can (k, ε, τ)-break IND for $\tau \leq$ poly (k) and $\varepsilon \geq 1/poly(k)$.

To achieve semantic security, a system should not leak any partial information about the plaintext of a given corresponding ciphertext. To be more specific, let f be a polynomial time computable function and $m \in \{0,1\}^n$ be a plaintext. Then, the public key cryptosystem is semantically secure if the probability that an adversary can guess $f(m)$ in polynomial time given the ciphertext is almost the same as the probability of guessing $f(m)$ without the ciphertext. We say that these two probabilities are almost the same if the difference is less than $1/p(n)$ for every polynomial p on input n. Thus, we can conclude that in a semantically secure public key cryptosystem, whatever information a polynomial time bounded adversary can compute about the plaintext given the ciphertext is also computable even without the ciphertext.

This idea can be formally verified through the following experiment called polynomial-time Indistinguishability (Goldwasser et al., 1984) experiment against an eavesdropper. Let $= (k, \varepsilon, \tau)$-be the public key encryption scheme and let A be a polynomial-time adversary. For any $n \in N$ as a security parameter.

1.   The adversary A outputs a pair of plaintexts (m_0, m_1). Both m_0 and m_1 are n-bit strings.
2.   Choose a key $k \leftarrow K(1^n)$ and a random $b \in \{0, 1\}$. Information of k and b cannot be leaked to A.
3.   Compute an encryption $c \leftarrow E_k(m_b)$.
4.   The adversary A receives c and guesses $b' \in \{0,1\}$.
5.   Return 1 if $b' = b$. Otherwise, return 0.

If the adversary outputs b' at random, the probability that the experiment outputs 1 should be 1/2. This cryptosystem has indistinguishable encryptions against an eavesdropper if any adversary whose computation power is no better than a probabilistic polynomial-time Turing machine cannot guess $b' = b$ with signi cantly higher probability than 1/2.

As we are in the public-key setting, it is worth noting that adversary $A = (A_1, A_2)$ is given the public-key pk and so can encrypt any message of its choice. In other words, the adversary can mount chosen-plaintext attacks (CPA). Hence, we write IND-CPA the security level offered by an IND-secure encryption scheme, emphasizing the fact that A has access to an encryption oracle.

Chosen-Ciphertext Attacks

IND-CPA security offers an adequate security level in the presence of a *passive* adversary. In a number of situations however (Shoup, 1998), this may prove to be insufficient in the presence of a more powerful adversary that can do more than merely eavesdropping the exchanged messages. The "right" security level against *active* attacks is that of IND-CCA security, or security against chosen-ciphertext attacks. The definition of the adversary's advantage readily extends to the IND-CCA model but the adversary $A = (A_1, A_2)$ now is given an adaptive access to a decryption oracle to which it can submit any ciphertext of its choice with the exception that A_2 may not query the decryption oracle on challenge ciphertext c.

There are two different types of CCA model. In chronological order, these are named non-adaptive chosen ciphertext attack(CCA1) and adaptive chosen ciphertext attack(CCA2). Recall that an adversary under chosen-ciphertext attack has an ability to access a decryption oracle so that he can decrypt the ciphertext that he has chosen. The difference between CCA1 and CCA2 lies in whether or not this ability is restricted by the challenge ciphertext c. Under CCA1, due to Naor and Yung (Naor et al., 1990) the adversary can access the decryption oracle only before he receives the challenge ciphertext c. That is, the adversary's queries to a decryption oracle cannot be adapted to the challenge c. This is the reason why the term `non-adaptive' is appended in the name of CCA1.

Under CCA2, due to Racko and Simon (1991), the adversary has an ability to access a decryption oracle, and now he can use this decrypting function even after he obtains the challenge ciphertext c.

The only restriction to this model is that an adversary cannot send c to the decryption oracle to verify the real message. In this model, an adversary can decide queries for the decryption oracle based on c, which is an extremely strong notion of security.

RSA IS NOT SEMANTICALLY SECURE

First, we focus on one of the most famous public key algorithms named RSA. The RSA scheme was originally introduced by Ron Rivest, Adi Shamir, and Leonard Adleman (1978) in 1978. The basic concept of this scheme is the fact that we believe a factoring problem of a large integer n, where n is the product of large random primes p and q, is computationally hard. The message space per single encryption is upper bounded in n, i.e., a block of the message should be an integer between 0 and n-1.

The RSA scheme involves a public key and a private key. These keys can be generated through the following procedure:

1. Pick two large primes p and q. Let $n = pq$.
2. Compute $\varphi(n) = (p-1)(q-1)$, where is the Euler's totient function.
3. Choose e, d $\in Z_{\varphi(n)}$ such that ed $\equiv$ 1 (mod (n)).
4. Public key: (n, e)
5. Private key: d

Let m be the plaintext, then the encryption of m is

$$c = m^e \bmod n$$

After receiving the ciphertext c from the sender, the decryption of c can be computed as

$$m = c^d \bmod n$$

It is believed that the private key d cannot be determined as long as $\varphi(n)$ is kept secret, and it is computationally infeasible to compute $\varphi(n)$ without factoring n. However, RSA has some weaknesses as regards to Semantic Security (Cha., 2010). First of all, a ciphertext encrypted by the RSA leaks some of the information in the message. Clearly, any deterministic encryption would not be able to overcome this weakness because there is only a unique encoding for each message. This could be a fatal defect for the public key encryptions as they are always vulnerable to the dictionary attack -an attacker can construct a dictionary which contains encryptions of every possible plaintext in the message space. Another known drawback of the plain RSA is its malleability. Any eavesdropper can construct the encryption of a transformed plaintext. Let m be the original plaintext and c be the encryption of the plaintext. Then, an adversary can compute

$$c' = c \times t^e \equiv m^e t^e \equiv (mt)^e \bmod n$$

for any t. If an adversary happens to know that this modification has a proper meaning, then he can encrypt a distorted message even though he does not know the plaintext m. For instance, setting t =1/2 instantly reduces m into half, and this kind of attack could be very critical if the plaintext was a numerical value such as price, date, or time. A non-malleable public key cryptosystem is semantically secure. As we now know that this attack can be a practical threat, NM-CPA should be achieved along with IND-CPA when designing a secure encryption scheme. One solution to achieve semantic security is to use a randomized padding scheme. As an easy example, we encrypt a message m along with a 10-bit random string r at the end of the message. With the help of the random string r, a ciphertext would become indistinguishable to the eavesdropper if the sender encrypts the same message twice and sends both ciphertexts to the receiver. After the decryption of the ciphertext, the plaintext m can be restored by removing the last 10-bits string of the decrypted message.

SECURING PUBLIC KEY SYSTEMS USING HASH FUNCTIONS

The following method strengthens a public key cryptosystem by appending to each ciphertext a tag that is correlated to the message to be enciphered. In this method tags are generated by the use of a one-way hash function.

Let us denote by G the cryptographically strong pseudo-random string generator based on the difficulty of computing discrete logarithms in finite fields. G stretches an n-bit input string into an output string whose length can be an arbitrary polynomial in n. This generator pro-duces $O(\log n)$ bits output at each exponentiation.

A user Alice's secret key is an element x_A chosen randomly from $[1, p- 1]$, and her public key is $y_A = g^{x_A}$ It is assumed that all messages to be enciphered are chosen from the set $\sum^P$, where $P = P(n)$ is an arbitrary polynomial with $P(n) \geq n$. Padding can be applied to messages whose lengths are less than n bits. In addition, let $l= l(n)$ be a polynomial which species the length of tags. It is recommended that l should be at least 64 for the sake of security.

Assume that h is a one-way hash function compressing input strings into l-bit output strings. A user Bob can use the following enciphering algorithm to send in secret a P-bit message m to Alice.

$E_{owh}(y_A, p, g, m)$

```
begin
      1.  x ∈_R [1, p - 1].
      2.  z = G(y_A^x)_[1..(P+l)]

      1.  t = h(m).
      2.  c₁ = gˣ.
      3.  c₂ = z ⊕(m || t)
      4.  output (c₁, c₂).
End
```

The deciphering algorithm for Alice, who possesses the secret key x_A, is as follows:

$D_{owh}(x_A, p, g, c_1, c_2)$

```
1. z' = G(c₁^xA)[1..(P+l)]
2. w = z' ⊕ c₂.
3. m' = w[1..P]
4. t'= w[(P=1)..(P+l)]
5. if h(m') = t' then output (m')
   else
      output ().
end
```

1. $z' = G(c_1^{x_A})_{[1..(P+l)]}$
2. $w = z' \oplus c_2.$
3. $m' = w_{[1..P]}$
4. $t' = w_{[(P=1)..(P+l)]}$
5. if $h(m') = t'$ then output (m')

SUMMARY

This chapter introduced security against Chosen Ciphertext Attacks as the strongest form of security against public key encryption schemes. It describes several solutions to secure public key systems against chosen ciphertext attacks. These solutions make use of hash functions for providing security against chosen ciphertext attacks.

REFERENCES

Abdalla, M., Bellare, M., & Rogaway, P. (2001). The Oracle Diffie-Hellman assumptions and an analysis of DHIES. In *CT-RSA 2001, LNCS* (Vol. 2020, pp. 143–158). Heidelberg: Springer. doi:10.1007/3-540-45353-9_12

Asokan, N., Shoup, V., & Waidner, M. (2000). Optimistic fair exchange of digital signatures. *IEEE Journal on Selected Areas in Communications*, 18(4), 593–610. doi:10.1109/49.839935

Bellare, M., Desai, A., Pointcheval, D., & Rogaway, A. (1998) Relations among notions of Security for public-key encryption schemes. In Advances in Cryptology CRYPTO '98 (pp. 26-45). doi:10.1007/BFb0055718

Bellare, M., Namprempre, C., Pointcheval, D., & Semanko, M. (2003). The one-more-RSA-inversion problems and the security of Chaums blind signature scheme. *Journal of Cryptology*, 16(3), 185–215. doi:10.1007/s00145-002-0120-1

Bellare, M., & Rogaway, P. (1994). Optimal Asymmetric Encryption, In Advances in Cryptology Eurocrypt '94 (pp. 92-111).

Bleichenbacher, D. (1998). Chosen ciphertext attacks against protocols based on the RSA encryption Standard pkcs #1. In *Advances in Cryptology CRYPTO '98.*

Cha, S. (2010), From semantic security to chosen ciphertext security. Iowa State University. Retrieved from http://lib.dr.iastate.edu/etd

Cramer, R., & Shoup, V. (2003). Design and Analysis of Practical Public Key Encryption Schemes Secure Against Chosen Ciphertext Attack. *SIAM Journal on Computing, 33*(1), 167–226. doi:10.1137/S0097539702403773

Dolev, D., Dwork, C., & Naor, M. (1991). Non-malleable cryptography. *Proceedings of the 23rd annual ACM Symposium on theory of computing* (pp. 542-552). doi:10.1145/103418.103474

Dolev, D., Dwork, C., & Naor, M. (2000). Non-malleable cryptography. *SIAM Journal on Computing, 30*(2), 391–437. doi:10.1137/S0097539795291562

Dwork, C., & Naor, M. (1996) Method for message authentication from non-malleable cryptosystems. U. S. Patent no. 05539826.

Goldwasser, S., & Micali, S. (1984). Probabilistic Encryption. *System Sciences, 28*, 270-299.

Naor, M., & Yung, M. (1990). Public-key cryptosystems provably secure against chosen ciphertext attacks. *Proceedings of the 22nd Annual ACM symposium on theory of computing* (pp. 427-437). doi:10.1145/100216.100273

Paillier, P. (2007). Impossibility proofs for RSA signatures in the standard model. Proceedings of CT-RSA 2007, LNCS (Vol. 4377, pp. 31–48). Heidelberg: Springer.

Paillier, P., & Villar, J. L. (2006). Trading one-wayness against chosen-ciphertext security in factoring-based encryption. Proceedings of ASIACRYPT '06, LNCS (Vol. 4284, pp. 252–266). Heidelberg: Springer. doi:10.1007/11935230_17

Racko, C., & Simon, D. (1991) Noninteractive zero-knowledge proof of knowledge and Chosen ciphertext attack. In Advances in cryptology, crypto '91 (pp. 433-444).

Rivest, R., Shamir, A., & Adleman, L. (1978) A method for obtaining digital signatures and public-key cryptosystems. Comm. of the ACM, 21(2), 120-126. doi:10.1145/359340.359342

Shoup, V. (1998). *Why chosen ciphertext security matters. Technical Report RZ 3076*. IBM Research.

Shoup, V. (1999). On formal models for secure key exchange. *Cryptology eprint archive report*. Retrieved from http://eprint.iacr.org

Zheng, Y., & Seberry, J. (1992). Practical approaches for attaining security against chosen-ciphertext attacks. Retrieved from http://coitweb.uncc.edu/~yzheng/publications/files/crypto92-immunize.pdf

KEY TERMS AND DEFINITIONS

Chosen Ciphertext Attack: An attack where an attacker can choose ciphertext of his choice and get corresponding plaintext.

Decryption Oracle: A program that will help an adversary to perform decryption of a given ciphertext.

Hash Functions: Hash functions convert the input message to a fixed size hash value.

Non-Malleability: The adversary uses a decryption oracle to get encryption of a different message.

Semantic Security: The adversary should not be able to get any partial information about the message given its ciphertext.

Chapter 12
Secure Two Party Computation

Kannan Balasubramanian
Mepco Schlenk Engineering College, India

ABSTRACT

The goal of secure two-party computation is to enable two parties to cooperatively evaluate a function that takes private data from both parties as input without exposing any of the private data. At the end of the computation, the participants learn nothing more than the output of the function. The two-party secure computation systems have three properties: (1) the application involves inputs from two independent parties; (2) each party wants to keep its own data secret; and (3) the participants agree to reveal the output of the computation. That is, the result itself does not imply too much information about either party's private input. Informally, the security requirements are that nothing is learned from the protocol other than the output (privacy), and that the output is distributed according to the prescribed functionality (correctness). The threat models in the two-party computation assume the presence of three different types of adversaries: 1) Semi honest, 2) Malicious and 3) Covert.

INTRODUCTION

The goal of secure two-party computation is to enable two parties to cooperatively evaluate a function that takes private data from both parties as input without exposing any of the private data. At the end of the computation, the participants learn nothing more than the output of the function. Secure computation has many important applications such as privacy-preserving biometric identification, set intersection and finding the kth ranked element. Practical solutions to the two-party computation are scarce due to the high runtime costs associated with traditional techniques and the effort required to build them. In this chapter, we review the threat models for the two-party computation and solutions for securing the two-party computation for each of the threat models.

MODEL OF TWO PARTY COMPUTATION

The two-party secure computation systems have three properties: (1) the application involves inputs from two independent parties; (2) each party wants to keep its own data secret; and (3) the participants agree

DOI: 10.4018/978-1-5225-2915-6.ch012

to reveal the output of the computation. That is, the result itself does not imply too much information about either party's private input.

More formally, in the setting of two-party computation, two parties with respective private inputs x and y, wish to jointly compute a functionality f $(x; y) = (f_1(x; y); f_2(x; y))$, such that the first party receives $f_1(x; y)$ and the second party receives $f_2(x; y)$. This functionality may be probabilistic, in which case f $(x; y)$ is a random variable. Informally, the security requirements are that nothing is learned from the protocol other than the output (*privacy*), and that the output is distributed according to the prescribed functionality (*correctness*).

THREAT MODELS

The threat models in the two-party computation assume the presence of three different types of adversaries (Huang, 2012): 1) Semi honest, 2) Malicious and 3) Covert.

The semi-honest (also known as honest-but-curious) threat model, assume that all parties follow the protocol as specified, but may attempt to learn additional information about the other party's input from the protocol transcript. It is usually unrealistic to assume passive adversaries who always obey the protocol specifications. To compromise the protocol security, an active adversary can deviate from the protocol in arbitrary ways, even at the risk of being caught. Informally speaking, a two-party computation protocol is said to be secure in the malicious threat model if the privacy and correctness properties are guaranteed even in presence of such active adversaries. In the covert model, a cheating adversary is "caught" with some constant probability, but with the remaining probability can (potentially) learn the honest party's entire input and arbitrarily bias the honest party's output. If an adversary is unwilling to take the risk of being caught, then such protocols will deter cheating altogether.

The first general solution for the problem of secure two-party computation in the presence of semi-honest adversaries was presented by (Yao, 1986). Later, solutions were provided for the multi-party and malicious adversarial cases by Goldreich et al. (Goldreich et al., 1987).

YAO'S PROTOCOL

Let f be a polynomial-time functionality (assume for now that it is deterministic), and let x and y be the parties' respective inputs. The first step is to view the function as a Boolean circuit C. In order to describe Yao's protocol, it is helpful to first recall how such a circuit is computed. Let x and y be the parties' inputs. Then, the circuit C $(x; y)$ is computed gate-by-gate, from the input wires to the output wires. Once the incoming wires to a gate g have obtained values $\alpha, \beta \in \{0,1\}$, it is possible to give the outgoing wires of the gate the value $g(\alpha ; \beta)$. The output of the circuit is given by the values obtained in the output wires of the circuit. Thus, essentially, computing a circuit involves allocating appropriate zero-one values to the *wires* of the circuit. In the description below, we refer to four different types of wires in a circuit: circuit-input wires (that receive the input values x and y), circuit-output wires (that carry the value C $(x; y)$), gate-input wires (that enter some gate g), and gate-output wires (that leave some gate g).

We now present a high-level description of Yao's protocol. The construction is actually a "compiler" that takes any polynomial-time functionality f, or actually a circuit C that computes f, and constructs a protocol for securely computing f in the presence of semi-honest adversaries. In a secure protocol, the only value learned by a party should be its output. Therefore, the values that are allocated to all wires that are not circuit-output, should not be learned by either party (these values may reveal information about the other party's input that could not be otherwise learned from the output). The basic idea behind Yao's protocol is to provide a method of computing a circuit so that values obtained on all wires other than circuit-output wires are never revealed. In order to do this, two random values are specified for every wire such that one value represents 0 and the other represents 1. For example, let w be the label of some wire. Then, two value k_w^0 and k_w^1 are chosen, where k_w^σ represents the bit. An important observation here is that even if one of the parties knows the value k_w obtained by the wire w, this does not help it to determine if $\sigma = 0$ or $\sigma = 1$ (because both k_w^0 and k_w^1 are identically distributed). Of course, the difficulty with such an idea is that it seems to make computation of the circuit impossible. That is, let g be a gate with incoming wires w_1 and w_2 and output wire w_3. Then, given two random values k_1^ς and k_2^τ, it does not seem possible to compute the gate because and are unknown. We therefore need a method of computing the value of the output wire of a gate (also a random value k_3^0 or k_3^1), given the value of the two input wires to that gate. In short, this method involves providing "garbled computation tables" that map the random input values to random output values. However, this mapping should have the property that given two input values, it is only possible to learn the output value that corresponds to the output of the gate (the other output value must be kept secret). This is accomplished by viewing the four possible inputs to the gate k_1^0; k_1^1; k_2^0; k_2^1 as encryption keys. Then, the output values k_3^0 and k_3^1 which are also keys, are encrypted under the appropriate keys from the incoming wires. For example, let g be an OR gate. Then, the key k_3^1 is encrypted under the pairs of keys associated with the values (1; 1), (1; 0) and (0; 1). In contrast, the key k_3^0 is encrypted under the pair of keys associated with (0; 0). Please refer to Table 1.

Notice that given the input wire keys k_1^α and k_2^β corresponding to α and β, and the four table values (found in the fourth column of Table 1), it is possible to decrypt and obtain the output wire key $k_3^{g(\alpha,\beta)}$. Furthermore, as required above, this is the only value that can be obtained (the other keys on the input wires are not known and so only a single table value can be decrypted). In other words, it is possible to compute the output key $k_3^{g(\alpha,\beta)}$ of a gate, and only that key, without learning anything about the real

Table 1. Garbled OR gate

Input wire w_1	Input wire w_2	Input wire w_3	Garbled Computation Table
k_1^0	k_2^0	k_3^0	$E_{k_1^0}\left(E_{k_2^0}\left(k_3^0\right)\right)$
k_1^0	k_2^1	k_3^1	$E_{k_1^0}\left(E_{k_2^1}\left(k_3^1\right)\right)$
k_1^1	k_2^0	k_3^1	$E_{k_1^1}\left(E_{k_2^0}\left(k_3^1\right)\right)$
k_1^1	k_2^1	k_3^1	$E_{k_1^1}\left(E_{k_2^1}\left(k_3^1\right)\right)$

values α, β or g(α ; β). (We note that the values of the table are randomly ordered so that a key's position does not reveal anything about the value that it is associated with. Despite this random ordering, the specific construction is such that given a pair of input wire keys, it is possible to locate the table entry that is encrypted by those keys.)

The above description only applies to the construction of a single garbled gate. A garbled circuit consists of garbled gates along with \output decryption tables". These tables map the random values on *circuit-output wires* back to their corresponding real values. That is, for a circuit-output wire w, the pairs $(0; k_w^0)$ and $(1; k_w^1)$ are provided. Then, after obtaining the key k_w on a circuit-output wire, it is possible to determine the actual output bit by comparing the key to the values in the output decryption table (or alternately in the output gates it is possible to directly encrypt 0 or 1 instead of k_w^0 or k_w^1). Notice that given the keys associated with inputs x and y, it is possible to (obliviously) compute the entire circuit gate-by-gate. Then, having obtained the keys on the circuit-output wires, these can be "decrypted" providing the result C $(x; y)$.

The informal description of Yao's protocol is as follows: In this protocol, one of the parties, henceforth the sender, constructs a garbled circuit and sends it to the other party, henceforth the receiver. The sender and receiver then interact so that the receiver obtains the input-wire keys that are associated with the inputs x and y (this interaction is described below). Given these keys, the receiver then computes the circuit as described, obtains the output and concludes the protocol.

It remains to describe how the receiver obtains the keys for the circuit-input wires. Here we differentiate between the inputs of the sender and the inputs of the receiver. Regarding the sender, it simply sends the receiver the values that correspond to its input. That is, if its ith input bit is 0 and the wire w_i receives this input, then the sender just hands the receiver the string k_i^0. It should be noted that since all of the keys are identically distributed, the receiver can learn nothing about the sender's input from these keys. Regarding the receiver, this is more problematic. The sender cannot hand it all of the keys pertaining to its input, because this would enable the receiver to compute more than just its output. (For a given input x of the sender, this would enable the receiver to compute C $(x; \tilde{y})$ for every $\tilde{y}$. This is much more information than a single value C $(x; y)$. On the other hand, the receiver cannot openly tell the sender which keys to send it, because then the sender would learn the receiver's input. The solution to this is to use a 1-out-of-2 oblivious transfer protocol (Even et al, 1985; Rabin, 1981). In such a protocol, a sender inputs two values x_0 and x_1 (in this case, k_w^0 and k_w^1 for some circuit-input wire w), and a receiver inputs a bit (in this case, corresponding to its appropriate input bit). The outcome of the protocol is that the receiver obtains the value x (in this case, the key k_w). Furthermore, the receiver learns nothing about the other value x_1, and the sender learns nothing about the receiver's input. By having the receiver obtain its keys in this way, we obtain that (a) the sender learns nothing of the receiver's input value, and (b) the receiver obtains only a single set of keys and so can compute the circuit on only a single value, as required. This completes the high-level description of Yao's protocol.

SECURE TWO-PARTY PROTOCOLS FOR SEMI-HONEST ADVERSARIES

The model that is considered here is that of two-party computation in the presence of *static semi-honest* adversaries. Such an adversary controls one of the parties (statically, and so at the onset of the computation) and follows the protocol specification exactly. However, it may try to learn more information than allowed by looking at the transcript of messages that it received.

Intuitively, a protocol is secure if whatever can be computed by a party participating in the protocol can be computed based on its input and output only. This is formalized according to the simulation paradigm. Informally, we require that a party's *view* in a protocol execution be simulatable given only its input and output. This then implies that the parties learn nothing from the protocol execution itself, as desired.

Definition of Security

Let $f = (f_1 ; f_2)$ be a probabilistic polynomial-time functionality and let π be a two-party protocol for computing f. The view of the ith party ($i \in \{1, 2\}$) during an execution of π on $(x; y)$ is denoted $view_i^\pi (x,y)$ and equals $(x; r^i ; m_1^i,\ldots, m_t^i)$, where r^i equals the contents of the ith party's internal random tape, and m_j^i represents the jth message that it received. The output of the ith party during an execution of on (x,y) is denoted $output_i (x,y)$ and can be computed from its own view of the execution. $output^\pi (x, y)$ is the denoted as $(output_1^\pi (x,y); output_2^\pi (x,y))$.

- **Security With Respect to Semi-Honest Behavior:** Let $f = (f_1; f_2)$ be a functionality. We say that securely computes f in the presence of static semi-honest adversaries if there exist probabilistic polynomial-time algorithms S_1 and S_2 such that

$$\left\{f\left(S_1\left(x, f_1\left(x, y\right)\right), f\left(x, y\right)\right)\right\}_{x,y\in\{0,1\}^*} \overset{c}{\equiv} \left\{\left(view_1^\pi\left(x, y\right), output^\pi\left(x, y\right)\right)\right\}_{x,y\in\{0,1\}^*}$$

$$\left\{f\left(S_2\left(x, f_2\left(x, y\right)\right), f\left(x, y\right)\right)\right\}_{x,y\in\{0,1\}^*} \overset{c}{\equiv} \left\{\left(\left(view_2^\pi\left(x, y\right), output^\pi\left(x, y\right)\right)\right)\right\}_{x,y\in\{0,1\}^*}$$

The above equations state that the view of a party can be simulated by a probabilistic polynomial-time algorithm given access to the party's input and output only. We emphasize that the adversary here is semi-honest and therefore the view is exactly according to the protocol definition. We note that it is not enough for the simulator S_i to generate a string indistinguishable from $view_i^\pi (x, y)$. Rather, the joint distribution of the simulator's output and the functionality output $f(x, y)$ must be indistinguishable from $(view_i^\pi (x, y);$ output $(x,y))$. This is necessary for probabilistic functionalities.

A simpler formulation for deterministic functionalities. In the case that the functionality f is deterministic, it suffices to require that simulator S_i generates the view of party P_i, without considering the joint distribution with the output. That is, we can require that there exist S_1 and S_2 such that:

$$\{S_1(x, f_1(x, y))\}_{x,y\in\{0,1\}^*} \overset{c}{\equiv} \{view_1^\pi(x, y)\}_{x,y\in\{0,1\}^*}$$

$$\{S_2(x, f_2(x, y))\}_{x,y\in\{0,1\}^*} \overset{c}{\equiv} \{view_2^\pi(x, y)\}_{x,y\in\{0,1\}^*}$$

The reason this suffices is that when f is deterministic, output $^\pi$ (x,y) must equal $f(x,y)$. A functionality $f =(f_1,f_2)$ is same-output if $f_1 = f_2$.

OBLIVIOUS TRANSFER

It can be shown that the secure two-party computation problem can be reduced to Oblivious transfer in the semi-honest model i.e., when parties are guaranteed to behave according to the protocols (Kilian, 1988). The notion of Oblivious Transfer (OT) was first introduced by Rabin (Ramin, 1981). In the original OT problem, the sender, Alice has a secret and the receiver will receive the secret with probability ½ and Alice does not know whether Bob received it not. The Oblivious Transfer notion has several versions which were shown to be equivalent to one another by Crepeau (1988) The 1-out-of-2 Oblivious Transfer protocol introduced by (Even et al., 1985) is a protocol between two parties, a sender Alice and a receiver Bob. Alice has two bits (b_0, b_1) and Bob wants to get one of the bits b_i of his choice. At the end of the protocol, Alice should not learn anything about i and Bob should not learn anything about the other bit.

1-out-of 2 Oblivious Transfer was further generalized to 1-out-of-n Oblivious Transfer by Brassard, Crepeau, and Robert (Brassard et al, 1986). 1-out-of-n Oblivious Transfer protocol refers to a protocol where at the beginning of the protocol one party Bob has n-inputs $X_1,\ldots, X_n$ and at the end of the protocol, the other party learns one of the inputs Xi for some $1 \leq i \leq n$ of her choice without learning about other inputs and without allowing Bob to learn anything about i.

YAO's GARBLED CIRCUIT IN THE MALICIOUS ADVERSARY MODEL

With respect to a semi-honest garbled circuit based protocol, malicious adversaries could launch attacks in several (but not limited to such) ways. A malicious generator might construct a faulty circuit that discloses the evaluator's private input. For example, a circuit for f of the adversaries' choice (rather than the supposed f) is actually transmitted so that the victim's secret input could be revealed directly.

In addition, more subtle attacks like selective failure also exist (Mohassel, 2006). In this attack, a malicious generator uses wire labels as inputs to the oblivious transfer that are inconsistent to those in garbled circuit construction. As a result, the evaluator's input can be inferred from whether the protocol execution completes successfully or not.

For example, a cheating generator choosing (w^0, w^1) to be the pair of labels of an input wire of the garbled circuit could use $(w^0, \tilde{w}^1)$, where $w^1 \neq \tilde{w}^1$, in the corresponding oblivious transfer. Consequently, if the evaluator's input is 0, she will get w^0 from OT and complete the evaluation. In contrast, if her input is 1, she gets $\tilde{w}^1$ and the execution will fail.

Since there are an unlimited number of ways an active adversary can deviate from the protocol, showing particular attacks are impossible is insufficient to prove the whole protocol is secure against any active attacks. Thus, the convention to formally define security in the fully malicious model is by comparing two protocols executing in two different worlds (i.e., the ideal world and the real world, respectively) (Goldreich, 2006). The ideal world features the presence of a trusted third party who is delegated to receive secret inputs, run the computation locally, and distribute the results. In contrast, the two parties simply run the secure computation protocol in the real world in the absence of any trusted party. A secure computation protocol $\prod$ is said to be secure if an adversary A corrupting a party in the real world obtains a distribution consisting of his view and the honest party's output, which is indistinguishable from the distribution of the ideal world outputs of both a probabilistic polynomial time simulator which corrupts the same party and the honest party. That is, no extra information is leaked by executing $\prod$ since whatever the adversary can learn (and affect) from a real-world execution are all achievable by a polynomial time simulator running the ideal world protocol.

There are three different ways to achieve security in the presence of malicious adversaries.

1. **Cut-and-Choose:** The basic idea is to prepare many (say greater than 200) executions of the protocol, among which some (e.g., 2/5th of) traces are selected to verify the participants have followed the protocol while the rest are used for actual execution. The majority function is applied to the results from all actual runs to produce the final output. The scheme can be proved cryptographically secure against all probabilistic polynomial time adversaries (Lindell et al, 2007; Shen et al, 2011).

2. **Commit-and-Prove:** The core idea, first suggested in (Goldreich et al., 1987), is to express every behavioral constraint in the protocol by an NP-language and prove that the constraints are satisfied using zero-knowledge proof of knowledge (ZKPoK) (Bellare et al., 1992). In another approach where the generator is asked to prove the correctness of the garbled circuit in zero knowledge before the evaluation starts (Jarecki, 2007). Note that only a single copy of the circuit needs to be constructed. Nevertheless, such scheme is believed to be much less efficient than cut-and-choose because hundreds of expensive asymmetric cryptographic operations are needed per garbled gate.

3. **MAC-then-Compute:** Nielsen et al. (2011) proposed a solution based on a technique called authenticated bits. Their key idea is to apply XOR-based message authentication code (MAC) to every bit throughout the collaborative computation, so that results remain authenticated only if both participants follow the protocol correctly. In other words, if a malicious participant deviates from the agreed protocol, the other party will notice and abort, but without risking any information leakage from the abortion. Hence, if the final result remains authenticated, it essentially proves that both parties behaved honestly. Although the protocol uses many expensive oblivious transfers (OT), an efficient OT extension protocol is devised to offset the cost via substituting expensive asymmetric operations with cheap symmetric ones.

OBLIVIOUS TRANSFER BASED PROTOCOL

In (Nielsen et.al, 2011), an approach for two party computation is described that uses the Oblivious Transfer approach. In this protocol, Alice holds secret shares x_A, y_A and Bob holds secret shares x_B, y_B of some bits x, y such that $x_A \oplus x_B = x$ and $y_A \oplus y_B = y$. Alice and Bob want to compute secret shares of $z = g(x, y)$ where g is some Boolean gate, for instance the AND gate: Alice and Bob need to compute a random sharing z_A, z_B of $z = xy = x_A y_A \oplus x_A y_B \oplus x_B y_A \oplus x_B y_B$. The parties can compute the AND of their local shares ($x_A y_A$ and $x_B y_B$), while they can use oblivious transfer (OT) to compute the cross products ($x_A y_B$ and $x_B y_A$). Now the parties can iterate for the next layer of the circuit, up to the end where they will reconstruct the output values by revealing their shares.

This protocol is secure against a semi-honest adversary: assuming the OT protocol to be secure, Alice and Bob learn nothing about the intermediate values of the computation. It is easy to see that if a large circuit is evaluated, then the protocol is not secure against a malicious adversary: any of the two parties could replace values on any of the internal wires, leading to a possibly incorrect output and/or leakage of information.

To overcome this, the protocol puts MACs on all bits. The starting point of the protocol is oblivious authentication of bits. One party, the key holder, holds a uniformly random global key $\Delta = \{0,1\}^k$. The other party, the MAC holder holds some secret bits (x,y, say). For each such bit, the key holder holds a corresponding uniformly local key ($K_x, K_y \in \{0,1\}^k$) and the MAC holder holds the corresponding MAC ($M_x = K_x \oplus x\Delta$, $M_y = K_y \oplus y\Delta$). The key holder does not know the bits and the MAC holder does not know the keys. It should be noted that $M_x \oplus M_y = (Kx \oplus Ky) \oplus (x \oplus y)\Delta$. The MAC holder can locally compute a MAC on $x \oplus y$ under the key $K_x \oplus K_y$ which is non-interactively computable by the key holder.

SUMMARY

In this chapter, we introduced the model for two party computation and the various of adversaries for the two-party computation protocol. We presented the Yao's protocol as an example of a secure two party computation problem. We discussed Oblivious transfer as another example of a two-party computation problem.

REFERENCES

Bellare, M., & Goldreich, O. (1992). On Defining Proofs of Knowledge. Proceedings of CRYPTO '92 (pp. 390-420).

Brassard, G., Crepeau, C., & Robert, J. (1986). All-or-nothing Disclosure of Secrets. In Advances in Cryptology, Crypto '86, LNCS (Vol. 263, pp. 234-238).

Crepeau, C. (1988). Equivalence between two flavors of oblivious transfers. In Advances in Cryptology CRYPTO '87, LNCS (Vol. *293*, pp. 239–247). doi:10.1007/3-540-48184-2_30

Even, S., Goldreich, O., & Lempel, A. (1985). A Randomized Protocol for Signing Contracts. Communications of the ACM, 28(6), 637-647.

Goldreich, O. (2004). Foundations of Cryptography (Vol 2. Basic Applications). Cambridge University Press.

Goldreich, O., Micali, S., & Wigderson, A. (1987). How to Play any Mental Game A Completeness Theorem for Protocols with Honest Majority. Proceedings of 19th STOC (pp. 218-229).

Huang, Y. (2012). Practical Secure Two-party Computation [Ph.D. Dissertation]. University of Virginia.

Jarecki, S., & Shmatikov, V. (2007). *Efficient two-party Secure Computation on Committed Inputs*. EuroCrypt. doi:10.1007/978-3-540-72540-4_6

Kilian, J. (1988). Founding Cryptography on oblivious transfer. *Proceedings of the Twentieth ACM symposium on Theory of Computing* (pp. 20-31).

Lindell, Y., & Pinkas, B. (2004). A Proof of Yao's Protocol for Secure Two-Party Computation. *Proceedings of the Electronic Colloquium on Computational Complexity.*

Lindell, Y., & Pinkas, B. (2007). *An Efficient Protocol for Secure Two-Party Computation in the Presence of Malicious Adversaries.* EuroCrypt. doi:10.1007/978-3-540-72540-4_4

Mohassel, P., & Franklin, M. (2006). Efficiency Tradeoffs for Malicious Two-Party Computation. *Proceedings of the International Conference on Theory and Practice of Public Key Cryptography* (pp. 458-473).

Nielsen, J. B., Nordholt, P. S., Orlandi, C., & Burra, S. S. (2011) A New Approach to Practical Active-Secure Two-Party Computation. Retrieved from http://eprint.iacr.org/2011/091

Rabin, M. (1981). How to Exchange Secrets by Oblivious Transfer (Tech. Memo TR-81). Aiken Computation Laboratory, Harvard University.

Shen, C. H., & Shelat, A. (2011). Two-output Secure Computation With Malicious Adversaries. Proceedings of EUROCRYPT.

Yao, A. (1986) How to generate and exchange secrets. Proceedings of the 27th FOCS (pp. 162-167).

KEY TERMS AND DEFINITIONS

Covert Adversaries: The cheating adversary is caught with some finite probability, but with the remaining probability can bias the honest party's output.

Garbled Circuits: The Garbled Circuits provides a solution for the secure two party computation model.

Malicious Adversary: The Malicious Adversary can launch the attack on several different ways.

Oblivious Transfer: A protocol between Alice and Bob that transfer secret values in a secure way.

Semi-Honest Adversaries: The adversary follow the protocols honestly. But they may try to get more information by looking at the transcripts of the messages exchanged.

Two-Party Computation: A model where two parties with two different inputs compute two different functions.

Chapter 13
Secure Multiparty Computation

Kannan Balasubramanian
Mepco Schlenk Engineering College, India

M. Rajakani
Mepco Schlenk Engineering College, India

ABSTRACT

The Secure Multiparty computation is characterized by computation by a set of multiple parties each participating using the private input they have. There are different types of models for Secure Multiparty computation based on assumption about the type of adversaries each model is assumed to protect against including Malicious and Covert Adversaries. The model may also assume a trusted setup with either using a Public Key Infrastructure or a using a Common Reference String. Secure Multiparty Computation has a number of applications including Scientific Computation, Database Querying and Data Mining.

INTRODUCTION

Secure Multiparty Computation (MPC) involves carrying out computation tasks by a set of parties based on the private inputs they each party has. Research in the MPC area has focused on only a limited set of problems. These computations could occur between mutually untrusted parties, or even between competitors. For example, customers might send to a remote database queries that contain private information or two competing financial organizations might jointly invest in a project that must satisfy both organizations' private constraints. To conduct such computations, one entity must usually know the inputs from all the participants; however, if nobody can be trusted enough to know all the inputs, privacy will become a primary concern. We present models for the Secure multiparty computation problem and provide examples for them. We also provide a classification of the Secure multiparty computation problems based on the type of adversaries against them.

DOI: 10.4018/978-1-5225-2915-6.ch013

SECURE MULTIPARTY COMPUTATION

In general, a secure multi-party computation problem deals with computing any probabilistic function on any input, in a distributed network where each participant holds one of the inputs, ensuring independence of the inputs, correctness of the computation, and that no more information is revealed to a participant in the computation than can be inferred from that participant's input and output. A common strategy is to assume the trustworthiness of the service providers, or to assume the existence of a trusted third party which is risky in todays' dynamic and malicious environment.

Examples of secure multiparty computation problems include privacy-preserving database querying, scientific computations, intrusion detection, statistical analysis, geometric computations, and data mining. It is possible to that a to systematically transform normal computations (not necessarily security related) to secure multi-party computations. The common property of the above three problems is the following: two or more parties want to conduct a computation based on their private inputs, but neither party is willing to disclose its own input to anybody else. The problem is how to conduct such a computation while preserving the privacy of the inputs. This problem is referred to as Secure Multi-party Computation problem or MPC (Yao, 1982).

A MODEL FOR SECURE MULTIPARTY COMPUTATION

Secure multi-party computation (MPC) can be defined as the problem of n players computing an agreed function of their inputs in a secure way, where security means guaranteeing the correctness of the output as well as the privacy of the players' inputs, even when some players cheat. Concretely, we assume we have inputs $x_1, ..., x_n$, where player i knows x_i, and we want to compute $f(x_1, ..., x_n) = (y_1, ..., y_n)$ such that player i is guaranteed to learn y_i, but can get nothing more than that.

An example is the Yao's millionaire's problem: two millionaires meet in the street and want to find out who is richer. Can they do this without having to reveal how many millions they each own? The function computed in this case is a simple comparison between two integers. If the result is that the first millionaire is richer, then he knows that the other guy has fewer millions than him, but this should be all the information he learns about the other guy's fortune

Another example is a voting scheme: here all players have an integer as input, designating the candidate they vote for, and the goal is to compute how many votes each candidate has received. We want to make sure that the correct result of the vote, but only this result, is made public. In these examples, all players learn the same result, i.e, $y_1 = ... = y_n$, but it can also be useful to have different results for different players. Consider for example the case of a blind signature scheme, which is useful in electronic cash systems. We can think of this as a two-party secure computation where the signer enters his private signing key sk as input, the user enters a message m to be signed, and the function $f(sk, m) = (y_1, y_2)$, where y_1 is for the signer and is empty, and where y_2 is for the user and the signature on m. Again, security means exactly what we want: the user gets the signature and nothing else, while the signer learns nothing new.

It is clear that if we can compute any function securely, we have a very powerful tool. However, some protocol problems require even more general ways of thinking. A secure payment system, for instance, cannot naturally be formulated as secure computation of a single function: what we want here is to continuously keep track of how much money each player has available and avoid cases where for instance people spend more money than they have. Such a system should behave like a secure general-purpose computer: it can receive inputs from the players at several points in time and each time it will produce results for each player computed in a specified way from the current inputs and from previously stored values.

A key tool for secure MPC, interesting in its own right, is verifiable secret sharing (VSS): a dealer distributes a secret value s among the players, where the dealer and/or some of the players may be cheating. It is guaranteed that if the dealer is honest, then the cheaters obtain no information about s, and all honest players are later able to reconstruct s, even against the actions of cheating players. Even if the dealer cheats, a unique such value s will be determined already at distribution time, and again this value is reconstructable even against the actions of the cheaters.

It is common to model cheating by considering an adversary who may corrupt some subset of the players. For concreteness, one may think of the adversary as a hacker who attempts to break into the players' computers. When a player is corrupted, the adversary gets all the data held by this player, including complete information on all actions and messages the player has received in the protocol so far. This may seem to be rather generous to the adversary, for example one might claim that the adversary will not learn that much, if the protocol instructs players to delete sensitive information when it is no longer needed. However, first other players cannot check that such information really is deleted, and second even if a player has every intention of deleting for example a key that is outdated, it may be quite difficult to ensure that the information really is gone and cannot be retrieved if the adversary breaks into this player's computer. Hence the standard definition of corruption gives the entire history of a corrupted player to the adversary.

One can distinguish between passive and active corruption. Passive corruption means that the adversary obtains the complete information held by the corrupted players, but the players still execute the protocol correctly. Active corruption means that the adversary takes full control of the corrupted players. It is (at least initially) unknown to the honest players which subset of players is corrupted. However, no protocol can be secure if any subset can be corrupted. For instance, we cannot even define security in a meaningful way if all players are corrupt. We therefore need a way to specify some limitation on the subsets the adversary can corrupt. For this, we define an adversary structure A, which is simply a family of subsets of the players. And we define an A-adversary to be an adversary that can only corrupt a subset of the players if that subset is in A. The adversary structure could for instance consist of all subsets with cardinality less than some threshold value t. In order for this to make sense, we must require for any adversary structure that if $C \in A$ and $B \subset C$, then $B \in A$. The intuition is that if the adversary is powerful enough to corrupt subset A, then it is reasonable to assume that he can also corrupt any subset of C.

Both passive and active adversaries may be static, meaning that the set of corrupted players is chosen once and for all before the protocol starts, or adaptive meaning that the adversary can at any time during the protocol choose to corrupt a new player based on all the information he has at the time, as long as the total corrupted set is in A.

Two basic models of communication have been considered in the literature. In the cryptographic model, the adversary is assumed to have access to all messages sent, however, he cannot modify messages exchanged between honest players. This means that security can only be guaranteed in a cryptographic sense, i.e. assuming that the adversary cannot solve some computational problem. In the information-theoretic model, it is assumed that the players can communicate over pairwise secure channels, in other words, the adversary gets no information at all about messages exchanged between honest players. Security can then be guaranteed even when the adversary has unbounded computing power.

For active adversaries, there is a further problem with broadcasting, namely if a protocol requires a player to broadcast a message to everyone, it does not suffice to just ask him to send the same message to all players. If he is corrupt, he may say different things to different players, and it may not be clear to the honest players if he did this or not One therefore in general has to make a distinction between the case where a broadcast channel is given for free as a part of the model, or whether such a channel has to be simulated by a subprotocol.

We assume throughout that communication is synchronous, i.e., processors have clocks that are to some extent synchronized, and when a message is sent, it will arrive before some time bound. In more detail, we assume that a protocol proceeds in rounds: in each round, each player may send a message to each other player, and all messages are delivered before the next round begins. We assume that in each round, the adversary first sees all messages sent by honest players to corrupt players (or in the cryptographic scenario, all messages sent). If he is adaptive, he may decide to corrupt some honest players at this point. And only then does he have to decide which messages he will send on behalf of the corrupted players. This fact that the adversary gets to see what honest players say before having to act himself is sometimes referred to as a rushing adversary.

In an asynchronous model of communication where message delivery or bounds on transit time is not guaranteed, it is still possible to solve most of the problems we consider here. However, we stick to synchronous communication – for simplicity, but also because problems can only be solved in a strictly weaker sense using asynchronous communication. Note, for instance, that if messages are not necessarily delivered, we cannot demand that a protocol generates any output.

To define the security of the multiparty protocol we define, in addition to the real world where the actual protocol and attacks on it take place, an ideal world which is basically a specification of what we would like the protocol to do. The idea is then to say that a protocol is good if what it produces cannot be distinguished from what we could get in the ideal scenario.

THE REAL AND THE IDEAL MODELS OF MULTI-PARTY COMPUTATION

The real world contains the environment Z and the players P_1, P_2, ..., P_n all of whom are modelled as interactive Turing machines (ITM's). The players communicate on a synchronous network using open channels or perfectly secure pairwise communication as specified earlier. In line with the discussion above, the environment Z should be thought of as a conglomerate of everything that is external to the the protocol execution. This includes the adversary, so therefore Z can do everything we described earlier for an adversary, i.e., it can corrupt players passively/actively and statically/adaptively, according to an adversary structure A. This is called a A-environment. The players follow their respective programs specified in protocol π, until they are corrupted and possibly taken over by Z. In addition to this, Z also communicates with the honest players, as follows: in every round Z sends a (possibly empty) input to every honest player, and at the end of every round each honest player computes a result that is then given to Z. When the protocol is finished, Z outputs a single bit. In addition to other inputs, all entities get as intitial input a security parameter value k, which is used to control the security level of the execution, e.g., the size of keys to use in the cryptographic scenario.

The ideal world contains the same environment we have in the real world, but there are no players. Instead, we have an ideal functionality F, and a simulator S. As mentioned above, F cannot be corrupted, and it will be programmed to carry out whatever task we want to execute securely, such as computing a function. F has an input and an output port for every player in the real protocol, and also has corrupt input/output ports, for communication with the environment/adversary.

The whole idea is that the environment Z we looked at in the real world should be able to act in the same way in the ideal world. Now, Z has two kinds of activities. First, it is allowed to send inputs to the honest players and see their outputs. We handle this by relaying these data directly to the relevant input/output ports of F. Second, Z expects to be able to attack the protocol by corrupting players, seeing all data they send/receive and possibly control their actions. For this purpose, we have the simulator S. Towards Z, S attempts to provide all the data Z would see in a real attack, namely internal data of newly corrupted players and protocol messages that corrupted players receive. We want Z to work exactly like it does in the real world, so therefore S must go through the protocol in the right time ordering and in every round show data to Z that look like what it would see in the real world. S is not allowed to rewind Z. The only help S gets to complete this job is that it gets to use the corrupt input/output ports of F i.e., it gets to provide inputs and see outputs on behalf of corrupted players.

To be precise, as soon as Z issues a request to corrupt player P_i, both S and F are notified about this. Then the following happens: S is given all input/outputs exchanged on the i'th input/output ports of F until now. F then stops using input/output port number i. Instead it expects S to provide inputs "on behalf of P_i" on the corrupt input port and sends output meant for P_i to S on the corrupt output port. One way of stating this is: we give to S exactly the data that the protocol is supposed to release to corrupt players, and based on this, it should be possible to simulate towards Z all the rest that corrupted players would see in a real protocol execution.

It is quite obvious that whatever functionality we could possibly wish for, could be securely realized simply by programming F appropriately. However, do not forget that the ideal world does not exist in real life, it only provides a specification of a functionality we would like to have. The point is that we can have confidence that any reasonable security requirement we could come up with will be automatically satisfied in the ideal world, precisely because everything is done by an incorruptible party - and so, if we can design a protocol that is in a strong sense equivalent to the ideal functionality, we know that usage of the protocol will guarantee the same security properties – even those we did not explicitly specify beforehand!

We can now start talking about what it means that a given protocol π securely realizes ideal functionality F. Note that the activities of Z have the same form in real as in ideal world. So, Z will output one bit in both cases. This bit is a random variable, whose distribution in the real world may depend on the programs of π, Z and also on the security parameter k and Z's input z. We call this variable $\text{REAL}_{\pi,Z}(k, z)$. Its distribution is taken over the random choices of all ITM's that take part. Similarly, in the ideal world, the bit output by Z is a random variable called $\text{IDEAL}_{F,S,Z}(k, z)$.

We say that π A-securely realizes F, if there exists a polynomial time simulator S such that for any A-environment Z and any input z, we have that

$$|\Pr(\text{REAL}_{\pi,\text{Adv}}(k, z) = 0) - \Pr(\text{IDEAL}_{F,S,\text{Adv}}(k, z) = 0)|$$

is negligible in k. Here, negligible in k means, as usual, that the entity in question is smaller than $1/f(k)$ for any polynomial $f()$ and all sufficiently large k.

There are several possible variants of this definition. The one we gave requires so-called statistical security, but can be made stronger by requiring that the two involved probabilities are equal for all k, and not just close. This is called perfect security. In both cases we consider all (potentially unbounded) adversaries and environments. For the cryptographic scenario, we need to restrict adversaries and environments to polynomial time, and we will only be able to prove protocols relative to some complexity assumption - we then speak of computational security.

PRIVACY PRESERVING SECURE MULTI-PARTY COMPUTATION PROBLEMS

Here we present a number of privacy preserving Multi-party computation models.

Scientific Computation

The following are scientific computation problems that fall into the Secure Multiparty Computation model.

Problem 1: Alice has m private linear equations represented by $M_1x = b_1$, and Bob has $n-m$ private linear equations represented by $M_2x = b_2$, where x is an n-dimensional vector. Alice and Bob want to find a vector x that satisfies both of Alice's and Bob's equations.

Problem 2: Alice has m1 private linear equations represented by $M_1x = b_1$, and Bob has m_2 private linear equations represented by $M_2x = b_2$, where x is an n-dimensional vector and $m_1 + m_2 > n$. Alice and Bob want to find a vector x that satisfies both of Alice's and Bob's equations. Since there are more conditions (equations) to be satisfied than degrees of freedom (variables), it is unlikely that they can all be satisfied. Therefore, they want to attempt to satisfy the equations as best as they can–that is, make the size of the residual vector r with components

$$r_j = b_j - \sum_{i=1}^{n} a_{ji} x_i$$

as small as possible (a_{ji} are the entries in the new matrix formed from M_1 and M_2). The least-squares criterion is the use of the Euclidean (or least-squares) norm for the size of r; that is, minimize

$$\sqrt{\sum_{j=1}^{m_1+m_2} r_j^2} = \|r\|_2$$

Problem 3: Alice has m1 private linear requirements represented by $M_1x \leq b_1$, and Bob has another m_2 private linear requirements represented by $M_2x \leq b_2$, where x is an n-dimensional vector. They want to minimize (maximize) the value of $a_1 x_1 + \cdots + a_n x_n$, for the known a1, . . ., an, and the solution $x = (x_1, \ldots, x_n)$ should satisfy all of Alice's and Bob's requirements.

Database Querying

The database Querying problem in the multiparty computation model is described below:

Alice has a string q, and Bob has a database of strings $T = \{t_1, \ldots, t_N\}$; Alice wants to know whether there exists a string t_i in Bob's database that "matches" q. The "match" could be an exact match or an approximate (closest) match. The privacy requirement is that Bob cannot know Alice's secret query q or the response to that query, and Alice cannot know Bob's database contents except for what could be derived from the query result.

Unlike exact pattern matching that produces "yes" and "no" answers, approximate pattern matching measures the difference between the two targets, and produces a score to indicate how different the two targets are. The metrics used to measure the difference usually are heuristic and are application-dependent. For example, in image template matching, $\sum_{i=1}^{n} (a_i - b_i)^2$ and $\sum_{i=1}^{n} |a_i - b_i|$ are often used to measure the difference between two sequences a and b. Solving approximate pattern matching problems under such privacy constraints is quite a nontrivial task. Consider the $\sum_{i=1}^{n} |a_i - b_i|$ metric as an example. The known Private Information Retrieval (PIR) techniques can be used by Alice to efficiently access each individual b_i without revealing to Bob anything about which b_i Alice accessed, but doing this for each individual b_i and then calculating $\sum_{i=1}^{n} |a_i - b_i|$ violates the requirement that Alice should know the total score $\sum_{i=1}^{n} |a_i - b_i|$ without knowing anything other than that score, i.e., without learning anything about the individual b_i values.

Intrusion Detection

The following is the description of the secure multi-party computation problem in Intrusion detection.

Problem 1: Alice has a profile database containing many known hacker's behaviors; Bob has collected a hacker's behavior from a recent break-in, and he wants to identify the hacker by matching this hacker's behavior with Alice's profile database. However, Bob does not want to disclose the hacker's actual behavior to Alice because that might disclose the vulnerability in his system because that behavior could be a successful series of actions that leads to the compromise of his system. On the other hand, Alice doesn't want to disclose the profile database because of the database contains confidential information. How could Alice and Bob cooperatively accomplish this task without sacrificing their privacy?

Problem 2: Two major financial organizations want to cooperate in preventing fraudulent intrusion into their computing system. To this end, they need to share data patterns relevant to fraudulent intrusion, but they do not want to share the data patterns since they are sensitive information. Therefore, combining the databases is not feasible. How can these two financial organizations conduct data mining operation or machine learning operation on the joint of their data while maintaining the privacy of the data.

Data Mining

The following problems are related to Data Mining.

Problem 1 (*Classification*): Alice has a private structured database D_1, and Bob has another private structured database D_2; both of the structured database are comprised of attribute-value pairs. Each row of the database is a transaction and each column is an attribute taking on different values. One of the attributes in the database is designated as the class attribute. How could Alice and Bob build a decision tree based on the $D_1 \cup D_2$ without disclosing the content of the database to the other party?

Given a decision tree, one can predict the class of new transactions for which the class is unknown. There are several proposed algorithms for generating decision trees; however, if the database D_1 or D_2 should be kept private from anybody other than the owner, those algorithms does not work because a default assumption for those algorithms is that the whole database is available. A new algorithm is needed to solve this new problem.

Problem 2 (*Data Clustering*): Alice has a private database D_1, and Bob has a private database D_2. They want to jointly perform data clustering on the union of D_1 and D_2.

The data clustering problem groups a set of data (without a predefined class attribute), based on the conceptual clustering principle: maximizing the intraclass similarity and minimizing the interclass similarity.

Problem 3 (*Mining Association Rules*): Alice has a private database D_1, and Bob has a private database D_2. They want to jointly identify association rules in the union of D_1 and D_2.

Alice has a private database D_1, and Bob has a private database D_2. They want to generalize, summarize or characterize the union of these two databases.

Other problems in secure multiparty computation are the selection problem (median or the kth ranked element, the sorting problem, the shortest path problem and polynomial interpolation.

VERIAFIABLE SECRET SHARING

VSS finds its origin in one of the classical cryptographic problems called secret sharing (Shamir, 1979). Secret sharing deals with the techniques to share secrets among parties in such a way that only designated subset of parties can reconstruct the shared secret and no other subset of parties can reconstruct the secret. It finds extensive use in key management, distributed storage system etc. To be more precise, secret sharing is a two phase protocol (sharing, reconstruction) carried out among n parties. In the sharing phase a special party called dealer shares a secret s among the n parties in such a way that later any designated subset of parties (specified by access structure) can reconstruct the shared secret s uniquely and no other subset of parties (specified by adversary structure) can reconstruct s.

Secret sharing is not very useful in real-life applications, since it makes an unrealistic assumption that all the parties behave honestly throughout in the system. That is, the parties in adversary structure behave like eavesdroppers who simply learn the information of other corrupted parties and try to obtain some information by manipulating the collected data. Some of the parties may stray away from their designated instructions to communicate/compute in any arbitrary fashion and collaborate among themselves in a centralized fashion to get some extra advantage. There are two main problems that may arise. In the sharing phase, the dealer may share no valid secret and get away with it. In the reconstruction phase, the bad/corrupted parties may input some wrong shares and prevent the reconstruction of secret. The above two problems clearly say that secret sharing is not equipped to tolerate malicious faults. After that, the notion of VSS was introduced by Chor, Goldwasser, Micali and Awerbuch in (Chor et al., 1985) to resolve this concern.

Informally, a VSS is a two phase protocol (Sharing and Reconstruction) carried out among n parties in the presence of a malicious/active adversary (how the corruption is done depends on different model discussed later). The goal of the VSS protocol is to share a secret, s among the n parties during the sharing phase in a way that would later allow for a unique reconstruction of this secret in the reconstruction phase, while preserving the secrecy of s until the reconstruction phase. In many applications one may treat VSS as a form of commitment where the commitment information is held in a distributed fashion by the parties. Most importantly, in the distributed setting the de-commitment is guaranteed, that is the committed value will be exposed. This is in contrast to the non-distributed setting where the committer can decide whether to expose the value or not.

A verifiable Secret Sharing (VSS) for a set P of players with secrecy structure S and secure against adversary structure A consists of two protocols, *Share* and *Reconstruct* such that even if the adversary corrupts players according to A, the following conditions hold:

1. If *Share* terminates successfully, then the Reconstruct protocol yields the same fixed value for all possible adversary strategies, i.e., the dealer is committed to a single value.
2. If the dealer is honest during Share, then Reconstruct always yields his input value.
3. If the dealer is honest, then the adversary cannot obtain any information about the shared secret.

To construct the Verifiable Secret Sharing Scheme, we need the k-out-of-k sharing scheme, i.e. one for k players such that only the complete set of players (and no proper subset) can reconstruct the secret. Such a scheme for any k and any domain of the secret s is obtained by splitting s into a random sum.

To assure that the dealer correctly shares a value, we only need to guarantee independently for each of the k shares, that all honest players receiving the share obtain the same value. This is easily achieved as follows: For each share s_i, all players receiving that share check pairwise whether the value received from the dealer is the same. If any inconsistency is detected, the players complain using broadcast, and the dealer must broadcast s_i to all the players. Secrecy cannot be violated, because a complaint is sent only if either the dealer is corrupted or a corrupted player received s_i, hence the adversary knew s_i already. After these checks, all honest players knowing s_i, hold the same value for s_i.

In the Reconstruct phase, all players send their shares (bilaterally) to all other players. Each player reconstructs each of the k shares $s_1, s_2, \ldots s_k$ and obtains the secret s.

MULTIPARTY COMPUTATION CLASSIFICATIONS

There are many protocol classifications based on the assumptions made. They are discussed below.

Trusted Setup

Some protocols require pre-sharing of certain information before the start of an execution. This information is independent from the actual protocol inputs on which the functionality is computed. Here we consider pre-sharing that is done in a trusted setup.

A common reference string (CRS) (Blum et.al., 1988) is a polynomial-length string that comes from a certain pre-specified distribution. All the involved parties must have access to the same string. Introducing a CRS makes it possible to remove some interaction from the protocol. For example, the random values that must be generated by one party and sent to another can be pre-shared before the execution starts.

A protocol may use a public key infrastructure (PKI), where a public and a secret key are issued to each party. The PKI can be used for various purposes such as signatures, commitments, and ensuring that only the intended receiver gets the message. Its advantage compared to a CRS is that it can be reused (unless it is used for certain tasks such as bit commitments, where the secret key is revealed), while in general, a CRS cannot be reused and a new instance has to be generated for each protocol run.

If there is no trusted setup, it is still possible to achieve the same properties that the trusted setup gives (for example, include a key exchange subprotocol), at the expense of an online protocol execution phase.

Existence of a Broadcast Channel

A broadcast channel allows a party to send the same message to all other parties in such a way that each receiver knows that each other (honest) party has received exactly the same message. If there is no explicit broadcast channel, it can still be modeled in some settings.

For example, if at least $2n/3 + 1$ of the n parties are honest, then a broadcast can be implemented as follows. If Pi wants to broadcast m, it sends (*init,i,m*) to all other parties. If a party Pj receives (*init,i,m*) from Pi, it sends (*echo,i,m*) to all parties (including itself). If a party Pj receives (*echo,i,m*) from at least $n/3 + 1$ different parties, then it sends (*echo,i,m*) to all parties too. If a party Pj receives (*echo,i,m*) from at least $2n/3+1$ different parties, then it accepts that Pi has broadcast m. It can be shown that if at least one party accepts m, then all the other honest parties do as well.

Assumption Level

The security of protocols can be based on the intractability of certain computational tasks. Some protocols use quite specific assumptions such as factoring or finding the minimal distance of vectors generated by a matrix over a finite field. In some cases, the intractability has not even been formally reduced to well-known open problems. Even if no efficient algorithm for solving these tasks is known right now, it may still be solved in the future.

Instead of assuming the hardness of a particular computational task, the security may be based on a more general assumption such as the existence of trapdoor functions. For a trapdoor function f, given an input x, it is easy to compute $f(x)$, but it is difficult to compute x from $f(x)$ unless a special trapdoor is known, which may depend on f itself, but not on x. A weaker assumption is the existence of one-way functions that do not require the existence of a trapdoor. When implementing a protocol, a specific one-way function f can be chosen. If it turns out that this particular f is not one-way, the protocol will not be immediately broken, as some other f can be used instead. In this case, the particular implementation becomes insecure, but not the whole protocol. It is not known if one-way functions exist. There are no computational problems whose hardness can be steadily proven, so in the best-case scenario no computational assumptions are used. The next level is statistical security, where the data may leak only with negligible probability. If the leakage probability is 0, then we have perfect security.

Maliciousness

Two intermediate levels between passive and active adversaries are the fail-stop adversary and covert adversary. A fail-stop adversary (Galil et al., 1988) follows the protocol similarly to the passive adversary, except for the possibility of aborting. This means that the adversary has the power to interrupt the protocol execution, but nothing more compared to the passive one. A covert adversary (Aumann et al., 2010) estimates the probability of being caught. It deviates from the protocol as long as this probability is sufficiently low.

Adversary Mobility

A static adversary chooses a set of corrupted parties before the protocol starts. After that, the set of corrupted parties stays immutable. An adaptive adversary adds parties to the malicious set during the execution of the protocol, until the threshold is reached. The choice of the next corrupted party depends on the state of the other parties corrupted so far. A mobile adversary can not only add new parties to the malicious set during the execution of the protocol, but also remove them, so that some other party can be corrupted instead.

Corrupted Parties

In the simplest case, a single adversary that corrupts a set of parties. In the case of mixed adversary security, different sets of parties can be corrupted by different adversaries. For example, it may happen that one of them is passive, and the other active. In the case of hybrid security, the protocol may tolerate different sets of corrupted parties with different capabilities. For example, one set of malicious parties is computationally bounded, while the other is not.

Fairness

If a protocol has the agreement property, then if at least one honest party receives its output, then all the other honest parties do as well. If a protocol has the fairness property, then if any party receives its output, then all the honest parties do as well.

Composability

If a protocol is secure in the stand-alone model, then it is secure only if it is executed once, and there are no other protocols running. For example, if one protocol uses PKI for commitments, the secret key is published when the commitment is opened, and the keys cannot be reused. Hence, the protocol can be run only once. If the protocol is sequentially composable, then it is secure regardless of any other instance of the same protocol running before and after it. However, there may still be problems if some other protocol is running in parallel. For example, a party P_1 may instantiate two protocol executions with P_2 and P_3, pretending to be P_3 for P_2. If P_2 requires proof that it indeed communicates with P_3, and sends a corresponding challenge to which only P_3 can respond, then P_1 may deliver this challenge to P_3 in a parallel protocol session in which it is the turn of P_1 to send the challenge.

A protocol that supports parallel composition is secure even if several instances are executed in parallel, regardless of the timings that the adversary inserts between the rounds of all the protocol runs. However, it can still be insecure in the presence of some other protocols. For example, a protocol that uses PKI for message transmission can be secure in parallel composition, but executing another protocol that uses the same PKI for commitments will break it. A universally composable (Canetti, 2001) protocol is secure, regardless of the environment.

SUMMARY

In this chapter, we introduced the model for secure multiparty computation and discussed problems in this category. We also provided a classification of secure multiparty computation based on the type of adversaries against that model.

REFERENCES

Aumann, Y., & Lindell, Y. (2010). Security against covert adversaries: Efficient protocols for realistic adversaries. *Journal of Cryptology, 23*(2), 281–343. doi:10.1007/s00145-009-9040-7

Blum, M., Feldman, P., & Micali, S. (1988). Non-interactive zero-knowledge and its applications. *Proceedings of the Twentieth Annual ACM Symposium on Theory of Computing STOC '88* (pp. 103–112). doi:10.1145/62212.62222

Canetti, R. (2001). Universally composable security: A new paradigm for cryptographic protocols. Proceedings of FOCS (pp. 136–145). IEEE Computer Society. doi:10.1109/SFCS.2001.959888

Chor, B., Goldwasser, S., Micali, S., & Awerbuch, B. (1985, May 6-8). Verifiable Secret Sharing and Achieving Simultaneity in the Presence of Faults (Extended Abstract). *Proceedings of the 17th Annual ACM Symposium on Theory of Computing*, Providence, Rhode Island, USA (pp. 383– 395). ACM Press.

Cramer, R., & Damgard, I. (2004). Multiparty Computation: An Introduction. Retrieved from http://citeseerx.ist.psu.edu/viewdoc/download?doi=10.1.1.91.6488&rep=rep1&type=pdf

Du, W., & Atallah, M. J. (2001). Secure Multi-party computation Problems And Their Applications: A Review and Open problems. Retrieved from http://www.cis.syr.edu/~wedu/Research/paper/nspw2001.pdf

Galil, Z., Haber, S., & Yung, M. (1988) Cryptographic computation: Secure fault-tolerant protocols and the public-key model (extended abstract). In Advances in Cryptology CRYPTO '87, LNCS (Vol. 293, pp. 135–155).

Laud, P., & Kamm, L. (2015). *Applications of Secure Multiparty Computation*. IOS Press.

Maurer, U. (2006). Secure Multi-party Computation made simple. *Discrete Applied Mathematics, Elsevier, 154*(2), 370–381. doi:10.1016/j.dam.2005.03.020

Patra, A. (2010). *Studies on Verifiable secret sharing, Byzantine Agreement, and Multiparty Computation* [Ph.D. Thesis]. Indian Institute of Technology, Madras.

Shamir, A. (1979). How to share a secret. *Communications of the ACM*, 22(11), 612–613. doi:10.1145/359168.359176

Yao, A. C. (1982). Protocols for Secure Computations. *Proceedings of the 23rd Annual IEEE Symposium on Foundations of Computer Science*.

KEY TERMS AND DEFINITIONS

Adversary: A malicious outsider who controls the behavior of one or more of the parties to disrupt the correct computation of the function.

Ideal Model: An ideal model is a model of computation where a simulator S can simulate the model of computation.

Multiparty Computation: A model of computation where parties P1, P2, …, Pn compute a function in a secure a way that all honest parties output the same value.

Real Model: In the real model of computation, the computation is carried out without the use of the simulator.

Secret Sharing: An example of a multiparty computation where a share of the secret is present with each party. The secret can be constructed only if k-out-of-n shares are reconstructed.

Universal Composability: A universal composable multiparty computation is secure regardless of the environment.

Verifiable Secret Sharing: The verifiable secret sharing scheme is a protocol for securely constructing the secret even when some of the parties are controlled by an adversary.

Chapter 14
Secure Bootstrapping Using the Trusted Platform Module

Kannan Balasubramanian
Mepco Schlenk Engineering College, India

Ahmed Mahmoud Abbas
The American University in Cairo, Egypt

ABSTRACT

The protection of Computer Hardware and Software using Cryptographic algorithms has assumed importance in the recent years. The Trusted Computing Group (TCG) has put forward certain conditions to be met by the computer hardware, software and firmware so that the devices may be considered trusted. The Trusted Platform Module is a hardware device that will authenticate the code modules contained in the Basic Input/Output System (BIOS) of a computer to ensure that the Computer System starts in a trustworthy state. This device can also protect against Memory Management attacks including Buffer Overflows and Memory Pointer attacks.

INTRODUCTION

This chapter examines the idea of Trusted Computing which is using security principles like confidentiality and integrity to the hardware and software of a computer system. The Trusted Computing Base is a set of devices that have been authenticated at the trusted source. The idea behind Trusted Computing is to secure the software and hardware of a computer system in a manner that will protect the system from malware and rootkits. The protection of physical memory during execution plays an important role in Trusted Computing. This chapter discusses a special device called the Trusted Platform Module that secures the Computer System against security attacks.

In order to lessen the demand on the CPU, many devices have built- in processors that operate autonomously-disk controllers, coprocessors, network cards, and more. Since each of these devices contains processing elements that could be replaced by compromised and infected firmware, it is important that the bootstrap process of a computer not only include the verification of the main host CPU

DOI: 10.4018/978-1-5225-2915-6.ch014

(Central Processing Unit) elements but also any and all firmware- driven devices that are attached to the computer at boot-up time.

Arbaugh, Farber, and Smith (1997) describe the essentials of a secure inheritance-based trust model that begins with the bootstrap. In their design, the integrity of each step of the bootstrap process is validated with digital signatures that were created using asymmetric cryptography in a secure and trusted environment back at the code origin. This approach, of course, requires that the signatures be checked by some processor, most likely the CPU. The first firmware component to run is the BIOS, or basic input-output system. This is typically stored in some form of rewriteable storage, since the BIOS must be updated to accommodate bug fixes. As such, an obvious attack avenue for this sort of implementation would be the compromise of the bootstrap process, its digital signatures (if not stored in ROM or Read Only Memory), and the BIOS that must authenticate them. Clearly, storing the digital signatures in ROM does not ultimately provide sufficient protection against such an attack if both the BIOS and the bootstrap can be altered.

The Trusted Computing Group has supported the use of a secure hardware device that can independently verify the BIOS and its verification. This allows remote verification that the operating system began with the computer in a trustworthy state. The trusted platform module (TPM) is an example of such a hardware device. In operation, the TPM employs hashing to create state signatures of code modules. During secure initialization, the TPM creates and stores a small code segment, the core root of trust for measurement (CRTM) in secure storage called the platform configuration register (PCR). Whenever the computer is reset, the CRTM is run first. The CRTM measures all executable firmware (including the BIOS) against the hash codes that were stored in the PCR during secure initialization. If successful, control is then transferred to the BIOS (which is now trusted), and the BIOS repeats the hash verification process for the initial program loader(IPL). The trusted IPL then measures code that it will load, and the process continues in this fashion through the remaining modules, such as the kernel, device drivers, and applications.

The process reflects the inheritance procedure that begins with the root and consecutively adds signatures for subsequent hardware and software modules whose integrity and trust are required in order to create a trusted computing environment. At this point, a remote administrator can issue a request to the TPM device, asking for the signatures of each module that is stored in the PCR. This enables the administrator to verify that the system was loaded correctly and can be trusted. The TPM itself cannot be verified, but, as hardware, it is more difficult to attack. Thus the degree of difficulty in attacking such a system has been raised. However, probing of the TPM is not detected, nor is the replacement of the TPM with compromised hardware that can subvert the authentication process. This is sometimes referred to as a remote attestation challenge or, more simply, attestation. Its purpose is to supply the net result of the attestation and trust-inheritance process to a remote system that seeks to ascribe a level of trust to the platform in question. The attestation process should not compromise user privacy in any way or include the transmission of personal user information.

In general it is better to trust hardware than to trust either firmware or software. Properly designed hardware can include tamper-evidence or tamper-protection capabilities, and the cost of creating a fake hardware device without the tamper protection included (or, alternatively, disabled) is quite high and often requires significant facilities and technical skill. Firmware and software, in contrast, are easily distributed, making them a much easier target for someone intent on compromising the bootstrap process. In fact, viruses and Trojan horses can be created that target exactly these firmware and software modules.

As with other security technologies, the human element often provides the easiest avenue for an attack. People can be compromised, bribed, tricked, or threatened. The use of such tactics could easily result in a target hard drive with valuable information being "loaned" to the attacker for a short period of time. During this period, an attacker could steal copies of sensitive data, plant system-level viruses, or add a "sleeper" function that is instantiated after a certain calendar date. Upon instantiation, the sleeper code could cause the disk to appear to malfunction, thereby causing the owner to send it in for additional or repeat service. Of course, the attacker knows the date on which this will occur and can arrange to conveniently appear at the compromised technician's workplace for another brief "loan."

The ultimate goal of a hardware attack is to obtain valuable data. Short of obtaining a target hardware device as described above, the next attack path would likely focus on the firmware. Unlike higher-level software, firmware is not overwritten by reinstalling software. It often requires a special-purpose software routine that "burns" the firmware into the device, a process rarely used by a typical user. However, it is not beyond the capability of an intent attacker. Like an operating system, firmware can be compromised. Nonetheless, an administrator should not assume that firmware can be trusted because it is harder to attack-history has shown that as users create security solutions that prevent one type of attack, attackers develop new solutions that sidestep the new protection. This will apply to firmware as well as to operating systems and applications.

There are several ways to launch an attack on firmware that can ultimately compromise an entire system. The most direct way is to provide a targeted user with the firmware update and the required "burning" code and convince him that he should install the update. A less direct way, although ultimately far more pervasive, is to insert an attacker in the device delivery process. This is likely to be a person or compromised firm that receives the hardware from the manufacturer and is responsible for either installing software or otherwise preparing and delivering the target device to the end user. During the period when the targeted devices are in the possession of the attacker or his firm, compromised firmware can be burned into the device before shipping.

An attack can occur closer to the user. For example, a company that provides software installation and configuration services could install compromised firmware. Maintenance crews can perform a similar function when devices are delivered to them for handling. Once an attacker has succeeded in installing compromised firmware, the user and system data will likely become available to the attacker in short order. Some devices can issue direct memory access (DMA) commands that allow it to read or write data present in memory, including sensitive data. Devices that are running compromised firmware can certainly deliver data that it is receiving to other locations over the network to which the computer is attached or, alternatively, store the data in a secret location that can be retrieved when the device is either later connected to the network or sent in for service.

THE TRUSTED COMPUTING BASE

To the extent possible, devices and their firmware should be included in the trusted computing base (TCB). The presence of a device in this base signifies that it has been authenticated at a trusted source (preferably at the manufacturing location), thereby conferring inheritance of trust to subsequent modules as described above. It is instructive to digress at this point to comment on some of the features present in the common-criteria (CC) process that have bearing on the inclusion of hardware and firmware in the TCB. Common criteria is an ISO/IEC standard for computer security. It is an assurance standard in which users can specify their computer-security requirements and vendors can use this information in the development of their products. It has developed a framework in which vendors can map functions within their products to certain functions required by users (these become the claims). Independent testing labs can then use the CC framework to test the product against the claims using this framework and assign a numerical grade to the product based on the results. The protection levels that can be achieved by products are graded from evaluation-assurance level (EAL) 1 through EAL 7, with higher numbers reflecting more demands upon the development of the security functions.

CC includes an auditing process that seeks to confirm that developers have achieved a certain level of security in the design and implementation of their product. This auditing process involves the careful examination of the company's security target (ST) by an independent group of security auditors in order to confirm that the target of evaluation (TOE) is adequately protected. (The TOE is the actual product that is being protected.) The ST essentially describes the security properties of the TOE by revealing the steps taken by the company to create the TOE.

In order to achieve a claimed level of security, the ST must demonstrate that certain security functional requirements (SFRs), individual security functions provided by the product, have been implemented in a secure manner. The process of auditing the SFRs (such as, for example, how an administrator might authenticate himself to the product's administration function modules) reveals interdependencies among them and can expose security risks that might not have been anticipated by the design team.

In anticipation of a subsequent audit and certification by the CC process, companies must make clear architectural decisions about which system components (hardware, firmware, and software) will reside within the boundary of the TOE and which will not. This process, and the subsequent auditing of module security and interdependence, would be a valuable addition to the development of secure and trusted components in the bootstrap process. By using such an organized procedure to determine the boundaries of the TCB (much like the boundaries of the TOE), developers are much less likely to inadvertently create systems with major attack points. Clearly, any hardware, firmware, or software element that is not included within the boundary of the TCB is automatically flagged as unsafe and can be treated accordingly by higher-level code.

The creation of a secure bootstrap process requires the establishment of trust and attestation at the manufacturing source, followed by the inheritance of that trust to any hardware, firmware, and bootstrap-critical software that has been designed to reside within the protected environment (the TCB). This creates a tree of trust whose origins are at the most elemental components of the bootstrap process, and the validation of those elements should be available through independent means from the manufacturer through a digital certificate. Attestation must also enable remote systems to challenge the trustworthiness of a platform.

Attention must be paid to dependencies of the components. Even if a component has been established as trusted, if it relies upon a separate element whose validity cannot be established, then the component can no longer be trusted and should be flagged as such. Higher-level functions should seek to establish the trustworthiness of each lower-level device and act accordingly-those devices that cannot be trusted should be constrained to gain access only to memory areas that are not secure or trusted, for example.

The proper development and implementation of a secure bootstrap process, including the establishment of trust at the point of manufacturing and the subsequent creation of inheritance trees within the TCB, reduces attack points to hardware only. (Attacks on any firmware and software components within the TCB would be detectable by the presence of an improper signature or invalid hash within the PCR.) Hardware attacks can be protected to some extent by using tamper-evident technologies that erase security-related information upon physical attack.

Secure bootstrapping provides the administrator with the ability to remotely detect attacks by checking hash signatures of the components. Patches to code can be verified through use of the trust-inheritance structure of the system, thereby providing an upgrade path that can be trusted. By limiting access of untrusted modules to nonsecure memory addresses only, the potential for buffer overflow attacks and unauthorized access to encryption keys can be nearly eliminated. In the hardware domain, tamper evidence can be implemented to provide protection of sensitive information. Implementation of secure bootstrapping provides the platform on which trust can be built, ultimately producing a more secure system and computing environment.

SECURE MEMORY MANAGEMENT

Secure memory management became an item of increased attention when buffer overflows were used to gain access to secure information or otherwise compromise the security of a system or application. Moreover, it became apparent that poor memory-management techniques by developers were leaving encryption keys and passwords in volatile memory after use, creating additional paths for attacks. Two technology factors have also contributed to the increased need for secure memory management. First, the increase of multitasking has increased the importance of proper isolation of memory between applications. Second, the use of the Internet to propagate viruses and Trojan-horse programs provided an easy attack path that could be exploited at arbitrary distances and at any time of day or night.

- **Buffer Overflows:** Applications reside in memory during operation. Poorly written software can inadvertently include code that attempts to store data beyond the boundaries assigned to the buffer. The result is that the program will over-write data in adjacent memory locations, causing incorrect results or a crash. Such undesirable behavior can be triggered by an attacker who writes code that will perform such a buffer overflow. Depending on the design of the system and its ability to prevent such a data excursion or recover from the error, an attacker may open various exploitation capabilities that are a consequence of the crash. In addition to writing data in adjacent memory locations, a sophisticated attacker can also create a malicious program that will overwrite the return address present on the stack. Upon completion of execution, a program retrieves the return address and proceeds to that location to continue running code. By overwriting the return address with an address that exists within the attack code, the program will obediently branch to the incorrect address and continue processing the attack code. A similar technique can be used by overwriting a function pointer. In both cases, the program has been diverted to perform the attacker's code. Buffer-overflow attacks can be minimized by writing code that carefully checks the bounds of allocated memory against the requested memory-write process to prevent excursions beyond the allocated space. This function can also be provided by a well-designed compiler.
- **Memory Pointer Attacks:** In a standard computer environment in which the memory-access privileges of applications are not enforced or restricted to application-specific bounds, memory pointers can be used by an attacker to redirect execution to malicious code. In this environment, memory pointers can point to any memory address. By placing malicious code at addresses commonly used by the operating system, an attacker can divert the 0s to perform malicious functions

without detection. An application dynamically allocates and releases memory at run-time. This memory is referred to as the "heap," and it usually includes data being used by the program. Data in the heap can be used by attackers in a somewhat different manner than a buffer-overflow attack. In particular, heap data include data structures that often include pointers.

- **Minimizing Memory Management Attacks:** Not only do memory exploits compromise the security of the target application, but they can also compromise the security of the target computer. Moreover, such an attack can also compromise the security of an entire network if its security policies, firewalls, and sharing of drives have not been administered properly. It is critical that an organization take steps to protect it against such attacks, since the impact may have far-reaching consequences. There is no substitute for secure programming practices. It is also inadvisable to rely solely on the compiler or run-time operating system to catch memory errors. Programmers need to ensure that memory management is being handled properly. The allocation, use, erasure, and subsequent release of dynamic memory must not be left to chance. Secure memory management begins with good security-minded programming practices. Although not a comprehensive list, the following comprises a reasonable representation of practices that will ultimately produce better memory management within applications:
  - Minimize the use of memory pointers.
  - Destroy memory pointers immediately after use.
  - Always allocate and release (free) memory within the same software module to minimize the possibility that memory will be forgotten.
  - Release memory only once.
  - Do not rely upon the operating system to clean memory-erase the
  - If global variables are used to store memory pointers, reset their contents to null after release of the related memory.
  - Make sure that the amount of memory requested by the allocation command is within the bounds allowed.
  - Check to assure that the amount of memory being requested in an will be large enough for the projected use.
  - Write code so that allocation errors are handled.
  - Initialize allocated memory within the code, rather than relying upon allocation the operating system to do so.

Attackers will seek to employ whatever techniques are available to obtain access to secure information (cryptographic keys, etc.). Although it is desirable that application developers employ best practices for secure memory management in order to prevent the use of their application for such attacks, platform developers cannot assume that this will always be the case. Therefore, techniques to create walls in memory between different operating applications will be a good first step in minimizing memory excursions beyond the bounds allocated to a specific application. The use of trusted platform module (TPM) technology will also help identify compromised systems and prevent the inadvertent trusting of such compromised platforms.

TRUSTED EXECUTION TECHNOLOGY

The characteristics of a hardware-based security system include attestation, process isolation, tamper-resistant storage of core secrets, and secure I0 paths. Using a mixture of these hardware-based protection techniques, Intel recently launched a secure computing initiative. Initially code-named LaGrande, the technology has been renamed the trusted execution technology (TET or TXT). TET is Intel's attempt to create a trusted platform. It provides a specification that defines how the TET hardware can be used to extend the trusted platform to include operating systems created by developers who employ the technology. Paying attention to attack vectors on memory and I0 devices, Intel has added hardware improvements and partitioning of secure space from all other space. Developers must be careful to follow Intel's specs in order to maximize the protection and added trust offered by the technology. The categories of enhanced protection offered by TET are listed below with a brief description of the conceptual goal for each.

- **Protected Execution:** In order to prevent unauthorized applications from gaining access to any information associated with a protected application, this capability isolates each application, its memory space, its return vectors, etc. This should limit or prevent the ability of unauthorized applications from altering information in the protected application.
- **Protected Storage:** Using the TPM, the TET system encrypts and stores keys and any sensitive data within the physically protected boundaries of the device. Not only are the TPM's mechanisms employed to protect this information, but the encryption keys used to protect the data also include information about the trustworthiness of the environment as an element of their creation. Should an untrustworthy environment be detected at a later date, this implementation will prevent the release of keys or other protected data from within the TPM.
- **Protected Input:** Communication between the processor and external devices, such as a keyboard, mouse, or USB device, can be compromised by malicious code. TET seeks to close this attack channel by introducing encryption between the processor and the external device, using keys that have been created in a trusted environment and that are stored in the TPM. This will prevent unauthorized persons from observing user typing activity (usually achieved through the use of keystroke-capture software), mouse movements, or communications with a USB device. On the processor side, each application must be enabled to accommodate the decryption process, thereby creating a secure channel between the external device and the application (with keys stored within the TPM).
- **Protected Graphics:** Screen captures and fake screens are eliminated by the TET system through the use of the protected execution environment. By creating rigid boundaries between applications and then allowing only trusted applications operating within the protected environment to gain access to the display-frame buffer, the ability of attackers to obtain (through the use of a screen-capture program) data from the display buffer is eliminated. Moreover, data displayed on the screen is only possible from the trusted application running within the protected environment. This eliminates pathways by which false screens can be displayed. Much like the protected input, this approach creates an encrypted and protected path between the application and the display.
- **Environment Authentication and Protected Launch:** Following the specifications of the TCG for correctly invoking a trusted environment, the TET system measures the software and hardware environment during the bootstrap process to assure than no components have been compromised. The hash-code signatures of trusted hardware and software components have been stored in the

TPM after being measured in a trusted environment before shipping and are compared to the signatures seen by the system during bootstrap. Using the processes described in previous chapters of this book, the TET system uses signature comparisons to control the launch of trusted applications and establishes the level of trust before communication with other platforms.

- **Domain Manager:** The TET system introduces a domain manager whose function is to manage the interaction of the hardware that is running in a specific instantiation of a protected environment with the software applications (also within the same environment) that require the interaction. A separate TET domain manager is invoked for each protected environment. In order to enforce separation of environments, domain managers cannot access one another's data, hardware, or other information.

- **Platform and Hardware Requirements:** In order to perform the security functions described above, the TET system must employ various hardware modules to achieve the desired security. At the very least, a TET-enabled system requires a properly implemented (and initialized) TPM, processor, keyboard, mouse, and display. The need for a specialized processor stems from the requirement that the system be able to create multiple, isolated execution environments. This will provide the user with the option of running any specific application in a standard partition or in a protected partition. As explained above, the latter option isolates the application from all others and protects its resources from access by any other application. Access by the application to certain resources (the display, keyboard, and mouse, for example) is protected by bidirectional encryption. Moreover, the specialized processor enforces domain separation, memory protection, and event handling. It must offer secure (encrypted) pathways to memory, graphics, keyboard, mouse, and the TPM.

Complementary hardware changes must, of course, be present on the related peripheral devices such as the keyboard, mouse, and display. With encrypted pathways between the processor and these devices, attacks that capture keystrokes, mouse clicks, or screen information should be defeated. Since the TPM is platform-specific from the moment of initialization by a trusted party (say, at the factory), changes to sensitive configuration elements (both hardware and software) will be detected. Moreover, the TPM provides physical and electronic protection of cryptographic keys, specific signatures and certificates, user-specific sensitive data, and (ideally) hardware-based key and random-number generation within a tamper-protected enclosure. As explained in the previous chapter, data that is protected by the TPM cannot be accessed unless the system is in a specified state and authorized commands have been issued.

Users need not employ the security features of the TET system in running their applications. Intel has designed the system so that users can elect to execute applications in a completely open and untrusted environment, as they do today. That is, the standard partition is identical to the manner in which applications are executed in today's unprotected environment. This standard partition provides a migration path, allowing existing applications that do not have the TET-required features to be executed as they are before users obtain the security-enhanced releases of the applications. By the same token, the TPM must be configured to require user election in order to activate the TPM system.

In addition to allowing users to employ their existing non-TPM-enabled applications on these new platforms as they have in the past, TET also enforces the control of the user over the invocation of the trusted environments and therefore the possible sharing of information with remote computers or authorities when trust needs to be established. Should a user elect to run an application in a protected environment, a parallel, coexisting environment (partition) will be created that runs TET- supported software and employs the new hardware. As explained above, applications running in this environment are completely isolated from one another and cannot view or access one another's memory, display, keyboard, or mouse data. The hardware components required to achieve this include the TET-enabled processor and related I0 chips required to encrypt and decrypt data from the keyboard, mouse, display, and any other TET-protected attachments. The TET domain manager enforces the isolation and protection of separate partitions. Applications need not be limited to either protected or unprotected mode. For example, applications can be developed that employ both environments, where I0 functions might be handled in the unprotected partition while the core, security-sensitive applications would be handled within a protected partition.

Of course, before the TET-protected environment can be loaded, the initial trust of the hardware and software modules must be established during the bootstrap process. The TET system provides three different paths for this. First, a user may decide to trust the initial configuration that has been delivered to him by the manufacturer or supplier. The user can create a secret phrase that only he knows and then seal this phrase into the initial trusted environment (within the TPM). The TET system provides the user with the ability to request and view the stored phrase upon booting. Any change to the trusted environment (through its examination of module hash codes within the PCM) would be intercepted and the secret message (or any other TPM-protected secrets) would not be available. The user would know immediately that the system cannot be trusted due to some change in these security-critical modules.

A second option employs a pluggable device (such as a USB or PCM- CIA device) that contains the measurements of the modules that were present during the trusted initial configuration. This device can then be used to measure the system independent of the TPM's result and provide the user with the results of the trust measurement. A third option is the extension of the second option to a remote party (that is, the use of a remote party to provide the validation of trustworthiness of the system's modules). Although this offers the advantage of remoteness (and the consequent difficulty of an attacker successfully compromising both the system and the remotely stored attributes), it introduces concerns about the protection of the communication channel between the two parties or the possible absence of the remote party due to network or local power problems. Reporting of the results would ideally be delivered through some independent path (a back channel) such as a web page or telephone dialup.

The TET system as implemented does not require reboot of the platform in order to establish a protected partition. In order to achieve this, the invocation of the protection turns off all running processes and begins the authentication of hardware and software modules as if the system were proceeding with a reboot. The process is comparable to an authenticated bootstrap process but differs in that any running processes are suspended, thereby allowing the authentication of elements to proceed without any possible interference from other processes. Upon successful completion, a protected partition is created and prior processes are allowed to proceed in the unprotected space. During release of a protected partition, the domain manager handles cleanup and release of memory and pointers and then finally terminates itself.

- **Unplanned Events:** It is possible that either a loss of power or an unexpected system reset may occur while a protected partition exists. Although the CPU might become unavailable, the contents of memory may remain intact. TET employs one of two actions to protect secret information in either of these situations. First, memory access is blocked upon reset or power loss, and, second, memory gets zeroed upon restoration of power. In the event that an unexpected "sleep" command has been received by the platform, the TET system encrypts all data in memory before releasing control to the hibernate or power-down sequence. On power-up, the encrypted pages can be decrypted and execution resumed if all other pointers are still valid. Otherwise, the user may need to restart his protected session.

- **Privacy and User Control:** As explained above, the TET system gives the user complete control over whether or not the protected partitions will be employed for any application and the extent to which the application might reside in both protected and unprotected partitions. The activation or deactivation of TET features and functions can only be performed with the complete knowledge of the user, thereby granting him control over his privacy. Moreover, the user maintains knowledge and control over any system-trust evaluations that are transmitted over any network. In keeping with this philosophy of user control and knowledge, systems that include TET are shipped with the TET system disabled (deactivated). In order to enable it, the user must give specific permission and take direct action. The user is able to employ certain security features within the TPM (such as cryptographic modules) without being required to enable remote authentication of the system's trust (attestation). Moreover, keys, attestation, and the TPM must not be used in a manner that compromises the user's privacy without his knowledge and prior approval.

THE CONCEPT OF TRUSTED COMPUTING

When they were first developed, general-purpose personal computers were not designed with security and trust as an integral part of the architecture. After all, computers then were completely stand-alone-data was transferred only through sharing of disks, which at that time was a relatively safe and trustworthy process. The Internet was developed by people who saw great potential in being able to share scientific and military information quickly and easily between computers. Security and the need for trust did not surface until viruses began to spread by disk, and, more significantly, these open computers were attached to networks. When networking was created back in the 1980s, it primarily served a function of enhanced communication and sharing of information between researchers within a laboratory or university department. As networking grew, it began to form connections between buildings, then between different universities, and ultimately between widely disparate organizations spanning the globe. As networking expanded, so did the realization that this new medium of interconnectivity introduced a significant degree of anonymity to the remote parties. Users were relying on trust. As viruses began to spread using these networks, the reliance on trust began to fade, and users sought ways to protect their computers and data. Moreover, as they are currently designed and implemented, if a user has access to a person's private information (for example, his online medical records at a hospital), he is completely free to copy that person's information and retransmit it to anyone anywhere. There is no inherited access control in today's Internet or PC file system.

Even with basic password protection implemented on a system, a simple screen-capture or keystroke-capture program, installed without the user's knowledge, can seize sensitive information in the background and forward it to a malicious attacker. A class of attack software that resides at the root of a PC is called a rootkit. The rootkit software resides in a hidden location on a PC without the user being aware of its presence. Rootkits hide themselves by modifying the operating system itself. This allows them to survive reboots of the system. They can replace normal system utility routines, adding their specific attack function to processes that are used frequently by the average user. This class of attack software can perform any of a number of malicious acts, including capturing and forwarding passwords, sending spam email designed to identify new attack targets, direct attacking of other machines on the local network, or opening a remote-control function that can be used by the attacker. Since local area networks are designed to allow easy communication between PCs and enable file and printer sharing, entire organizations are often placed at risk once a rootkit has been established on any one of the machines in the office. Depending on the nature of the business, this may introduce legal liability due to the potential loss of private user information.

Rootkits are now quite common and readily available on several web sites. They have become sufficiently easy to use that nonexpert users can develop them using such available software packages. The nastier versions employ virtualization techniques (such as those used by legitimate companies like VMWare) in which a normal OS runs. This gives the rootkit access to all information while evading detection. Botnets (from "robot network") are becoming an increasingly common attack mode. In this type of attack, a virus is placed on the target computer that allows a hacker to remotely command the computer to perform any of a number of functions. The network robots can launch denial-of-service attacks on targeted computers, send spam emails to members of the mailing lists present on each machine, or capture and forward password and account information to the attacker. Botnets consisting of thousands of computers are not uncommon, making them a very effective means to launch denial-of-service attacks. Computers infected with botnet software are particularly dangerous to systems that employ trust, since they tend to undermine the trust of all of the computers that include the commandeered computer as a member of the trusted circle. It is estimated that one in every four computers worldwide has a botnet infection.

Current computer systems and networks employ an unspoken hierarchy of trust. When logging into a business's website to enter personal information, the user must decide if he trusts that remote business to protect his information. The user must also decide if he trusts the business to have properly protected itself against viruses and Trojan horses. Even if the answer is "yes" to both, he must also decide if he trusts the business's employees to protect his information. By the same token, can the business's affiliates be trusted to protect his information? All of these "trust" decisions must be made by the user, often without much supporting information. Organizations that claim to protect private user information must have a mechanism in place to enforce that protection. Moreover, the organization must have a mechanism in place to enforce the policy amongst its affiliates who might have access to that information.

Ultimately, a system must be "trusted" to behave e the way the user expects it to behave, including the manner in which information is being protected. Once such a system has been established and the user community at large accepts the system as being truly "trustworthy," its extension to the networked world is straightforward. Trusted machines that can demonstrate their trustworthiness to the satisfaction of the broad user community can then limit trusted functions to other platforms that have similarly established themselves as trusted. Platforms that are not trusted can be separated and treated as suspect.

Today, the movement towards increased mobility by the technology workforce increases the demand for secure and trusted communication over networks. Remote workers have the ability to maintain productivity while far from their home office, accessing data and support information remotely. As a result, the hosting systems back at the home office must employ technologies that protect against unauthorized users trying to gain access. Web interfaces must be carefully secured against bugs and vulnerabilities. Electronic commerce, such as online bill paying, fund transfers, and other banking functions, has increased dramatically in the past decade. Shopping online and subsequent purchasing of goods now rivals "brick and mortar" stores during holiday seasons. This increased dependence on electronic networks further heightens the urgency for hardware-based protection of information, authentication of users, and establishment of high degrees of trust in local and remote computing systems. The economic impact of failure to protect such information is demonstrated almost daily by the loss of private information, identity theft, and hacking.

This unprotected, nontrusted environment needs a low-cost module that is tamper-evident and can protect central security information (such as cryptographic keys) against theft or alteration by attackers. With this capability, a system could in principle, measure the integrity of the hardware and software modules resident on the system and create certificates that certify those modules. Such a module cannot be software-based, since such solutions cannot possibly provide protection against physical attacks. A security module that establishes trust that can be inherited by its software and hardware modules must be hardware-based. Moreover, such a module should be low-cost, and a process must be established to assure that it can only be deployed on systems that are worthy of trust. Failure to do so would cause a contaminated system to assert itself as "trustworthy," and its impact on other systems could possibly spread. The hardware module should be dedicated and independent of the host operating system during its security operations.

The term "trusted computing" is a general term used by the IT industry when referring to the creation of platforms (PCs, etc.) that have special hardware whose function includes cryptography, validation, and authentication of hardware and software modules and certification of the trustworthiness of the platform to the user and other remote devices. This hardware element also aids in the protection of secure data within the device. Through its ability to control the execution of processes (preventing untrusted processes or at least notifying the user that they are not trusted), trusted computing systems should prevent viruses and piracy. But there is an additional concern, raised by privacy-rights groups and others, that the entire trusted-computing paradigm will reside in the hands of a few large manufacturers.

Currently, the technical and policy standards regarding trusted computing are handled by a consortium of large manufacturers of electronics and software (such as Microsoft, IBM, HP, Intel, AMD, and others). User groups have formed to ask for regulation of trusted computing (and others have asked for its outright rejection), but there is little movement in these deliberations at this time.

THE TRUSTED PLATFORM MODULE

In 1999, a group of leading IT and PC companies created the Trusted Computing Platform Alliance (TCPA). The founding members included Compaq, Hewlett-Packard, IBM, Intel, and Microsoft. This group set as its objective a definition of a trusted computing platform with special attention to ensuring privacy and security. It should be noted that there are groups that are opposed to the TCPA approach, citing privacy rights, freedom of speech, and other concerns (http://www.againsttcpa.org).

Any system that employs trust must ultimately rely upon a person or group of people that must be trusted. When examined carefully, all systems have at their root an administrator, programmer, or manufacturer that must be declared trustworthy. To the extent that this is not true, all of the subsequent trust dependencies fall. It is probably best to establish that trust by using groups of people rather than a single person. It is less likely that all of the people in a group will agree to deliver compromised systems (this would be a conspiracy), but of course nothing can ever be guaranteed. At some point, trust-based systems rely on people. At its core, the group defined a Trusted Platform Module (TPM), which would handle all software- and hardware-related security features, including storage and protection of keys, auditing of surrounding hardware and software components, and creation of certificates of trust that can then be viewed either remotely by administrators or employed as part of any associated trusted process.

The TPM must, by its nature, employ very high security tools to protect its keys, certificates, and other security-related contents. It must protect this information against unauthorized external access, physical and software attacks, and replacement by altered or otherwise copied versions of the TPM. In doing so, it establishes a root of trust at a fundamental level of the computing system.

The TPM assumes that software must be isolated from outside interference in order to be trusted. Moreover, it assumes that proper behavior implies trust. This carries the implicit assumption that all possible behaviors have been tested-failure to do so could allow the existence of a path for compromise.

The TCPA defined a core root of trust (CRT) as its most basic building block from which all trust is derived for a specific PC. In order to protect that fundamental role, the CRT is required to be a static portion of code that is a component of the platform's initialization routine. It must be executed first as part of the bootstrap process. This places the machine in a known initial state that can be compared to a trusted initial state that has been independently confirmed. Since software alone cannot be protected against physical attacks, the TPM must be a hardware device, such as an application-specific integrated circuit (ASIC) or dedicated chip on the motherboard of the platform. With these two constraints (CRT and physical device), the TPM becomes the root from which all trust is built for the platform.

A proper implementation of the TPM must include strong physical protection (tamper evidence and tamper resistance) so that its contents are protected against physical attack. As mentioned above, the cryptographic keys that control critical resources (root access, secure memory routines, administration functions, etc.) must be stored within the TPM. Ideally, a true random-number generator would reside within the TPM (to be distinguished from software-based pseudo-random-number generators), and associated functions such as critical cryptography, hashing, and the creation of digital signatures or certificates should be performed within the TPM bounds. Data traveling into and out of the TPM should be cryptographically secure. The TPM should be not only physically bound to the host platform but also bound through manufacturer-owned signed digital certificates that are stored at the time of initialization at the factory so that swapping of the TPM module would be easily detected. Keys never leave the TPM, and data of any sort that is protected by the TPM can only be decrypted when the system is in a specified state and a specific authorized command is issued.

The startup of the TPM has three basic options:

- **Clear:** the TPM is requested to start with default values that have been set by the TPM owner.
- **State:** The TPM is instructed to recover some previously saved state and continue operations from this state
- **Deactivate:** The TPM is turned off and will not process any further commands until the reset command is issued by the TPM owner.

STRUCTURE OF THE TPM

The architecture of the TPM, as specified by the TCG, requires that a trusted platform execute a specific series of steps upon power-up. First, the CRT must be authenticated. Since the CRT resides at the most fundamental level of a trusted platform, this step is critical. If the CRT is authentic, then the secure bootstrap process executes the instructions contained within the CRT. This process feeds forward-the executed steps determine the validity of subsequent steps and proceed to execute those in turn. This maintains the "known state" condition of the system during the boot process.

In the event that the authentication steps fail at any point, there are two options. First, the system can be shut down. This is generally not the option of choice, since it leaves the user completely without functionality. The second option is to allow the system to complete its startup process but leave it in a state that cannot be trusted (unauthenticated). In this second option, none of the secure information can be accessed, but the user retains some basic level of functionality. This TPM structure enables the CRT to establish authentication of itself, its modules and hardware, and, to some extent, software applications. The creation of this authenticated state allows the platform to join a worldwide network of trusted platforms, thereby creating a network of more secure machines. To the extent that secure memory management and input/output control is included, the trust is strengthened by forcing the isolation of applications and their allocated memory, thereby avoiding exposure to buffer-overflow attacks and other attack vectors that employ memory techniques.

Each TPM includes a 2048-bit RSA key pair (the endorsement key, or EK) that is created before delivery to the end user. When the EK is created, a credential is also created that can be used to verify the validity of the EK. The TPM is designed to prevent alternation or subsequent generation of EKs once configuration has been completed at the factory. The private key portion of the EK can never leave the TPM or be viewed outside of the protected confines of the hardware module.

The EK is used for verification of the initial state of the TPM and is bound to the platform. It acts as a root of trust for reporting when remote attestation is invoked. The system also creates attestation identity keys (AIKs) that are based upon the EK and can be created by the owner at any time, The user can create multiple AIK identities, thereby allowing enhanced privacy, using different identities for different operations. Since the EK is platform-specific, the AIK cannot be migrated from one platform to another. The TPM must be shipped without an owner. Initialization of the TPM by the end user should require his physical presence, and he must reset all old secrets (excluding the platform-specific EK). Since the TPM hardware includes secure storage combined with tamper resistance, the storage of keys and other user-critical information enjoys the protection afforded by a hardware solution.

THE TPM'S PRIMARY ROLES

Since the primary role of the TPM is to act as the root of trust for the platform, it must check and verify the integrity of the system's hardware and software during the boot process. Armed with this, it should provide authentication and status information to local and remote (authenticated) administrators as well as to software programs that request such information. It must provide a secure storage location for the user's private keys and private data and control over these items to the authenticated user. Some cautionary notes are in order here. The functionality of the TPM does not span all of the security-related functions. For example, the TPM relies upon the host system for information regarding host software. In checking the integrity of the host software, the TPM posts a request to the host, which then proceeds to "measure" the integrity of the identified software. The TPM does not have a means to independently verify that the host measured the requested software.

The TPM does not have control over the PC's hardware functionality. That is, the TPM cannot demand a physical reset of the PC, nor is it able to prevent programs from accessing portions of the PC's memory. The latter must be provided by a proper implementation of secure memory management. The user controls the activation and deactivation of the TPM. When deactivated, the user's PC is not trusted, nor are any of its applications or its communications with the outside world (such as over the Internet).

Ownership of the TPM is not the same as a "super user"-the TPM can be deactivated, and ownership does not automatically grant access to all operations. All protected operations require authorization. The owner and users control the use of all keys stored within the TPM. The owner must not foster a false sense of security about the protection of encrypted data on his hard drive. Data encrypted on the user's hard drive using encryption keys that are stored within the TPM are no stronger than the strength of the keys themselves. Although the keys are stored in physically secure memory within the TPM, which provides a heightened degree of protection, dictionary attacks and other hacking techniques sidestep the acquisition of the cryptographic keys and instead rely upon bruteforce methods to guess the key. Therefore, it is incumbent upon the user to employ strong cryptographic keys, generated using the techniques described earlier in this book, with the maximum key lengths allowed by the system. Technological solutions, whether hardware- or software-based, do not prevent a malicious user from simply writing down information from the screen and passing it on to others.

TPM AND ROOTKITS

Although there are a variety of rootkit detection and removal tools available, these require continual vigilance by the user, running the detector frequently, adding it to scheduled tasks, etc. The TCG has devoted resources to the development of standards that provide significant protection against rootkits.

As explained above, when the PC boots, the TPM measures the BIOS, the boot loader, any critical applications within the operating system, critical hardware devices, etc. Since these measurements were made at the time of manufacture at a trusted location (the point of origin of the PC) and stored within secure, immutable memory within the TPM, any changes to the signatures are immediately detected. The system is flagged as not trustworthy, and the user is so notified. The recommendation is that the PC be repaired.

COMPLICATIONS INTRODUCED BY TPM

As explained above, the most effective TPM is one which has been bound to the specific hardware and software configuration that was present at the time it was initialized. The owner subsequently assumed responsibility for the TPM. Keys, software hash codes, and user permissions were bound to the original platform configuration. Hardware devices fail, and depending on which device has failed, there may be complications introduced by the presence of the TPM system. Similar issues arise with hardware upgrades. In the event of hard-drive failure or corruption of files, the user may have no choice but to remove and replace the hard drive or otherwise replace critical files with restored files. This most likely will require the owner to perform individual backup and restore operations though the TPM, effecting a manual migration to the new configuration. This can be time-consuming and may present an opportunity for errors or oversights.

The motherboard itself might fail. There must be a migration path of data from one TPM to another, although it should be a requirement that the source and target motherboards be the same model and manufacturer. This will likely require an approval step by the manufacturer. Cryptographic keys that were used to encrypt files on the (failed) hard drive will have to be migrated to the new drive, along with the images of the encrypted files. This will require authorization of migration by the owner and subsequent acceptance of migration by the user (who may or may not be the same person). Migration to a new PC for upgrade purposes similarly will require that the owner authorize the migration. In the case of a single platform with multiple users, each user will subsequently have to consent to the migration individually. This introduces an administrative burden that can be minimized by a carefully architected TPM application interface, but even such an interface will not eliminate the approval stage.

RESIDUAL VULNERABILITIES

The introduction of TPM technology onto the motherboard of a platform raises the degree of protection and trust that can be ascribed to the system. Nonetheless, there remain some obvious paths of attack that are not addressed by TPM. Access to the frame buffer that drives the user's display is an attack avenue that is not addressed by the TPM. In this attack, the attacker accesses the video memory buffer and captures screen shots of the user's work. Memory can often be accessed in unprotected systems through the use of DMA commands or buffer overflows. Proper secure memory management will protect against this type of attack.

Key-capture routines are not detected or eliminated by TPM. TPM currently employs SHA-1 in creating nonreversible hash-code summaries of software modules and other information it wishes to authenticate at a later date. Unfortunately, as explained in earlier chapters, SHA-1 was recently broken by hackers. This raises immediate concerns about the strength of TPM against attacks. The use of SHA-1 by TPM should be replaced as soon as possible by a stronger hash algorithm (such as secure hash algorithm 256, or SHA 256), which has been certified by the National Security Agency.

PRIVACY AND DIGITAL RIGHTS MANAGEMENT

To the extent that a TPM implementation includes the protection of user's digital-rights-management ("DRM") keys, it is appropriate to review the issues surrounding this controversial topic. The protection of a user's privacy, creating a trusted platform, and limiting a user's access to information have created some emotionally charged debates in recent years. Security and privacy are often interpreted as attempts to address the same thing. For clarity, throughout this book, the term "security" means the protection of information assets through the use of technology. "Privacy" means a user's right to be able to choose when personal data is collected, used, or shared. Clearly one must employ security to achieve privacy, but the desire of a user to protect his privacy using security does not give other parties the right to collect, use, or share that user's private information without his consent.

One problem that has enjoyed a great deal of scrutiny is the theft and distribution of copyrighted material that is owned by a content creator (a music label or motion-picture company, for example). In addition to the music and motion-picture industries, the theft of software is not far behind on the list of providers concerned about such theft. In response to this problem, these industries have created digital-rights-management (DRM) technology, which seeks to control the ability of users to make or otherwise distribute copies of music, movies, and software. Although effective, DRM is viewed by some users as awkward and limiting and by others as an invasion of their privacy. In the music field, for example, users have been long accustomed to being able to purchase (for example) a record album and then make copies of specific songs (or the entire album) onto other media, such as audio tapes or MP3 players.

Some users feel that once they have purchased the album, they are free to copy it as they choose, In effect, these users feel that, once purchased, the album becomes personal data.

The digital world introduces a new twist to this concept, however. In the case of a record album, the users are purchasing a reasonable copy of the original music (which was mixed and recorded onto master tapes from which the albums are subsequently "cut"), The rendering of the music onto an album suffers some alteration of the spectral content of the audio tracks. Records are not an exact duplicate of the original recording. If the studios create digitized copies that are then burned onto compact disks, these copies are as close to a true replication of the original music as possible (limited perhaps by the conversion of analog tape tracks to digital format). If the original recordings are captured digitally and recorded in digital form, the subsequent copies are likely to be an even closer approximation of the original content.

Digital copies subsequently burned onto CDs do not lose any of the integrity offered by the original CD, unless compression technology was employed to reduce the storage space required per track (as is the case with MP3 files, which employ compression at the expense of fidelity). The propagation of these copies is largely viewed by the music industry as lost revenue; it asserts that all of the illegal copies would have been purchased had proper DRM technology been implemented. Others argue that these illegal copies were obtained due to their low or nonexistent cost. Had these same people been required to purchase legitimate copies, it is argued, these users would likely not have purchased the content at all. The true lost revenue lies somewhere between these two extremes. DRM introduces encryption keys and certificates that can be bound to specific platforms or players, and copies can be limited to that platform only. DRM usually includes a migration path so that users can enjoy their music on other platforms, but the migration disables the music on the previous platform. In the most common implementation, only one platform can play DRM-protected content at any given time. DRM-protected music was initially widely used by the music industry, but complaints by users regarding the awkward restrictions caused a gradual withdrawal from its use. Online purchases of MP3 music files were estimated at somewhere between 10 and 20 percent of all music sales revenue in 2007, so the music industry tends to be responsive to customer demands regarding the use of DRM in the purchased files. The motion-picture industry has also introduced DRM technology to limit copying of digital movies to backup versions only. Microsoft has introduced a form of DRM into document control, allowing the creator to control the ability of others to print or forward the file to others.

Another issue that is often voiced with respect to DRM is the user's privacy. Some groups argue that the purchase of music or movie content should remain anonymous, protecting the user's privacy. User groups often voice concerns about the invasion of privacy regarding DRM implementations that employ information about the user. There are fears that the migration process is equivalent to a tracking system that records what platforms are being used by which users for specific content. Finally, there is a concern amongst some users that the owners of software applications could conceivably track a user's migration of purchased software as it is moved from one platform to another. Some users assert that information and content (such as software) should not be protected from their legitimate owners. Rather, it is felt that the legitimate owners should have full control over their purchased content. The issues surrounding control and privacy often get mixed with the trust and privacy issues that are being addressed by TPM. As a result, some users are reluctant to employ the technology for fear that the originating organization might track or otherwise seek to control access of users of their products. This fear has fostered a mistrust of any technology that touches user privacy.

The use of hardware-based system authentication and verification on booting of a platform by the TPM technology is a solid step forward towards the development of systems that are secure against hacking and theft of sensitive information. By moving the functionality of TPM to the root level during the boot process and employing careful practices to initialize such systems with trusted software, firmware, and hardware, TPM will likely provide a solid foundation upon which other hardware-based security technologies can be built. Issues and concerns remain that need to be addressed. At this time, there is nothing to assure a user that the TPM system will allow him to run applications produced by a competitor of the system's manufacturer. Content providers could, in principle, examine the elements reported within the attestation and refuse service or content to users who are running competitive applications or parallel operating systems. Manufacturers or software providers could conceivably use the remote attestation to require the user to pay some charge in order to enable the operation of such competing software. Such fees could be asked of the application developers themselves in order to allow their applications to run on the systems.

TPM's strong, hardware-based protection of secrets could act as a double-edged sword, preventing users and bonafide government agencies alike from verifying what is actually occurring within the TPM validation process. How would a user truly know that the TPM is actually checking and not simply returning a conclusion that the system should be trusted? How can users convince themselves that there are no back doors in the code or the TPM itself? How will users be able to exercise their rights to fair use of legally purchased DRM-protected content? Will migration paths be provided for the originals and the legal copies? On the sensitive matter of user privacy, a user's privacy is best protected by introducing and employing carefully conceived and tested hardware-based security technologies. Programmers must be careful to consider user privacy during the development of these applications. Such applications should protect user content and allow ease of use by rightful owners, preferably without resorting to tracking of user activities. The determination of a user's identity through hardware security technologies (as opposed to software-only applications) should be sufficiently unique that the user will be confident that spoofing cannot occur. Legal recourse can be added to complement but not replace properly implemented hardware security technologies. The use of independent, nonprofit monitoring and enforcement organizations should be considered as a means to defuse the user community's concerns that the technology only serves to protect the creators of software. Finally, the user should be notified of the intent to share or transmit his personal information, and his approval must be granted before such sharing can occur.

SUMMARY

This chapter introduced the notion of Trusted Computing by adding Security of the hardware and software of a computer system. The use of a Trusted Platform Module was discussed to secure the devices of a computer System.

REFERENCES

Arbaugh, W. A., Farber, D. J., & Smith, J. M. (1997). A secure and reliable bootstrap architecture. *Proceedings of the 1997 IEEE Symposium on Security and Privacy* (pp. 65-71).

Dube, R. (2008). *Hardware-based Computer Security Techniques to Defeat Hackers, From Biometrics to Quantum Cryptography*. John Wiley & Sons. doi:10.1002/9780470425497

The Trusted Computing Group. (2003, October). TPM Main: Part 1 Design Principles. Retrieved from https://trustedcomputinggroup.org/wp-content/uploads/TPM-Main-Part-1-Design-Principles_v1.2_rev116_01032011.pdf

The Trusted Computing Group. (n. d.) Retrieved from: http://www.trustedcomputinggroup.org

KEY TERMS AND DEFINITIONS

Botnets: The Botnet is a malicious program planted on a computer that allows a hacker to remotely control a computer to perform certain functions.

Buffer Overflow Attacks: A buffer overflow attack occurs when software attempts to store data beyond the boundaries assigned to the buffer.

Memory Pointer Attacks: Memory pointer attacks can be used by an attacker to redirect execution to malicious code.

Rootkits: A type of malicious software that allows the user to get root or administrator privileges and once the root privileges are obtained, they can hide the intrusion and privileged access.

Secure Bootstrapping: The security of bootstrap process is validated with use of digital signatures that were created in a trusted environment.

Trusted Computing: The trusted Computing concept aims to protect the hardware by enforcing specific behaviors and protects the system against unauthorized changes and attacks such as malware and rootkits.

Trusted Execution: Trusted Execution is a hardware-based security system which includes attestation, process isolation, tamper-resistant storage of core secrets and secure I/O paths.

Trusted Platform Module: The TPM is an international Standard for a secure coprocessor which is a dedicated microcontroller designed to secure hardware by integrating cryptographic keys into it.

Chapter 15
Experiments with the Cryptool Software

Kannan Balasubramanian
Mepco Schlenk Engineering College, India

ABSTRACT

Researchers have developed many different types of software for implementing Cryptography algorithms. One such software is Cryptool. This software can be used to demonstrate many Classical Cryptosystems and symmetric-Key Cryptosystems like DES and AES. This software can be used to demonstrate Public Key Cryptosystems like RSA and ECC as well as many hash algorithms like MD5, SHA-1, SHA-256, and SHA-512. The usage of the algorithms and sample input and outputs obtained from the software are included for the beginners and learners to the area of Cryptography.

INTRODUCTION

The Cryptool (www.cryptool.org) is a software for learning and understanding Cryptographic algorithms. The Cryptool comes in two versions: Cryptool1 and Cryptool2 which are very different although both are meant for introducing Cryptography algorithms for beginners. There is also a Java version which is available for users. The Online Version of Cryptool (www.cryptool-online.org) is useful for Beginners. The algorithms that can be learnt from Cryptool are discussed in this paper. The mysterytwisterc3 web page (www.mysterytwisterc3.org) lists a number of cryptography challenges for the learners.

CRYPTOOL 1

The Cryptool 1 software supports Cryptography algorithms under the following major headings:

1. Encrypt/Decrypt
2. Digital Signatures/PKI
3. Individual Procedures
4. Analysis

DOI: 10.4018/978-1-5225-2915-6.ch015

The algorithms in each of the above classes are discussed below:

Encrypt/Decrypt: Under this category, four different groups of algorithms are presented: Symmetric(classic), Symmetric(Modern), Asymmetric and Hybrid. The Classical symmetrical algorithms supported are: Caesar/Rot-13, Vegenere, Hill, Substitution/Atbash, Playfair, ADFGVX, Byte Addition, XOR, Vernam/OTP, Homophone, Permutation/Transposition, Solitaire, Scytale/Rail Fence.

The inputs to the above algorithms and the output from the Classical Symmetrical algorithms are presented below:

Caesar/Rot-13:
Input: ABCDEFGHIJKLMNOPQRSTUVWXYZ
Key: 3
Output: DEFGHIJKLMNOPQRSTUVWXYZABC (for Caesar)
NOPQRSTUVWXYZABCDEFGHIJKLM (for Rot-13, No Key is Required)
Vegenere:
Input: ABCDEFGHIJKLMNOPQRSTUVWXYZ
Key: ABCDEFGHIJKLMNOPQRSTUVWXYZ
Output: ACEGIKMOQSUWYACEGIKMOQSUWY
Hill:
Input: ABCDEFGHIJKLMNOPQRSTUVWXYZ

Key: $\begin{pmatrix} G & T \\ B & Q \end{pmatrix}$

Output: KUCOUIMCEWWQOKGEYYQSIMAGSA
Substitution:
Input: SUBSTITUTION
Key: KEY
Output: RTERSGSTSGNM
Atbash:
Input: ABCDEFGHIJKLMNOPQRSTUVWXYZ
Output: ZYXWVUTSRQPONMLKJIHGFEDCBA
Playfair:
Input: AB CD EF GH IX IK LM NO PQ RS TU VW XY ZX
Output: BC DE AK HI HY KF MN OP LU ST UQ WX YZ VY
ADFGVX:
Input: ABCDEFGHIJKLMNOPQRSTUVWXYZ
Password: PASSWORD
Output: AVFAVFAGDXGDXFAVFAVAADFFGVADDFGGAADFFGVDXGDXGDADDFGG
Vernam/OTP:
Input: ONETIMEPAD
Key: ABCDEFGHIJKLMNOPQRSTUVWXYZ
Output: 0E 0C 06 10 0C 0B 02 18 08 0E (in Hexadecimal format)
Homophone:
Input: ABCDEFGHIJKLMNOPQRSTUVWXYZ
Key: random key

Output: 98 A8 67 EB DA 4B 91 2B 96 C7 5F 13 46 D6 2A E7 08 BD F4 1F 0F B3 CD 8F 21 E1 (in hexadecimal Format)

Permutation/Transposition:

Input: ABCDEFGHIJKLMNOPQRSTUVWXYZ

KEY: Key

Output: JKLMNOPQRABCDEFGHISTUVWXYZ

Solitaire:

Input: ABCDEFGHIJKLMNOPQRSTUVWXYZ

Keystream: 4,49,10,24,8,51,44,6,4,33,20,39,19,34,42,21,21,18,24,36,52,51,49,25,8,3

Output: EYMBM EYNMQ EYFVE KLJQD UUTWG C

Scytale/Rail Fence:

Input: ABCDEFGHIJKLMNOPQRSTUVWXYZ

Key: 2

Output: EVYEM KBLMJ EQYDN UMUQT EWYGF C (Scytale)

EYMBM EYNMQ EYFVE KLJQD UUTWG C (Rail Fence)

The Modern Symmetrical algorithms presented are: IDEA, RC2,RC4, DES(ECB), DES(CBC), Triple-DES(ECB),Triple-DES(CBC),Rijndael(AES),MARS,RC6,Serpent,TwoFish, DESX, DESL, DESXL and AES (Self-extracting). The Inputs to and the outputs from these algorithms are given below:

IDEA:

Input: Cryptool

Key: 11 22 33 44 55 66 77 99 11 22 33 44 55 66 77 88 (128 Bits)

Output: 9C AF FC 90 C9 E8 4F B5 0B 73 70 87 43 81 D0 7D

RC2:

Input: Cryptool

Key: 1A (8 bits)

Output: 7D AA 21 9C 15 6A 92 40 51 35 1A 2E 8D B2 73 D7

RC4:

Input: 123456

Key: 1A

Output: D0 DD F7 66 A0 10 ED 3D

DES(ECB):

Input:011010001

Key: 11 22 33 44 55 66 77 88 (64 bits, effectively 56 bits)

Output: 56 BE 29 A6 60 45 CA B8 CB F6 AE 6B 34 72 1D F2

DES(CBC):

Input: 011010001

Key: 11 22 33 44 55 66 77 88 (64 bits, effectively 56 bits)

Output: 56 BE 29 A6 60 45 CA B8 1B EE BE F1 DC D1 A4 36

Triple-DES(ECB):

Input: 011010001

Key: 11 22 33 44 55 66 77 88 99 11 22 33 44 55 66 77 (128 bits, effectively 112 bits)

Output: 79 8C CA 19 83 CC B0 48 6F 80 C7 D9 A2 B8 91 45

Triple-DES (CBC):
Input: 011010001
Key: 11 22 33 44 55 66 77 88 99 11 22 33 44 55 66 77 (128 bits, effectively 112 bits)
Output: 79 8C CA 19 83 CC B0 48 D5 24 C6 63 AA 8C A3 82
Rijndael (AES)
Input: 011010001
Key: 11 22 33 44 55 66 77 88 99 11 22 33 44 55 66 77
Output: 04 A8 E9 F0 AC 40 EA 97 25 95 05 D5 9B FC 7A 92

The Cryptool also provides commands for performing Digital signatures, Hash value generation using MD2, MD4, MD5, SHA, SHA-1, SHA-256, SHA-512 RIPEMD-160 algorithms and Demonstration of RSA Cryptosystem. For more details on the algorithms supported, please refer to (http://vanilla47. com/PDFs/Cryptography/Cryptoanalysis/CRYPTOLOGY_WITH_CRYPTOOL.pdf) where examples for the following are provided.

1. Encryption with RSA / Prime number tests / Hybrid encryption and digital certificates / SSL
2. Digital signature visualized
3. Attack on RSA encryption (small modulus N)
4. Analysis of encryption in PSION 5
5. Weak DES keys
6. Locating key material ("NSA key")
7. Attack on digital signature through hash collision search
8. Authentication in a client-server environment
9. Demonstration of a side-channel attack (on hybrid encryption protocol)
10. Attack on RSA using lattice reduction
11. Random analysis with 3-D visualization
12. Secret Sharing using the Chinese Remainder Theorem (CRT) and Shamir
13. Implementation of CRT in astronomy (solving systems of linear modular equations)
14. Visualization of symmetric encryption methods using ANIMAL
15. Visualizations of AES
16. Visualization of Enigma encryption
17. Visualization of Secure Email with S/MIME
18. Generation of a message authentication code (HMAC)
19. Hash demonstration
20. Educational tool for number theory and asymmetric encryption
21. Point addition on elliptic curves
22. Password quality meter (PQM) and password entropy
23. Brute force analysis
24. Scytale / Rail Fence
25. Hill encryption / Hill analysis
26. CrypTool online help / Menu tree of the program

The Cryptool 2 provides the following additional features:

- Comprehensive visualization on the topic of prime numbers
- GNFS (General number field sieve)
- Encryption and automated cryptanalysis of the Enigma machine (and possibly of Sigaba as well)
- Cube attack (I. Dinur and A. Shamir: "Cube Attacks on Tweakable Black Box Polynomials", 2008)
- Demonstration of Bleichenbacher's and Kuehn's RSA signature forgery
- Demonstration of virtual credit card numbers (as an educational tool against credit card abuse)
- WEP encryption and WEP analysis
- Mass pattern search
- Framework for distributed cryptanalysis
- Demonstration of SOA security (SOAP messages with WS-Security)
- Framework to create and analyze LFSR stream ciphers

DIFFIE-HELLMAN DEMONSTRATION

An example demonstration of the Diffie-Hellman Key Exchange protocol using Cryptool 1 is shown below:

Prime module p: 164459422689066624301172996805743844245560635639783704470073336199 1165383163799

Generator g: 153403059147030478498401777935904837680388691336381731679529925197362735476062

Alice's Secret Key: 551486549656166387047447927534748872866689140412659099827107889 48131730336318

Alice's Public Key: 128692569121742575345074563003669402745617398629635402008872777 857244648699493

Bob's Secret Key: 237846997079934938728652553870751337045394789062684412619133580 7580431859921

Bob's Public Key: 145602284636130097651880749308999887901331283947669389418131294229575595022888

Alice's Shared Key: 242952302750278304536593038867925011192652574394458301363791427 0952483432437

Bob's Shared Key: 242952302750278304536593038867925011192652574394458301363791427 0952483432437

RSA DEMONSTRATION

An example demonstration of RSA Cryptosystem is given below:

- **Prime Number p:** 382827809005832557
- **Prime Number q:** 1040092401029253827
- **RSA Modulus N:** 398176295049644985709545024613445639
- **Phi(N)=(p-1)(q-1):** 398176295049644984286624814578359256
- **Public key e:** 2^16+1

- **Private key *d*:** 32559115692983314323085011235262939 3
- **Message to be Encrypted:** security
- **Message in base 10 format:** 234050992983447108487388101975248 0
- **Encrypted message:** 1477911470124797400213199001069408 59

HASH FUNCTIONS

The following examples demonstrates the use of hash functions MD2, MD4, MD5, SHA, SHA-1, SHA-256, SHA-512, RIPEMD-160 using the Cryptool Software:

MD2:
Input: Cryptool
Hash Output: 1C 5F 74 F8 70 AC E9 86 5E 1C 31 AE 2A 62 D8 89
MD4:
Input: Cryptool
Hash Output: 45 31 66 39 64 39 A4 62 B1 BA AC 04 70 42 32 12
MD5:
Input: Cryptool
Hash Output: C3 79 C3 84 FD C0 22 85 B1 E5 BA ED 5D EF 29 AF
SHA:
Input: Cryptool
Hash Output: 51 29 44 8E 72 F4 F8 4E D7 A5 66 46 61 F9 2E AE 5F DF 07 CE
SHA-1:
Input: Cryptool
Hash Output: 0B 35 DC 41 55 58 F3 0F CB 53 DC 5C AD F4 C9 06 4E 10 35 FE
SHA-256:
Input: Cryptool
Hash Output: 98 71 BC 92 E5 7C 34 18 43 17 49 AD 00 DF 5C 08 A9 8B 13 5E 04 E1 02 5D 4F FF
60 BF 00 CD 9C 12
SHA-512:
Input: Cryptool
Hash Output: E0 8E 82 F8 2D C9 9A 8A 4F 0F 9A FE 1B 04 8C 55 DD D2 82 BA D5 30 00 2C 5F EF
87 76 D9 AD 2D 68 20 91 1B 53 4B 13 2D 67 53 17 8D E1 D9 1D E3 DA C1 C7 38 D1 58 6D
2A 25 44 C5 73 CD 71 0D B1 84
RIPEMD-160:
Input: Cryptool
Hash Output: 76 8E 3F 64 26 67 AD 31 B4 3E A8 71 B2 E0 E0 8B CA A9 EE D1

CRYPTANALYSIS

The following input was analysed for the various frequency analysis tests:
   File: startingexample-en.txt

CrypTool (Starting example for the CrypTool version family 1.x)

CrypTool is a comprehensive free educational program about cryptography and cryptanalysis offering extensive online help and many visualizations.

This is a text file, created in order to help you to make your first steps with CrypTool.

1. *As a first step, it is recommended you read the included online help, this will provide a useful oversight of all available functions within this application. The starting page of the online help can be accessed via the menu "Help -> Starting Page" at the top right of the screen or using the search keyword "Starting page" within the index of the online help.*

    Press F1 to start the online help everywhere in CrypTool.

Table 1. Histogram Analysis of <startingexample-en>. File size 1619 bytes. (Descending sorted on frequency)

No.	Substring	Frequency (in %)	Frequency
1	E	13.0120	162
2	T	9.1566	114
3	I	7.4699	93
4	A	7.1486	89
5	N	7.1486	89
6	O	7.1486	89
7	R	5.7831	72
8	S	5.3012	66
9	L	5.1406	64
10	H	4.9799	62
11	P	4.2570	53
12	C	3.4538	43
13	D	2.8916	36
14	U	2.8112	35
15	Y	2.6506	33
16	G	2.4096	30
17	F	2.1687	27
18	M	2.0884	26
19	V	1.6064	20
20	W	1.5261	19
21	B	0.8032	10
22	X	0.6426	8
23	K	0.2410	3
24	J	0.0803	1
25	Z	0.0803	1

2. *A possible next step would be to encrypt a file with the Caesar algorithm. This can be done via the menu "Crypt/Decrypt -> Symmetric (Classic)".*

3. *There are several examples (tutorials) provided within the online help which provide an easy way to gain an understanding of cryptology. These examples can be found via the menu "Help -> Scenarios (Tutorials)".*

4. *You can also develop your knowledge by:*
   a. *Navigating through the menus. You can press F1 at any selected menu item to get further information.*
   b. *Reading the included Readme file (see the menu "Help -> Readme").*
   c. *Viewing the included colorful presentation (This presentation can be found on several ways: e.g. in the "Help" menu of this application, or via the "Documentation" section found at the "Starting" page of the online help).*
   d. *Viewing the webpage www.cryptool.org.*

Table 2. Diagram Analysis of <startingexample-en>. File size 1619 bytes (Descending sorted on frequency)

No.	Substring	Frequency (in %)	Frequency
1	HE	4.2424	42
2	TH	4.1414	41
3	IN	3.1313	31
4	ON	2.0202	20
5	TO	1.8182	18
6	EN	1.6162	16
7	RE	1.6162	16
8	TI	1.6162	16
9	CR	1.5152	15
10	AN	1.4141	14
11	EL	1.4141	14
12	RY	1.4141	14
13	AT	1.3131	13
14	PT	1.3131	13
15	YP	1.3131	13
16	DE	1.2121	12
17	IO	1.2121	12
18	LP	1.2121	12
19	ME	1.2121	12
20	NG	1.2121	12
21	OU	1.2121	12
22	ST	1.2121	12
23	ER	1.1111	11
24	IS	1.1111	11
25	OR	1.1111	11

July 2010
The CrypTool team
The results of various frequency tests are given in the tables.
The Histogram analysis of the above text is given in Table 1.
Diagram Analysis of the input text (Table 2).

SUMMARY

The Cryptool provides a very easy to use interface and various functions including cryptanalysis of classical and modern encryption algorithms.

REFERENCES

Buchmann, J. (2004). *Introduction to Cryptography* (2nd ed.). Springer. doi:10.1007/978-1-4419-9003-7

Joux, A. (2009). *Algorithmic Cryptanalysis*. Chapman/Hall &CRC. doi:10.1201/9781420070033

Menezes, A. J., van Oorschot, P. C., & Vanstone, S. A. (1999). *Handbook of Applied Cryptography*. CRC Press.

Singh, S. (1999). *The Codebook*. DoubleDay.

KEY TERMS AND DEFINITIONS

Ciphertext: The output from an encryption algorithm using English Language characters or in binary form.

Classical Encryption: Techniques whereby English Language Plaintexts are converted to ciphertexts.

Cryptanalysis: The process of guessing the key used in an encryption algorithm or the plaintext used in the encryption.

Digital Signature: The encryption of the hash of a message using signer's private key.

Hash Algorithms: The Hash algorithms convert their binary input to a fixed size hash output.

Modern Encryption: Techniques which take binary input and convert them to a binary ciphertext.

Plaintext: The input to an encryption algorithm in plain English or in binary form.

Chapter 16
A Software Library for Multi Precision Arithmetic

Kannan Balasubramanian
Mepco Schlenk Engineering College, India

Ahmed Mahmoud Abbas
The American University in Cairo, Egypt

ABSTRACT

The most prevalent need for multiple precision arithmetic, often referred to as "bignum" math, is within the implementation of public key cryptography algorithms. Algorithms such as RSA and Diffie-Hellman require integers of significant magnitude to resist known cryptanalytic attacks. As of now, a typical RSA modulus would be at least greater than 10^309. However, modern programming languages such as ISO C and Java only provide intrinsic support for integers that are relatively small and single precision. This chapter describe the modules provided by one such library for the C Programming Language.

INTRODUCTION

The use of Public Key Algorithms like RSA require use of arbitrarily long numbers and arithmetic on those numbers. The existing programming languages cannot easily support the numbers handled by these algorithms. There are many tools for doing Multiple Precision arithmetic. This chapter discusses the use of one such tool called the 'bignum' math library. This library of routines can be easily integrated with any C program and the routines can be used to perform multiple precision arithmetic.

ARIHEMTIC ON BIG INTEGERS

The most prevalent need for multiple precision arithmetic, often referred to as "bignum" math, is within the implementation of public key cryptography algorithms. Algorithms such as RSA (Rivest et al,1978) and Diffie-Hellman (1976) require integers of significant magnitude to resist known cryptanalytic attacks. For example, at the time of this writing a typical RSA modulus would be at least greater than

DOI: 10.4018/978-1-5225-2915-6.ch016

10^{309}. However, modern programming languages such as ISO C (ISO/IEC 9899:1999) and Java (http://java.sun.com) only provide intrinsic support for integers that are relatively small and single precision.

The largest data type guaranteed to be provided by the ISO C programming language can only represent values up to 10^{19}. On its own, the C language is insufficient to accommodate the magnitude required for the problem at hand. An RSA modulus of magnitude 10^{19} could be trivially factored on the average desktop computer, rendering any protocol based on the algorithm insecure. Multiple precision algorithms solve this problem by extending the range of representable integers while using single precision data types.

Most advancements in fast multiple precision arithmetic stem from the need for faster and more efficient cryptographic primitives. Faster modular reduction and exponentiation algorithms such as Barrett's reduction algorithm, can render algorithms such as RSA and Diffie-Hellman more efficient. In fact, several major companies such as RSA Security, Certicom, and Entrust have built entire product lines on the implementation and deployment of efficient algorithms.

The benefit of multiple precision representations over single or fixed precision representations is that no precision is lost while representing the result of an operation that requires excess precision. For example, the product of two n-bit integers requires at least $2n$ bits of precision to be represented faithfully. A multiple precision algorithm would augment the precision of the destination to accommodate the result, while a single precision system would truncate excess bits to maintain a fixed level of precision.

A PACKAGE FOR MULTIPLE PRECISION ARITHMETIC

A package for using multiple Precision Arithmetic called the LibTomMath (Denis, 2006) that can be used with C programs is described. Appendix A (http://www.opensource.apple.com/source/Heimdal/Heimdal-247.7/lib/hcrypto/libtommath/tommath.h)lists all the function calls that can be made using this library. A multiple precision integer of n-digits shall be denoted as $x = (x_{n-1}, \ldots x_1, x_0) \beta$ and represents the integer $x \equiv \sum_{i=0}^{n-1} x_i \beta^i$. The term "mp_int" shall refer to a composite structure that contains the digits of the integer it represents, and auxiliary data required to manipulate the data., It is assumed that a "multiple precision integer" and an "mp_int" are assumed synonymous. The structure of mp_int is used in the LibTomMath package is given below:

```
typedef struct {
int used,alloc, sign;
mp_digit *dp;
}mp_init;
```

- The *used* parameter denotes how many digits of the array *dp* contain the digits used to represent a given integer. The *used* count must be positive (or zero) and may not exceed the *alloc* count.
- The *alloc* parameter denotes how many digits are available in the array to use by functions before it has to increase in size. When the *used* count of a result exceeds the *alloc* count, all the algorithms will automatically increase the size of the array to accommodate the precision of the result.

- The pointer *dp* points to a dynamically allocated array of digits that represent the given multiple precision integer. It is padded with (*alloc* − *used*) zero digits. The array is maintained in a least significant digit order. For example, if *dp* contains {a, b, c, . . .} where dp_0 = a, dp_1 = b, dp_2 = c,… then it would represent the integer a + bβ + cβ² + .
- The *sign* parameter denotes the sign as either zero/positive (MP_ZPOS) or negative (MP_NEG).

Several rules are placed on the state of an mp_int structure and are assumed to be followed for reasons of efficiency. The only exceptions are when the structure is passed to initialization functions such as mp_init() and mp_init_copy().

- The value of *alloc* may not be less than one. That is, *dp* always points to a previously allocated array of digits.
- The value of *used* may not exceed *alloc* and must be greater than or equal to zero.
- The value of *used* implies the digit at index (*used* − 1) of the *dp* array is non-zero. That is, leading zero digits in the most significant positions must be trimmed.
- Digits in the *dp* array at and above the *used* location must be zero.
- The value of *sign* must be MP_ZPOS if *used* is zero; this represents the mp_int value of zero.

Appendix B lists a demo program (http://www.opensource.apple.com/source/Heimdal/Heimdal-247.7/lib/hcrypto/libtommath/demo/demo.c) that illustrates how the function calls in this package can be used.

THE BIGINTEGER CLASS IN JAVA

The BigInteger Class in Java which is part of the java.math package can be used to represent arbitralily long integers. Appendix C (http://www.java2s.com/Code/Java/Security/SimpleRSApublickeyencryption-algorithmimplementation.htm) lists an RSA implementation using the BigInteger class in java.

OTHER IMPLEMENTATIONS

A javascript library provided in (http://ats.oka.nu/titaniumcore/js/crypto/readme.txt) can be used for cryptographic algorithms. Another javascript library aimed at using large numbers is provided in (http://www-cs-students.stanford.edu/~tjw/jsbn/).

SUMMARY

This chapter examined the Bignum math library for performing arithmetic using arbitrarily long integers. The appendices contain information about how to use this library and provides an example program for using these routines.

REFERENCES

Denis, T. S., & Rose, G. (2006). *BigNum Math Implementing Cryptographic Multiple Precision Arithmetic*. Syngress.

Diffie, W., & Hellman, M. E. (1976). New Directions in Cryptography. *IEEE Transactions on Information Theory, 22(6),* 29–40.

Rivest, R. L., Shamir, A., & Adleman, L. (1978). A method for obtaining Digital Signatures and Public-Key Cryptosystems. *Communications of the ACM, 12*(2), 120–126. doi:10.1145/359340.359342

KEY TERMS AND DEFINITIONS

Fixed Precision Arithmetic: Arithmetic that uses only fixed precision (e.g., certain number of decimal digits). The Programming Languages that support fixed Precision arithmetic cannot support arbitrarily long integers.

Modular Reduction and Exponentiation: The modular reduction and exponentiation algorithms are important in the implementation of cryptographic algorithms. For example, the RSA algorithm uses a very large integer as its modulus which is a product of two large prime numbers.

Multiple Precision Arithmetic: Arithmetic that involves arbitrarily long integers. Most Programming Languages have limitations regarding the size of the integers that can be used in the calculation.

APPENDIX A

Multiple Precision Arithmetic

```
The to mmath.h header file defining the functions that can be called from
LibTomMath #ifndef BN_H_ #define BN_H_ #include <stdio.h> #include <string.h>
#include <stdlib.h> #include <ctype.h> #include <limits.h>
#include <tommath_class.h>
#ifndef MIN
   #define MIN(x,y) ((x)<(y)?(x):(y))
#endif
#ifndef MAX
   #define MAX(x,y) ((x)>(y)?(x):(y))
#endif
#ifdef __cplusplus
extern "C" {
/* C++ compilers don't like assigning void * to mp_digit * */
#define  OPT_CAST(x)  (x *)
#else
/* C on the other hand doesn't care */
#define  OPT_CAST(x)
#endif
/* detect 64-bit mode if possible */
#if defined(__x86_64__)
   #if !(defined(MP_64BIT) && defined(MP_16BIT) && defined(MP_8BIT))
      #define MP_64BIT
   #endif
#endif
/* some default configurations.
 *
 * A "mp_digit" must be able to hold DIGIT_BIT + 1 bits
 * A "mp_word" must be able to hold 2*DIGIT_BIT + 1 bits
 *
 * At the very least a mp_digit must be able to hold 7 bits
 * [any size beyond that is ok provided it doesn't overflow the data type]
 */
#ifdef MP_8BIT
   typedef unsigned char      mp_digit;
   typedef unsigned short     mp_word;
#elif defined(MP_16BIT)
   typedef unsigned short     mp_digit;
   typedef unsigned long      mp_word;
#elif defined(MP_64BIT)
```

```
   /* for GCC only on supported platforms */
#ifndef CRYPT
   typedef unsigned long long ulong64;
   typedef signed long long   long64;
#endif
   typedef unsigned long      mp_digit;
   typedef unsigned long      mp_word __attribute__ ((mode(TI)));
   #define DIGIT_BIT          60
#else
   /* this is the default case, 28-bit digits */
   /* this is to make porting into LibTomCrypt easier:-) */
#ifndef CRYPT
   #if defined(_MSC_VER) || defined(__BORLANDC__)
      typedef unsigned __int64   ulong64;
      typedef signed __int64     long64;
   #else
      typedef unsigned long long ulong64;
      typedef signed long long   long64;
   #endif
#endif
   typedef unsigned long      mp_digit;
   typedef ulong64            mp_word;
#ifdef MP_31BIT
   /* this is an extension that uses 31-bit digits */
   #define DIGIT_BIT          31
#else
   /* default case is 28-bit digits, defines MP_28BIT as a handy macro to test
*/
   #define DIGIT_BIT          28
   #define MP_28BIT
#endif
#endif
/* define heap macros */
#ifndef CRYPT
   /* default to libc stuff */
   #ifndef XMALLOC
      #define XMALLOC  malloc
      #define XFREE    free
      #define XREALLOC realloc
      #define XCALLOC  calloc
   #else
      /* prototypes for our heap functions */
      extern void *XMALLOC(size_t n);
```

```
      extern void *XREALLOC(void *p, size_t n);
      extern void *XCALLOC(size_t n, size_t s);
      extern void XFREE(void *p);
   #endif
#endif
/* otherwise the bits per digit is calculated automatically from the size of a
mp_digit */
#ifndef DIGIT_BIT
   #define DIGIT_BIT        ((int)((CHAR_BIT * sizeof(mp_digit) - 1)))  /* bits
per digit */
#endif
#define MP_DIGIT_BIT     DIGIT_BIT
#define MP_MASK          ((((mp_digit)1)<<((mp_digit)DIGIT_BIT))-((mp_dig-
it)1))
#define MP_DIGIT_MAX     MP_MASK
/* equalities */
#define MP_LT          -1   /* less than */
#define MP_EQ           0   /* equal to */
#define MP_GT           1   /* greater than */
#define MP_ZPOS         0   /* positive integer */
#define MP_NEG          1   /* negative */
#define MP_OKAY         0   /* ok result */
#define MP_MEM         -2   /* out of mem */
#define MP_VAL         -3   /* invalid input */
#define MP_RANGE       MP_VAL
#define MP_YES          1   /* yes response */
#define MP_NO           0   /* no response */
/* Primality generation flags */
#define LTM_PRIME_BBS      0x0001 /* BBS style prime */
#define LTM_PRIME_SAFE     0x0002 /* Safe prime (p-1)/2 == prime */
#define LTM_PRIME_2MSB_ON  0x0008 /* force 2nd MSB to 1 */
typedef int            mp_err;
/* you'll have to tune these... */
extern int KARATSUBA_MUL_CUTOFF,
           KARATSUBA_SQR_CUTOFF,
           TOOM_MUL_CUTOFF,
           TOOM_SQR_CUTOFF;
/* define this to use lower memory usage routines (exptmods mostly) */
/* #define MP_LOW_MEM */
/* default precision */
#ifndef MP_PREC
   #ifndef MP_LOW_MEM
      #define MP_PREC                  32      /* default digits of precision */
```

```
   #else
      #define MP_PREC                    8       /* default digits of precision */
   #endif
#endif
/* size of comba arrays, should be at least 2 * 2**(BITS_PER_WORD - BITS_PER_
DIGIT*2) */
#define MP_WARRAY               (1 << (sizeof(mp_word) * CHAR_BIT - 2 * DIGIT_
BIT + 1))
/* the infamous mp_int structure */
typedef struct  {
    int used, alloc, sign;
    mp_digit *dp;
} mp_int;
/* callback for mp_prime_random, should fill dst with random bytes and return
how many read [upto len] */
typedef int ltm_prime_callback(unsigned char *dst, int len, void *dat);
#define USED(m)     ((m)->used)
#define DIGIT(m,k) ((m)->dp[(k)])
#define SIGN(m)     ((m)->sign)
/* error code to char* string */
char *mp_error_to_string(int code);
/* ---> init and deinit bignum functions <--- */
/* init a bignum */
int mp_init(mp_int *a);
/* free a bignum */
void mp_clear(mp_int *a);
/* init a null terminated series of arguments */
int mp_init_multi(mp_int *mp, ...);
/* clear a null terminated series of arguments */
void mp_clear_multi(mp_int *mp, ...);
/* exchange two ints */
void mp_exch(mp_int *a, mp_int *b);
/* shrink ram required for a bignum */
int mp_shrink(mp_int *a);
/* grow an int to a given size */
int mp_grow(mp_int *a, int size);
/* init to a given number of digits */
int mp_init_size(mp_int *a, int size);
/* ---> Basic Manipulations <--- */
#define mp_iszero(a) (((a)->used == 0) ? MP_YES: MP_NO)
#define mp_iseven(a) (((a)->used > 0 && (((a)->dp[0] & 1) == 0)) ? MP_YES:
MP_NO)
#define mp_isodd(a)   (((a)->used > 0 && (((a)->dp[0] & 1) == 1)) ? MP_YES:
```

```
MP_NO)
#define mp_isneg(a)   (((a)->sign) ? MP_YES: MP_NO)
/* set to zero */
void mp_zero(mp_int *a);
/* set to zero, multi */
void mp_zero_multi(mp_int *a, ...);
/* set to a digit */
void mp_set(mp_int *a, mp_digit b);
/* set a 32-bit const */
int mp_set_int(mp_int *a, unsigned long b);
/* get a 32-bit value */
unsigned long mp_get_int(mp_int * a);
/* initialize and set a digit */
int mp_init_set (mp_int * a, mp_digit b);
/* initialize and set 32-bit value */
int mp_init_set_int (mp_int * a, unsigned long b);
/* copy, b = a */
int mp_copy(mp_int *a, mp_int *b);
/* inits and copies, a = b */
int mp_init_copy(mp_int *a, mp_int *b);
/* trim unused digits */
void mp_clamp(mp_int *a);
/* ---> digit manipulation <--- */
/* right shift by "b" digits */
void mp_rshd(mp_int *a, int b);
/* left shift by "b" digits */
int mp_lshd(mp_int *a, int b);
/* c = a / 2**b */
int mp_div_2d(mp_int *a, int b, mp_int *c, mp_int *d);
/* b = a/2 */
int mp_div_2(mp_int *a, mp_int *b);
/* c = a * 2**b */
int mp_mul_2d(mp_int *a, int b, mp_int *c);
/* b = a*2 */
int mp_mul_2(mp_int *a, mp_int *b);
/* c = a mod 2**d */
int mp_mod_2d(mp_int *a, int b, mp_int *c);
/* computes a = 2**b */
int mp_2expt(mp_int *a, int b);
/* Counts the number of lsbs which are zero before the first zero bit */
int mp_cnt_lsb(mp_int *a);
/* I Love Earth! */
/* makes a pseudo-random int of a given size */
```

```
int mp_rand(mp_int *a, int digits);
/* ---> binary operations <--- */
/* c = a XOR b  */
int mp_xor(mp_int *a, mp_int *b, mp_int *c);
/* c = a OR b */
int mp_or(mp_int *a, mp_int *b, mp_int *c);
/* c = a AND b */
int mp_and(mp_int *a, mp_int *b, mp_int *c);
/* ---> Basic arithmetic <--- */
/* b = -a */
int mp_neg(mp_int *a, mp_int *b);
/* b = |a| */
int mp_abs(mp_int *a, mp_int *b);
/* compare a to b */
int mp_cmp(mp_int *a, mp_int *b);
/* compare |a| to |b| */
int mp_cmp_mag(mp_int *a, mp_int *b);
/* c = a + b */
int mp_add(mp_int *a, mp_int *b, mp_int *c);
/* c = a - b */
int mp_sub(mp_int *a, mp_int *b, mp_int *c);
/* c = a * b */
int mp_mul(mp_int *a, mp_int *b, mp_int *c);
/* b = a*a  */
int mp_sqr(mp_int *a, mp_int *b);
/* a/b => cb + d == a */
int mp_div(mp_int *a, mp_int *b, mp_int *c, mp_int *d);
/* c = a mod b, 0 <= c < b  */
int mp_mod(mp_int *a, mp_int *b, mp_int *c);
/* ---> single digit functions <--- */
/* compare against a single digit */
int mp_cmp_d(mp_int *a, mp_digit b);
/* c = a + b */
int mp_add_d(mp_int *a, mp_digit b, mp_int *c);
/* c = a - b */
int mp_sub_d(mp_int *a, mp_digit b, mp_int *c);
/* c = a * b */
int mp_mul_d(mp_int *a, mp_digit b, mp_int *c);
/* a/b => cb + d == a */
int mp_div_d(mp_int *a, mp_digit b, mp_int *c, mp_digit *d);
/* a/3 => 3c + d == a */
int mp_div_3(mp_int *a, mp_int *c, mp_digit *d);
/* c = a**b */
```

```
int mp_expt_d(mp_int *a, mp_digit b, mp_int *c);
/* c = a mod b, 0 <= c < b  */
int mp_mod_d(mp_int *a, mp_digit b, mp_digit *c);
/* ---> number theory <--- */
/* d = a + b (mod c) */
int mp_addmod(mp_int *a, mp_int *b, mp_int *c, mp_int *d);
/* d = a - b (mod c) */
int mp_submod(mp_int *a, mp_int *b, mp_int *c, mp_int *d);
/* d = a * b (mod c) */
int mp_mulmod(mp_int *a, mp_int *b, mp_int *c, mp_int *d);
/* c = a * a (mod b) */
int mp_sqrmod(mp_int *a, mp_int *b, mp_int *c);
/* c = 1/a (mod b) */
int mp_invmod(mp_int *a, mp_int *b, mp_int *c);
/* c = (a, b) */
int mp_gcd(mp_int *a, mp_int *b, mp_int *c);
/* produces value such that U1*a + U2*b = U3 */
int mp_exteuclid(mp_int *a, mp_int *b, mp_int *U1, mp_int *U2, mp_int *U3);
/* c = [a, b] or (a*b)/(a, b) */
int mp_lcm(mp_int *a, mp_int *b, mp_int *c);
/* finds one of the b'th root of a, such that |c|**b <= |a|
 *
 * returns error if a < 0 and b is even
 */
int mp_n_root(mp_int *a, mp_digit b, mp_int *c);
/* special sqrt algo */
int mp_sqrt(mp_int *arg, mp_int *ret);
/* is number a square? */
int mp_is_square(mp_int *arg, int *ret);
/* computes the jacobi c = (a | n) (or Legendre if b is prime)  */
int mp_jacobi(mp_int *a, mp_int *n, int *c);
/* used to setup the Barrett reduction for a given modulus b */
int mp_reduce_setup(mp_int *a, mp_int *b);
/* Barrett Reduction, computes a (mod b) with a precomputed value c
 *
 * Assumes that 0 < a <= b*b, note if 0 > a > -(b*b) then you can merely
 * compute the reduction as -1 * mp_reduce(mp_abs(a)) [pseudo code].
 */
int mp_reduce(mp_int *a, mp_int *b, mp_int *c);
/* setups the montgomery reduction */
int mp_montgomery_setup(mp_int *a, mp_digit *mp);
/* computes a = B**n mod b without division or multiplication useful for
 * normalizing numbers in a Montgomery system.
```

```
 */
int mp_montgomery_calc_normalization(mp_int *a, mp_int *b);
/* computes x/R == x (mod N) via Montgomery Reduction */
int mp_montgomery_reduce(mp_int *a, mp_int *m, mp_digit mp);
/* returns 1 if a is a valid DR modulus */
int mp_dr_is_modulus(mp_int *a);
/* sets the value of "d" required for mp_dr_reduce */
void mp_dr_setup(mp_int *a, mp_digit *d);
/* reduces a modulo b using the Diminished Radix method */
int mp_dr_reduce(mp_int *a, mp_int *b, mp_digit mp);
/* returns true if a can be reduced with mp_reduce_2k */
int mp_reduce_is_2k(mp_int *a);
/* determines k value for 2k reduction */
int mp_reduce_2k_setup(mp_int *a, mp_digit *d);
/* reduces a modulo b where b is of the form 2**p - k [0 <= a] */
int mp_reduce_2k(mp_int *a, mp_int *n, mp_digit d);
/* returns true if a can be reduced with mp_reduce_2k_l */
int mp_reduce_is_2k_l(mp_int *a);
/* determines k value for 2k reduction */
int mp_reduce_2k_setup_l(mp_int *a, mp_int *d);
/* reduces a modulo b where b is of the form 2**p - k [0 <= a] */
int mp_reduce_2k_l(mp_int *a, mp_int *n, mp_int *d);
/* d = a**b (mod c) */
int mp_exptmod(mp_int *a, mp_int *b, mp_int *c, mp_int *d);
/* ---> Primes <--- */
/* number of primes */
#ifdef MP_8BIT
    #define PRIME_SIZE      31
#else
    #define PRIME_SIZE      256
#endif
/* table of first PRIME_SIZE primes */
extern const mp_digit ltm_prime_tab[];
/* result=1 if a is divisible by one of the first PRIME_SIZE primes */
int mp_prime_is_divisible(mp_int *a, int *result);
/* performs one Fermat test of "a" using base "b".
 * Sets result to 0 if composite or 1 if probable prime
 */
int mp_prime_fermat(mp_int *a, mp_int *b, int *result);
/* performs one Miller-Rabin test of "a" using base "b".
 * Sets result to 0 if composite or 1 if probable prime
 */
int mp_prime_miller_rabin(mp_int *a, mp_int *b, int *result);
```

```
/* This gives [for a given bit size] the number of trials required
 * such that Miller-Rabin gives a prob of failure lower than 2^-96
 */
int mp_prime_rabin_miller_trials(int size);
/* performs t rounds of Miller-Rabin on "a" using the first
 * t prime bases.  Also performs an initial sieve of trial
 * division.  Determines if "a" is prime with probability
 * of error no more than (1/4)**t.
 *
 * Sets result to 1 if probably prime, 0 otherwise
 */
int mp_prime_is_prime(mp_int *a, int t, int *result);
/* finds the next prime after the number "a" using "t" trials
 * of Miller-Rabin.
 *
 * bbs_style = 1 means the prime must be congruent to 3 mod 4
 */
int mp_prime_next_prime(mp_int *a, int t, int bbs_style);
/* makes a truly random prime of a given size (bytes),
 * call with bbs = 1 if you want it to be congruent to 3 mod 4
 *
 * You have to supply a callback which fills in a buffer with random bytes.
"dat" is a parameter you can
 * have passed to the callback (e.g. a state or something).  This function
doesn't use "dat" itself
 * so it can be NULL
 *
 * The prime generated will be larger than 2^(8*size).
 */
#define mp_prime_random(a, t, size, bbs, cb, dat) mp_prime_random_ex(a, t,
((size) * 8) + 1, (bbs==1)?LTM_PRIME_BBS:0, cb, dat)
/* makes a truly random prime of a given size (bits),
 *
 * Flags are as follows:
 *
 *   LTM_PRIME_BBS      - make prime congruent to 3 mod 4
 *   LTM_PRIME_SAFE     - make sure (p-1)/2 is prime as well (implies LTM_
PRIME_BBS)
 *   LTM_PRIME_2MSB_OFF - make the 2nd highest bit zero
 *   LTM_PRIME_2MSB_ON  - make the 2nd highest bit one
 *
 * You have to supply a callback which fills in a buffer with random bytes.
"dat" is a parameter you can
```

```
 * have passed to the callback (e.g. a state or something).  This function
doesn't use "dat" itself
 * so it can be NULL
 *
 */
int mp_prime_random_ex(mp_int *a, int t, int size, int flags, ltm_prime_call-
back cb, void *dat);
int mp_find_prime(mp_int *a);
int mp_isprime(mp_int *a);
/* ---> radix conversion <--- */
int mp_count_bits(mp_int *a);
int mp_unsigned_bin_size(mp_int *a);
int mp_read_unsigned_bin(mp_int *a, const unsigned char *b, int c);
int mp_to_unsigned_bin(mp_int *a, unsigned char *b);
int mp_to_unsigned_bin_n (mp_int * a, unsigned char *b, unsigned long *out-
len);
int mp_signed_bin_size(mp_int *a);
int mp_read_signed_bin(mp_int *a, const unsigned char *b, int c);
int mp_to_signed_bin(mp_int *a,  unsigned char *b);
int mp_to_signed_bin_n (mp_int * a, unsigned char *b, unsigned long *outlen);
int mp_read_radix(mp_int *a, const char *str, int radix);
int mp_toradix(mp_int *a, char *str, int radix);
int mp_toradix_n(mp_int * a, char *str, int radix, int maxlen);
int mp_radix_size(mp_int *a, int radix, int *size);
int mp_fread(mp_int *a, int radix, FILE *stream);
int mp_fwrite(mp_int *a, int radix, FILE *stream);
#define mp_read_raw(mp, str, len) mp_read_signed_bin((mp), (str), (len))
#define mp_raw_size(mp)           mp_signed_bin_size(mp)
#define mp_toraw(mp, str)         mp_to_signed_bin((mp), (str))
#define mp_read_mag(mp, str, len) mp_read_unsigned_bin((mp), (str), (len))
#define mp_mag_size(mp)           mp_unsigned_bin_size(mp)
#define mp_tomag(mp, str)         mp_to_unsigned_bin((mp), (str))
#define mp_tobinary(M, S)  mp_toradix((M), (S), 2)
#define mp_tooctal(M, S)   mp_toradix((M), (S), 8)
#define mp_todecimal(M, S) mp_toradix((M), (S), 10)
#define mp_tohex(M, S)     mp_toradix((M), (S), 16)
/* lowlevel functions, do not call! */
int s_mp_add(mp_int *a, mp_int *b, mp_int *c);
int s_mp_sub(mp_int *a, mp_int *b, mp_int *c);
#define s_mp_mul(a, b, c) s_mp_mul_digs(a, b, c, (a)->used + (b)->used + 1)
int fast_s_mp_mul_digs(mp_int *a, mp_int *b, mp_int *c, int digs);
int s_mp_mul_digs(mp_int *a, mp_int *b, mp_int *c, int digs);
int fast_s_mp_mul_high_digs(mp_int *a, mp_int *b, mp_int *c, int digs);
```

```
int s_mp_mul_high_digs(mp_int *a, mp_int *b, mp_int *c, int digs);
int fast_s_mp_sqr(mp_int *a, mp_int *b);
int s_mp_sqr(mp_int *a, mp_int *b);
int mp_karatsuba_mul(mp_int *a, mp_int *b, mp_int *c);
int mp_toom_mul(mp_int *a, mp_int *b, mp_int *c);
int mp_karatsuba_sqr(mp_int *a, mp_int *b);
int mp_toom_sqr(mp_int *a, mp_int *b);
int fast_mp_invmod(mp_int *a, mp_int *b, mp_int *c);
int mp_invmod_slow (mp_int * a, mp_int * b, mp_int * c);
int fast_mp_montgomery_reduce(mp_int *a, mp_int *m, mp_digit mp);
int mp_exptmod_fast(mp_int *G, mp_int *X, mp_int *P, mp_int *Y, int mode);
int s_mp_exptmod (mp_int * G, mp_int * X, mp_int * P, mp_int * Y, int mode);
void bn_reverse(unsigned char *s, int len);
extern const char *mp_s_rmap;
#ifdef __cplusplus
   }
#endif
#endif
/* $Source: /cvs/libtom/libtommath/tommath.h,v $ */
/* $Revision: 1.8 $ */
/* $Date: 2006/03/31 14:18:44 $ */
```

APPENDIX B

A Demo Program for Illustrating the Use of the LibTomMath Procedure Calls

```
#include <time.h>
#ifdef IOWNANATHLON
#include <unistd.h>
#define SLEEP sleep(4)
#else
#define SLEEP
#endif
#include "tommath.h"
void ndraw(mp_int * a, char *name)
{
   char buf[16000];
   printf("%s: ", name);
   mp_toradix(a, buf, 10);
   printf("%s\n", buf);
}
```

```c
static void draw(mp_int * a)
{
   ndraw(a, "");
}
unsigned long lfsr = 0xAAAAAAAAUL;
int lbit(void)
{
   if (lfsr & 0x80000000UL) {
      lfsr = ((lfsr << 1) ^ 0x8000001BUL) & 0xFFFFFFFFUL;
      return 1;
   } else {
      lfsr <<= 1;
      return 0;
   }
}
int myrng(unsigned char *dst, int len, void *dat)
{
   int x;
   for (x = 0; x < len; x++)
      dst[x] = rand() & 0xFF;
   return len;
}
char cmd[4096], buf[4096];
int main(void)
{
   mp_int a, b, c, d, e, f;
   unsigned long expt_n, add_n, sub_n, mul_n, div_n, sqr_n, mul2d_n, div2d_n,
      gcd_n, lcm_n, inv_n, div2_n, mul2_n, add_d_n, sub_d_n, t;
   unsigned rr;
   int i, n, err, cnt, ix, old_kara_m, old_kara_s;
   mp_digit mp;
   mp_init(&a);
   mp_init(&b);
   mp_init(&c);
   mp_init(&d);
   mp_init(&e);
   mp_init(&f);
   srand(time(NULL));
#if 0
   // test montgomery
   printf("Testing montgomery...\n");
   for (i = 1; i < 10; i++) {
      printf("Testing digit size: %d\n", i);
```

```
    for (n = 0; n < 1000; n++) {
        mp_rand(&a, i);
        a.dp[0] |= 1;
        // let's see if R is right
        mp_montgomery_calc_normalization(&b, &a);
        mp_montgomery_setup(&a, &mp);
        // now test a random reduction
        for (ix = 0; ix < 100; ix++) {
            mp_rand(&c, 1 + abs(rand()) % (2*i));
            mp_copy(&c, &d);
            mp_copy(&c, &e);
            mp_mod(&d, &a, &d);
            mp_montgomery_reduce(&c, &a, mp);
            mp_mulmod(&c, &b, &a, &c);
            if (mp_cmp(&c, &d) != MP_EQ) {
printf("d = e mod a, c = e MOD a\n");
mp_todecimal(&a, buf); printf("a = %s\n", buf);
mp_todecimal(&e, buf); printf("e = %s\n", buf);
mp_todecimal(&d, buf); printf("d = %s\n", buf);
mp_todecimal(&c, buf); printf("c = %s\n", buf);
printf("compare no compare!\n"); exit(EXIT_FAILURE); }
            }
        }
    }
    printf("done\n");
    // test mp_get_int
    printf("Testing: mp_get_int\n");
    for (i = 0; i < 1000; ++i) {
        t = ((unsigned long) rand() * rand() + 1) & 0xFFFFFFFF;
        mp_set_int(&a, t);
        if (t != mp_get_int(&a)) {
            printf("mp_get_int() bad result!\n");
            return 1;
        }
    }
    mp_set_int(&a, 0);
    if (mp_get_int(&a) != 0) {
        printf("mp_get_int() bad result!\n");
        return 1;
    }
    mp_set_int(&a, 0xffffffff);
    if (mp_get_int(&a) != 0xffffffff) {
        printf("mp_get_int() bad result!\n");
```

```
        return 1;
    }
// test mp_sqrt
printf("Testing: mp_sqrt\n");
for (i = 0; i < 1000; ++i) {
    printf("%6d\r", i);
    fflush(stdout);
    n = (rand() & 15) + 1;
    mp_rand(&a, n);
    if (mp_sqrt(&a, &b) != MP_OKAY) {
        printf("mp_sqrt() error!\n");
        return 1;
    }
    mp_n_root(&a, 2, &a);
    if (mp_cmp_mag(&b, &a) != MP_EQ) {
        printf("mp_sqrt() bad result!\n");
        return 1;
    }
}
printf("\nTesting: mp_is_square\n");
for (i = 0; i < 1000; ++i) {
    printf("%6d\r", i);
    fflush(stdout);
    /* test mp_is_square false negatives */
    n = (rand() & 7) + 1;
    mp_rand(&a, n);
    mp_sqr(&a, &a);
    if (mp_is_square(&a, &n) != MP_OKAY) {
        printf("fn:mp_is_square() error!\n");
        return 1;
    }
    if (n == 0) {
        printf("fn:mp_is_square() bad result!\n");
        return 1;
    }
    /* test for false positives */
    mp_add_d(&a, 1, &a);
    if (mp_is_square(&a, &n) != MP_OKAY) {
        printf("fp:mp_is_square() error!\n");
        return 1;
    }
    if (n == 1) {
        printf("fp:mp_is_square() bad result!\n");
```

```
        return 1;
    }
}
printf("\n\n");
/* test for size */
for (ix = 10; ix < 128; ix++) {
    printf("Testing (not safe-prime): %9d bits    \r", ix);
    fflush(stdout);
    err =
        mp_prime_random_ex(&a, 8, ix,
                           (rand() & 1) ? LTM_PRIME_2MSB_OFF:
                           LTM_PRIME_2MSB_ON, myrng, NULL);
    if (err != MP_OKAY) {
        printf("failed with err code %d\n", err);
        return EXIT_FAILURE;
    }
    if (mp_count_bits(&a) != ix) {
        printf("Prime is %d not %d bits!!!\n", mp_count_bits(&a), ix);
        return EXIT_FAILURE;
    }
}
for (ix = 16; ix < 128; ix++) {
    printf("Testing ( safe-prime): %9d bits    \r", ix);
    fflush(stdout);
    err =
        mp_prime_random_ex(&a, 8, ix,
                           ((rand() & 1) ? LTM_PRIME_2MSB_OFF:
                            LTM_PRIME_2MSB_ON) | LTM_PRIME_SAFE, myrng,
                           NULL);
    if (err != MP_OKAY) {
        printf("failed with err code %d\n", err);
        return EXIT_FAILURE;
    }
    if (mp_count_bits(&a) != ix) {
        printf("Prime is %d not %d bits!!!\n", mp_count_bits(&a), ix);
        return EXIT_FAILURE;
    }
    /* let's see if it's really a safe prime */
    mp_sub_d(&a, 1, &a);
    mp_div_2(&a, &a);
    mp_prime_is_prime(&a, 8, &cnt);
    if (cnt != MP_YES) {
        printf("sub is not prime!\n");
```

```
            return EXIT_FAILURE;
      }
   }
   printf("\n\n");
   mp_read_radix(&a, "123456", 10);
   mp_toradix_n(&a, buf, 10, 3);
   printf("a == %s\n", buf);
   mp_toradix_n(&a, buf, 10, 4);
   printf("a == %s\n", buf);
   mp_toradix_n(&a, buf, 10, 30);
   printf("a == %s\n", buf);
#if 0
   for (;;) {
      fgets(buf, sizeof(buf), stdin);
      mp_read_radix(&a, buf, 10);
      mp_prime_next_prime(&a, 5, 1);
      mp_toradix(&a, buf, 10);
      printf("%s, %lu\n", buf, a.dp[0] & 3);
   }
#endif
   /* test mp_cnt_lsb */
   printf("testing mp_cnt_lsb...\n");
   mp_set(&a, 1);
   for (ix = 0; ix < 1024; ix++) {
      if (mp_cnt_lsb(&a) != ix) {
         printf("Failed at %d, %d\n", ix, mp_cnt_lsb(&a));
         return 0;
      }
      mp_mul_2(&a, &a);
   }
/* test mp_reduce_2k */
   printf("Testing mp_reduce_2k...\n");
   for (cnt = 3; cnt <= 128; ++cnt) {
     mp_digit tmp;
     mp_2expt(&a, cnt);
     mp_sub_d(&a, 2, &a);            /* a = 2**cnt - 2 */
     printf("\nTesting %4d bits", cnt);
     printf("(%d)", mp_reduce_is_2k(&a));
     mp_reduce_2k_setup(&a, &tmp);
     printf("(%d)", tmp);
     for (ix = 0; ix < 1000; ix++) {
        if (!(ix & 127)) {
           printf(".");
```

```
            fflush(stdout);
        }
        mp_rand(&b, (cnt / DIGIT_BIT + 1) * 2);
        mp_copy(&c, &b);
        mp_mod(&c, &a, &c);
        mp_reduce_2k(&b, &a, 2);
        if (mp_cmp(&c, &b)) {
            printf("FAILED\n");
            exit(0);
        }
    }
}
/* test mp_div_3  */
    printf("Testing mp_div_3...\n");
    mp_set(&d, 3);
    for (cnt = 0; cnt < 10000;) {
        mp_digit r1, r2;
        if (!(++cnt & 127))
            printf("%9d\r", cnt);
        mp_rand(&a, abs(rand()) % 128 + 1);
        mp_div(&a, &d, &b, &e);
        mp_div_3(&a, &c, &r2);
        if (mp_cmp(&b, &c) || mp_cmp_d(&e, r2)) {
            printf("\n\nmp_div_3 => Failure\n");
        }
    }
    printf("\n\nPassed div_3 testing\n");
/* test the DR reduction */
    printf("testing mp_dr_reduce...\n");
    for (cnt = 2; cnt < 32; cnt++) {
        printf("%d digit modulus\n", cnt);
        mp_grow(&a, cnt);
        mp_zero(&a);
        for (ix = 1; ix < cnt; ix++) {
            a.dp[ix] = MP_MASK;
        }
        a.used = cnt;
        a.dp[0] = 3;
        mp_rand(&b, cnt - 1);
        mp_copy(&b, &c);
        rr = 0;
        do {
            if (!(rr & 127)) {
```

```
                printf("%9lu\r", rr);
                fflush(stdout);
            }
            mp_sqr(&b, &b);
            mp_add_d(&b, 1, &b);
            mp_copy(&b, &c);
            mp_mod(&b, &a, &b);
            mp_dr_reduce(&c, &a, (((mp_digit) 1) << DIGIT_BIT) - a.dp[0]);
            if (mp_cmp(&b, &c) != MP_EQ) {
                printf("Failed on trial %lu\n", rr);
                exit(-1);
            }
        } while (++rr < 500);
        printf("Passed DR test for %d digits\n", cnt);
    }
#endif
/* test the mp_reduce_2k_l code */
#if 0
#if 0
/* first load P with 2^1024 - 0x2A434 B9FDEC95 D8F9D550 FFFFFFFF FFFFFFFF */
    mp_2expt(&a, 1024);
    mp_read_radix(&b, "2A434B9FDEC95D8F9D550FFFFFFFFFFFFFFFF", 16);
    mp_sub(&a, &b, &a);
#elif 1
/*  p = 2^2048 - 0x1 00000000 00000000 00000000 00000000 4945DDBF 8EA2A91D
5776399B B83E188F  */
    mp_2expt(&a, 2048);
    mp_read_radix(&b,
                  "100000000000000000000000000000000000004945DDBF8EA2A91D5776399B-
B83E188F",
                  16);
    mp_sub(&a, &b, &a);
#endif
    mp_todecimal(&a, buf);
    printf("p==%s\n", buf);
/* now mp_reduce_is_2k_l() should return */
    if (mp_reduce_is_2k_l(&a) != 1) {
        printf("mp_reduce_is_2k_l() return 0, should be 1\n");
        return EXIT_FAILURE;
    }
    mp_reduce_2k_setup_l(&a, &d);
    /* now do a million square+1 to see if it varies */
    mp_rand(&b, 64);
```

```
   mp_mod(&b, &a, &b);
   mp_copy(&b, &c);
   printf("testing mp_reduce_2k_l...");
   fflush(stdout);
   for (cnt = 0; cnt < (1UL << 20); cnt++) {
      mp_sqr(&b, &b);
      mp_add_d(&b, 1, &b);
      mp_reduce_2k_l(&b, &a, &d);
      mp_sqr(&c, &c);
      mp_add_d(&c, 1, &c);
      mp_mod(&c, &a, &c);
      if (mp_cmp(&b, &c) != MP_EQ) {
         printf("mp_reduce_2k_l() failed at step %lu\n", cnt);
         mp_tohex(&b, buf);
         printf("b == %s\n", buf);
         mp_tohex(&c, buf);
         printf("c == %s\n", buf);
         return EXIT_FAILURE;
      }
   }
   printf("...Passed\n");
#endif
   div2_n = mul2_n = inv_n = expt_n = lcm_n = gcd_n = add_n =
      sub_n = mul_n = div_n = sqr_n = mul2d_n = div2d_n = cnt = add_d_n =
      sub_d_n = 0;
   /* force KARA and TOOM to enable despite cutoffs */
   KARATSUBA_SQR_CUTOFF = KARATSUBA_MUL_CUTOFF = 8;
   TOOM_SQR_CUTOFF = TOOM_MUL_CUTOFF = 16;
   for (;;) {
      /* randomly clear and re-init one variable, this has the affect of trim-
ing the alloc space */
      switch (abs(rand()) % 7) {
      case 0:
         mp_clear(&a);
         mp_init(&a);
         break;
      case 1:
         mp_clear(&b);
         mp_init(&b);
         break;
      case 2:
         mp_clear(&c);
         mp_init(&c);
```

```
            break;
        case 3:
            mp_clear(&d);
            mp_init(&d);
            break;
        case 4:
            mp_clear(&e);
            mp_init(&e);
            break;
        case 5:
            mp_clear(&f);
            mp_init(&f);
            break;
        case 6:
            break;                          /* don't clear any */
        }
        printf
            ("%4lu/%4lu/%4lu/%4lu/%4lu/%4lu/%4lu/%4lu/%4lu/%4lu/%4lu/%4lu/%4lu/%4
lu/%4lu ",
                add_n, sub_n, mul_n, div_n, sqr_n, mul2d_n, div2d_n, gcd_n, lcm_n,
                expt_n, inv_n, div2_n, mul2_n, add_d_n, sub_d_n);
        fgets(cmd, 4095, stdin);
        cmd[strlen(cmd) - 1] = 0;
        printf("%s   ]\r", cmd);
        fflush(stdout);
        if (!strcmp(cmd, "mul2d")) {
            ++mul2d_n;
            fgets(buf, 4095, stdin);
            mp_read_radix(&a, buf, 64);
            fgets(buf, 4095, stdin);
            sscanf(buf, "%d", &rr);
            fgets(buf, 4095, stdin);
            mp_read_radix(&b, buf, 64);
            mp_mul_2d(&a, rr, &a);
            a.sign = b.sign;
            if (mp_cmp(&a, &b) != MP_EQ) {
                printf("mul2d failed, rr == %d\n", rr);
                draw(&a);
                draw(&b);
                return 0;
            }
        } else if (!strcmp(cmd, "div2d")) {
            ++div2d_n;
```

```
        fgets(buf, 4095, stdin);
        mp_read_radix(&a, buf, 64);
        fgets(buf, 4095, stdin);
        sscanf(buf, "%d", &rr);
        fgets(buf, 4095, stdin);
        mp_read_radix(&b, buf, 64);
        mp_div_2d(&a, rr, &a, &e);
        a.sign = b.sign;
        if (a.used == b.used && a.used == 0) {
            a.sign = b.sign = MP_ZPOS;
        }
        if (mp_cmp(&a, &b) != MP_EQ) {
            printf("div2d failed, rr == %d\n", rr);
            draw(&a);
            draw(&b);
            return 0;
        }
    } else if (!strcmp(cmd, "add")) {
        ++add_n;
        fgets(buf, 4095, stdin);
        mp_read_radix(&a, buf, 64);
        fgets(buf, 4095, stdin);
        mp_read_radix(&b, buf, 64);
        fgets(buf, 4095, stdin);
        mp_read_radix(&c, buf, 64);
        mp_copy(&a, &d);
        mp_add(&d, &b, &d);
        if (mp_cmp(&c, &d) != MP_EQ) {
            printf("add %lu failure!\n", add_n);
            draw(&a);
            draw(&b);
            draw(&c);
            draw(&d);
            return 0;
        }
        /* test the sign/unsigned storage functions */
        rr = mp_signed_bin_size(&c);
        mp_to_signed_bin(&c, (unsigned char *) cmd);
        memset(cmd + rr, rand() & 255, sizeof(cmd) - rr);
        mp_read_signed_bin(&d, (unsigned char *) cmd, rr);
        if (mp_cmp(&c, &d) != MP_EQ) {
            printf("mp_signed_bin failure!\n");
            draw(&c);
```

```
        draw(&d);
        return 0;
    }
    rr = mp_unsigned_bin_size(&c);
    mp_to_unsigned_bin(&c, (unsigned char *) cmd);
    memset(cmd + rr, rand() & 255, sizeof(cmd) - rr);
    mp_read_unsigned_bin(&d, (unsigned char *) cmd, rr);
    if (mp_cmp_mag(&c, &d) != MP_EQ) {
        printf("mp_unsigned_bin failure!\n");
        draw(&c);
        draw(&d);
        return 0;
    }
} else if (!strcmp(cmd, "sub")) {
    ++sub_n;
    fgets(buf, 4095, stdin);
    mp_read_radix(&a, buf, 64);
    fgets(buf, 4095, stdin);
    mp_read_radix(&b, buf, 64);
    fgets(buf, 4095, stdin);
    mp_read_radix(&c, buf, 64);
    mp_copy(&a, &d);
    mp_sub(&d, &b, &d);
    if (mp_cmp(&c, &d) != MP_EQ) {
        printf("sub %lu failure!\n", sub_n);
        draw(&a);
        draw(&b);
        draw(&c);
        draw(&d);
        return 0;
    }
} else if (!strcmp(cmd, "mul")) {
    ++mul_n;
    fgets(buf, 4095, stdin);
    mp_read_radix(&a, buf, 64);
    fgets(buf, 4095, stdin);
    mp_read_radix(&b, buf, 64);
    fgets(buf, 4095, stdin);
    mp_read_radix(&c, buf, 64);
    mp_copy(&a, &d);
    mp_mul(&d, &b, &d);
    if (mp_cmp(&c, &d) != MP_EQ) {
        printf("mul %lu failure!\n", mul_n);
```

```
        draw(&a);
        draw(&b);
        draw(&c);
        draw(&d);
        return 0;
    }
} else if (!strcmp(cmd, "div")) {
    ++div_n;
    fgets(buf, 4095, stdin);
    mp_read_radix(&a, buf, 64);
    fgets(buf, 4095, stdin);
    mp_read_radix(&b, buf, 64);
    fgets(buf, 4095, stdin);
    mp_read_radix(&c, buf, 64);
    fgets(buf, 4095, stdin);
    mp_read_radix(&d, buf, 64);
    mp_div(&a, &b, &e, &f);
    if (mp_cmp(&c, &e) != MP_EQ || mp_cmp(&d, &f) != MP_EQ) {
        printf("div %lu %d, %d, failure!\n", div_n, mp_cmp(&c, &e),
                mp_cmp(&d, &f));
        draw(&a);
        draw(&b);
        draw(&c);
        draw(&d);
        draw(&e);
        draw(&f);
        return 0;
    }
} else if (!strcmp(cmd, "sqr")) {
    ++sqr_n;
    fgets(buf, 4095, stdin);
    mp_read_radix(&a, buf, 64);
    fgets(buf, 4095, stdin);
    mp_read_radix(&b, buf, 64);
    mp_copy(&a, &c);
    mp_sqr(&c, &c);
    if (mp_cmp(&b, &c) != MP_EQ) {
        printf("sqr %lu failure!\n", sqr_n);
        draw(&a);
        draw(&b);
        draw(&c);
        return 0;
    }
```

```
    } else if (!strcmp(cmd, "gcd")) {
        ++gcd_n;
        fgets(buf, 4095, stdin);
        mp_read_radix(&a, buf, 64);
        fgets(buf, 4095, stdin);
        mp_read_radix(&b, buf, 64);
        fgets(buf, 4095, stdin);
        mp_read_radix(&c, buf, 64);
        mp_copy(&a, &d);
        mp_gcd(&d, &b, &d);
        d.sign = c.sign;
        if (mp_cmp(&c, &d) != MP_EQ) {
            printf("gcd %lu failure!\n", gcd_n);
            draw(&a);
            draw(&b);
            draw(&c);
            draw(&d);
            return 0;
        }
    } else if (!strcmp(cmd, "lcm")) {
        ++lcm_n;
        fgets(buf, 4095, stdin);
        mp_read_radix(&a, buf, 64);
        fgets(buf, 4095, stdin);
        mp_read_radix(&b, buf, 64);
        fgets(buf, 4095, stdin);
        mp_read_radix(&c, buf, 64);
        mp_copy(&a, &d);
        mp_lcm(&d, &b, &d);
        d.sign = c.sign;
        if (mp_cmp(&c, &d) != MP_EQ) {
            printf("lcm %lu failure!\n", lcm_n);
            draw(&a);
            draw(&b);
            draw(&c);
            draw(&d);
            return 0;
        }
    } else if (!strcmp(cmd, "expt")) {
        ++expt_n;
        fgets(buf, 4095, stdin);
        mp_read_radix(&a, buf, 64);
        fgets(buf, 4095, stdin);
```

```
    mp_read_radix(&b, buf, 64);
    fgets(buf, 4095, stdin);
    mp_read_radix(&c, buf, 64);
    fgets(buf, 4095, stdin);
    mp_read_radix(&d, buf, 64);
    mp_copy(&a, &e);
    mp_exptmod(&e, &b, &c, &e);
    if (mp_cmp(&d, &e) != MP_EQ) {
        printf("expt %lu failure!\n", expt_n);
        draw(&a);
        draw(&b);
        draw(&c);
        draw(&d);
        draw(&e);
        return 0;
    }
} else if (!strcmp(cmd, "invmod")) {
    ++inv_n;
    fgets(buf, 4095, stdin);
    mp_read_radix(&a, buf, 64);
    fgets(buf, 4095, stdin);
    mp_read_radix(&b, buf, 64);
    fgets(buf, 4095, stdin);
    mp_read_radix(&c, buf, 64);
    mp_invmod(&a, &b, &d);
    mp_mulmod(&d, &a, &b, &e);
    if (mp_cmp_d(&e, 1) != MP_EQ) {
        printf("inv [wrong value from MPI?!] failure\n");
        draw(&a);
        draw(&b);
        draw(&c);
        draw(&d);
        mp_gcd(&a, &b, &e);
        draw(&e);
        return 0;
    }
} else if (!strcmp(cmd, "div2")) {
    ++div2_n;
    fgets(buf, 4095, stdin);
    mp_read_radix(&a, buf, 64);
    fgets(buf, 4095, stdin);
    mp_read_radix(&b, buf, 64);
    mp_div_2(&a, &c);
```

```
      if (mp_cmp(&c, &b) != MP_EQ) {
         printf("div_2%lu failure\n", div2_n);
         draw(&a);
         draw(&b);
         draw(&c);
         return 0;
      }
   } else if (!strcmp(cmd, "mul2")) {
      ++mul2_n;
      fgets(buf, 4095, stdin);
      mp_read_radix(&a, buf, 64);
      fgets(buf, 4095, stdin);
      mp_read_radix(&b, buf, 64);
      mp_mul_2(&a, &c);
      if (mp_cmp(&c, &b) != MP_EQ) {
         printf("mul_2%lu failure\n", mul2_n);
         draw(&a);
         draw(&b);
         draw(&c);
         return 0;
      }
   } else if (!strcmp(cmd, "add_d")) {
      ++add_d_n;
      fgets(buf, 4095, stdin);
      mp_read_radix(&a, buf, 64);
      fgets(buf, 4095, stdin);
      sscanf(buf, "%d", &ix);
      fgets(buf, 4095, stdin);
      mp_read_radix(&b, buf, 64);
      mp_add_d(&a, ix, &c);
      if (mp_cmp(&b, &c) != MP_EQ) {
         printf("add_d %lu failure\n", add_d_n);
         draw(&a);
         draw(&b);
         draw(&c);
         printf("d == %d\n", ix);
         return 0;
      }
   } else if (!strcmp(cmd, "sub_d")) {
      ++sub_d_n;
      fgets(buf, 4095, stdin);
      mp_read_radix(&a, buf, 64);
      fgets(buf, 4095, stdin);
```

```
        sscanf(buf, "%d", &ix);
        fgets(buf, 4095, stdin);
        mp_read_radix(&b, buf, 64);
        mp_sub_d(&a, ix, &c);
        if (mp_cmp(&b, &c) != MP_EQ) {
            printf("sub_d %lu failure\n", sub_d_n);
            draw(&a);
            draw(&b);
            draw(&c);
            printf("d == %d\n", ix);
            return 0;
        }
    }
  }
  return 0;
}
/* $Source: /cvs/libtom/libtommath/demo/demo.c,v $ */
/* $Revision: 1.3 $ */
/* $Date: 2005/06/24 11:32:07 $ */
```

APPENDIX C

A Simple RSA Implementation Using the Java BigInteger Class

```
/*-------------------------------------------
import java.math.BigInteger;
import java.security.SecureRandom;
public class RSA {
  private BigInteger n, d, e;
  private int bitlen = 1024;
  /** Create an instance that can encrypt using someone elses public key. */
  public RSA(BigInteger newn, BigInteger newe) {
    n = newn;
    e = newe;
  }
  /** Create an instance that can both encrypt and decrypt. */
  public RSA(int bits) {
    bitlen = bits;
    SecureRandom r = new SecureRandom();
    BigInteger p = new BigInteger(bitlen / 2, 100, r);
    BigInteger q = new BigInteger(bitlen / 2, 100, r);
```

```java
   n = p.multiply(q);
   BigInteger m = (p.subtract(BigInteger.ONE)).multiply(q
       .subtract(BigInteger.ONE));
   e = new BigInteger("3");
   while (m.gcd(e).intValue() > 1) {
     e = e.add(new BigInteger("2"));
   }
   d = e.modInverse(m);
}
/** Encrypt the given plaintext message. */
public synchronized String encrypt(String message) {
   return (new BigInteger(message.getBytes())).modPow(e, n).toString();
}
/** Encrypt the given plaintext message. */
public synchronized BigInteger encrypt(BigInteger message) {
   return message.modPow(e, n);
}
/** Decrypt the given ciphertext message. */
public synchronized String decrypt(String message) {
   return new String((new BigInteger(message)).modPow(d, n).toByteArray());
}
/** Decrypt the given ciphertext message. */
public synchronized BigInteger decrypt(BigInteger message) {
   return message.modPow(d, n);
}
/** Generate a new public and private key set. */
public synchronized void generateKeys() {
   SecureRandom r = new SecureRandom();
   BigInteger p = new BigInteger(bitlen / 2, 100, r);
   BigInteger q = new BigInteger(bitlen / 2, 100, r);
   n = p.multiply(q);
   BigInteger m = (p.subtract(BigInteger.ONE)).multiply(q
       .subtract(BigInteger.ONE));
   e = new BigInteger("3");
   while (m.gcd(e).intValue() > 1) {
     e = e.add(new BigInteger("2"));
   }
   d = e.modInverse(m);
}
/** Return the modulus. */
public synchronized BigInteger getN() {
   return n;
}
```

```
/** Return the public key. */
public synchronized BigInteger getE() {
  return e;
}
/** Trivial test program. */
public static void main(String[] args) {
  RSA rsa = new RSA(1024);
  String text1 = "Yellow and Black Border Collies";
  System.out.println("Plaintext: " + text1);
  BigInteger plaintext = new BigInteger(text1.getBytes());
  BigInteger ciphertext = rsa.encrypt(plaintext);
  System.out.println("Ciphertext: " + ciphertext);
  plaintext = rsa.decrypt(ciphertext);
  String text2 = new String(plaintext.toByteArray());
  System.out.println("Plaintext: " + text2);
}
}
```

Chapter 17
Integer Factoring Algorithms

Kannan Balasubramanian
Mepco Schlenk Engineering College, India

Ahmed Mahmoud Abbas
The American University in Cairo, India

ABSTRACT

Most cryptographic systems are based on an underlying difficult problem. The RSA cryptosystem and many other cryptosystems rely on the fact that factoring a large composite number into two prime numbers is a hard problem. The are many algorithms for factoring integers. This chapter presents some of the basic algorithms for integer factorization like the Trial Division, Fermat's Algorithm. Pollard's Rho Method, Pollard's p-1 method and the Elliptic Curve Method. The Number Field Sieve algorithm along with Special Number field Sieve and the General Number Field Sieve are also used in factoring large numbers. Other factoring algorithms discussed in this chapter are the Continued Fractions Algorithms and the Quadratic Sieve Algorithm.

INTRODUCTION

Integer factoring has become very important in the area of Cryptography since the widely used public key cryptosystem is based on the difficulty of factoring large integers. Various techniques have been evolved to tackle the integer factoring problem like the trial division, pollard's rho method, pollard's p-1 method, Elliptic Curve method and the Fermat's method. To speed up the factorization, various other algorithms are used nowadays including the Number Field Sieve, Generalized Number Field Sieve, the Continued Fractions method and the Quadratic Sieve. This chapter discusses each of these algorithms and compares them based on their performance of these algorithms in terms of the number of digits they are able to factorize.

THE FACTORIZATION PROBLEM

Factoring a positive integer n means finding positive integers u and v such that the product of u and v equals n, and such that both u and v are greater than 1. Such u and v are called *factors* (or *divisors*) of n,

DOI: 10.4018/978-1-5225-2915-6.ch017

and $n = u \cdot v$ is called a *factorization* of n. Positive integers that can be factored are called *composites*. Positive integers greater than 1 that cannot be factored are called *primes*. A factorization of a composite number is not necessarily unique. But the *prime factorization* of a number—writing it as a product of prime numbers—is unique, up to the order of the factors.

We are interested in finding just a factorization. The prime factorization can be obtained by further factoring the factors that happen to be composite. Factoring a composite integer is believed to be a hard problem. This is, of course, not the case for *all* composites—composites with small factors are easy to factor—but, in general, the problem seems to be difficult. As yet there is no firm mathematical ground on which this assumption can be based. The only evidence that factoring is hard consists of our failure so far to find a fast and practical factoring algorithm.

This relation between factoring and cryptography is one of the main reasons why people are interested in evaluating the practical difficulty of the integer factorization problem. Currently the limits of our factoring capabilities lie around 130 decimal digits (Lenstra, 2000). Factoring hard integers in that range requires enormous amounts of computing power. A cheap and convenient way to get the computing power needed is to distribute the computation over the Internet. This approach was first used in 1988 to factor a 100-digit integer (Lenstra, 1990), since then to factor many integers in the 100 to 120 digit range, and in 1994 to factor the famous 129-digit RSA-challenge number. Most recently, in 1996 a 130-digit number was factored, partially using a World Wide Web interface (Cowie et.al., 1996).

In this chapter, we illustrate the basic steps involved in the factoring methods used to obtain the factorizations just mentioned and we explain how these methods can be run in parallel on a loosely coupled computer network, such as the Internet. We distinguish two main types of factoring methods: those that work quickly if one is lucky, and those that are almost guaranteed to work no matter how unlucky one is. The latter are referred to as *general-purpose algorithms* and have an expected run time that depends solely on the size of the number n being factored. The former are called *special-purpose algorithms*; they have an expected run time that also depends on the properties of the— unknown—factors of n. When evaluating the security of factoring-based cryptosystems, people employ general-purpose factoring algorithms.

SPECIAL PURPOSE FACTORING ALGORITHMS

We briefly discuss five of the most important special purpose factoring methods: *trial division*, *Pollard's rho method*, *Pollard's p- 1 method*, the *elliptic curve method* and *Fermat's method*. We assume that n denotes the number to be factored. We also assume that n is composite and not a prime power.

- **Trial Division:** The smallest prime factor p of n can in principle be found by trying if n is divisible by 2,3,5, 7, 11, 13, 17, ..., i.e., all primes in succession, until p is reached. If we assume that a table of all primes p is available (which can be generated in approximately p steps using for instance the *sieve of Erathostenes* (Knuth, 1981)), this process takes $\pi(p)$ division attempts (so-called 'trial divisions'), where π is the prime counting function. Because $\pi(p) \approx p/s^2$ finding the factor p of n in this way takes at least approximately p steps—how many precisely depends on how we count the cost of each trial division. Even for fairly small p, say $p > 10^6$, trial division is already quite inefficient compared to other methods.

Since n has at least one factor $\leq \sqrt{n}$ factoring n using trial division takes approximately n operations, in the worst case. For many composites trial division is therefore infeasible as factoring method. For most numbers it is very effective, however, because most numbers have small factors: 88% of all positive integers have a factor < 100, and almost 92% have a factor < 1000.

- **Pollard's Rho Method:** Pollard's rho method (Pollard, 1975) is based on a combination of two ideas that are also useful for various other factoring methods. The first idea is the well known *birthday paradox*: a group of at least 23 (randomly selected) people contains two persons with the same birthday in more than 50% of the cases. More generally, if numbers are picked at random from a set containing p numbers, the probability of picking the same number twice exceeds 50% after $1.177\sqrt{p}$ numbers have been picked. The first duplicate can be expected after $c.\sqrt{p}$ numbers have been selected, for some small constant c. The second idea is the following: if p is some unknown divisor of n and x and y are two integers that are suspected to be identical modulo p, i.e., $x \equiv y \bmod p$, then this can be checked by computing $\gcd(|x-y|,n)$ More importantly, this computation may reveal a factorization of n, unless x and y are also identical modulo n.

These ideas can be combined into a factoring algorithm in the following way: Generate a sequence in $\{0,1,\ldots n-1\}$ by randomly selecting x_0 and by defining x_i as the least non-negative remainder of x_{i-1}^2 $+1 \bmod n$. Since p divides n the least non-negative remainders $x_i \bmod p$ and $x_j \bmod p$ are equal if and only if x_i and x_j are identical modulo p. Since the $x_i \bmod p$ behave more or less as random integers in $\{0, 1,\ldots p-1\}$ we can expect to factor n by computing $\gcd(|x_i - x_j|, n)$ for $i \neq j$ after about $c.\sqrt{p}$ elements of the sequence have been computed.

This suggests that approximately $(c\sqrt{p})^2/2$ pairs x_i, x_j have to be considered. However, this can easily be avoided by only computing $\gcd(|x_i - x_{2i}|, n)$, for $i = 0,1,\ldots$, i.e., by generating two copies of the sequence, one at the regular speed and one at the double speed, until the sequence 'bites in its own tail' (which explains the 'rho' (ρ) in the name of the method); this can be expected to result in a factorization of n after approximately $2\sqrt{p}$ gcd computations.

The most remarkable success of Pollard's rho method so far was the discovery in 1980 by Brent and Pollard of the factorization of the Eighth Fermat number $2^{2^n} + 1$.

Pollard's p-1 method: Pollard's p-1 method (Pollard, J.M.,1974) follows very roughly from Pollard's rho method by replacing the birthday paradox by Fermat's little theorem. Let p again be a prime factor of n. For any integer a, with $1 < a < p$, we have according to Fermat's little theorem, that $a^{p-1} \equiv 1 \bmod p$, so that $a^{k(p-1)} \equiv 1^k \equiv 1 \bmod p$ for any integer k. Therefore, for any multiple of m of $p-1$, we have that $a^m \equiv 1 \bmod p$ i.e., p divides a^m-1. Thus computing a $\gcd(a^m-1, n)$ might reveal a factorization of n. It should be noted that it is sufficient to compute $\gcd((a^m-n)\bmod n,n)$ and that p divides $(a^m-1 \bmod n)$ because p divides n.

It remains to find a multiple $m > 1$ of $p-1$. The idea is that one simply hopes that p-1 is B-smooth for some relatively small bound B i.e., p-1 has only prime factors $\leq$ B. (An integer is said to be smooth with respect to S, if it can be completely factored using the elements of S. This would imply that m of the form $\prod_{q \leq B} q$ with the product ranging over prime powers q, could be a multiple of $p-1$. Since $a^m-1 \bmod$ n for such m can be computed in time roughly proportional to the largest prime factor in p-1. This is going to be efficient for which p-1 is smooth. For fast ways to implement Pollard's p-1 methods and variations of this method the reader is referred to (Montgomery, 1987).

- **Elliptic Curve Method:** The major disadvantage of Pollard's p - 1 method is that it only works efficiently if the number to be factored happens to have a factor p for which p -1 is B-smooth, for some reasonably small bound B. So, it only works for 'lucky' n. The elliptic curve method (Lenstra, 1987) can be regarded as a variation of the p - 1 method that does not have this disadvantage. It consists of any number of trials, where each trial can be lucky—and factor n—independently of the other trials: a trial is successful if some random number close to some prime factor of n is smooth. Thus, the probability of success of each trial depends only on the size and not on any other fixed properties of the factors of n.

During each trial an elliptic curve modulo n is selected at random. For any prime p dividing n, any point a on the curve satisfies an equation that is similar to Fermat's little theorem, with two important differences. In the first place, and this is why the elliptic curve method is so powerful, the exponent p -1 is replaced by some random number p' close to p - 1. Secondly, the exponentiation is not a regular integer exponentiation modulo n: since a is not an integer but a point on a curve, other operations have to be performed on it to 'exponentiate on the curve'. The number of elementary arithmetic operations to be carried out for such an exponentiation is a constant multiple of the number of operations needed for a regular integer exponentiation modulo n with the same exponent.

- **Fermat's Method:** In Fermat's method one attempts to solve a *congruence of squares*, i.e., integers x and y such that x^2 - y^2 is a *multiple* of n. Namely, if n divides x^2 - y^2, it also divides $(x - y)$ $(x + y) = x^2$ - y^2. Therefore, the factors of n must be factors of x - y, or they must be factors of x + y, or some of them must be factors of x - y and some must be factors of x + y. In the first case, n is a factor of x - y, which can be checked easily. In the second case, n is a factor of x + y, which can also be checked easily. If neither of those cases hold, then the factors of n must be split, in some way, among x - y and x + y. This gives us a way to find factors of n because we have an efficient method to find out which factors n and x- y have in common, and which factors n and x + y have in common.

THE NUMBER FIELD SIEVE ALGORITHM

The Number Field Sieve (NFS) is currently the fastest classical algorithm for factoring a large integer into its prime cofactors (Lenstra, et al, 1993). Continued study of the practical implementations of the NFS is of significant interest for the security assessment of common public-key cryptosystems, chief among them being the RSA algorithm. Continued study of the practical implementations of the NFS is of significant interest for the security assessment of common public-key cryptosystems, chief among them being the RSA algorithm. The security of the RSA encryption algorithm relies on the fact that integer factorization is difficult. Improvements to the NFS algorithm are of significant practical importance, and factoring milestones are followed by the applied cryptography community. Signi can't milestones include the factoring of a 512-bit RSA modulus by the general NFS (GNFS) in 2000 (Cavallar, et al,

2000), 2^{1039}-1 by the special NFS (SNFS) in 2007 (Aoki, et al, 2007), and a 768-bit RSA modulus in 2010 (Kleinjung, et al, 2010).

Using the SNFS, the complete factorization of the Mersenne number, 2^{1061}- 1, has been determined. Prior this this effort, this number had no known factors. Although easier than the factorization of RSA-768, this represents a new largest factorization using SNFS, and the largest factorization to date using publicly available software. NFS is comprised of five basic steps: polynomial selection, sieving for relations, ltering of relations, linear algebra, and square root. The steps are explained below (Childers, 2012):

1. **Polynomial Selection:** Polynomial selection consists of finding two polynomials that share a common root modulo the number being factored. For this SNFS factorization, selection of appropriate polynomials is trivial. The polynomials f(x) = x^6-2 and g(x) = x-2^{177} share the common root 2^{177} modulo 2^{1061}-1

2. **Sieving:** Sieving was by far the most computationally intensive step in this factorization. Although sieving is somewhat memory intensive, requiring one to two gigabytes per process, the individual sieving tasks do not need to interact.

3. **Filtering:** Filtering was performed using the MSIEVE software library (Papadapoulous, 2012). Filtering started with the set of approximately 671 million unique relations. Following the singleton and clique removal steps, the matrix had approximate 282 million rows.

4. **Linear Algebra:** The MSIEVE software library uses the block Lanczos algorithm (Montogomery, 1995) for the linear algebra

5. **Square Root:** MSIEVE uses a straightforward, but memory-intensive, algorithm for the algebraic square root. This involves multiplying all the relations involved in a non-trivial dependency from the linear algebra modulo the monic algebraic polynomial f(x).

Results: The number 2^{1061}-1 is the product of 143-digit and 177-digit prime numbers, P143 and P177, where

P143= 46817226351072266562077767067500697230161897921425283287506897630383940041368 23139211681544651517684724209800447157458585228039804732079435644433

P 177= 5277396428112339175588382160735346093125228962547079720105831757604670549896 4928727027865497640526434935113822732260526319797755339363514620374643318804671877 17179256707148303247

THE GENERAL NUMBER FIELD SIEVE ALGORITHM(GNFS)

The SNFS works on special type of composites, namely integers of the form: r^e-s, for small integers r, s and integer e and the GNFS works on all types of composites. The difference between SNFS and GNFS is in the polynomial selection part of the algorithm, where the special numbers which SNFS can be applied to, make a special class of polynomials especially attractive and the work in the square root step is also more complex for the GNFS.

The steps of the algorithm are as follows:

Algorithm: GNFS

Input: Composite integer n.
Output: A nontrivial factor p of n.
Step 1: (Polynomial Selection)

Find an irreducible polynomial $f(x)$ with root m, i.e, $f(m) \equiv 0 \pmod{n}$, $f(x) \in Z[x]$.

Step 2: (Factor bases)

Choose the size for the factor bases and set up the rational factor base, algebraic factor base and the quadratic character base.

Step 3: (Sieving)

Find pairs of integers (a, b) with the following properties:

- $\gcd(a, b) = 1$
- $a + bm$ is smooth over the rational factor base
- $b^{\deg(f)}f(a/b)$ is smooth over the algebraic factor base

A pair (a, b) with these properties is called a relation. The purpose of the sieving stage is to collect as many relations as possible (at least one larger than the elements in all of the bases combined).

Step 4: (Linear Algebra)

Filter the results from the sieving by removing duplicates and the relations containing a prime ideal not present in any of the other relations. The relations are put into relation-sets and a very large sparse matrix over GF(2) is constructed. The matrix is reduced resulting in some dependencies, ie. elements which lead to a square modulo n.

Step 5: (Square root)

Calculate the rational square root, i.e., y with $y^2 = \displaystyle\prod_{(a,b)\in S} (a - bm)$

Calculate the algebraic square root i.e, x with $x^2 = \displaystyle\prod_{(a,b)\in S} (a - b\alpha)$ where α is a root of $f(x)$.

p can then be found by $\gcd(n, x - y)$ and $\gcd(n, x + y)$.

THE CONTINUED FRACTIONS ALGORITHM(CFRAC)

To describe the Continued Fractions algorithm, the following definitions are required.

- **Legendre's Congruence:** $x^2 \equiv y^2 \bmod n, 0 \le x \le y \le n, \; x \ne y, \; x + y \ne n$. If we have integers x and y which satisfy Legendre's Congruence then $\gcd(n, x - y)$ and $\gcd(n, x + y)$ are possibly nontrivial factors of n.

- **Continued Fraction of Square Root of n:** The square root $\sqrt{n}$ of a square free integer n has a periodic continued fraction of the form

$$\sqrt{n} = [a_0, \overline{a_1, \ldots a_n, 2a_0}]$$

Furthermore we have $0 \le a_i \le 2\sqrt{n}$

- **Convergents of a Continued Fraction:** The convergents P_n/Q_n of a simple continued fraction are defined as:

$$\frac{P_0}{Q_0} = \frac{q_0}{1}, \; \frac{P_1}{Q_1} = \frac{q_{0_1} q_1 + 1}{q_1}, \ldots, \; \frac{P_i}{Q_i} = \frac{q_i P_{i-1} + P_{i-2}}{q_i Q_{i-1} + Q_{i-2}}, i \ge 2$$

Algorithm: CFRAC

Input: Composite integer n.
Output: A nontrivial factor p of n.
Step 1: (Setting up factor base)

Construct the factor base *fb* with all primes below some chosen limit.

Step 2: (Finding Relations)

Compute the continued fraction expansion of $\sqrt{n}$. For each congruent P_i/Q_i compute the corresponding integer $W = P_i^2 - Q_i^2 n$ and if it is *fb*-smooth, store a vector of its prime factorization as its relation. When we have obtained more relations than elements in *fb*, we can proceed to the next step.

Step 3: (Finding Squares)

From the relations we can use Gaussian Elimination over GF(2) and find x and y that satisfy Legendre'Congruence.

Step 4: (gcd)

p can then be found (with a probability 2/3) as $p = \gcd(n, x \pm y)$

The Continued Fractions algorithms uses the convergents of the continued fraction of n and the ones that are smooth over the factor base are kept as relations. The relations are put through a linear algebra step and the ones that yield a square are then used for the gcd step.

THE QUADRATIC SIEVE ALGORITHM

One of the shortcomings of the CFRAC algorithm is that a lot of useless divisions are performed. In (Pomerance, 1985), another algorithm called Quadratic Sieve algorithm is presented that avoids a lot of the useless divisions in the CFRAC algorithm.

Algorithm: QS

Input: Composite integer n.
Output: A nontrivial factor p of n.
Step 1: (Setting up factor base)

Construct the factor base *fb* with all primes p_i below some chosen limit B and which has Legendre symbol $\left(\dfrac{n}{p_i} \right) = 1$.

Step 2: (Finding Relations)

Compute the polynomial Q(x) and define a sieving interbal [-M;M].
Compute $Q(x_i)$ for $x_i \in$ [-M;M]
If $Q(x_i)$ is smooth over the factor base, store x_i as a relation.
Go on to the next step when there are more relations stored than the number of elements in the factor base.

Step 3: (Finding Squares)

From the relations we can use Gaussian Elimination over GF(2) and find x and y that satisfy Legendre'Congruence.

Step 4: (gcd)

p can then be found (with a probability 2/3) as $p = \gcd(n, x \pm y)$

FACTORING CHALLENGES

The RSA numbers webpage (https://en.wikipedia.org/wiki/RSA_numbers) provides the current status regarding the RSA factoring challenges that have been solved and the others that have not been solved.
The small RSA challenges webpage(http://www.loria.fr/~zimmerma/records/rsa.html) lists the following numbers:

RSA-59= 71641520761751435455133616475667090434063332228247871795429

RSA-79= 7293469445285646172092483905177589838606665884410340391954917800303813280 275279

RSA-99= 2567243932811370362436185481696927471681339978306745745605643210744948925 761057 43931776484232708881

RSA119= 5551975077871790827710938021229009352731163006895690063564832463524902860 251720 95023692554648430351832073994158412570 91

The following factoring challenges were listed on the Great Factoring Challenge:
128-bit RSA

Modulus=3081629384434678807576923726100716606 61

256-bit RSA

Modulus=10644421035331445949477617690675461467865299540310463617357821539589 71 47761517

512-bit RSA

Modulus=9978518573603876093789324998666265401107033139797543804288209530518842420 0808760757799832603966566286378966191828314762912905151465240465230284758666724 19

768-bit RSA

Modulus=1139795849900923923354271059604307494555491892673422185149471786568450 88 36 7200309758971432753871671063396422419968309975002399256010074067651730677598 69 2601 61235508638297620399480722593446865428382081962554168639762935230730604239 73

1024-bit RSA

Modulus=135475910240232261321675456529140759144516177876761672134498277465708747 52 5087233245135068420553906863774343232846114200440928785995673673713968910253 43 2672 3589062209692618286024109804122742114195910488645434932408235747195549708 519 289389 15752404867450141760790762070326006945313068083053014321461750291189 159

2048-bit RSA

Modulus=2325585876231366968091927968582533782710021760908832203037251847673439 73 90 9626683560790701279996704968112811606745425688916523929131365419005500844481906776 3268680985221049515927292389861051877339432549238353510687159209861806716746149796 37752963939659380976360308550138194090029222794204392277182870944908547678 9 60033091 64487515764967294009703608877258178304741161112222325594801577470749338 2 6714151519

937488618005508633115479401103518447317803715170660750447008282473243035 2467509551 614116344180057741832511158214977264605112951261874522934571181490 52 88450942831424 285753833986718938630295146077713803941905910743507

4096-bit RSA

Modulus=938526311360739833086461038829310111015989546988043619323285662886971235 82 644890138036629691554576482893328111680177869244449382711632813844244951177753455 2 067560347078549609760810239779140450264304649109141789448063030926854801115778535 6 700499763819838733750946192998999813871367558740066538422941375746591752666094188 9 357072281894025247202832408611788703413041283568184216632841159025854460777424571 2 880103916531526460135345754804456359689082457325574735312314625407274179987017793 8 148089013343595488032048834437536060495736892819062058577148522762291268276200461 7 625541861838591141926085339217945956436487813057186391829827138361714990178182904 9 915144449393594340870311559838614828254853925913240368167632956395100293761485146 3 000932533562233419554979902868479981012465632227235048338834286434436054722539119 1 937162646002410629539652942740518414440586204568499956209044 726172349486625929803 9 376775826752134202521536034602508998391927173084715169491068832471823083219871411 5 057018011007217524634097648303912264283007044031798735411919528095183041644394542 5 140021820621010142963905679455139315860276895906727817218926964548510714202137684 9 270761596906287867558867704258825820241451162605541745494326239501092685160622524 5 64030592281

8192-bit RSA

Modulus=953727866679589993242730584141014275507643236061430112362661425395236558 6 85 36615766069940820775958394325795076080067238605176872358593633548092245722115714 66 72635298836289306025492112254490482819292209213287036540288157450066071910490044 52 97881176949135119878573239330637717669848619536386060219048268463638746215198704 49 69790949491282158429629022142786527173004231319543694721439681163878583206295995 47 30381775438149487467404847059257210269293617286284247952183316677872020738727821 46 46814820760175382154743709592023997331397691281518525207065235050829816785383875 49 55989757615323704785141641806214218228651461127440466475845988982249925861142397 6 65795807386784009253629173423335214017486387553832200075638484073732749021118789 48 82742567264985442135247598191865799665857412389606190799148531675047810577610506 68 60453521641597401733120946704733515334698041805722823547743545136832121557221448 78 29015998362679758166853186531787770178143110449966357019031170276356162605097148 64 67792844033695129315061172327734237880334624945146255354253725581986575497336739 50 02917676160083110941358181594433617334155309605956675175141141469067943516348309 73 15168539663350881125838223807440133242106347124122646992409938007849230996341648 17 05153644879193040513203684939725287447811899187890823267786911627907594917852859 80 04349198490795410506399966511206400577205401685348000914677242518506381138109773 23 95376429037614513167010972546131245792335014677568158996014869835344502005914581 41 93374568402180395032163944771658315986558749714150150872147490833253124116399659 45 15114521180528613260050511402417058302437702750655872156452210561836826689432780 45 59704922839062471842491492991701386822040100158356419205019401793795792749344386 19

3429532518553826376793865329576039237086082712792780492061261406149385587531427556 9526354908432647378407723718238441787238223345037521324998859680116571349114295554 7853294136946045090373631258728555574327772274939813214294412651731282063286557086 8076528388461343630417033895578075151016317523662848554246079305319694841206963780 7319916317082425956865796096231480354590760973029690799887240997768092621572807092 2660118717568676209731826300989426988720067888015952558563931613652927968196225962 5005088340319798086177482479784054060780821571964836150881294382490869202151678017 7631861963443147777980093720340500449715710127462449355211107928253098250439243737 7283910961513316359327352722435355837730167362213365826773651825205522815074453141 06211596893107

FACTORING TOOLS

The webpage (http://www.numberempire.com/numberfactorizer.php) has a number factorizer tool that can factor integers up to 60 digits. Another website that may be useful for factoring is (http://www.alpertron.com.ar/). A good program that may be useful in factoring is yafu (http://sourceforge.net/projects/yafu). The website (http://pgnfs.org) website provides an implementation of the General Number Field Sieve. The website (http://gilchrist.ca/jeff/factoring/nfs_beginners_guide.html) provides instructions as to how to use the GGNFS and MSIEVE library.

FACTORING RECORDS

The largest number factored has been RSA-768, a 232-digit number from RSA's challenge list. The factors of this number presented below were found using the Number field Sieve algorithm(http://www.loria.fr/~zimmerma/records/rsa768.txt)

RSA-768 = 1230186684530117755130494958384962720772853569595334792197322452151726400 5072636575187452021997864693899564749427740638459251925573263034537315482685079170 26122142913461670429214311602221240479274737794080665351419597459856902143413

Both factors of this number have 384-bits or 116 digits:

334780716989568987860441698482126908177047949837137685689124313889828837938780028 761471165253174308773781446799489

*

367460436667995904282446337996279526322791581643430876426760322838157396665112792 3 3373417143396810270092798736308917

For the other factoring records, please refer to the webpage (http://www.cryptoworld.com/Factor-Records.html)

238

SUMMARY

This chapter discussed the special purpose factoring algorithms like the trial division, Pollard's rho method, Pollard's p-1 method, Elliptic Curve method and the Fermat's method. This chapter also surveyed the commonly used algorithms like the Number Field Sieve, The Generalized Number Field Sieve, the Continued Fractions method and the Quadratic Sieve algorithm that are currently used for solving the factorization problem and compared their performance in terms of the number of digits they are able to factorize.

REFERENCES

Aoki, K., Franke, J., Kleinjung, T., Lenstra, A. K., & Osvik, D. A. (2007). A kilobit special number field sieve factorization. In *Advances in Cryptology ASIACRYPT '07*. Berlin: Springer. doi:10.1007/978-3-540-76900-2_1

Cavallar, S., Dodson, B., Lenstra, A. K., Lioen, W. M., Montgomery, P. L., Murphy, B., & Zimmermann, P. et al. (2000). Factorization of a 512-bit RSA modulus. In *Advances in Cryptology, EUROCRYPT 2000*. Berlin: Springer. doi:10.1007/3-540-45539-6_1

Childers, G. (2012). Factorization of a 1061-bit number by the special number field sieve. Cryptology ePrint Archive, Report 2012/444.

Cowie, J., Dodson, B., Elkenbracht–Huizing, R. M., Lenstra, A. K., Montgomery, P. L., & Zayer, J. (1996). A World Wide Number Field Sieve factoring record: On to 512 bits. In *Advances in Cryptography Asiacrypt '96, LNCS* (Vol. *1163*, pp. 382–394). doi:10.1007/BFb0034863

Kleinjung, T., Aoki, K., Franke, J., Lenstra, A., Thome, E., Bos, J., … Zimmermann, P. (2010). Factorization of a 768-bit RSA modulus (Cryptology ePrint Archive, Report 2010/006).

Knuth, D. E. (1981). Art of computer programming: Vol. 2. *Seminumerical Algorithms* (2nd ed.). Reading, Massachusetts: Addison-Wesley.

Lenstra, A. K. (2000). Integer Factoring, Designs. *Codes and Cryptography*, *19*(2/3), 101–128. doi:10.1023/A:1008397921377

Lenstra, A. K., & Lenstra, H. W. Jr. (1993). The development of the number field sieve. In *Lecture Notes in Mathematics* (Vol. 1554). Berlin, Heidelberg: Springer-Verlag. doi:10.1007/BFb0091534

Lenstra, A. K., & Manasse, M. S. (1990). Factoring by electronic mail. In *Advances in Cryptology, Eurocrypt '89, LNCS* (Vol. *434*, pp. 355–371). doi:10.1007/3-540-46885-4_35

Lenstra, H.W., Jr. (1987). Factoring integers with elliptic curves. *Ann. of Math*, *126*, 649–673.

Montgomery, P. L. (1987). Speeding the Pollard and the Elliptic Curve methods of factorization. *Mathematics of Computation*, *48*(177), 243–264. doi:10.1090/S0025-5718-1987-0866113-7

Montgomery, P. L. (1995), A block Lanczos algorithm for finding dependencies over GF(2). *Proceedings of the 14th annual international conference on theory and application of cryptographic techniques* (pp. 106-120). Springer-Verlag.

Papadopoulos, J. (2012). MSIEVE 2012. Retrieved from http://sourceforge.net/projects/msieve/

Pollard, J. M. (1974). Theorems on factororization and primality testing. *Proceedings of the Cambridge Philosophical Society*, *76*(03), 521–528. doi:10.1017/S0305004100049252

Pollard, J. M. (1975). A Monte Carlo method for factorization. *BIT Numerical Mathematics*, *15*(3), 331–334. doi:10.1007/BF01933667

Pomerance, C. (1985) The quadratic sieve factoring algorithm. In T. Beth, N. Cot, & I. Ingemarsson (Eds.), Advances in cryptology: EUROCRYPT '84, LNCS (Vol. 209, pp. 169–182). Springer-Verlag.

KEY TERMS AND DEFINITIONS

Factoring Problem: The integer factoring problem factorizes an integer into its prime factors. If the integer to be factored consists of only two prime numbers, then its factorization is considered very difficult.

Factoring Records: The factoring records indicate the current status of factorization of integers into two component prime numbers. The Wikipedia page RSA Numbers indicate that numbers up to 232 decimal digits have been factored using current computers.

General Purpose Factoring Algorithms: The general purpose factoring algorithms do not assume anything about the factors of the number being factored.

Number Field Sieve: The Number Field Sieve, Special Number Field Sieve and Generalized Number Field Sieve algorithms have been used successfully in the factorization of large RSA composite numbers.

Special Purpose Factoring Algorithms: The Special Purpose Factoring Algorithms rely on some special properties of the factors being factored.

The Continued Fractions Algorithm: A factoring algorithm based on the continued fraction representation of large decimal numbers.

The Quadratic Sieve Algorithm: A factoring algorithms based on the idea factoring over a set of rimes called the factoring base.

Chapter 18
The Quadratic Sieve Algorithm for Integer Factoring

Kannan Balasubramanian
Mepco Schlenk Engineering College, India

M. Rajakani
Mepco Schlenk Engineering College, India

ABSTRACT

At the time when RSA was invented in 1977, factoring integers with as few as 80 decimal digits was intractable. The first major breakthrough was quadratic sieve, a relatively simple factoring algorithm invented by Carl Pomerance in 1981, which can factor numbers up to 100 digits and more. It's still the best-known method for numbers under 110 digits or so; for larger numbers, the general number field sieve (GNFS) is now used. However, the general number field sieve is extremely complicated, for even the most basic implementation. However, GNFS is based on the same fundamental ideas as quadratic sieve. The fundamentals of the Quadratic Sieve algorithm are discussed in this chapter.

INTRODUCTION

At the time when RSA was invented in 1977, factoring integers with as few as 80 decimal digits was intractable; all known algorithms were either too slow or required the number to have a special form. This made even small, 256-bit keys relatively secure. The first major breakthrough was quadratic sieve, a relatively simple factoring algorithm invented by Carl Pomerance in 1981, which can factor numbers up to 100 digits and more. It's still the best-known method for numbers under 110 digits or so; for larger numbers, the general number field sieve (GNFS) is now used. However, the general number field sieve is extremely complicated, and requires extensive explanation and background for even the most basic implementation. However, GNFS is based on the same fundamental ideas as quadratic sieve. The chapter discusses the fundamentals of the Quadratic Sieve algorithm.

DOI: 10.4018/978-1-5225-2915-6.ch018

FINDING A SUBSET OF INTEGERS WHOSE PRODUCT IS A SQUARE

Suppose I give you a set of integers and I ask you to find a subset of those integers whose product is a square, if one exists. For example, given the set $\{10, 24, 35, 52, 54, 78\}$, the product $24\times52\times78$ is 97344 $= 312^2$. The brute-force solution, trying every subset, is too expensive because there are an exponential number of subsets.

Another approach is based on prime factorizations and linear algebra. First, we factor each of the input numbers into prime factors; for now, we will assume that these numbers are easy to factor. For the above example set, we get:

$10 = 2 \times 5$

$24 = 2^3 \times 3$

$35 = 5 \times 7$

$52 = 2^2 \times 13$

$54 = 2 \times 3^3$

$78 = 2 \times 3 \times 13$

When you multiply two numbers written as prime factorizations, you simply add the exponents of the primes used. For example, the exponent of 2 in $24\times52\times78$ is 6, because it's 3 in 24, 2 in 52, and 1 in 78. A number is a square if and only if all the exponents in its prime factorization are even. Suppose we write the above factorizations as vectors, where the kth entry corresponds to the exponent of the kth prime number. We get:

$[1\ 0\ 1\ 0\ 0\ 0]$

$[3\ 1\ 0\ 0\ 0\ 0]$

$[0\ 0\ 1\ 1\ 0\ 0]$

$[2\ 0\ 0\ 0\ 0\ 1]$

$[1\ 3\ 0\ 0\ 0\ 0]$

$[1\ 1\ 0\ 0\ 0\ 1]$

Now, multiplying numbers is as simple as adding vectors. If we add rows 2, 4, and 6, we get $[6\ 2\ 0\ 0\ 0\ 2]$, which has all even exponents and so must be a square. In more familiar terms, we want the last bit of each entry in the sum to be zero. But in this case, we don't need to store all of the numbers above, only the last bit of each number. This gives us the following:

[1 0 1 0 0 0]

[1 1 0 0 0 0]

[0 0 1 1 0 0]

[0 0 0 0 0 1]

[1 1 0 0 0 0]

[1 1 0 0 0 1]

Moreover, since we're only interested in last bits, we can perform all our addition using one-bit integers with wraparound semantics (in other words, mod 2). If we add rows 2, 4, and 6 in this way, we get [0 0 0 0 0 0 0], the zero vector. In fact, all squares correspond to the zero vector.

Let's rephrase this as a matrix equation problem. If we transpose the above matrix, so that rows become columns, we get this:

[1 1 0 0 1 1]

[0 1 0 0 1 1]

[1 0 1 0 0 0]

[0 0 1 0 0 0]

[0 0 0 0 0 0]

[0 0 0 1 0 1]

Call this matrix A. If we multiply A by the vector [0 1 0 1 0 1], using one-bit integer arithmetic, we get the zero vector. This tells us precisely which numbers we need to multiply to get a square. So, our goal is to find a nonzero vector x such that $Ax=0$ (remember, all arithmetic here is with one-bit integers).

If you've had a course in linear algebra, this problem should look very familiar; it's the problem of finding the null space of a matrix, the set of vectors such that $Ax=0$. The problem can be solved using row reduction (Gaussian elimination). We row reduce the matrix, and then assign values to the free variables in a way that gives us a nonzero solution. The other variables will be determined by these values and the matrix. You probably studied this problem using rational numbers, not one-bit integers, but it turns out row reduction works just as well for these. For example, if we add row 1 to row 3 in the above matrix, we get the following:

[1 1 0 0 1 1]

[0 1 0 0 1 1]

[0 1 1 0 1 1]

[0 0 1 0 0 0]

[0 0 0 0 0 0]

[0 0 0 1 0 1]

Completing the row reduction, we eventually end up with this matrix:

[1 0 0 0 0 0]

[0 1 0 0 1 1]

[0 0 1 0 0 0]

[0 0 0 1 0 1]

[0 0 0 0 0 0]

[0 0 0 0 0 0]

If we turn this back into a system of equations and rearrange, we get this:

$x_1 = 0$

$x_2 = -x_5 - x_6$

$x_3 = 0$

$x_4 = -x_6$

Suppose we choose $x_5 = 0$, $x_6 = 1$. From the above equations, it follows that the first four vectors have the values 0, 1, 0, and 1 (remember, one-bit integer arithmetic). This gives us our final vector, [0 1 0 1 0 1]. If we were to choose $x_5 = 1$ and $x_6 = 0$ instead, we'd get a different solution: [0 1 0 0 1 0], corresponding to $24 \times 54 = 1296 = 36^2$. Moreover, a theorem of linear algebra tells us precisely how many input numbers we need to guarantee that a square can be found: as long as we have more columns than rows, the null space is guaranteed to be nontrivial, so that we have a nonzero solution. In other words, we just need more numbers than prime factors used by those numbers. As this case shows, though, this isn't a necessary condition.

The one remaining problem with this method is that if one of the numbers in our set happens to have very large factors, our matrix will have a large number of rows, which requires a lot of storage and makes row reduction inefficient. To avoid this, we require that the input numbers are *B-smooth*, meaning that they only have small factors less than some integer B. This also makes them easy to factor.

FERMAT'S METHOD: FACTORING USING A DIFFERENCE OF SQUARES

Although not efficient in general, the Fermat's method embodies the same basic idea as quadratic sieve and works great for numbers with factors close to their square root.

The idea is to find two numbers a and b such that $a^2 - b^2 = n$, the number we wish to factor. If we can do this, simple algebra tells us that $(a+b)(a-b) = n$. If we're lucky, this is a nontrivial factorization of n; if we're not so lucky, one of them is 1 and the other is n. The concept behind Fermat's algorithm is to search for an integer a such that $a^2 - n$ is a square. If we find such an a, it follows that:

$$a^2 - (a^2 - n) = n$$

Hence, we have a difference of squares equal to n. The search is a straightforward linear search: we begin with the ceiling of the square root of n, the smallest possible number such that $a^2 - n$ is positive, and increment a until $a^2 - n$ becomes a square. If this ever happens, we try to factor n as $(a - \mathrm{sqrt}(a^2 - n))(a + \mathrm{sqrt}(a^2 - n))$; if the factorization is trivial, we continue incrementing a.

Here's an example of Fermat's method. Let $n = 5959$; a starts out at 78. The numbers $78^2 - 5959$ and $79^2 - 5959$ are not squares, but $80^2 - 5959 = 441 = 21^2$. Hence $(80-21)(80+21) = 5959$, and this gives the nontrivial factorization $59 \times 101 = 5959$. The reason Fermat's method is slow is because simply performing a linear search of all possible a hoping that we'll hit one with $a^2 - n$ square is a poor strategy — there just aren't that many squares around to hit. A better way of going about it is to proactively compute an a having this property (actually a similar property). The key is to notice that if we take a number of $a^2 - n$ values, none of which are squares themselves, and multiply them, we may get a square, say S. Let A be the product of the corresponding values of a. Basic algebra shows that $A^2 - S$ is a multiple of n. Hence, $(A - \mathrm{sqrt}(S))(A + \mathrm{sqrt}(S))$ is a factorization of *some multiple* of n; in other words, at least one of these shares a factor with n. By computing the greatest common divisor (GCD) of each with n using Euclid's algorithm, we can identify this factor. Again, it may be trivial (just n itself); if so we try again with a different square.

All that remains is, given a list of $a^2 - n$ values, to find a subset whose product is a square. But this is precisely an instance of the problem discussed in the last section. Unfortunately, recall that that the method we came up with there is not efficient for numbers with large factors; the matrix becomes too large. What do we do? We simply throw away numbers with large factors! Theoretical results show that there are a fairly large number of values in the sequence a^2-n that are smooth (recall that smooth numbers have only small factors). This gives us a new factoring method that works pretty well up to a point.

For example, consider the number 90283. If we start a at 301 and increment it up to 360 while computing a^2-n, we get the following values:

318, 921, 1526, 2133, 2742, 3353, 3966, 4581, 5198, 5817, 6438, 7061, 7686, 8313, 8942, 9573, 10206, 10841, 11478, 12117, 12758, 13401, 14046, 14693, 15342, 15993, 16646, 17301, 17958, 18617, 19278, 19941, 20606, 21273, 21942, 22613, 23286, 23961, 24638, 25317, 25998, 26681, 27366, 28053, 28742, 29433, 30126, 30821, 31518, 32217, 32918, 33621, 34326, 35033, 35742, 36453, 37166, 37881, 38598, 39317

None of these are squares (the first square occurs at $a=398$); however, if we factor each value we will discover that 7 of these values have no factor larger than 43:

6438, 10206, 16646, 19278, 19941, 30821, 35742

If we take these 7 values and feed them to the algorithm described in the last section, it finds a square: $19278 \times 19941 \times 30821 \times 35742 = 423481541612104836 = 650754594^2$. The corresponding original a were 331, 332, 348, and 355, and their product is 13576057680. Now, we can factor the number:

$(13576057680-650754594)(13576057680+650754594) = 12925303086 \times 14226812274$ is a multiple of 90283

GCD(90283, 12925303086) = 137

GCD(90283, 14226812274) = 659

$137 \times 659 = 90283$.

MAKING IT FASTER: SIEVING FOR SMOOTH NUMBERS

The factorization algorithm above is considerably better than Fermat's algorithm, but if we try to scale up the size of number we factor, we quickly encounter a bottleneck: finding the smooth numbers in the sequence. Only 7 of the 60 values we computed in our last example were 43-smooth (actually we were lucky to get a square with so few vectors). As the size of the number that we're factoring grows, so does the size of the numbers in the sequence, and the proportion of smooth numbers rapidly shrinks. Although finding smooth numbers doesn't require completely factoring every number in the sequence (we only have to test primes up to the smoothness limit), it's still too expensive to test every number in the sequence this way.

The key is to observe that the prime factors of the sequence a^2-n follow a predictable sequence. Let's take a look at the prime factorizations of the first ten or so numbers in our example sequence above:

$318 = 2 \times 3 \times 53$

$921 = 3 \times 307$

$1526 = 2 \times 7 \times 109$

$2133 = 3^3 \times 79$

$2742 = 2 \times 3 \times 457$

$3353 = 7 \times 479$

$3966 = 2 \times 3 \times 661$

$4581 = 3^2 \times 509$

$5198 = 2 \times 23 \times 113$

$5817 = 3 \times 7 \times 277$

The most obvious pattern is that every other number is even, beginning with the first one. This should be no surprise, since we're effectively adding $2a+1$ to get each new number, which is always odd. Also, you'll notice that the first and second numbers are divisible by 3, as are the fourth and fifth, the seventh and eighth, and so on. If you look at the larger list, you'll notice similar patterns for larger primes; for example, the 3rd and 6th numbers are divisible by 7, and every 7th number after each of them as well. And, mysteriously, not one number in our entire sequence is divisible by 5!

So, what's going on? The answer involves what number theorists call *quadratic residues*. A number a is called a *quadratic residue mod p* if there is some square S such that $S-a$ is divisible by p. Half of all numbers are quadratic residues mod p, regardless of the value of p, and there's a simple formula for determining whether or not a particular number is: just take a, raise it to the power $(p-1)/2$, and then take the remainder after division by p. Then a is a quadratic residue mod p if and only if the answer is 1. Although this computation seems to involve very large values, in fact we can compute it quite quickly using "exponentiation by squaring" combined with frequent remainder operations.

This explains why none of our values are divisible by 5. If we compute $90283^{(5-1)/2}$ mod 5, we get 4, which is not 1 (remember that 90283 is our original n to be factored). Thus, there is no square such that $S-n$ is divisible by 5; but all numbers in our sequence have this form. In practice, this means we can compute just once ahead of time which factors may occur in the sequence (primes p such that n is a quadratic residue mod p), and ignore all others.

For our next mystery, why is it that given a number in the sequence divisible by p, every pth number after that is also divisible by p? Well, simple algebra shows that if $a^2-n=kp$, then:

$$(a+p)^2-n = (a^2-n)+p(2a+p) = kp+p(2a+p).$$

But this does not explain why it always seems to be the case that there are *exactly two* different initial values of a such that $a^2 - n$ is divisible by p (with the exception of $p=2$). For example, in our sequence above the 3rd and 6th values were divisible by 7. The answer again is quadratic residues: it can be shown that the modular equation $x^2 \equiv y \pmod{p}$ has exactly two solutions (if it has any), and in fact there is an efficient algorithm for computing these two solutions called the 'Shanks-Tonelli algorithm. I won't go into it here since it requires some background in number theory, but for small primes it isn't really needed; it suffices to test the first p numbers to see which are divisible by p. For larger primes, it becomes important to avoid this expensive scan.

Recall the "Sieve of Eratosthenes" algorithm for locating prime numbers. It starts with a list of numbers, then crosses off all numbers not divisible by 2 except 2, then does the same for 3, 5, and so on until it's done. The numbers that remain must be prime. When attempting to find a list of prime numbers, this strategy is much more efficient than running even the most advanced primality test on each number individually.

We take a similar strategy here: we begin with a table of the original values in the sequence. We then visit all the numbers divisible by 2 and divide out a factor of 2. We do the same for each power of 2 up to the size of the sequence. We then do the same for every other prime up to our smoothness bound (43 in our example). In the end, the smooth numbers and only the smooth numbers will have become 1. Since we visit less and less list elements as the prime factor increases, the overall work is much less. For example, here's our original list from the above example:

318, 921, 1526, 2133, 2742, 3353, 3966, 4581, 5198, 5817, 6438, 7061, 7686, 8313, 8942, 9573, 10206, 10841, 11478, 12117, 12758, 13401, 14046, 14693, 15342, 15993, 16646, 17301, 17958, 18617, 19278, 19941, 20606, 21273, 21942, 22613, 23286, 23961, 24638, 25317, 25998, 26681, 27366, 28053, 28742, 29433, 30126, 30821, 31518, 32217, 32918, 33621, 34326, 35033, 35742, 36453, 37166, 37881, 38598, 39317

We visit elements 1, 3, 5, and so on, dividing out 2. Here's the list after this first pass is complete:

159, 921, 763, 2133, 1371, 3353, 1983, 4581, 2599, 5817, 3219, 7061, 3843, 8313, 4471, 9573, 5103, 10841, 5739, 12117, 6379, 13401, 7023, 14693, 7671, 15993, 8323, 17301, 8979, 18617, 9639, 19941, 10303, 21273, 10971, 22613, 11643, 23961, 12319, 25317, 12999, 26681, 13683, 28053, 14371, 29433, 15063, 30821, 15759, 32217, 16459, 33621, 17163, 35033, 17871, 36453, 18583, 37881, 19299, 39317

Here it is after dividing out the prime factors 3, 5, 7, 11, 13, and 17:

53, 307, 109, 79, 457, 479, 661, 509, 2599, 277, 1073, 7061, 61, 163, 263, 3191, 1, 10841, 1913, 577, 6379, 1489, 2341, 2099, 2557, 1777, 1189, 5767, 2993, 18617, 1, 23, 10303, 1013, 1219, 22613, 3881, 163, 12319, 2813, 619, 26681, 4561, 1039, 2053, 9811, 5021, 37, 103, 10739, 16459, 1601, 1907, 35033, 851, 12151, 18583, 1403, 919, 39317

We see a couple 1's have already appeared; these are 17-smooth numbers. When we get all the way up through 43, we have:

53, 307, 109, 79, 457, 479, 661, 509, 113, 277, 1, 307, 61, 163, 263, 3191, 1, 293, 1913, 577, 6379, 1489, 2341, 2099, 2557, 1777, 1, 5767, 73, 18617, 1, 1, 10303, 1013, 53, 22613, 3881, 163, 12319, 97, 619, 26681, 4561, 1039, 2053, 9811, 5021, 1, 103, 10739, 16459, 1601, 1907, 35033, 1, 419, 18583, 61, 919, 39317

We see several numbers set to 53 or 61; these would be smooth if we raised our bound a little bit.

This sieving process is where quadratic sieve gets its name from. This drastically decreases the overall work needed to find a sufficient number of smooth numbers, making it practical for very large numbers. This basic implementation could probably handle numbers up to 50-60 digits.

IMPROVEMENTS AND OPTIMIZATIONS

Quadratic sieve admits a number of "bells and whistles" to dramatically improve its runtime in practice. We mention only a few of the most important ones here. The simple row reduction method of Gaussian elimination is not able to accommodate the very large smoothness bounds needed to factor large numbers, which often range in the millions, mostly due to space limitations; such matrices, if stored explicitly, would require trillions of bits. However, this method is wasteful, because most of the entries in the matrix are zero (they must be; each number has no more than $\log_2 n$ prime factors). Instead of using an actual two-dimensional array, we can just keep a list for each column that lists the positions of the 1 bits in that column. We then use a method well-suited to reducing sparse matrices such as the Lanczos algorithm. This still requires a fair amount of space; it's common to use block algorithms that work on small portions of the matrix at one time, storing the rest of the matrix on disk. The matrix step is notoriously difficult to parallelize and for large problems is often done on a single high-performance supercomputer.

The most expensive step by far is the sieving, which can require scanning billions of numbers to locate the needed smooth numbers. A common trick is to only track the approximate logarithm of each number, usually in fixed-point arithmetic. Then, when visiting each number, instead of performing an expensive division we only have to subtract. This introduces a bit of rounding error into the algorithm, but that's okay; by rounding consistently in the correct direction, we can ensure that we don't miss any smooth numbers and only capture a few spurious numbers that we can quickly check and reject. Because the logarithms of small primes are small, and require visiting more numbers than any others, primes like 2 and 3 are often dropped altogether.

Another problem is that $a^2 - n$ grows fairly quickly; because smaller numbers are more likely to be smooth, we get diminishing returns as we scan higher in the sequence. To get around this, we scan values of not just the sequence $a^2 - n$ but also a number of similar sequences such as $(Ca+b)^2 - n$ for suitable constants C, b. This variation is called the multiple polynomial quadratic sieve, since each of these sequences can be seen as the values of polynomial in a.

Finally, although the matrix step does not admit simple parallelization due to many data dependencies, the sieving step is perfectly suited to massive parallelization. Each processor or machine simply takes a portion of the sequence to scan for smooth numbers by itself, returning the small quantity of smooth numbers that it discovers to a central processor. As soon as the central processor has accumulated enough smooth numbers, it asks all the workers to stop. In the multiple polynomial variant, it's common to assign some of the polynomials to each machine.

One peculiar idea for massively parallelizing the sieving step, invented by Adi Shamir, is to use not computers but a specially constructed sieving device based on light emitters and sensors called "TWINKLE". The concept is that we have a light for each prime number whose intensity is proportional to the logarithm of that prime. Each light turns on just two times every p cycles, corresponding to the two square roots of n mod p. A sensor senses the combined intensity of all the lights together, and if this is close enough to the logarithm of the current value, that value is a smooth number candidate.

THE QUADRATIC SIEVE ALGORITHM

The quadratic sieve algorithm is based on the concept of a factor base which is a small set of prime numbers used in sieving. The Fermat's method of factorization we check x^2 mod N to be a perfect square.

However, this task of finding congruence of squares is almost impractical for large numbers as there are $\sqrt{N}$ squares less than N. A simpler method introduced in (Dixon, 1981). In this method, a bound B and factor base P which is a set of prime numbers less than or equal to B. We randomly pick a positive integer z such that z^2 is B-smooth. A positive integer is called B-smooth if none of its prime factors is greater than B. Written mathematically,

$$z^2 \equiv \sum_{P_i \in P} p_i^{q_i} \bmod N$$

Then after collecting relations a little bit more than the size of the factor base, check a combination on the right-hand side that their multiplication is a square. Remember, in order for a number to be a square, the exponents of the primes on the right-hand side must be even. You can use Gaussian elimination to determine this step. Finally, the calculation produces a congruence of the form $a \equiv b^2$ mod N and the Fermat theorem can then be applied.

The Quadratic sieve algorithm is an Integer factorization algorithm developed by Carl Pomerance as an improvement to Dixon's factorization method (Pomerance, 1982). As of today, it is the second fastest algorithm after General number field sieve and still is regarded as the fastest for numbers less than 100 digits.

The quadratic sieve algorithm has two phases: the data collection and data processing phase. During the data collection phase, all necessary in-formation that may lead to factorization of a number is gathered. These information are pairs of integers x and $Q(x)$ that meet the condition $x^2 \equiv y^2$ mod N. During data processing phase, the data is placed in matrix then the algorithm attempts to find the factors by search for congruence of squares.

As in Dixon's factorization method, the basic idea is, in order to factor a number N, find two numbers x and y such that $x^2 \equiv y^2$ mod N and $x \not\equiv \pm y$ mod N. This implies a $(x - y)(x + y) \equiv 0(mod N)$, and can be simply computed as $(x - y; N)$ using the Euclidean Algorithm to check if this divisor is nontrivial. At least, the chance that the factor is nontrivial is greater than half.

During the first data collection pahse, the algorithm attempts to find pairs of integers x and $Q(x)$ that satisfy the condition $x^2 \equiv y^2$ mod N. It chooses a set of primes called *factor base*, and tries to find x such that the remainder of $Q(x) = x^2$mod N factorizes completely over the factor base. The x values are said to be smooth over the factor base. One technique used by QS to speed-up finding the above relations is to take x as close as the square root of n. This ensures that $Q(x)$ is smaller and as a result have greater chance of being smooth.

$$Q(x) = \left(\left\lceil \sqrt{N} \right\rceil + x\right)^2 - N \text{ x is a small integer}$$

$$Q(x) \approx 2x \left\lceil \sqrt{N} \right\rceil$$

Simply increasing the size of the factor base can also increase the chance of smoothness. The next step is to compute $Q(x_1)$, $Q(x_2)$, ..., $Q(x_k)$ for a set of values $x_1, x_2, ..., x_k$. From the set of values $Q(x)$, pick a subset such that $Q(x_{i1})$, $Q(x_{i2})$, ..., $Q(x_{ir}) \equiv (x_{i1} x_{i2}, ..., x_{ir})^2 \pmod{N}$.

The steps of the Quadratic Sieve Algorithm are summarized as follows:

Algorithm: Quadratic Sieve Algorithm

1. *Input*: number N to be factored
2. *Output*: two factors of N
3. Choose a bound B
4. Let $\prod(B)$ = the number of primes less than or equal to B. Call those prime numbers as $p_1 \ldots p_k$.
5. Find $\prod(B)$ +1 numbers a_i so that $a_i^2 \bmod N = b_i$ is B-smooth meaning $b_i = p_1^{q_{i1}} p_2^{q_{i2}} \ldots p_k^{q_{ik}}$
6. Represent b_i as matrix $b_i = (q_{i1} \bmod 2, q_{i2} \bmod 2, \ldots\ldots q_{ik} \bmod 2)$
7. Use Linear Algebra to find a subset of those vectors b_i which add to the zero vector.
8. Multiply to all corresponding a_i and corresponding b_i to produce $a^2 \equiv b^2 \bmod N$ where $a = \prod a_i$ and $b^2 = \prod b_i$
9. *If* gcd($a+b$, N) is non-trivial then
   return gcd($a+b$, N) as one factor of N
   return N/gcd($a+b$,N) as the other factor of N
   else
   Try different set of b_i or different a_i
   endif

SUMMARY

This chapter discussed the Quadratic Sieve algorithm and its implementations. This chapter discussed improvements and optimizations that can be made for this algorithm.

REFERENCES

Dixon, J. D. (1981). Asymptotically Fast Factorization of Integers. *Mathematics of Computation, 36*(153), 255. doi:10.1090/S0025-5718-1981-0595059-1

Garrett, S. L. (2008). *On the Quadratic Sieve* [Master's Thesis]. University of North Carolina at Greensboro.

Ghebregiorgish, S. T. (2012). *Quadratic Sieve Integer Factorization using Hadoop* [Master's Thesis]. University of Stavanger.

Jansen, P. L. (2005). *Integer Factorization* [Master's Thesis]. University of Copenhagen.

Microsoft. (2006) Factoring large numbers with quadratic sieve. *Microsoft developer.* Retrieved from https://blogs.msdn.microsoft.com/devdev/2006/06/19/factoring-large-numbers-with-quadratic-sieve/

Pomerance, C. (1982). Analysis and Comparison of Some Integer Factoring Algorithms, in Computational Methods in Number Theory, Part I. In H.W. Lenstra, Jr. And R. Tiejdeman, (Eds.), Math, Centre Tract 154, Amsterdam (pp. 89-139).

Seibert, C. (2011). Integer Factorization using the Quadratic Sieve. *Proceedings of MICS '11.* Retrieved from micsymposium.org/mics_2011_proceedings/mics2011_submission_28.pdf

Shamir, A. (1999). Factoring Large numbers with the TWINKLE Device. Retrieved from http://link.springer.com/content/pdf/10.1007%2F3-540-48059-5_2.pdf

KEY TERMS AND DEFINITIONS

B-Smooth: Numbers that can be factored over the factor base.

Factor Base: A set of prime numbers used in the Sieving algorithm.

Sieving: A step in the factorization algorithms to find factors of a number.

The Quadratic Sieve, The Number Field Sieve, The Generalized Number Field Sieve: The QS, NFS and GNFS are algorithms for integer factorization.

Related References

To continue our tradition of advancing research on topics in the field of engineering, we have compiled a list of recommended IGI Global readings. These references will provide additional information and guidance to further enrich your knowledge and assist you with your own research and future publications.

Abawajy, J. H., Pathan, M., Rahman, M., Pathan, A., & Deris, M. M. (2013). *Network and traffic engineering in emerging distributed computing applications.* Hershey, PA: IGI Global. doi:10.4018/978-1-4666-1888-6

Abu-Faraj, Z. O. (2012). Bioengineering/biomedical engineering education. In Z. Abu-Faraj (Ed.), Handbook of research on biomedical engineering education and advanced bioengineering learning: Interdisciplinary concepts (pp. 1–59). Hershey, PA: IGI Global. doi:10.4018/978-1-4666-0122-2.ch001

Abu-Nimeh, S., & Mead, N. R. (2012). Combining security and privacy in requirements engineering. In T. Chou (Ed.), Information assurance and security technologies for risk assessment and threat management: Advances (pp. 273–290). Hershey, PA: IGI Global. doi:10.4018/978-1-61350-507-6.ch011

Abu-Taieh, E., El Sheikh, A., & Jafari, M. (2012). *Technology engineering and management in aviation: Advancements and discoveries.* Hershey, PA: IGI Global. doi:10.4018/978-1-60960-887-3

Achumba, I. E., Azzi, D., & Stocker, J. (2010). Low-cost virtual laboratory workbench for electronic engineering. *International Journal of Virtual and Personal Learning Environments, 1*(4), 1–17. doi:10.4018/jvple.2010100101

Achumba, I. E., Azzi, D., & Stocker, J. (2012). Low-cost virtual laboratory workbench for electronic engineering. In M. Thomas (Ed.), Design, implementation, and evaluation of virtual learning environments (pp. 201–217). Hershey, PA: IGI Global. doi:10.4018/978-1-4666-1770-4.ch014

Addo-Tenkorang, R., & Eyob, E. (2013). Engineer-to-order: A maturity concurrent engineering best practice in improving supply chains. In Industrial engineering: Concepts, methodologies, tools, and applications (pp. 1780-1796). Hershey, PA: IGI Global. doi:10.4018/978-1-4666-1945-6.ch095

Aguilera, A., & Davim, J. (2014). *Research developments in wood engineering and technology.* Hershey, PA: IGI Global. doi:10.4018/978-1-4666-4554-7

Aharoni, A., & Reinhartz-Berger, I. (2013). Semi-automatic composition of situational methods. In K. Siau (Ed.), Innovations in database design, web applications, and information systems management (pp. 335–364). Hershey, PA: IGI Global. doi:10.4018/978-1-4666-2044-5.ch013

Ahmad, M., Jung, L. T., & Zaman, N. (2014). A comparative analysis of software engineering approaches for sequence analysis. In Software design and development: Concepts, methodologies, tools, and applications (pp. 1093–1102). Hershey, PA: IGI Global. doi:10.4018/978-1-4666-4301-7.ch053

Ahrens, A., Bassus, O., & Zaščerinska, J. (2014). Enterprise 2.0 in engineering curriculum. In M. Cruz-Cunha, F. Moreira, & J. Varajão (Eds.), Handbook of research on enterprise 2.0: Technological, social, and organizational dimensions (pp. 599–617). Hershey, PA: IGI Global. doi:10.4018/978-1-4666-4373-4.ch031

Akbar, D. (2012). Community engagement in engineering education: Needs and learning outcomes. In M. Rasul (Ed.), Developments in engineering education standards: Advanced curriculum innovations (pp. 301–317). Hershey, PA: IGI Global. doi:10.4018/978-1-4666-0951-8.ch017

Alam, F., Subic, A., Plumb, G., Shortis, M., & Chandra, R. P. (2012). An innovative offshore delivery of an undergraduate mechanical engineering program. In M. Rasul (Ed.), Developments in engineering education standards: Advanced curriculum innovations (pp. 233–245). Hershey, PA: IGI Global. doi:10.4018/978-1-4666-0951-8.ch013

Ali, D. F., Patil, A., & Nordin, M. S. (2012). Visualization skills in engineering education: Issues, developments, and enhancement. In A. Patil, H. Eijkman, & E. Bhattacharyya (Eds.), New media communication skills for engineers and IT professionals: Trans-national and trans-cultural demands (pp. 175–203). Hershey, PA: IGI Global. doi:10.4018/978-1-4666-0243-4.ch011

Aljawarneh, S. (2013). Cloud security engineering: Avoiding security threats the right way. In S. Aljawarneh (Ed.), Cloud computing advancements in design, implementation, and technologies (pp. 147–153). Hershey, PA: IGI Global. doi:10.4018/978-1-4666-1879-4.ch010

Alkhatib, G. (2012). *Models for capitalizing on web engineering advancements: Trends and discoveries.* Hershey, PA: IGI Global. doi:10.4018/978-1-4666-0023-2

Allee, T., Handorf, A., & Li, W. (2010). Electrospinning: Development and biomedical applications. In A. Shukla & R. Tiwari (Eds.), Intelligent medical technologies and biomedical engineering: Tools and applications (pp. 48–78). Hershey, PA: IGI Global. doi:10.4018/978-1-61520-977-4.ch003

Alsmadi, I. (2014). Website performance measurement: Process and product metrics. In Software design and development: Concepts, methodologies, tools, and applications (pp. 1801–1827). Hershey, PA: IGI Global. doi:10.4018/978-1-4666-4301-7.ch086

Altarawneh, H., Alamaro, S., & El Sheikh, A. (2012). Web engineering and business intelligence: Agile web engineering development and practice. In A. Rahman El Sheikh & M. Alnoukari (Eds.), Business intelligence and agile methodologies for knowledge-based organizations: Cross-disciplinary applications (pp. 313–344). Hershey, PA: IGI Global. doi:10.4018/978-1-61350-050-7.ch015

Altarawneh, H., & El-Shiekh, A. (2010). Web engineering in small Jordanian web development firms: An XP based process model. In A. Tatnall (Ed.), Web technologies: Concepts, methodologies, tools, and applications (pp. 1696–1707). Hershey, PA: IGI Global. doi:10.4018/978-1-60566-982-3.ch091

Alzoabi, Z. (2014). Agile software: Body of knowledge. In Software design and development: Concepts, methodologies, tools, and applications (pp. 96–116). Hershey, PA: IGI Global. doi:10.4018/978-1-4666-4301-7.ch006

Andrade-Campos, A. (2013). Development of an optimization framework for parameter identification and shape optimization problems in engineering. In J. Davim (Ed.), Dynamic methods and process advancements in mechanical, manufacturing, and materials engineering (pp. 1–24). Hershey, PA: IGI Global. doi:10.4018/978-1-4666-1867-1.ch001

Andreatos, A. (2012). Educating the 21st century's engineers and IT professionals. In A. Patil, H. Eijkman, & E. Bhattacharyya (Eds.), New media communication skills for engineers and IT professionals: Trans-national and trans-cultural demands (pp. 132–159). Hershey, PA: IGI Global. doi:10.4018/978-1-4666-0243-4.ch009

Annamalai, C., & Ramayah, T. (2013). Reengineering for enterprise resource planning (ERP) systems implementation: An empirical analysis of assessing critical success factors (CSFs) of manufacturing organizations. In Industrial engineering: Concepts, methodologies, tools, and applications (pp. 791-806). Hershey, PA: IGI Global. doi:10.4018/978-1-4666-1945-6.ch044

Antchev, M. (2010). Other applications of converters and systems of converters. In Technologies for electrical power conversion, efficiency, and distribution: Methods and processes (pp. 270–299). Hershey, PA: IGI Global. doi:10.4018/978-1-61520-647-6.ch011

Anzelotti, G., & Valizadeh, M. (2010). Purpose-oriented small software: A case study for some engineering subjects. In R. Luppicini & A. Haghi (Eds.), Cases on digital technologies in higher education: Issues and challenges (pp. 164–178). Hershey, PA: IGI Global. doi:10.4018/978-1-61520-869-2.ch012

Anzelotti, G., & Valizadeh, M. (2010). Sights inside the virtual engineering education. In D. Russell & A. Haghi (Eds.), Web-based engineering education: Critical design and effective tools (pp. 160–174). Hershey, PA: IGI Global. doi:10.4018/978-1-61520-659-9.ch012

Asadi, M., Mohabbati, B., Gašević, D., Bagheri, E., & Hatala, M. (2012). Developing semantically-enabled families of method-oriented architectures. *International Journal of Information System Modeling and Design*, *3*(4), 1–26. doi:10.4018/jismd.2012100101

Augusti, G., & Feyo de Azevedo, S. (2011). Qualification frameworks and field-specific approaches to quality assurance: Initiatives in engineering and technical education. *International Journal of Quality Assurance in Engineering and Technology Education*, *1*(1), 44–57. doi:10.4018/ijqaete.2011010104

Aung, Z., & Nyunt, K. K. (2014). Constructive knowledge management model and information retrieval methods for software engineering. In Software design and development: Concepts, methodologies, tools, and applications (pp. 253–269). Hershey, PA: IGI Global. doi:10.4018/978-1-4666-4301-7.ch014

Azad, A. K., Auer, M. E., & Harward, V. (2012). *Internet accessible remote laboratories: Scalable e-learning tools for engineering and science disciplines.* Hershey, PA: IGI Global. doi:10.4018/978-1-61350-186-3

Azar, A. T. (2013). Overview of biomedical engineering. In Bioinformatics: Concepts, methodologies, tools, and applications (pp. 1-28). Hershey, PA: Medical Information Science Reference. doi:10.4018/978-1-4666-3604-0.ch001

Badr, K. B., Badr, A. B., & Ahmad, M. N. (2013). Phases in ontology building methodologies: A recent review. In M. Nazir Ahmad, R. Colomb, & M. Abdullah (Eds.), Ontology-based applications for enterprise systems and knowledge management (pp. 100–123). Hershey, PA: IGI Global. doi:10.4018/978-1-4666-1993-7.ch006

Baer, W., & Renfro, C. (2013). Information sources and collection planning for engineering. In S. Holder (Ed.), Library collection development for professional programs: Trends and best practices (pp. 128–144). Hershey, PA: IGI Global. doi:10.4018/978-1-4666-1897-8.ch008

Baghdadi, Y., & Kraiem, N. (2014). Business process modeling with services: reverse engineering databases. In R. Perez-Castillo & M. Piattini (Eds.), Uncovering essential software artifacts through business process archeology (pp. 177–200). Hershey, PA: IGI Global. doi:10.4018/978-1-4666-4667-4.ch007

Bakopoulou, A., Leyhausen, G., Geurtsen, W., & Koidis, P. (2013). Dental tissue engineering research and translational approaches towards clinical application. In A. Daskalaki (Ed.), Medical advancements in aging and regenerative technologies: Clinical tools and applications (pp. 279–312). Hershey, PA: IGI Global. doi:10.4018/978-1-4666-2506-8.ch013

Baporikar, N. (2012). Developing right graduate attributes through project-based teaching. In M. Rasul (Ed.), Developments in engineering education standards: Advanced curriculum innovations (pp. 64–79). Hershey, PA: IGI Global. doi:10.4018/978-1-4666-0951-8.ch004

Baraldi, E., & Nadin, G. (2012). "Network process re-engineering" in a home textile network: The importance of business relationships and actor bonds. In T. Choi (Ed.), Fashion supply chain management: Industry and business analysis (pp. 212–234). Hershey, PA: IGI Global. doi:10.4018/978-1-60960-756-2.ch012

Barbu, M. C., Hasener, J., & Bernardy, G. (2014). Modern testing of wood-based panels, process control, and modeling. In A. Aguilera & J. Davim (Eds.), Research developments in wood engineering and technology (pp. 90–130). Hershey, PA: IGI Global. doi:10.4018/978-1-4666-4554-7.ch003

Bas, T. G. (2013). Dual market(ing) in bio-engineering high technology new products: The risk of uncertainty and failure. *International Journal of Measurement Technologies and Instrumentation Engineering*, *3*(2), 63–74. doi:10.4018/ijmtie.2013040104

Bedi, P., Gandotra, V., & Singhal, A. (2014). Innovative strategies for secure software development. In Software design and development: Concepts, methodologies, tools, and applications (pp. 2099–2119). Hershey, PA: IGI Global. doi:10.4018/978-1-4666-4301-7.ch097

Bellatreche, L. (2010). *Data warehousing design and advanced engineering applications: Methods for complex construction*. Hershey, PA: IGI Global. doi:10.4018/978-1-60566-756-0

Bhattacharyya, S., & Dutta, P. (2013). Handbook of research on computational intelligence for engineering, science, and business (Vols. 1–2). Hershey, PA: IGI Global. doi:10.4018/978-1-4666-2518-1

Blicblau, A. S., & Richards, D. (2012). Development of real world project skills for engineering students. *International Journal of Quality Assurance in Engineering and Technology Education*, 2(1), 1–13. doi:10.4018/ijqaete.2012010101

Boci, E. S., Sarkani, S., & Mazzuchi, T. A. (2013). Development of a complex geospatial/RF design model in support of service volume engineering design. In M. Bartolacci & S. Powell (Eds.), Advancements and innovations in wireless communications and network technologies (pp. 56–67). Hershey, PA: IGI Global. doi:10.4018/978-1-4666-2154-1.ch005

Boudreaux, A., & Primeaux, B. (2014). Modular game engine design. In Software design and development: Concepts, methodologies, tools, and applications (pp. 1179–1199). Hershey, PA: IGI Global. doi:10.4018/978-1-4666-4301-7.ch058

Boudriga, N., & Hamdi, M. (2014). *Security engineering techniques and solutions for information systems: Management and implementation*. Hershey, PA: IGI Global. doi:10.4018/978-1-61520-803-6

Brad, S. (2010). Competitive design of web-based courses in engineering education. In D. Russell & A. Haghi (Eds.), Web-based engineering education: Critical design and effective tools (pp. 119–148). Hershey, PA: IGI Global. doi:10.4018/978-1-61520-659-9.ch010

Brad, S. (2010). Designing effective web-based courses in engineering. In R. Luppicini & A. Haghi (Eds.), Cases on digital technologies in higher education: Issues and challenges (pp. 217–240). Hershey, PA: IGI Global. doi:10.4018/978-1-61520-869-2.ch016

Bradford, M., Gingras, R., & Hornby, J. (2010). Business process reengineering and ERP: Weapons for the global organization. In K. St.Amant (Ed.), IT outsourcing: Concepts, methodologies, tools, and applications (pp. 211–228). Hershey, PA: IGI Global. doi:10.4018/978-1-60566-770-6.ch012

Brennan, R. W., Hugo, R., & Rosehart, W. D. (2012). CDIO as an enabler for graduate attributes assessment: A Canadian case study. *International Journal of Quality Assurance in Engineering and Technology Education*, 2(2), 45–54. doi:10.4018/ijqaete.2012040105

Burnett, M. (2012). End-user software engineering and why it matters. In A. Dwivedi & S. Clarke (Eds.), End-user computing, development, and software engineering: New challenges (pp. 185–201). Hershey, PA: IGI Global. doi:10.4018/978-1-4666-0140-6.ch009

Burns, G. U., & Chisohlm, C. (2011). Engineering professional development related to sustainability of quality. *International Journal of Quality Assurance in Engineering and Technology Education*, 1(1), 15–29. doi:10.4018/ijqaete.2011010102

Byrne, D., Kelly, L., & Jones, G. J. (2014). Multiple multimodal mobile devices: Lessons learned from engineering lifelong solutions. In Software design and development: Concepts, methodologies, tools, and applications (pp. 2014–2032). Hershey, PA: IGI Global. doi:10.4018/978-1-4666-4301-7.ch093

Cervera, M., Albert, M., Torres, V., & Pelechano, V. (2012). A model-driven approach for the design and implementation of software development methods. *International Journal of Information System Modeling and Design*, 3(4), 86–103. doi:10.4018/jismd.2012100105

Chang, L., Levy, M., & Powell, P. (2011). Small firm process re-engineering success. In M. Tavana (Ed.), Managing adaptability, intervention, and people in enterprise information systems (pp. 138–155). Hershey, PA: IGI Global. doi:10.4018/978-1-60960-529-2.ch007

Chinyemba, F. (2011). Mobility of engineering and technology professionals and its impact on the quality of engineering and technology education: The case of Chinhoyi University of Technology, Zimbabwe. *International Journal of Quality Assurance in Engineering and Technology Education*, *1*(2), 35–49. doi:10.4018/ijqaete.2011070104

Chinyemba, F. (2011). Mobility of engineering and technology professionals and its impact on the quality of engineering and technology education: The case of Chinhoyi University of Technology, Zimbabwe. *International Journal of Quality Assurance in Engineering and Technology Education*, *1*(2), 35–49. doi:10.4018/ijqaete.2011070104

Chiong, R. (2010). *Nature-inspired informatics for intelligent applications and knowledge discovery: Implications in business, science, and engineering*. Hershey, PA: IGI Global. doi:10.4018/978-1-60566-705-8

Chiprianov, V., Kermarrec, Y., & Rouvrais, S. (2014). Integrating DSLs into a software engineering process: Application to collaborative construction of telecom services. In Software design and development: Concepts, methodologies, tools, and applications (pp. 570–595). Hershey, PA: IGI Global. doi:10.4018/978-1-4666-4301-7.ch028

Chis, M. (2010). Introduction: A survey of the evolutionary computation techniques for software engineering. In M. Chis (Ed.), Evolutionary computation and optimization algorithms in software engineering: Applications and techniques (pp. 1–12). Hershey, PA: IGI Global. doi:10.4018/978-1-61520-809-8.ch001

Chiu, D. K. (2013). *Mobile and web innovations in systems and service-oriented engineering*. Hershey, PA: IGI Global. doi:10.4018/978-1-4666-2470-2

Chu, P. K., & Wu, S. (2012). Biomaterials. In Z. Abu-Faraj (Ed.), Handbook of research on biomedical engineering education and advanced bioengineering learning: Interdisciplinary concepts (pp. 238–283). Hershey, PA: IGI Global. doi:10.4018/978-1-4666-0122-2.ch006

Cimellaro, G. P. (2013). Optimal placement of controller for seismic structures. In N. Lagaros, V. Plevris, & C. Mitropoulou (Eds.), Design optimization of active and passive structural control systems (pp. 1–33). Hershey, PA: IGI Global. doi:10.4018/978-1-4666-2029-2.ch001

Clark, R., & Andrews, J. (2012). Engineering the future. In M. Rasul (Ed.), Developments in engineering education standards: Advanced curriculum innovations (pp. 143–155). Hershey, PA: IGI Global. doi:10.4018/978-1-4666-0951-8.ch008

Clark, T., & Willans, J. (2013). Software language engineering with XMF and XModeler. In M. Mernik (Ed.), Formal and practical aspects of domain-specific languages: Recent developments (pp. 311–340). Hershey, PA: IGI Global. doi:10.4018/978-1-4666-2092-6.ch011

Coll, R. K., & Zegwaard, K. E. (2012). Enculturation into engineering professional practice: Using legitimate peripheral participation to develop communication skills in engineering students. In A. Patil, H. Eijkman, & E. Bhattacharyya (Eds.), New media communication skills for engineers and IT professionals: Trans-national and trans-cultural demands (pp. 22–33). Hershey, PA: IGI Global. doi:10.4018/978-1-4666-0243-4.ch003

Coll, R. K., & Zegwaard, K. E. (2012). Enculturation into engineering professional practice: Using legitimate peripheral participation to develop communication skills in engineering students. In A. Patil, H. Eijkman, & E. Bhattacharyya (Eds.), New media communication skills for engineers and IT professionals: Trans-national and trans-cultural demands (pp. 22–33). Hershey, PA: IGI Global. doi:10.4018/978-1-4666-0243-4.ch003

Colomb, R. M. (2013). Representation of action is a primary requirement in ontologies for interoperating information systems. In M. Nazir Ahmad, R. Colomb, & M. Abdullah (Eds.), Ontology-based applications for enterprise systems and knowledge management (pp. 68–76). Hershey, PA: IGI Global. doi:10.4018/978-1-4666-1993-7.ch004

Cooklev, T. (2013). The role of standards in engineering education. In K. Jakobs (Ed.), Innovations in organizational IT specification and standards development (pp. 129–137). Hershey, PA: IGI Global. doi:10.4018/978-1-4666-2160-2.ch007

Costa, L., Loughran, N., & Grønmo, R. (2014). Model-driven engineering, services and interactive real-time applications. In Software design and development: Concepts, methodologies, tools, and applications (pp. 178–202). Hershey, PA: IGI Global. doi:10.4018/978-1-4666-4301-7.ch010

Dai, Y., Chakraborty, B., & Shi, M. (2011). *Kansei engineering and soft computing: Theory and practice*. Hershey, PA: IGI Global. doi:10.4018/978-1-61692-797-4

Daud, M. F., Taib, J. M., & Shariffudin, R. S. (2012). Assessing mechanical engineering undergraduates' conceptual knowledge in three dimensional computer aided design (3D CAD). In K. Yusof, N. Azli, A. Kosnin, S. Yusof, & Y. Yusof (Eds.), Outcome-based science, technology, engineering, and mathematics education: Innovative practices (pp. 350–363). Hershey, PA: IGI Global. doi:10.4018/978-1-4666-1809-1.ch017

Daugherty, A., Hires, W. E., & Braunstein, S. G. (2013). Collection development for the college of engineering at Louisiana State University libraries: Liaison responsibilities and duties. In S. Holder (Ed.), Library collection development for professional programs: Trends and best practices (pp. 291–305). Hershey, PA: IGI Global. doi:10.4018/978-1-4666-1897-8.ch017

Davim, J. (2013). *Dynamic methods and process advancements in mechanical, manufacturing, and materials engineering*. Hershey, PA: IGI Global. doi:10.4018/978-1-4666-1867-1

de Vere, I., & Melles, G. (2013). Integrating 'designerly' ways with engineering science: A catalyst for change within product design and development. In Industrial engineering: Concepts, methodologies, tools, and applications (pp. 56-78). Hershey, PA: IGI Global. doi:10.4018/978-1-4666-1945-6.ch005 del Sagrado Martinez, J., & del Aguila Cano, I. M. (2010). A Bayesian network for predicting the need for a requirements review. In F. Meziane & S. Vadera (Eds.), Artificial intelligence applications for improved software engineering development: New prospects (pp. 106–128). Hershey, PA: IGI Global. doi:10.4018/978-1-60566-758-4.ch006

Dhar-Bhattacharjee, S., & Takruri-Rizk, H. (2012). An Indo-British comparison. In C. Romm Livermore (Ed.), *Gender and social computing: Interactions, differences and relationships* (pp. 50–71). Hershey, PA: Information Science Publishing. doi:10.4018/978-1-60960-759-3.ch004

Díaz, V. G., Lovelle, J. M., García-Bustelo, B. C., & Martinez, O. S. (2014). *Advances and applications in model-driven engineering*. Hershey, PA: IGI Global. doi:10.4018/978-1-4666-4494-6

Dogru, A., Senkul, P., & Kaya, O. (2012). Modern approaches to software engineering in the compositional era. In Machine learning: Concepts, methodologies, tools and applications (pp. 1903–1923). Hershey, PA: IGI Global. doi:10.4018/978-1-60960-818-7.ch803

Dogru, A. H., & Biçer, V. (2011). *Modern software engineering concepts and practices: Advanced approaches*. Hershey, PA: IGI Global. doi:10.4018/978-1-60960-215-4

Doll, W. J., & Deng, X. (2013). Antecedents of improvisation in IT-enabled engineering work. In A. Dwivedi & S. Clarke (Eds.), Innovative strategies and approaches for end-user computing advancements (pp. 242–264). Hershey, PA: IGI Global. doi:10.4018/978-1-4666-2059-9.ch013

Dominguez, U., & Magdaleno, J. (2011). Industrial training in engineering education in Spain. In P. Keleher, A. Patil, & R. Harreveld (Eds.), Work-integrated learning in engineering, built environment and technology: Diversity of practice in practice (pp. 72–84). Hershey, PA: IGI Global. doi:10.4018/978-1-60960-547-6.ch004

Dormido, S., Vargas, H., & Sánchez, J. (2013). AutomatL@bs consortium: A Spanish network of web-based labs for control engineering education. In Industrial engineering: Concepts, methodologies, tools, and applications (pp. 679–699). Hershey, PA: IGI Global. doi:10.4018/978-1-4666-1945-6.ch039

Dyro, J. F. (2012). Clinical engineering. In Z. Abu-Faraj (Ed.), Handbook of research on biomedical engineering education and advanced bioengineering learning: Interdisciplinary concepts (pp. 521–576). Hershey, PA: IGI Global. doi:10.4018/978-1-4666-0122-2.ch012

Easton, J. M., Davies, J. R., & Roberts, C. (2011). Ontology engineering the whats, whys, and hows of data exchange. *International Journal of Decision Support System Technology*, *3*(1), 40–53. doi:10.4018/jdsst.2011010103

Eijkman, H., & Kayali, O. (2011). Addressing the politics of accreditation in engineering education: The benefits of soft systems thinking. *International Journal of Quality Assurance in Engineering and Technology Education*, *1*(2), 1–10. doi:10.4018/ijqaete.2011070101

El-Khalili, N. H. (2013). Teaching agile software engineering using problem-based learning. *International Journal of Information and Communication Technology Education*, *9*(3), 1–12. doi:10.4018/jicte.2013070101

Favre, L. M. (2010). MDA-based object-oriented reverse engineering. In L. Favre (Ed.), Model driven architecture for reverse engineering technologies: Strategic directions and system evolution (pp. 199–229). Hershey, PA: IGI Global. doi:10.4018/978-1-61520-649-0.ch010

Favre, L. M. (2010). Reverse engineering and MDA: An introduction. In L. Favre (Ed.), Model driven architecture for reverse engineering technologies: Strategic directions and system evolution (pp. 1–14). Hershey, PA: IGI Global. doi:10.4018/978-1-61520-649-0.ch001

Fenton, N., Hearty, P., Neil, M., & Radlinski, L. (2010). Software project and quality modelling using Bayesian networks. In F. Meziane & S. Vadera (Eds.), Artificial intelligence applications for improved software engineering development: New prospects (pp. 1–25). Hershey, PA: IGI Global. doi:10.4018/978-1-60566-758-4.ch001

Ferreira, R., Brisolara, L., Mattos, J. C., Spech, E., & Cota, E. (2010). Engineering embedded software: From application modeling to software synthesis. In L. Gomes & J. Fernandes (Eds.), Behavioral modeling for embedded systems and technologies: Applications for design and implementation (pp. 245–270). Hershey, PA: IGI Global. doi:10.4018/978-1-60566-750-8.ch010

Ferreira da Silva Oliveira, M., Wehrmeister, M. A., Assis do Nascimento, F., & Pereira, C. E. (2010). High-level design space exploration of embedded systems using the model-driven engineering and aspect-oriented design approaches. In L. Gomes & J. Fernandes (Eds.), Behavioral modeling for embedded systems and technologies: Applications for design and implementation (pp. 114–146). Hershey, PA: IGI Global. doi:10.4018/978-1-60566-750-8.ch005

Ferris, T. L. (2013). Engineering design as research. In Industrial engineering: Concepts, methodologies, tools, and applications (pp. 1766–1779). Hershey, PA: IGI Global. doi:10.4018/978-1-4666-1945-6.ch094

Frank, M. (2010). Capacity for engineering systems thinking (CEST): Literature review, principles for assessing and the reliability and validity of an assessing tool. In M. Hunter (Ed.), Strategic information systems: Concepts, methodologies, tools, and applications (pp. 1171–1183). Hershey, PA: IGI Global. doi:10.4018/978-1-60566-677-8.ch076

Fraser, D. (2012). A case study of curriculum development in engineering: Insights gained over two decades. In K. Yusof, N. Azli, A. Kosnin, S. Yusof, & Y. Yusof (Eds.), Outcome-based science, technology, engineering, and mathematics education: Innovative practices (pp. 27–49). Hershey, PA: IGI Global. doi:10.4018/978-1-4666-1809-1.ch002

Fraser, D. (2012). Curriculum initiatives to help engineering students learn and develop. In K. Yusof, N. Azli, A. Kosnin, S. Yusof, & Y. Yusof (Eds.), Outcome-based science, technology, engineering, and mathematics education: Innovative practices (pp. 85–106). Hershey, PA: IGI Global. doi:10.4018/978-1-4666-1809-1.ch005

Fries, T. P. (2014). Reengineering structured legacy system documentation to UML object-oriented artifacts. In Software design and development: Concepts, methodologies, tools, and applications (pp. 749–771). Hershey, PA: IGI Global. doi:10.4018/978-1-4666-4301-7.ch036

Funabashi, M. (2014). Transdisciplinary science and technology and service systems. In M. Kosaka & K. Shirahada (Eds.), Progressive trends in knowledge and system-based science for service innovation (pp. 101–127). Hershey, PA: IGI Global. doi:10.4018/978-1-4666-4663-6.ch006

Gaetano, L., Puppato, D., & Balestra, G. (2012). Modeling clinical engineering activities to support healthcare technology management. In A. Kolker & P. Story (Eds.), Management engineering for effective healthcare delivery: Principles and applications (pp. 113–131). Hershey, PA: IGI Global. doi:10.4018/978-1-60960-872-9.ch005

Galvão, T. A., Neto, F., & Bonates, M. F. (2013). eRiskGame: A persistent browser-based game for supporting project-based learning in the risk management context. In Industrial engineering: Concepts, methodologies, tools, and applications (pp. 1243-1259). Hershey, PA: IGI Global. doi:10.4018/978-1-4666-1945-6.ch067

Garousi, V., Shahnewaz, S., & Krishnamurthy, D. (2013). UML-driven software performance engineering: A systematic mapping and trend analysis. In V. Díaz, J. Lovelle, B. García-Bustelo, & O. Martínez (Eds.), Progressions and innovations in model-driven software engineering (pp. 18–64). Hershey, PA: IGI Global. doi:10.4018/978-1-4666-4217-1.ch002

Ge, W., Yang, N., Wang, W., & Li, J. (2011). Interfacial interactions: Drag. In S. Pannala, M. Syamlal, & T. O'Brien (Eds.), Computational gas-solids flows and reacting systems: Theory, methods and practice (pp. 128–177). Hershey, PA: IGI Global. doi:10.4018/978-1-61520-651-3.ch004

Génova, G., Llorens, J., & Morato, J. (2014). Software engineering research: The need to strengthen and broaden the classical scientific method. In Software design and development: Concepts, methodologies, tools, and applications (pp. 1639–1658). Hershey, PA: IGI Global. doi:10.4018/978-1-4666-4301-7.ch079

Genvigir, E. C., & Vijaykumar, N. L. (2010). Requirements traceability. In M. Ramachandran & R. de Carvalho (Eds.), Handbook of research on software engineering and productivity technologies: Implications of globalization (pp. 102–120). Hershey, PA: IGI Global. doi:10.4018/978-1-60566-731-7.ch008

Ghosh, S. (2010). Online automated essay grading system as a web based learning (WBL) tool in engineering education. In D. Russell & A. Haghi (Eds.), Web-based engineering education: Critical design and effective tools (pp. 53–62). Hershey, PA: IGI Global. doi:10.4018/978-1-61520-659-9.ch005

Gill, A. Q., & Bunker, D. (2013). SaaS requirements engineering for agile development. In X. Wang, N. Ali, I. Ramos, & R. Vidgen (Eds.), Agile and lean service-oriented development: Foundations, theory, and practice (pp. 64–93). Hershey, PA: IGI Global. doi:10.4018/978-1-4666-2503-7.ch004

Giraldo, F. D., Villegas, M. L., & Collazos, C. A. (2014). The use of HCI approaches into distributed CSCL activities applied to software engineering courses. In Software design and development: Concepts, methodologies, tools, and applications (pp. 2033–2050). Hershey, PA: IGI Global. doi:10.4018/978-1-4666-4301-7.ch094

Girardi, R., & Leite, A. (2011). Knowledge engineering support for agent-oriented software reuse. In M. Ramachandran (Ed.), Knowledge engineering for software development life cycles: Support technologies and applications (pp. 177–195). Hershey, PA: IGI Global. doi:10.4018/978-1-60960-509-4.ch010

Goodhew, P. (2013). Why get your engineering programme accredited? In Industrial engineering: Concepts, methodologies, tools, and applications (pp. 18–20). Hershey, PA: IGI Global. doi:10.4018/978-1-4666-1945-6.ch002

Goossenaerts, J., Possel-Dölken, F., & Popplewell, K. (2011). Vision, trends, gaps and a broad roadmap for future engineering. In I. Management Association (Ed.),Global business: Concepts, methodologies, tools and applications (pp. 2229-2243). Hershey, PA: Business Science Reference. doi:10.4018/978-1-60960-587-2.ch802

Goyal, S. B., & Prakash, N. (2013). Functional method engineering. *International Journal of Information System Modeling and Design, 4*(1), 79–103. doi:10.4018/jismd.2013010104

Gunasekaran, A., & Shea, T. (2010). Requirements management for ERP projects. In Organizational advancements through enterprise information systems: Emerging applications and developments (pp. 29–45). Hershey, PA: IGI Global. doi:10.4018/978-1-60566-968-7.ch003

Gustavsson, I., Claesson, L., Nilsson, K., Zackrisson, J., Zubia, J. G., & Jayo, U. H. … Claesson, I. (2012). The VISIR open lab platform. In A. Azad, M. Auer, & V. Harward (Eds.), Internet accessible remote laboratories: Scalable e-learning tools for engineering and science disciplines (pp. 294-317). Hershey, PA: IGI Global. doi:10.4018/978-1-61350-186-3.ch015

Habib, M. K., & Davim, J. (2013). *Engineering creative design in robotics and mechatronics*. Hershey, PA: IGI Global. doi:10.4018/978-1-4666-4225-6

Haghi, A. K. (2013). *Methodologies and applications for chemoinformatics and chemical engineering*. Hershey, PA: IGI Global. doi:10.4018/978-1-4666-4010-8

Haghi, A. K., & Noroozi, B. (2010). Adapting engineering education to the new century. In D. Russell & A. Haghi (Eds.), Web-based engineering education: Critical design and effective tools (pp. 30–41). Hershey, PA: IGI Global. doi:10.4018/978-1-61520-659-9.ch003

Haghpanahi, M., Nikkhoo, M., & Peirovi, H. A. (2010). Computer aided tissue engineering from modeling to manufacturing. In A. Lazakidou (Ed.), Biocomputation and biomedical informatics: Case studies and applications (pp. 75–88). Hershey, PA: IGI Global. doi:10.4018/978-1-60566-768-3.ch004

Hepsø, I. L., Rindal, A., & Waldal, K. (2013). The introduction of a hand-held platform in an engineering and fabrication company. In T. Rosendahl & V. Hepsø (Eds.), Integrated operations in the oil and gas industry: Sustainability and capability development (pp. 246–260). Hershey, PA: IGI Global. doi:10.4018/978-1-4666-2002-5.ch015

Hernández-López, A., Colomo-Palacios, R., García-Crespo, Á., & Cabezas-Isla, F. (2013). Software engineering productivity: Concepts, issues and challenges. In J. Wang (Ed.), Perspectives and techniques for improving information technology project management (pp. 69–79). Hershey, PA: IGI Global. doi:10.4018/978-1-4666-2800-7.ch006

Herrmann, A., & Morali, A. (2012). Interplay of security requirements engineering and reverse engineering in the maintenance of undocumented software. In J. Rech & C. Bunse (Eds.), Emerging technologies for the evolution and maintenance of software models (pp. 57–91). Hershey, PA: IGI Global. doi:10.4018/978-1-61350-438-3.ch003

Hochrainer, M., & Ziegler, F. (2013). Tuned liquid column gas damper in structural control: The salient features of a general purpose damping device and its application in buildings, bridges, and dams. In N. Lagaros, V. Plevris, & C. Mitropoulou (Eds.), Design optimization of active and passive structural control systems (pp. 150–179). Hershey, PA: IGI Global. doi:10.4018/978-1-4666-2029-2.ch007

Hochstein, L., Schott, B., & Graybill, R. B. (2013). Computational engineering in the cloud: Benefits and challenges. In A. Dwivedi & S. Clarke (Eds.), Innovative strategies and approaches for end-user computing advancements (pp. 314–332). Hershey, PA: IGI Global. doi:10.4018/978-1-4666-2059-9.ch017

Höhn, S., Lowis, L., Jürjens, J., & Accorsi, R. (2010). Identification of vulnerabilities in web services using model-based security. In C. Gutiérrez, E. Fernández-Medina, & M. Piattini (Eds.), Web services security development and architecture: Theoretical and practical issues (pp. 1–32). Hershey, PA: IGI Global. doi:10.4018/978-1-60566-950-2.ch001

Holton, D. L., & Verma, A. (2010). Designing animated simulations and web-based assessments to improve electrical engineering education. In D. Russell & A. Haghi (Eds.), Web-based engineering education: Critical design and effective tools (pp. 77–95). Hershey, PA: IGI Global. doi:10.4018/978-1-61520-659-9.ch007

Honnutagi, A. R., Sonar, R., & Babu, S. (2012). Quality accreditation system for Indian engineering education using knowledge management and system dynamics. *International Journal of Quality Assurance in Engineering and Technology Education*, 2(3), 47–61. doi:10.4018/ijqaete.2012070105

Hua, G. B. (2013). Business process re-engineering. In Implementing IT business strategy in the construction industry (pp. 118–140). Hershey, PA: IGI Global. doi:10.4018/978-1-4666-4185-3.ch006

Hussein, B., Hage-Diab, A., Hammoud, M., Kawtharani, A., El-Hage, H., & Haj-Ali, A. (2014). Management response to improve the educational performance of engineering students: The case of the lebanese international university. In G. Khoury & M. Khoury (Eds.), Cases on management and organizational behavior in an Arab context (pp. 91–110). Hershey, PA: IGI Global. doi:10.4018/978-1-4666-5067-1.ch006

Hussey, M., Wu, B., & Xu, X. (2011). Co-operation models for industries and software education institutions. In *Software industry-oriented education practices and curriculum development: Experiences and lessons* (pp. 39–56). Hershey, PA: Information Science Publishing. doi:10.4018/978-1-60960-797-5.ch003

Hussey, M., Wu, B., & Xu, X. (2011). Curriculum issues in industry oriented software engineering education. In *Software industry-oriented education practices and curriculum development: Experiences and lessons* (pp. 153–165). Hershey, PA: Information Science Publishing. doi:10.4018/978-1-60960-797-5.ch010

Hussey, M., Wu, B., & Xu, X. (2011). Industry oriented curriculum and syllabus creation for software engineering series courses in the school of software. In *Software industry-oriented education practices and curriculum development: Experiences and lessons* (pp. 98–109). Hershey, PA: Information Science Publishing. doi:10.4018/978-1-60960-797-5.ch006

Ilyas, Q. M. (2013). Ontology augmented software engineering. In K. Buragga & N. Zaman (Eds.), Software development techniques for constructive information systems design (pp. 406–413). Hershey, PA: IGI Global. doi:10.4018/978-1-4666-3679-8.ch023

Islam, S., Mouratidis, H., Kalloniatis, C., Hudic, A., & Zechner, L. (2013). Model based process to support security and privacy requirements engineering. *International Journal of Secure Software Engineering*, *3*(3), 1–22. doi:10.4018/jsse.2012070101

Jahan, K., Everett, J. W., Tang, G., Farrell, S., Zhang, H., Wenger, A., & Noori, M. (2010). Use of living systems to teach basic engineering concepts. In D. Russell & A. Haghi (Eds.), Web-based engineering education: Critical design and effective tools (pp. 96–107). Hershey, PA: IGI Global. doi:10.4018/978-1-61520-659-9.ch008

Jakovljevic, M. (2013). A conceptual model of creativity, invention, and innovation (MCII) for entrepreneurial engineers. In S. Buckley & M. Jakovljevic (Eds.), Knowledge management innovations for interdisciplinary education: Organizational applications (pp. 66–87). Hershey, PA: IGI Global. doi:10.4018/978-1-4666-1969-2.ch004

Jaroucheh, Z., Liu, X., & Smith, S. (2014). A software engineering framework for context-aware service-based processes in pervasive environments. In Software design and development: Concepts, methodologies, tools, and applications (pp. 71–95). Hershey, PA: IGI Global. doi:10.4018/978-1-4666-4301-7.ch005

Joiner, R., Iacovides, I., Darling, J., Diament, A., Drew, B., Duddley, J., . . . Gavin, C. (2013). Racing academy: A case study of a digital game for supporting students learning of physics and engineering. In Y. Baek & N. Whitton (Eds.), Cases on digital game-based learning: Methods, models, and strategies (pp. 509–523). Hershey, PA: IGI Global. doi:10.4018/978-1-4666-2848-9.ch026

Jordan, M. E. (2014). Interweaving the digital and physical worlds in collaborative project-based learning experiences. In D. Loveless, B. Griffith, M. Bérci, E. Ortlieb, & P. Sullivan (Eds.), Academic knowledge construction and multimodal curriculum development (pp. 265–282). Hershey, PA: IGI Global. doi:10.4018/978-1-4666-4797-8.ch017

Juang, Y. (2010). WIRE: A highly interactive blended learning for engineering education. In D. Russell & A. Haghi (Eds.), Web-based engineering education: Critical design and effective tools (pp. 149–159). Hershey, PA: IGI Global. doi:10.4018/978-1-61520-659-9.ch011

Kadry, S. (2013). *Diagnostics and prognostics of engineering systems: Methods and techniques*. Hershey, PA: IGI Global. doi:10.4018/978-1-4666-2095-7

Kamboj, A., Kumar, S., & Singh, H. (2012). Design and development of hybrid stir casting process. *International Journal of Applied Industrial Engineering*, *1*(2), 1–6. doi:10.4018/ijaie.2012070101

Kamthan, P. (2010). A methodology for integrating the social web environment in software engineering education. In S. Dasgupta (Ed.), Social computing: Concepts, methodologies, tools, and applications (pp. 457–471). Hershey, PA: IGI Global. doi:10.4018/978-1-60566-984-7.ch031

Kamthan, P. (2010). A social web perspective of software engineering education. In S. Murugesan (Ed.), Handbook of research on web 2.0, 3.0, and X.0: Technologies, business, and social applications (pp. 472–495). Hershey, PA: IGI Global. doi:10.4018/978-1-60566-384-5.ch026

Kamthan, P. (2010). On the prospects and concerns of pattern-oriented web engineering. In G. Alkhatib & D. Rine (Eds.), Web engineering advancements and trends: Building new dimensions of information technology (pp. 97–128). Hershey, PA: IGI Global. doi:10.4018/978-1-60566-719-5.ch006

Kamthan, P. (2011). Using the social web environment for software engineering education. In L. Tomei (Ed.), Online courses and ICT in education: Emerging practices and applications (pp. 23–45). Hershey, PA: IGI Global. doi:10.4018/978-1-60960-150-8.ch003

Kamthan, P. (2013). An exploration of the social web environment for collaborative software engineering education. In N. Karacapilidis, M. Raisinghani, & E. Ng (Eds.), Web-based and blended educational tools and innovations (pp. 1–23). Hershey, PA: IGI Global. doi:10.4018/978-1-4666-2023-0.ch001

Kapos, G., Dalakas, V., Nikolaidou, M., & Anagnostopoulos, D. (2014). An integrated framework to simulate SysML models using DEVS simulators. In P. Fonseca i Casas (Ed.), Formal languages for computer simulation: Transdisciplinary models and applications (pp. 305–332). Hershey, PA: IGI Global. doi:10.4018/978-1-4666-4369-7.ch010

Karlsson, F., & Ågerfalk, P. J. (2011). Towards structured flexibility in information systems development: Devising a method for method configuration. In K. Siau (Ed.), Theoretical and practical advances in information systems development: Emerging trends and approaches (pp. 214–238). Hershey, PA: IGI Global. doi:10.4018/978-1-60960-521-6.ch010

Karpati, P., Sindre, G., & Matulevicius, R. (2012). Comparing misuse case and mal-activity diagrams for modelling social engineering attacks. *International Journal of Secure Software Engineering*, *3*(2), 54–73. doi:10.4018/jsse.2012040103

Keleher, P., & Patil, A. (2012). Conducting an effective residential school for an undergraduate materials science and engineering course. *International Journal of Quality Assurance in Engineering and Technology Education*, *2*(3), 41–46. doi:10.4018/ijqaete.2012070104

Ker, H. W. (2012). Engineering education and attitudes toward mathematics: A comparative study. *International Journal of Quality Assurance in Engineering and Technology Education*, *2*(1), 63–76. doi:10.4018/ijqaete.2012010105

Kinsner, W. (2012). Challenges in the design of adoptive, intelligent and cognitive systems. In Y. Wang (Ed.), Software and intelligent sciences: New transdisciplinary findings (pp. 47–67). Hershey, PA: IGI Global. doi:10.4018/978-1-4666-0261-8.ch004

Kirikova, M. (2011). Domain modeling approaches in IS engineering. In J. Osis & E. Asnina (Eds.), Model-driven domain analysis and software development: Architectures and functions (pp. 388–406). Hershey, PA: IGI Global. doi:10.4018/978-1-61692-874-2.ch018

Kljajic, M., & Farr, J. V. (2010). Importance of systems engineering in the development of information systems. In D. Paradice (Ed.), Emerging systems approaches in information technologies: Concepts, theories, and applications (pp. 51–66). Hershey, PA: IGI Global. doi:10.4018/978-1-60566-976-2.ch004

Kljajic, M., & Farr, J. V. (2010). The role of systems engineering in the development of information systems. In M. Hunter (Ed.), Strategic information systems: Concepts, methodologies, tools, and applications (pp. 369–381). Hershey, PA: IGI Global. doi:10.4018/978-1-60566-677-8.ch026

Knoell, H. D. (2010). User participation in the quality assurance of requirements specifications: An evaluation of traditional models and animated systems engineering techniques. In M. Hunter (Ed.), Strategic information systems: Concepts, methodologies, tools, and applications (pp. 1623–1638). Hershey, PA: IGI Global. doi:10.4018/978-1-60566-677-8.ch106

Kof, L. (2010). From textual scenarios to message sequence charts. In F. Meziane & S. Vadera (Eds.), Artificial intelligence applications for improved software engineering development: New prospects (pp. 83–105). Hershey, PA: IGI Global. doi:10.4018/978-1-60566-758-4.ch005

Köhler, B., Gluchow, M., & Brügge, B. (2014). Teaching basic software engineering to senior high school students. In K-12 education: Concepts, methodologies, tools, and applications (pp. 1634–1649). Hershey, PA: IGI Global. doi:10.4018/978-1-4666-4502-8.ch094

Kolker, A. (2012). Efficient managerial decision-making in healthcare settings: Examples and fundamental principles. In A. Kolker & P. Story (Eds.), Management engineering for effective healthcare delivery: Principles and applications (pp. 1–45). Hershey, PA: IGI Global. doi:10.4018/978-1-60960-872-9.ch001

Kolker, A., & Story, P. (2012). *Management engineering for effective healthcare delivery: Principles and applications*. Hershey, PA: IGI Global. doi:10.4018/978-1-60960-872-9

Kornyshova, E., Deneckère, R., & Claudepierre, B. (2013). Towards method component contextualization. In J. Krogstie (Ed.), Frameworks for developing efficient information systems: Models, theory, and practice (pp. 337–368). Hershey, PA: IGI Global. doi:10.4018/978-1-4666-4161-7.ch015

Krishnan, S. (2012). Problem-based learning curricula in engineering. In M. Rasul (Ed.), Developments in engineering education standards: Advanced curriculum innovations (pp. 23–40). Hershey, PA: IGI Global. doi:10.4018/978-1-4666-0951-8.ch002

Ku, H., & Thonglek, S. (2011). Running a successful practice school: Challenges and lessons learned. In P. Keleher, A. Patil, & R. Harreveld (Eds.), Work-integrated learning in engineering, built environment and technology: Diversity of practice in practice (pp. 131–163). Hershey, PA: IGI Global. doi:10.4018/978-1-60960-547-6.ch007

Lacuesta, R., Fernández-Sanz, L., & Romay, M. D. (2014). Requirements specification as basis for mobile software quality assurance. In Software design and development: Concepts, methodologies, tools, and applications (pp. 719–732). Hershey, PA: IGI Global. doi:10.4018/978-1-4666-4301-7.ch034

Lai, A., Zhang, C., & Busovaca, S. (2013). 2-SQUARE: A web-based enhancement of SQUARE privacy and security requirements engineering. *International Journal of Software Innovation*, 1(1), 41–53. doi:10.4018/ijsi.2013010104

Lane, J. A., Petkov, D., & Mora, M. (2010). Software engineering and the systems approach: A conversation with Barry Boehm. In M. Hunter (Ed.), Strategic information systems: Concepts, methodologies, tools, and applications (pp. 333–337). Hershey, PA: IGI Global. doi:10.4018/978-1-60566-677-8.ch024

Lansiquot, R. D. (2013). *Cases on interdisciplinary research trends in science, technology, engineering, and mathematics: Studies on urban classrooms*. Hershey, PA: IGI Global. doi:10.4018/978-1-4666-2214-2

Laribi, S., Le Bris, A., Huang, L. M., Olsson, P., & Guillemoles, J. F. (2013). Phononic engineering for hot carrier solar cells. In L. Fara & M. Yamaguchi (Eds.), Advanced solar cell materials, technology, modeling, and simulation (pp. 214–242). Hershey, PA: IGI Global. doi:10.4018/978-1-4666-1927-2.ch012

Lee, C. K., & Sidhu, M. S. (2013). Computer-aided engineering education: New learning approaches and technologies. In V. Wang (Ed.), Handbook of research on teaching and learning in K-20 education (pp. 317–340). Hershey, PA: IGI Global. doi:10.4018/978-1-4666-4249-2.ch019

Lee, J., Ma, S., Lee, S., Wu, C., & Lee, C. L. (2014). Towards a high-availability-driven service composition framework. In Software design and development: Concepts, methodologies, tools, and applications (pp. 1498–1520). Hershey, PA: IGI Global. doi:10.4018/978-1-4666-4301-7.ch073

Leng, J., Rhyne, T., & Sharrock, W. (2012). Visualization: Future technology and practices for computational science and engineering. In J. Leng & W. Sharrock (Eds.), Handbook of research on computational science and engineering: Theory and practice (pp. 381–413). Hershey, PA: IGI Global. doi:10.4018/978-1-61350-116-0.ch016

Leng, J., & Sharrock, W. (2012). Handbook of research on computational science and engineering: Theory and practice (Vols. 1–2). Hershey, PA: IGI Global. doi:10.4018/978-1-61350-116-0

Li, Z. J. (2013). Prototyping of robotic systems in surgical procedures and automated manufacturing processes. In Industrial engineering: Concepts, methodologies, tools, and applications (pp. 1969–1987). Hershey, PA: IGI Global. doi:10.4018/978-1-4666-1945-6.ch106

Lladó, C. M., Bonet, P., & Smith, C. U. (2014). Towards a multi-formalism multi-solution framework for model-driven performance engineering. In M. Gribaudo & M. Iacono (Eds.), Theory and application of multi-formalism modeling (pp. 34–55). Hershey, PA: IGI Global. doi:10.4018/978-1-4666-4659-9.ch003

Loo, A. (2013). *Distributed computing innovations for business, engineering, and science*. Hershey, PA: IGI Global. doi:10.4018/978-1-4666-2533-4

Ma, Z. M. (2011). Engineering design knowledge management. In D. Schwartz & D. Te'eni (Eds.), Encyclopedia of knowledge management (2nd ed., pp. 263–269). Hershey, PA: IGI Global. doi:10.4018/978-1-59904-931-1.ch025

Maiti, C. K., & Maiti, A. (2013). Teaching technology computer aided design (TCAD) online. In Industrial engineering: Concepts, methodologies, tools, and applications (pp. 1043-1063). Hershey, PA: IGI Global. doi:10.4018/978-1-4666-1945-6.ch057

Male, S. A. (2012). Generic engineering competencies required by engineers graduating in Australia: The competencies of engineering graduates (CEG) project. In M. Rasul (Ed.), Developments in engineering education standards: Advanced curriculum innovations (pp. 41–63). Hershey, PA: IGI Global. doi:10.4018/978-1-4666-0951-8.ch003

Malmqvist, J. (2012). A comparison of the CDIO and EUR-ACE quality assurance systems. *International Journal of Quality Assurance in Engineering and Technology Education*, 2(2), 9–22. doi:10.4018/ijqaete.2012040102

Management Association. I. (2012). Computer engineering: Concepts, methodologies, tools and applications (4 Volumes). Hershey, PA: IGI Global. doi:10.4018/978-1-61350-456-7

Management Association. I. (2013). Industrial engineering: Concepts, methodologies, tools, and applications (3 Volumes). Hershey, PA: IGI Global. doi:10.4018/978-1-4666-1945-6

Maree, D. J., & Maree, M. (2010). Factors contributing to the success of women working in science, engineering and technology (SET) careers. In A. Cater-Steel & E. Cater (Eds.), Women in engineering, science and technology: Education and career challenges (pp. 183–210). Hershey, PA: IGI Global. doi:10.4018/978-1-61520-657-5.ch009

Marichal, G. N., & González, E. J. (2012). Intelligent MAS in system engineering and robotics. In Machine learning: Concepts, methodologies, tools and applications (pp. 175–182). Hershey, PA: IGI Global. doi:10.4018/978-1-60960-818-7.ch204

Martinez, L., Favre, L., & Pereira, C. (2013). Architecture-driven modernization for software reverse engineering technologies. In V. Díaz, J. Lovelle, B. García-Bustelo, & O. Martínez (Eds.), Progressions and innovations in model-driven software engineering (pp. 288–307). Hershey, PA: IGI Global. doi:10.4018/978-1-4666-4217-1.ch012

Matanovic, D. (2014). The macondo 252 disaster: Causes and consequences. In D. Matanovic, N. Gaurina-Medjimurec, & K. Simon (Eds.), Risk analysis for prevention of hazardous situations in petroleum and natural gas engineering (pp. 115–131). Hershey, PA: IGI Global. doi:10.4018/978-1-4666-4777-0.ch006

Matanovic, D., Gaurina-Medjimurec, N., & Simon, K. (2014). *Risk analysis for prevention of hazardous situations in petroleum and natural gas engineering*. Hershey, PA: IGI Global. doi:10.4018/978-1-4666-4777-0

Matsuo, T., & Fujimoto, T. (2012). Analogical thinking based instruction method in IT professional education. In R. Colomo-Palacios (Ed.), *Professional advancements and management trends in the IT sector* (pp. 95–108). Hershey, PA: Information Science Publishing. doi:10.4018/978-1-4666-0924-2.ch007

Mazo, R., Salinesi, C., Diaz, D., Djebbi, O., & Lora-Michiels, A. (2012). Constraints: The heart of domain and application engineering in the product lines engineering strategy. *International Journal of Information System Modeling and Design*, 3(2), 33–68. doi:10.4018/jismd.2012040102

Mead, N. R. (2010). Benefits and challenges in the use of case studies for security requirements engineering methods. *International Journal of Secure Software Engineering*, 1(1), 74–91. doi:10.4018/jsse.2010102005

Méausoone, P., & Aguilera, A. (2014). Inventory of experimental works on cutting tools' life for the wood industry. In A. Aguilera & J. Davim (Eds.), Research developments in wood engineering and technology (pp. 320–342). Hershey, PA: IGI Global. doi:10.4018/978-1-4666-4554-7.ch009

Medlin, B. D., & Cazier, J. (2011). Obtaining patient's information from hospital employees through social engineering techniques: An investigative study. In H. Nemati (Ed.), Pervasive information security and privacy developments: Trends and advancements (pp. 77–89). Hershey, PA: IGI Global. doi:10.4018/978-1-61692-000-5.ch006

Meziane, F., & Vadera, S. (2010). *Artificial intelligence applications for improved software engineering development: new prospects*. Hershey, PA: IGI Global. doi:10.4018/978-1-60566-758-4

Meziane, F., & Vadera, S. (2012). Artificial intelligence in software engineering: Current developments and future prospects. In Machine learning: Concepts, methodologies, tools and applications (pp. 1215–1236). Hershey, PA: IGI Global. doi:10.4018/978-1-60960-818-7.ch504

Milanovic, N. (2011). *Engineering reliable service oriented architecture: Managing complexity and service level agreements*. Hershey, PA: IGI Global. doi:10.4018/978-1-60960-493-6

Miller, W. S., & Summers, J. D. (2013). Tool and information centric design process modeling: Three case studies. In Industrial engineering: Concepts, methodologies, tools, and applications (pp. 1613–1637). Hershey, PA: IGI Global. doi:10.4018/978-1-4666-1945-6.ch086

Mishra, B., & Shukla, K. K. (2014). Data mining techniques for software quality prediction. In Software design and development: Concepts, methodologies, tools, and applications (pp. 401–428). Hershey, PA: IGI Global. doi:10.4018/978-1-4666-4301-7.ch021

Mishra, S. (2011). Social and ethical concerns of biomedical engineering research and practice. In A. Shukla & R. Tiwari (Eds.), Biomedical engineering and information systems: Technologies, tools and applications (pp. 54–80). Hershey, PA: IGI Global. doi:10.4018/978-1-61692-004-3.ch003

Moeller, D. P., & Sitzmann, D. (2012). Online computer engineering: combining blended e-learning in engineering with lifelong learning. In M. Rasul (Ed.), Developments in engineering education standards: Advanced curriculum innovations (pp. 194–215). Hershey, PA: IGI Global. doi:10.4018/978-1-4666-0951-8.ch011

Moeller, D. P., & Vakilzadian, H. (2012). Technology-enhanced learning standard through integration of modeling and simulation into engineering study programs. In M. Rasul (Ed.), Developments in engineering education standards: Advanced curriculum innovations (pp. 157–177). Hershey, PA: IGI Global. doi:10.4018/978-1-4666-0951-8.ch009

Mohan Baral, L., Kifor, C. V., Bondrea, I., & Oprean, C. (2012). Introducing problem based learning (PBL) in textile engineering education and assessing its influence on six sigma project implementation. *International Journal of Quality Assurance in Engineering and Technology Education*, 2(4), 38–48. doi:10.4018/ijqaete.2012100104

Moore, S., May, D., & Wold, K. (2012). Developing cultural competency in engineering through transnational distance learning. In R. Hogan (Ed.), Transnational distance learning and building new markets for universities (pp. 210–228). Hershey, PA: IGI Global. doi:10.4018/978-1-4666-0206-9.ch013

Mora, M., Gelman, O., Frank, M., Paradice, D. B., & Cervantes, F. (2010). Toward an interdisciplinary engineering and management of complex IT-intensive organizational systems: A systems view. In D. Paradice (Ed.), Emerging systems approaches in information technologies: Concepts, theories, and applications (pp. 1–24). Hershey, PA: IGI Global. doi:10.4018/978-1-60566-976-2.ch001

Mora, M., O'Connor, R., Raisinghani, M. S., Macías-Luévano, J., & Gelman, O. (2013). An IT service engineering and management framework (ITS-EMF). In P. Ordóñez de Pablos & R. Tennyson (Eds.), Best practices and new perspectives in service science and management (pp. 76–91). Hershey, PA: IGI Global. doi:10.4018/978-1-4666-3894-5.ch005

Moser, T., Biffl, S., Sunindyo, W. D., & Winkler, D. (2013). Integrating production automation expert knowledge across engineering domains. In N. Bessis (Ed.), Development of distributed systems from design to application and maintenance (pp. 152–167). Hershey, PA: IGI Global. doi:10.4018/978-1-4666-2647-8.ch009

Mouratidis, H. (2011). *Software engineering for secure systems: Industrial and research perspectives.* Hershey, PA: IGI Global. doi:10.4018/978-1-61520-837-1

Mourtos, N. J. (2012). Defining, teaching, and assessing engineering design skills. *International Journal of Quality Assurance in Engineering and Technology Education*, 2(1), 14–30. doi:10.4018/ijqaete.2012010102

Moustafa, A. (2012). Damage assessment of inelastic structures under simulated critical earthquakes. In V. Plevris, C. Mitropoulou, & N. Lagaros (Eds.), Structural seismic design optimization and earthquake engineering: Formulations and applications (pp. 128–151). Hershey, PA: IGI Global. doi:10.4018/978-1-4666-1640-0.ch006

Nasir, M. H., Alias, N. A., Fauzi, S. S., & Massatu, M. H. (2012). Implementation of the personal software process in academic settings and current support tools. In S. Fauzi, M. Nasir, N. Ramli, & S. Sahibuddin (Eds.), Software process improvement and management: Approaches and tools for practical development (pp. 117–148). Hershey, PA: IGI Global. doi:10.4018/978-1-61350-141-2.ch007

Nhlabatsi, A., Nuseibeh, B., & Yu, Y. (2012). Security requirements engineering for evolving software systems: A survey. In K. Khan (Ed.), Security-aware systems applications and software development methods (pp. 108–128). Hershey, PA: IGI Global. doi:10.4018/978-1-4666-1580-9.ch007

Noroozi, B., Valizadeh, M., & Sorial, G. A. (2010). Designing of e-learning for engineering education in developing countries: Key issues and success factors. In D. Russell & A. Haghi (Eds.), Web-based engineering education: Critical design and effective tools (pp. 1–19). Hershey, PA: IGI Global. doi:10.4018/978-1-61520-659-9.ch001

Oh Navarro, E. (2011). On the role of learning theories in furthering software engineering education. In Instructional design: Concepts, methodologies, tools and applications (pp. 1645–1666). Hershey, PA: IGI Global. doi:10.4018/978-1-60960-503-2.ch709

Onwubiko, C. (2014). Modelling situation awareness information and system requirements for the mission using goal-oriented task analysis approach. In Software design and development: Concepts, methodologies, tools, and applications (pp. 460–478). Hershey, PA: IGI Global. doi:10.4018/978-1-4666-4301-7.ch023

Osis, J., & Asnina, E. (2011). Is modeling a treatment for the weakness of software engineering? In J. Osis & E. Asnina (Eds.), Model-driven domain analysis and software development: Architectures and functions (pp. 1–14). Hershey, PA: IGI Global. doi:10.4018/978-1-61692-874-2.ch001

Othman, R., & Awang, Z. (2012). Using multiple methods in assessing oral communication skills in the final year project design course of an undergraduate engineering program. In K. Yusof, N. Azli, A. Kosnin, S. Yusof, & Y. Yusof (Eds.), Outcome-based science, technology, engineering, and mathematics education: Innovative practices (pp. 263–287). Hershey, PA: IGI Global. doi:10.4018/978-1-4666-1809-1.ch013

Ozcelik, Y. (2010). IT-enabled reengineering: Productivity impacts. In K. St.Amant (Ed.), IT outsourcing: Concepts, methodologies, tools, and applications (pp. 371–376). Hershey, PA: IGI Global. doi:10.4018/978-1-60566-770-6.ch022

Ožvoldová, M., & Schauer, F. (2012). Remote experiments in freshman engineering education by integrated e-learning. In A. Azad, M. Auer, & V. Harward (Eds.), Internet accessible remote laboratories: Scalable e-learning tools for engineering and science disciplines (pp. 60–83). Hershey, PA: IGI Global. doi:10.4018/978-1-61350-186-3.ch004

Paay, J., Pedell, S., Sterling, L., Vetere, F., & Howard, S. (2011). The benefit of ambiguity in understanding goals in requirements modelling. *International Journal of People-Oriented Programming*, *1*(2), 24–49. doi:10.4018/ijpop.2011070102

Palmer, S., & Holt, D. (2010). Online discussion in engineering education: Student responses and learning outcomes. In L. Shedletsky & J. Aitken (Eds.), Cases on online discussion and interaction: Experiences and outcomes (pp. 105–122). Hershey, PA: IGI Global. doi:10.4018/978-1-61520-863-0.ch005

Pandian, A., Ismail, S. A., & Abdullah, A. S. (2012). Communication framework to empower 21st century engineers and IT professionals. In A. Patil, H. Eijkman, & E. Bhattacharyya (Eds.), New media communication skills for engineers and IT professionals: Trans-national and trans-cultural demands (pp. 34–54). Hershey, PA: IGI Global. doi:10.4018/978-1-4666-0243-4.ch004

Pasupathy, K. S. (2010). Systems engineering and health informatics: Context, content, and implementation. In S. Kabene (Ed.), Healthcare and the effect of technology: Developments, challenges and advancements (pp. 123–144). Hershey, PA: IGI Global. doi:10.4018/978-1-61520-733-6.ch009

Pasupathy, K. S. (2010). Transforming healthcare: Leveraging the complementarities of health informatics and systems engineering. *International Journal of Healthcare Delivery Reform Initiatives*, *2*(2), 35–55. doi:10.4018/jhdri.2010040103

Pasupathy, K. S. (2011). Systems engineering and health informatics. In Clinical technologies: Concepts, methodologies, tools and applications (pp. 1684–1705). Hershey, PA: IGI Global. doi:10.4018/978-1-60960-561-2.ch606

Patel, C., & Ramachandran, M. (2010). Story card process improvement framework for agile requirements. In M. Ramachandran & R. de Carvalho (Eds.), Handbook of research on software engineering and productivity technologies: Implications of globalization (pp. 61–54). Hershey, PA: IGI Global. doi:10.4018/978-1-60566-731-7.ch006

Patro, C. S. (2012). A study on adaptability of total quality management in engineering education sector. *International Journal of Quality Assurance in Engineering and Technology Education*, *2*(4), 25–37. doi:10.4018/ijqaete.2012100103

Peña de Carrillo, C. I., Choquet, C., Després, C., Iksal, S., Jacoboni, P., & Lekira, A. ... Thi-Ngoc, D. P. (2014). Engineering and reengineering of technology enhanced learning scenarios using context awareness processes. In Software design and development: Concepts, methodologies, tools, and applications (pp. 1289-1313). Hershey, PA: Information Science Reference. doi:10.4018/978-1-4666-4301-7.ch063

Peng, F., & Li, H. (2011). A steganalysis method for 2D engineering graphics based on the statistic of geometric features. *International Journal of Digital Crime and Forensics*, *3*(2), 35–40. doi:10.4018/jdcf.2011040103

Pérez, J. L., Rabuñal, J., & Abella, F. M. (2012). Soft computing techniques in civil engineering: Time series prediction. In Computer engineering: Concepts, methodologies, tools and applications (pp. 1982–1997). Hershey, PA: IGI Global. doi:10.4018/978-1-61350-456-7.ch811

Pérez-Castillo, R., Rodríguez de Guzmán, I. G., & Piattini, M. (2011). Architecture-driven modernization. In A. Dogru & V. Biçer (Eds.), Modern software engineering concepts and practices: Advanced approaches (pp. 75–103). Hershey, PA: IGI Global. doi:10.4018/978-1-60960-215-4.ch004

Pérez-Castillo, R., Rodríguez de Guzmán, I. G., & Piattini, M. (2012). Model-driven reengineering. In J. Rech & C. Bunse (Eds.), Emerging technologies for the evolution and maintenance of software models (pp. 200–229). Hershey, PA: IGI Global. doi:10.4018/978-1-61350-438-3.ch008

Petkov, D., Edgar-Nevill, D., Madachy, R., & O'Connor, R. (2010). Information systems, software engineering, and systems thinking: Challenges and opportunities. In M. Hunter (Ed.), Strategic information systems: Concepts, methodologies, tools, and applications (pp. 315–332). Hershey, PA: IGI Global. doi:10.4018/978-1-60566-677-8.ch023

Petkov, D., Edgar-Nevill, D., Madachy, R., & O'Connor, R. (2012). Towards a wider application of the systems approach in information systems and software engineering. In Computer engineering: Concepts, methodologies, tools and applications (pp. 1627–1645). Hershey, PA: IGI Global. doi:10.4018/978-1-61350-456-7.ch701

Petre, L., Sere, K., & Troubitsyna, E. (2012). *Dependability and computer engineering: Concepts for software-intensive systems*. Hershey, PA: IGI Global. doi:10.4018/978-1-60960-747-0

Poels, G., Decreus, K., Roelens, B., & Snoeck, M. (2013). Investigating goal-oriented requirements engineering for business processes. *Journal of Database Management*, *24*(2), 35–71. doi:10.4018/jdm.2013040103

Polgar, J., & Adamson, G. (2011). *New generation of portal software and engineering: Emerging technologies*. Hershey, PA: IGI Global. doi:10.4018/978-1-60960-571-1

Power, C., Freire, A. P., & Petrie, H. (2011). Integrating accessibility evaluation into web engineering processes. In G. Alkhatib (Ed.), Web engineered applications for evolving organizations: Emerging knowledge (pp. 315–339). Hershey, PA: IGI Global. doi:10.4018/978-1-60960-523-0.ch018

Praeg, C. (2011). Framework for IT service value engineering: Managing value and IT service quality. In C. Praeg & D. Spath (Eds.), Quality management for IT services: Perspectives on business and process performance (pp. 274–297). Hershey, PA: IGI Global. doi:10.4018/978-1-61692-889-6.ch016

Prescott, J., & Bogg, J. (2013). *Gendered occupational differences in science, engineering, and technology careers.* Hershey, PA: IGI Global. doi:10.4018/978-1-4666-2107-7

Prpic, J. K., & Moore, G. (2012). E-portfolios as a quantitative and qualitative means of demonstrating learning outcomes and competencies in engineering. In K. Yusof, N. Azli, A. Kosnin, S. Yusof, & Y. Yusof (Eds.), Outcome-based science, technology, engineering, and mathematics education: Innovative practices (pp. 124–154). Hershey, PA: IGI Global. doi:10.4018/978-1-4666-1809-1.ch007

Puteh, M. M., & Ismail, K. (2012). Quality assurance through innovation policy: The pedagogical implications on engineering education. In Human resources management: Concepts, methodologies, tools, and applications (pp. 40–49). Hershey, PA: IGI Global. doi:10.4018/978-1-4666-1601-1.ch004

Puthanpurayil, A. M., Dhakal, R. P., & Carr, A. J. (2013). Optimal passive damper positioning techniques: State-of-the-art. In N. Lagaros, V. Plevris, & C. Mitropoulou (Eds.), Design optimization of active and passive structural control systems (pp. 85–111). Hershey, PA: IGI Global. doi:10.4018/978-1-4666-2029-2.ch004

Ramachandran, M. (2010). Knowledge engineering support for software requirements, architectures and components. In F. Meziane & S. Vadera (Eds.), Artificial intelligence applications for improved software engineering development: New prospects (pp. 129–145). Hershey, PA: IGI Global. doi:10.4018/978-1-60566-758-4.ch007

Ramachandran, M. (2011). *Knowledge engineering for software development life cycles: Support technologies and applications.* Hershey, PA: IGI Global. doi:10.4018/978-1-60960-509-4

Ramachandran, M., & de Carvalho, R. (2010). *Handbook of research on software engineering and productivity technologies: Implications of globalization.* Hershey, PA: IGI Global. doi:10.4018/978-1-60566-731-7

Rasul, M., Nouwens, F., Swift, R., Martin, F., & Greensill, C. V. (2012). Assessment of final year engineering projects: A pilot investigation on issues and best practice. In M. Rasul (Ed.), Developments in engineering education standards: Advanced curriculum innovations (pp. 80–104). Hershey, PA: IGI Global. doi:10.4018/978-1-4666-0951-8.ch005

Razali, Z. B., & Trevelyan, J. (2012). An evaluation of students' practical intelligence and ability to diagnose equipment faults. In K. Yusof, N. Azli, A. Kosnin, S. Yusof, & Y. Yusof (Eds.), Outcome-based science, technology, engineering, and mathematics education: Innovative practices (pp. 328–349). Hershey, PA: IGI Global. doi:10.4018/978-1-4666-1809-1.ch016

Reimann, D. (2011). Shaping interactive media with the sewing machine: Smart textile as an artistic context to engage girls in technology and engineering education. *International Journal of Art, Culture and Design Technologies, 1*(1), 12–21. doi:10.4018/ijacdt.2011010102

Rikkilä, J. (2014). Agile, lean, and service-oriented development, continuum, or chasm. In Software design and development: concepts, methodologies, tools, and applications (pp. 132–163). Hershey, PA: IGI Global. doi:10.4018/978-1-4666-4301-7.ch008

Rocci, L. (2010). Engineering and environmental technoethics. In R. Luppicini (Ed.), Technoethics and the evolving knowledge society: Ethical issues in technological design, research, development, and innovation (pp. 146–162). Hershey, PA: IGI Global. doi:10.4018/978-1-60566-952-6.ch008

Rodrigues, D., Estrella, J. C., Monaco, F. J., Branco, K. R., Antunes, N., & Vieira, M. (2012). Engineering secure web services. In V. Cardellini, E. Casalicchio, K. Castelo Branco, J. Estrella, & F. Monaco (Eds.), Performance and dependability in service computing: Concepts, techniques and research directions (pp. 360–380). Hershey, PA: IGI Global. doi:10.4018/978-1-60960-794-4.ch016

Rodríguez, J., Fernández-Medina, E., Piattini, M., & Mellado, D. (2011). A security requirements engineering tool for domain engineering in software product lines. In N. Milanovic (Ed.), Non-functional properties in service oriented architecture: Requirements, models and methods (pp. 73–92). Hershey, PA: IGI Global. doi:10.4018/978-1-60566-794-2.ch004

Rojko, A., Zürcher, T., Hercog, D., & Stebler, R. (2012). Implementation of remote laboratories for industrial education. In A. Azad, M. Auer, & V. Harward (Eds.), Internet accessible remote laboratories: Scalable e-learning tools for engineering and science disciplines (pp. 84–107). Hershey, PA: IGI Global. doi:10.4018/978-1-61350-186-3.ch005

Rosado, D. G., Mellado, D., Fernandez-Medina, E., & Piattini, M. G. (2013). *Security engineering for cloud computing: Approaches and tools*. Hershey, PA: IGI Global. doi:10.4018/978-1-4666-2125-1

Rose, S., Lauder, M., Schlereth, M., & Schürr, A. (2011). A multidimensional approach for concurrent model-driven automation engineering. In J. Osis & E. Asnina (Eds.), Model-driven domain analysis and software development: Architectures and functions (pp. 90–113). Hershey, PA: IGI Global. doi:10.4018/978-1-61692-874-2.ch005

Russell, C. (2012). Conceptual mapping, visualisation, and systems thinking in engineering. In A. Patil, H. Eijkman, & E. Bhattacharyya (Eds.), New media communication skills for engineers and IT professionals: Trans-national and trans-cultural demands (pp. 72–93). Hershey, PA: IGI Global. doi:10.4018/978-1-4666-0243-4.ch006

Russell, D., & Haghi, A. (2010). *Web-based engineering education: Critical design and effective tools*. Hershey, PA: IGI Global. doi:10.4018/978-1-61520-659-9

Russo, B., Scotto, M., Sillitti, A., & Succi, G. (2010). Improving agile methods. In B. Russo, M. Scotto, A. Sillitti, & G. Succi (Eds.), Agile technologies in open source development (pp. 189–231). Hershey, PA: IGI Global. doi:10.4018/978-1-59904-681-5.ch012

Russo, B., Scotto, M., Sillitti, A., & Succi, G. (2010). Requirements management. In B. Russo, M. Scotto, A. Sillitti, & G. Succi (Eds.), Agile technologies in open source development (pp. 268–286). Hershey, PA: IGI Global. doi:10.4018/978-1-59904-681-5.ch015

Russo, M. T. (2012). Humanities in engineering education. In M. Rasul (Ed.), Developments in engineering education standards: Advanced curriculum innovations (pp. 285–300). Hershey, PA: IGI Global. doi:10.4018/978-1-4666-0951-8.ch016

Saidane, A., & Guelfi, N. (2014). Towards test-driven and architecture model-based security and resilience engineering. In Software design and development: Concepts, methodologies, tools, and applications (pp. 2072–2098). Hershey, PA: IGI Global. doi:10.4018/978-1-4666-4301-7.ch096

Sala, N. (2012). Virtual reality in architecture, in engineering and beyond. In E. Abu-Taieh, A. El Sheikh, & M. Jafari (Eds.), Technology engineering and management in aviation: Advancements and discoveries (pp. 336–345). Hershey, PA: IGI Global. doi:10.4018/978-1-60960-887-3.ch020

Salzmann, C., Gillet, D., Esquembre, F., Vargas, H., Sánchez, J., & Dormido, S. (2012). Web 2.0 open remote and virtual laboratories in engineering education. In A. Okada, T. Connolly, & P. Scott (Eds.), Collaborative learning 2.0: Open educational resources (pp. 369–390). Hershey, PA: IGI Global. doi:10.4018/978-1-4666-0300-4.ch020

Samaras, G. (2012). Human-centered systems engineering: Managing stakeholder dissonance in healthcare delivery. In A. Kolker & P. Story (Eds.), Management engineering for effective healthcare delivery: Principles and applications (pp. 148–171). Hershey, PA: IGI Global. doi:10.4018/978-1-60960-872-9.ch007

Sampaio, A. Z., Henriques, P. G., Cruz, C. O., & Martins, O. P. (2011). Interactive models based on virtual reality technology used in civil engineering education. In G. Vincenti & J. Braman (Eds.), Teaching through multi-user virtual environments: Applying dynamic elements to the modern classroom (pp. 387–413). Hershey, PA: IGI Global. doi:10.4018/978-1-61692-822-3.ch021

Sanabria, S. J., Furrer, R., Neuenschwander, J., Niemz, P., & Sennhauser, U. (2014). Bonding defect imaging in glulam with novel air-coupled ultrasound testing. In A. Aguilera & J. Davim (Eds.), Research developments in wood engineering and technology (pp. 221–246). Hershey, PA: IGI Global. doi:10.4018/978-1-4666-4554-7.ch006

Sánchez de la Rosa, J. L., Miranda, S. A., & González, C. S. (2013). Evaluation of transversal competences of the engineering students and their relation to the enterprise requirements. In K. Patel & S. Vij (Eds.), Enterprise resource planning models for the education sector: Applications and methodologies (pp. 1–17). Hershey, PA: IGI Global. doi:10.4018/978-1-4666-2193-0.ch001

Sarirete, A., & Chikh, A. (2012). A knowledge management process in communities of practice of engineering based on the SECI model for knowledge. In E. Ng, N. Karacapilidis, & M. Raisinghani (Eds.), Evaluating the impact of technology on learning, teaching, and designing curriculum: Emerging trends (pp. 134–149). Hershey, PA: IGI Global. doi:10.4018/978-1-4666-0032-4.ch009

Sass, L. (2013). Direct building manufacturing of homes with digital fabrication. In Industrial engineering: Concepts, methodologies, tools, and applications (pp. 1231–1242). Hershey, PA: IGI Global. doi:10.4018/978-1-4666-1945-6.ch066

Sauvet, B., Boukhicha, M., Balan, A., Hwang, G., Taverna, D., Shukla, A., & Régnier, S. (2012). Selective pick-and-place of thin film by robotic micromanipulation. *International Journal of Intelligent Mechatronics and Robotics*, 2(3), 24–37. doi:10.4018/ijimr.2012070103

Schnabel, M. A. (2013). Learning parametric designing. In Industrial engineering: Concepts, methodologies, tools, and applications (pp. 197–210). Hershey, PA: IGI Global. doi:10.4018/978-1-4666-1945-6.ch013

Schrödl, H., & Wind, S. (2013). Requirements engineering for cloud application development. In A. Bento & A. Aggarwal (Eds.), Cloud computing service and deployment models: Layers and management (pp. 137–150). Hershey, PA: IGI Global. doi:10.4018/978-1-4666-2187-9.ch007

Schulz, T., Radlinski, L., Gorges, T., & Rosenstiel, W. (2011). Software process model using dynamic bayesian networks. In M. Ramachandran (Ed.), Knowledge engineering for software development life cycles: Support technologies and applications (pp. 289–310). Hershey, PA: IGI Global. doi:10.4018/978-1-60960-509-4.ch016

Sevillian, D. B. (2013). Aircraft development and design: Enhancing product safety through effective human factors engineering design solutions. In Industrial engineering: Concepts, methodologies, tools, and applications (pp. 858–886). Hershey, PA: IGI Global. doi:10.4018/978-1-4666-1945-6.ch048

Shan, T. C., & Hua, W. W. (2010). Strategic technology engineering planning. In M. Hunter (Ed.), Strategic information systems: Concepts, methodologies, tools, and applications (pp. 414–434). Hershey, PA: IGI Global. doi:10.4018/978-1-60566-677-8.ch029

Sharma, A., & Maurer, F. (2014). A roadmap for software engineering for the cloud: Results of a systematic review. In Software design and development: Concepts, methodologies, tools, and applications (pp. 1–16). Hershey, PA: IGI Global. doi:10.4018/978-1-4666-4301-7.ch001

Sharma, N., Singh, K., & Goyal, D. (2014). Software engineering, process improvement, and experience management: Is the nexus productive? Clues from the Indian giants. In Software design and development: Concepts, methodologies, tools, and applications (pp. 1401–1414). Hershey, PA: IGI Global. doi:10.4018/978-1-4666-4301-7.ch068

Shirk, S., Arreola, V., Wobig, C., & Russell, K. (2012). Girls' e-mentoring in science, engineering, and technology based at the University of Illinois at Chicago women in science and engineering (WISE) program. In Computer engineering: Concepts, Methodologies, tools and applications (pp. 1144-1163). Hershey, PA: IGI Global. doi:10.4018/978-1-61350-456-7.ch505

Shukla, A., & Tiwari, R. (2011). *Biomedical engineering and information systems: Technologies, tools and applications*. Hershey, PA: IGI Global. doi:10.4018/978-1-61692-004-3

Sidhu, M. S. (2010). Challenges and trends of TAPS packages in enhancing engineering education. In M. Sidhu (Ed.), Technology-assisted problem solving for engineering education: Interactive multimedia applications (pp. 158–166). Hershey, PA: IGI Global. doi:10.4018/978-1-60566-764-5.ch011

Sidhu, M. S. (2010). Evaluation of TAPS packages. In M. Sidhu (Ed.), Technology-assisted problem solving for engineering education: Interactive multimedia applications (pp. 128–147). Hershey, PA: IGI Global. doi:10.4018/978-1-60566-764-5.ch009

Sidhu, M. S. (2010). Technology assisted problem solving packages: A new approach to learning, visualizing, and problem solving in engineering. In M. Sidhu (Ed.), Technology-assisted problem solving for engineering education: Interactive multimedia applications (pp. 69–90). Hershey, PA: IGI Global. doi:10.4018/978-1-60566-764-5.ch006

Sidhu, M. S. (2010). *Technology-assisted problem solving for engineering education: Interactive multimedia applications*. Hershey, PA: IGI Global. doi:10.4018/978-1-60566-764-5

Sidhu, M. S., & Kang, L. C. (2012). Emerging trends and technologies for enhancing engineering education: An overview. In L. Tomei (Ed.), Advancing education with information communication technologies: Facilitating new trends (pp. 320–330). Hershey, PA: IGI Global. doi:10.4018/978-1-61350-468-0.ch026

Sidhu, M. S., & Kang, L. C. (2012). New trends and futuristic information communication technologies for engineering education. In S. Chhabra (Ed.), ICTs for advancing rural communities and human development: Addressing the digital divide (pp. 251–262). Hershey, PA: IGI Global. doi:10.4018/978-1-4666-0047-8.ch017

Simonette, M. J., & Spina, E. (2014). Enabling IT innovation through soft systems engineering. In M. Pańkowska (Ed.), Frameworks of IT prosumption for business development (pp. 64–72). Hershey, PA: IGI Global. doi:10.4018/978-1-4666-4313-0.ch005

Singh, T., Verma, M. K., & Singh, R. (2014). Role of emotional intelligence in academic achievement: An empirical study on engineering students. In P. Ordóñez de Pablos & R. Tennyson (Eds.), Strategic approaches for human capital management and development in a turbulent economy (pp. 255–263). Hershey, PA: IGI Global. doi:10.4018/978-1-4666-4530-1.ch016

Smolnik, S., Teuteberg, F., & Thomas, O. (2012). *Semantic technologies for business and information systems engineering: Concepts and applications*. Hershey, PA: IGI Global. doi:10.4018/978-1-60960-126-3

Solemon, B., Sahibuddin, S., & Ghani, A. A. (2014). Requirements engineering process improvement and related models. In Software design and development: Concepts, methodologies, tools, and applications (pp. 203–218). Hershey, PA: IGI Global. doi:10.4018/978-1-4666-4301-7.ch011

Sorial, G. A., & Noroozi, B. (2012). Improvement of engineering students education by e-learning. In Virtual learning environments: Concepts, methodologies, tools and applications (pp. 870–883). Hershey, PA: IGI Global. doi:10.4018/978-1-4666-0011-9.ch414

Srinivasan, A., López-Ribot, J. L., & Ramasubramanian, A. K. (2011). Microfluidic applications in vascular bioengineering. In A. Shukla & R. Tiwari (Eds.), Biomedical engineering and information systems: Technologies, tools and applications (pp. 1–30). Hershey, PA: IGI Global. doi:10.4018/978-1-61692-004-3.ch001

Steinbuch, R. (2013). Evolutionary optimization of passive compensators to improve earthquake resistance. In N. Lagaros, V. Plevris, & C. Mitropoulou (Eds.), Design optimization of active and passive structural control systems (pp. 250–273). Hershey, PA: IGI Global. doi:10.4018/978-1-4666-2029-2.ch011

Stephenson, S. V., & Sage, A. P. (2010). Information and knowledge perspectives in systems engineering and management for innovation and productivity through enterprise resource planning. In M. Hunter (Ed.), Strategic information systems: Concepts, methodologies, tools, and applications (pp. 338–368). Hershey, PA: IGI Global. doi:10.4018/978-1-60566-677-8.ch025

Strasser, T., Zoitl, A., & Rooker, M. (2013). Zero-downtime reconfiguration of distributed control logic in industrial automation and control. In Industrial engineering: Concepts, methodologies, tools, and applications (pp. 2024–2051). Hershey, PA: IGI Global. doi:10.4018/978-1-4666-1945-6.ch109

Sudeikat, J., & Renz, W. (2010). Building complex adaptive systems: On engineering self-organizing multi-agent systems. In M. Hunter (Ed.), Strategic information systems: Concepts, methodologies, tools, and applications (pp. 767–787). Hershey, PA: IGI Global. doi:10.4018/978-1-60566-677-8.ch050

Sugiyama, S., & Burgess, L. (2012). Principle for engineering service based system by swirl computing. In X. Liu & Y. Li (Eds.), Advanced design approaches to emerging software systems: Principles, methodologies and tools (pp. 48–60). Hershey, PA: IGI Global. doi:10.4018/978-1-60960-735-7.ch003

Sun, Z., Han, J., Dong, D., & Zhao, S. (2010). Engineering of experience based trust for e-commerce. In M. Wang & Z. Sun (Eds.), Handbook of research on complex dynamic process management: Techniques for adaptability in turbulent environments (pp. 342–367). Hershey, PA: IGI Global. doi:10.4018/978-1-60566-669-3.ch014

Sunindyo, W. D., Moser, T., Winkler, D., Mordinyi, R., & Biffl, S. (2013). Workflow validation framework in collaborative engineering environments. In A. Loo (Ed.), Distributed computing innovations for business, engineering, and science (pp. 285–299). Hershey, PA: IGI Global. doi:10.4018/978-1-4666-2533-4.ch015

Szeto, A. Y. (2014). Assistive technology and rehabilitation engineering. In Assistive technologies: Concepts, methodologies, tools, and applications (pp. 277–331). Hershey, PA: IGI Global. doi:10.4018/978-1-4666-4422-9.ch015

Takruri-Rizk, H., Sappleton, N., & Dhar-Bhattacharjee, S. (2010). Progression of UK women engineers: Aids and hurdles. In A. Cater-Steel & E. Cater (Eds.), Women in engineering, science and technology: Education and career challenges (pp. 280–300). Hershey, PA: IGI Global. doi:10.4018/978-1-61520-657-5.ch013

Tekinerdogan, B., & Aksit, M. (2011). A comparative analysis of software engineering with mature engineering disciplines using a problem-solving perspective. In A. Dogru & V. Biçer (Eds.), Modern software engineering concepts and practices: Advanced approaches (pp. 1–18). Hershey, PA: IGI Global. doi:10.4018/978-1-60960-215-4.ch001

Tellioglu, H. (2012). About representational artifacts and their role in engineering. In G. Viscusi, G. Campagnolo, & Y. Curzi (Eds.), Phenomenology, organizational politics, and IT design: The social study of information systems (pp. 111–130). Hershey, PA: IGI Global. doi:10.4018/978-1-4666-0303-5.ch007

Terawaki, Y., Takahashi, Y., Kodama, Y., & Yana, K. (2013). The development of educational environment suited to the Japan-specific educational service using requirements engineering techniques: Case study of running Sakai with PostgreSQL. In V. Kumar & F. Lin (Eds.), System and technology advancements in distance learning (pp. 261–270). Hershey, PA: IGI Global. doi:10.4018/978-1-4666-2032-2.ch019

Thomas, K. D., & Muga, H. E. (2012). Sustainability: The new 21st century general education requirement for engineers. In M. Rasul (Ed.), Developments in engineering education standards: Advanced curriculum innovations (pp. 263–284). Hershey, PA: IGI Global. doi:10.4018/978-1-4666-0951-8.ch015

Trigo, B., Olguin, G., & Matai, P. (2010). The use of applets in an engineering chemistry course: Advantages and new ideas. In D. Russell & A. Haghi (Eds.), Web-based engineering education: Critical design and effective tools (pp. 108–118). Hershey, PA: IGI Global. doi:10.4018/978-1-61520-659-9.ch009

Tsadimas, A., Nikolaidou, M., & Anagnostopoulos, D. (2014). Model-based system design using SysML: The role of the evaluation diagram. In P. Fonseca i Casas (Ed.), Formal languages for computer simulation: Transdisciplinary models and applications (pp. 236–266). Hershey, PA: IGI Global. doi:10.4018/978-1-4666-4369-7.ch008

Unhelkar, B., Ghanbary, A., & Younessi, H. (2010). *Collaborative business process engineering and global organizations: Frameworks for service integration.* Hershey, PA: IGI Global. doi:10.4018/978-1-60566-689-1

Uziak, J., Oladiran, M. T., & Kommula, V. P. (2012). Integrating general education courses into engineering curriculum: Students' perspective. In M. Rasul (Ed.), Developments in engineering education standards: Advanced curriculum innovations (pp. 247–262). Hershey, PA: IGI Global. doi:10.4018/978-1-4666-0951-8.ch014

Valizadeh, M., Anzelotti, G., & Salehi, A. S. (2010). Web-based approaches in engineering education. In R. Luppicini & A. Haghi (Eds.), Cases on digital technologies in higher education: Issues and challenges (pp. 241–256). Hershey, PA: IGI Global. doi:10.4018/978-1-61520-869-2.ch017

Valizadeh, M., Anzelotti, G., & Salehi, S. (2010). Web-based training: An applicable tool for engineering education. In D. Russell & A. Haghi (Eds.), Web-based engineering education: Critical design and effective tools (pp. 186–198). Hershey, PA: IGI Global. doi:10.4018/978-1-61520-659-9.ch014

Valverde, R., Toleman, M., & Cater-Steel, A. (2010). Design science: A case study in information systems re-engineering. In M. Hunter (Ed.), Strategic information systems: Concepts, methodologies, tools, and applications (pp. 490–503). Hershey, PA: IGI Global. doi:10.4018/978-1-60566-677-8.ch033

Vaquero, L. M., Rodero-Merino, L., Cáceres, J., Chapman, C., Lindner, M., & Galán, F. (2012). Principles, methodology and tools for engineering cloud computing systems. In X. Liu & Y. Li (Eds.), Advanced design approaches to emerging software systems: Principles, methodologies and tools (pp. 250–273). Hershey, PA: IGI Global. doi:10.4018/978-1-60960-735-7.ch012

Vargas, E. P. (2014). Quality, improvement and measurements in high risk software. In Software design and development: Concepts, methodologies, tools, and applications (pp. 733–748). Hershey, PA: IGI Global. doi:10.4018/978-1-4666-4301-7.ch035

Vasant, P. (2013). *Meta-heuristics optimization algorithms in engineering, business, economics, and finance.* Hershey, PA: IGI Global. doi:10.4018/978-1-4666-2086-5

Venkatraman, S. (2013). Software engineering research gaps in the cloud. *Journal of Information Technology Research, 6*(1), 1–19. doi:10.4018/jitr.2013010101

Villazón-Terrazas, B. C., Suárez-Figueroa, M., & Gómez-Pérez, A. (2012). A pattern-based method for re-engineering non-ontological resources into ontologies. In A. Sheth (Ed.), Semantic-enabled advancements on the web: Applications across industries (pp. 17–54). Hershey, PA: IGI Global. doi:10.4018/978-1-4666-0185-7.ch002

Vinod, J. S. (2010). Dem simulations in geotechnical earthquake engineering education. *International Journal of Geotechnical Earthquake Engineering, 1*(1), 61–69. doi:10.4018/jgee.2010090804

Virdi, J. (2014). Business risk analysis: Obsolescence management in requirements engineering. In Software design and development: Concepts, methodologies, tools, and applications (pp. 1736–1763). Hershey, PA: IGI Global. doi:10.4018/978-1-4666-4301-7.ch083

Walk, S., Pöschko, J., Strohmaier, M., Andrews, K., Tudorache, T., Noy, N. F., & Musen, M. A. et al. (2013). PragmatiX: An interactive tool for visualizing the creation process behind collaboratively engineered ontologies. *International Journal on Semantic Web and Information Systems*, *9*(1), 45–78. doi:10.4018/jswis.2013010103 PMID:24465189

Wang, J. (2013). Architects and engineers. In Challenging ICT applications in architecture, engineering, and industrial design education (pp. 48–64). Hershey, PA: IGI Global. doi:10.4018/978-1-4666-1999-9.ch003

Wang, J. (2013). *Challenging ICT applications in architecture, engineering, and industrial design education*. Hershey, PA: IGI Global. doi:10.4018/978-1-4666-1999-9

Wang, J. (2013). Pedagogy and curriculum in architecture and engineering. In Challenging ICT applications in architecture, engineering, and industrial design education (pp. 65–92). Hershey, PA: IGI Global. doi:10.4018/978-1-4666-1999-9.ch004

Wang, J. (2013). Professionalism in architecture and engineering. In Challenging ICT applications in architecture, engineering, and industrial design education (pp. 137–156). Hershey, PA: IGI Global. doi:10.4018/978-1-4666-1999-9.ch007

Wang, J. (2013). Reviewing engineers and introducing industrial designers. In Challenging ICT applications in architecture, engineering, and industrial design education (pp. 111–136). Hershey, PA: IGI Global. doi:10.4018/978-1-4666-1999-9.ch006

Wang, Y. (2010). On cognitive properties of human factors and error models in engineering and socialization. In Y. Wang (Ed.), Discoveries and breakthroughs in cognitive informatics and natural intelligence (pp. 93–109). Hershey, PA: IGI Global. doi:10.4018/978-1-60566-902-1.ch006

Wang, Y. (2012). Convergence of software science and computational intelligence: A new transdisciplinary research field. In Y. Wang (Ed.), Software and intelligent sciences: New transdisciplinary findings (pp. 1–13). Hershey, PA: IGI Global. doi:10.4018/978-1-4666-0261-8.ch001

Wang, Y., & Patel, S. (2012). Exploring the cognitive foundations of software engineering. In Y. Wang (Ed.), Software and intelligent sciences: New transdisciplinary findings (pp. 232–251). Hershey, PA: IGI Global. doi:10.4018/978-1-4666-0261-8.ch014

Wei, J., Chen, J., & Zhu, Q. (2010). Service science, management and engineering education: A unified model for university. *International Journal of Service Science, Management, Engineering, and Technology*, *1*(2), 51–69. doi:10.4018/jssmet.2010040104

Weigang, L., Barros, A. D., & Romani de Oliveira, I. (2010). *Computational models, software engineering, and advanced technologies in air transportation: Next generation applications*. Hershey, PA: IGI Global. doi:10.4018/978-1-60566-800-0

Westh Nicolajsen, H. (2010). Limitations and perspectives on use of e-services in engineering consulting. In Electronic services: Concepts, methodologies, tools and applications (pp. 1280–1295). Hershey, PA: IGI Global. doi:10.4018/978-1-61520-967-5.ch078

Wilson, R., & Younis, H. (2013). *Business strategies for electrical infrastructure engineering: Capital project implementation.* Hershey, PA: IGI Global. doi:10.4018/978-1-4666-2839-7

Winter, A. (2010). The smart women – smart state strategy: A policy on women's participation in science, engineering and technology in Queensland, Australia. In A. Cater-Steel & E. Cater (Eds.), Women in engineering, science and technology: Education and career challenges (pp. 1–20). Hershey, PA: IGI Global. doi:10.4018/978-1-61520-657-5.ch001

Winter, R., & van Beijnum, I. (2014). Inter-domain traffic engineering using the origin preference attribute. In M. Boucadair & D. Binet (Eds.), Solutions for sustaining scalability in internet growth (pp. 18–38). Hershey, PA: IGI Global. doi:10.4018/978-1-4666-4305-5.ch002

Worth, D., Greenough, C., & Chin, S. (2014). Pragmatic software engineering for computational science. In Software design and development: Concepts, methodologies, tools, and applications (pp. 663–694). Hershey, PA: IGI Global. doi:10.4018/978-1-4666-4301-7.ch032

Wu, J. (2013). *Biomedical engineering and cognitive neuroscience for healthcare: Interdisciplinary applications.* Hershey, PA: IGI Global. doi:10.4018/978-1-4666-2113-8

Wu, Y., & Koszalka, T. A. (2013). Instructional design of an advanced interactive discovery environment: Exploring team communication and technology use in virtual collaborative engineering problem solving. In Industrial engineering: Concepts, methodologies, tools, and applications (pp. 117–136). Hershey, PA: IGI Global. doi:10.4018/978-1-4666-1945-6.ch009

Yadav, V. (2011). Research review: Globally distributed requirements engineering and agility. *International Journal of Innovation in the Digital Economy*, 2(1), 1–11. doi:10.4018/jide.2011010101

Yang, J. J., Liu, J. F., Kurokawa, T., Kitamura, N., Yasuda, K., & Gong, J. P. (2013). Tough double-network hydrogels as scaffolds for tissue engineering: Cell behavior in vitro and in vivo test. In J. Wu (Ed.), Technological advancements in biomedicine for healthcare applications (pp. 213–222). Hershey, PA: IGI Global. doi:10.4018/978-1-4666-2196-1.ch023

Yeoh, W., Gao, J., & Koronios, A. (2010). Empirical investigation of critical success factors for implementing business intelligence systems in multiple engineering asset management organisations. In M. Hunter (Ed.), Strategic information systems: Concepts, methodologies, tools, and applications (pp. 2039–2063). Hershey, PA: IGI Global. doi:10.4018/978-1-60566-677-8.ch129

Yerrick, R., Lund, C., & Lee, Y. (2013). Online simulator use in the preparing chemical engineers. *International Journal of Online Pedagogy and Course Design*, 3(2), 1–24. doi:10.4018/ijopcd.2013040101

Yilmaz, A. E., & Yilmaz, I. B. (2012). Natural language processing techniques in requirements engineering. In Computer engineering: Concepts, methodologies, tools and applications (pp. 533–545). Hershey, PA: IGI Global. doi:10.4018/978-1-61350-456-7.ch303

Yong, E. (2012). Literature review skills for undergraduate engineering students in large classes. In K. Yusof, N. Azli, A. Kosnin, S. Yusof, & Y. Yusof (Eds.), Outcome-based science, technology, engineering, and mathematics education: Innovative practices (pp. 240–261). Hershey, PA: IGI Global. doi:10.4018/978-1-4666-1809-1.ch012

Yun, H., Xu, J., Xiong, J., & Wei, M. (2013). A knowledge engineering approach to develop domain ontology. In V. Kumar & F. Lin (Eds.), System and technology advancements in distance learning (pp. 55–70). Hershey, PA: IGI Global. doi:10.4018/978-1-4666-2032-2.ch004

Zardari, S., Faniyi, F., & Bahsoon, R. (2013). Using obstacles for systematically modeling, analysing, and mitigating risks in cloud adoption. In I. Mistrik, A. Tang, R. Bahsoon, & J. Stafford (Eds.), Aligning enterprise, system, and software architectures (pp. 275–296). Hershey, PA: IGI Global. doi:10.4018/978-1-4666-2199-2.ch014

Zaščerinska, J., Ahrens, A., & Bassus, O. (2012). Enterprise 2.0 and 3.0 in education: Engineering and business students' view. In M. Cruz-Cunha, P. Gonçalves, N. Lopes, E. Miranda, & G. Putnik (Eds.), Handbook of research on business social networking: Organizational, managerial, and technological dimensions (pp. 472–494). Hershey, PA: IGI Global. doi:10.4018/978-1-61350-168-9.ch025

Zaščerinska, J., Ahrens, A., & Bassus, O. (2012). Enterprise 2.0 and 3.0 in education: Engineering and business students' view. In M. Cruz-Cunha, P. Gonçalves, N. Lopes, E. Miranda, & G. Putnik (Eds.), Handbook of research on business social networking: Organizational, managerial, and technological dimensions (pp. 472–494). Hershey, PA: IGI Global. doi:10.4018/978-1-61350-168-9.ch025

Zhang, D. (2012). Machine learning and value-based software engineering. In Y. Wang (Ed.), Software and intelligent sciences: New transdisciplinary findings (pp. 287–301). Hershey, PA: IGI Global. doi:10.4018/978-1-4666-0261-8.ch017

Zhang, H., Xu, C., Su, W., & Luo, H. (2014). Routing optimization for inter-domain traffic engineering under identifier network. In M. Boucadair & D. Binet (Eds.), Solutions for sustaining scalability in internet growth (pp. 127–147). Hershey, PA: IGI Global. doi:10.4018/978-1-4666-4305-5.ch007

Zhong, Y. (2013). Processing of 3D unstructured measurement data for reverse engineering. In S. Sirouspour (Ed.), Advanced engineering and computational methodologies for intelligent mechatronics and robotics (pp. 118–127). Hershey, PA: IGI Global. doi:10.4018/978-1-4666-3634-7.ch008

Zhou, Z., Wang, H., & Lou, P. (2010). *Manufacturing intelligence for industrial engineering: Methods for system self-organization, learning, and adaptation.* Hershey, PA: IGI Global. doi:10.4018/978-1-60566-864-2

Zhu, L., Jayaram, U., & Kim, O. (2011). Online semantic knowledge management for product design based on product engineering ontologies. *International Journal on Semantic Web and Information Systems*, *7*(4), 36–61. doi:10.4018/jswis.2011100102

Compilation of References

Abdalla, M., Bellare, M., & Rogaway, P. (2001). The oracle Diffie-Hellman assumptions and an analysis of DHIES. In Topics in Cryptology, LNCS (Vol. *2020*, pp. 143–158). doi:10.1007/3-540-45353-9_12

Ahila, S., & Shunmuganathan, K.L. (2014). State Of Art in Homomorphic Encryption Schemes. *Int. Journal of Engineering Research and Applications, 4*(2), 37-43.

Al-Ahmad, M.A., & Alshaikhli, I.F. (2013). Broad view of Cryptographic Hash Functions. *International Journal of Computer Science Issues, 10*(4).

Al-Riyami, S. S., & Paterson, K. G. (2003). Certificateless public key cryptography. Proceedings of Asiacrypt 2003. doi:10.1007/978-3-540-40061-5_29

Amir, Y., & Stanton, J. (1998). The Spread wide area group communication system (Tech. Rep. 98-4). Johns Hopkins University, Center of Networking and Distributed Systems.

Amir, Y., Kim, Y., Nita-Rotaru, C., Schultz, J. L., Stanton, J., & Tsudik, G. (2004). Secure group communication using robust contributory key agreement. *IEEE Transactions on Parallel and Distributed Systems, 15*(5), 468–480. doi:10.1109/TPDS.2004.1278104

Anderson, R. J. (2001). *Security Engineering*. New York: Wiley &sons.

Anshel, I., Anshel, M., & Goldfeld, D. (1999). An algebraic method for public-key cryptography. *Math. Res. Lett, 6*(3), 287–291. doi:10.4310/MRL.1999.v6.n3.a3

Aoki, K., Franke, J., Kleinjung, T., Lenstra, A. K., & Osvik, D. A. (2007). A kilobit special number field sieve factorization. In *Advances in Cryptology ASIACRYPT '07*. Berlin: Springer. doi:10.1007/978-3-540-76900-2_1

Arbaugh, W. A., Farber, D. J., & Smith, J. M. (1997). A secure and reliable bootstrap architecture. *Proceedings of the 1997 IEEE Symposium on Security and Privacy* (pp. 65-71).

Aronsson, H. (1995). *Zero Knowledge Protocols and Small Systems*. Retrieved from Http://www.tml.tkk.fi/Opinnot/Tik-110.501/1995/zeroknowledge.html

Asokan, N., Shoup, V., & Waidner, M. (2000). Optimistic fair exchange of digital signatures. *IEEE Journal on Selected Areas in Communications, 18*(4), 593–610. doi:10.1109/49.839935

Aumann, Y., & Lindell, Y. (2010). Security against covert adversaries: Efficient protocols for realistic adversaries. *Journal of Cryptology, 23*(2), 281–343. doi:10.1007/s00145-009-9040-7

Bao, F., Deng, R. H., & Zhu, H. (2003). Variations of Diffie-Hellman problem. In Information and Communications Security, LNCS (Vol. *2836*, pp. 301–312). doi:10.1007/978-3-540-39927-8_28

Baretto, P. S. L. M., & Rijmen, V. (2003). *The Whirlpool Hash Function.*

Bellare, M., & Goldreich, O. (1992). On Defining Proofs of Knowledge. Proceedings of CRYPTO '92 (pp. 390-420).

Bellare, M., & Rogaway, P. (1994). Optimal Asymmetric Encryption, In Advances in Cryptology Eurocrypt '94 (pp. 92-111).

Bellare, M., Canetti, R., & Krawczyk, H. (1996a). Pseudorandom Functions Revisited: The Cascade Construction and Its Concrete Security. Proceedings of FOCS (pp. 514-523).

Bellare, M., Canetti, R., & Krawczyk, H. (1996b). Keying Hash Functions for Message Authentication. *Proceedings of CRYPTO '96* (pp. 1-15).

Bellare, M., Desai, A., Pointcheval, D., & Rogaway, A. (1998) Relations among notions of Security for public-key encryption schemes. In Advances in Cryptology CRYPTO '98 (pp. 26-45). doi:10.1007/BFb0055718

Bellare, M., Kilian, J., & Rogaway, P. (1994). *The security of Cipher Block Chaining. Proc. of Crypto'94, LNCS (Vol. 839).* Springer-Verlag.

Bellare, M., Namprempre, C., Pointcheval, D., & Semanko, M. (2003). The one-more-RSA-inversion problems and the security of Chaums blind signature scheme. *Journal of Cryptology, 16*(3), 185–215. doi:10.1007/s00145-002-0120-1

Bellare, M., & Rogaway, P. (1993). Random Oracles are practical: a paradigm for designing efficient protocols. *Proc. of ACM CCS* '93 (pp. 62-73). doi:10.1145/168588.168596

Benaloh, J. C. (1987). *Verifiable Secret Ballot Elections* [PhD thesis]. Yale University.

Bernhard, D. (2014). *Zero Knowledge Proofs in Theory and Practice* [Ph.D. dissertation]. University of Bristol.

Bernstein, D.J., Buchmann, J., & Damen, E. (Eds.). (2009). *Post-Quantum Cryptography.* Springer-Verlag.

Bhargav, Y., & Moorthy, P. S. (2013). Homomorphic Recommendations for Data Packing- A Survey. *International Journal of Computer Science and Mobile Applications, 1*(5), 18-37.

Biham, E. (1996), How to forge DES-encrypted messages in 2^{28} steps (technical Report CS-0884). Computer Science Department, Technion, Haifa, Israel.

Biham, E., & Shamir, A. (1997) Differential fault analysis of secret key cryptosystems. In B. Kaliski (Ed.), Proc. of Advances in Cryptology – Crypto '97, LNCS (Vol. 1294, pp. 513–525). doi:10.1007/BFb0052259

Biswas, G. P. (2008). Diffie-Hellman Technique: Extended to multiple two-party keys and one multi-party key. *IET Information Security, 2*(1), 12–18. doi:10.1049/iet-ifs:20060142

Black, J., Halevi, S., Krawczyk, H., Krovetz, T., & Rogaway, P. (1999). *UMAC: Fast and Secure Message Authentication. Proc. Crypto '99, LNCS (Vol. 1666).* Springer-Verlag.

Black, J., & Rogaway, P. (2000). *CBC MACs for Arbitrary-Length Messages: The Three-Key Constructions. Proc. Crypto '00, LNCS (Vol. 1880).* Springer-Verlag.

Blaze, M., Diffie, W., Rivest, R., Schneier, B., Shimomura, T., Thompson, E., & Wiener, M. (1996). Minimal key lengths for symmetric ciphers to provide adequate commercial security. Retrieved from http://www.schneier.com/paper-keylength.html

Bleichenbacher, D. (1998). Chosen ciphertext attacks against protocols based on the RSA encryption Standard pkcs #1. In *Advances in Cryptology CRYPTO '98.*

Blomer,J., and Seifert,J.P. (2002) Fault based cryptanalysis of the advanced encryption standard (AES).

Blum, M., Feldman, P., & Micali, S. (1988). Non-interactive zero-knowledge and its applications. *Proceedings of the Twentieth Annual ACM Symposium on Theory of Computing STOC '88* (pp. 103–112). doi:10.1145/62212.62222

Boneh, D., & Boyen, X. (2004a). Short Signatures Without Random Oracles. In *Eurocrypt 2004, LNCS* (Vol. 3027, pp. 56-73). Springer-Verlag.

Boneh, D., & Boyen, X. (2004c). Efficient Selective-ID Secure Identity-Based Encryption Without Random Oracles. In *Eurocrypt 2004, LNCS* (Vol. 3027, pp. 223-238). Springer-Verlag.

Boneh, D., & Franklin, M. (2001). Identity-Based Encryption from the Weil Pairing. *Proceedings of CRYPTO 2001*, 213-229. doi:10.1007/3-540-44647-8_13

Boneh, D., Boyen, X., & Goh, E. (2005a). Hierarchical Identity Based Encryption with Constant Size Ciphertext. In *Eurocrypt 2005, LNCS* (Vol. 3494, pp. 440-456). Springer-Verlag.

Boneh, D., Boyen, X., & Shacham, H. (2004b). Short Group Signatures. In *Crypto 2004, LNCS* (Vol. 3152, pp. 41-55). Springer-Verlag.

Boneh, D., DeMillo, R. A., & Lipton, R. J. (1997). On the importance of checking crypto-graphic protocols for faults. In W. Fumy (Ed.), Advances in Cryptology - EUROCRYPT '97, Konstanz, Germany LNCS (Vol. 1233, pp. 37–51). Springer.

Boneh, D., Gentry, C., & Waters, B. (2005b). Collution Resistant Broadcast Encryption with Short Ciphertexts and Private Keys. In *Crypto 2005, LNCS* (Vol. 3621, pp. 258-275). Springer-Verlag.

Boneh, D., & Franklin, M. K. (2003). Identity-based encryption from the Weil pairing. *SIAM Journal on Computing*, *32*(3), 586–615. doi:10.1137/S0097539701398521

Boneh, D., Gentry, C., Halevi, S., Wang, F., & Wu, D. J. (2013). Private Database Queries Using Somewhat Homomorphic Encryption. Proceedings of *ACNS '13* (pp. 102–118).

Bosselaers, A. (1992). Integrity Primitives for Secure Information Systems, Final Report of RACE Integrity Primitives Evaluation.

Boyd, C. (1988). A new multiple key cipher and an improved voting scheme. *Lecture Notes in Computer Science*, *434*, 617–625. doi:10.1007/3-540-46885-4_58

Brassard, G., Crepeau, C., & Robert, J. (1986). All-or-nothing Disclosure of Secrets. In Advances in Cryptology, Crypto '86, LNCS (Vol. 263, pp. 234-238).

Bresson, E., Chevassut, O., & Pointcheval, D. (2002a). Group Diffie-Hellman secure against dictionary attacks. In Zheng (Ed.), Proc. of Asiacrypt '02. Springer.

Bresson, E., Chevassut, O., & Pointcheval, D. (2002b). Dynamic Group Diffie-Hellman key exchange under standard assumptions. In L.R. Knudsen (Ed.), Proceedings of Eurocrypt '02, LNCS (Vol. 2332, pp. 321-326).

Bresson, E., Chevassut, O., Pointcheval, D., & Quisquater, J.-J. (2001b). Provably authenticated group Diffie-Hellman Exchange-The dynamic case. In C. Boyd (Ed.), Proc. of Asiacrypt '01, LNCS (Vol. 2248, pp. 290-309).

Bresson, E., Chevassut, O., Pointcheval, D., & Quisquater, J.-J. (2001a). Provably authenticated group Diffie-Hellman Exchange. In P. Samarati (Ed.), *Proc. of ACM CCS '01* (pp. 255-264).

Buchman, J., Dahmen, E., Ereth, S., Hulsing, A., & Ruckert, M. (2011a). On the Security of the Winternitz One-Time Signature Scheme. *AFRICACRYPT'11 Proceedings of the 4th International Conference on Progrewss in Cryptology in Africa*. Retrieved from: https://eprint.iacr.org/2011/191.pdf

Buchmann, J. (2004). *Introduction to Cryptography* (2nd ed.). Springer. doi:10.1007/978-1-4419-9003-7

Buchmann, J., & Hülsing, A. (2011b). XMSS — A Practical Forward Secure Signature Scheme based on Minimal Security Assumptions. In B.-Y. Yang (Ed.), *Post-Quantum Cryptography* (Vol. 7071). Springer. doi:10.1007/978-3-642-25405-5_8

Burmester, M., & Desmedt, Y. (1994, May). A secure and efficient conference key distribution system. In *Advances in Cryptology EUROCRYPT'94*.

Canetti, R. (2001). Universally composable security: A new paradigm for cryptographic protocols. Proceedings of FOCS (pp. 136–145). IEEE Computer Society. doi:10.1109/SFCS.2001.959888

Canetti, R. (2002). Universally composable Security: A New paradigm for cryptographic protocols, Proceedings of the 34th STOC (pp. 494-503).

Canetti, R., Dwork, C., Naor, M., & Ostrovsky, R. (1996). Deniable Encryption. Retrieved from https://eprint.iacr.org/1996/002.ps

Canetti, R. (2000). Security and Composition of Multiparty Cryptography Protocols. *Journal of Cryptology*, *13*(1), 143–202. doi:10.1007/s001459910006

Caronni, G., Waldvogel, M., Sun, D., Weiler, N., & Plattner, B. (1999). The VersaKey framework: Versatile group key management. *IEEE Journal on Selected Areas in Communications*, *17*, 9.

Carter, L., & Wegman, M. N. (1979). Universal Classes of Hash Functions. *Journal of CSS*, *18*(20), 143–154.

Cash, D., Kiltz, E., & Shoup, V. (2009). The Twin Diffie-Hellman problem and its applications. Retrieved from https://eprint.iacr.org/2008/067

Castagnos, G. (2007). An Efficient Probabilistic Public-Key Cryptosystem over Quadratic Fields Quotients. *Finite Fields and Their Applications*, *13*(3), 563–576. doi:10.1016/j.ffa.2006.05.004

Cavallar, S., Dodson, B., Lenstra, A. K., Lioen, W. M., Montgomery, P. L., Murphy, B., & Zimmermann, P. et al. (2000). Factorization of a 512-bit RSA modulus. In *Advances in Cryptology, EUROCRYPT 2000*. Berlin: Springer. doi:10.1007/3-540-45539-6_1

Cha, S. (2010), From semantic security to chosen ciphertext security. Iowa State University. Retrieved from http://lib.dr.iastate.edu/etd

Cha, J. C., Ko, K. H., Lee, S. J., Han, J. W., & Cheon, J. H. (2001). An efficient Implementation of Braid Groups. *Proceedings of ASIACRYPT '01*, LNCS (Vol. *2248*, pp. 144–156). doi:10.1007/3-540-45682-1_9

Chaum, D. L. (1981). Untraceable electronic mail, return address, and digital pseudonym. *Communications of the ACM*, *24*(2), 84–90.

Chaum, D. L. (1988). Elections with unconditionally-secret ballots and disruption equivalent to breaking RSA. *Proceedings of EUROCRYPT '88*.

Chevassut, O., Fouque, P.-A., Gaudry, P., & Pointcheval, D. (2005). Key derivation and randomness extraction. Retrieved from http://eprint.iacr.org/2005/061

Childers, G. (2012). Factorization of a 1061-bit number by the special number field sieve. Cryptology ePrint Archive, Report 2012/444.

Choi, S. J., & Youn, H. Y. (2004). A novel data encryption and distribution approach for high security and availability using LU decomposition. In Computational Science and Its Applications, *LNCS* (Vol. *3046*, pp. 637–646).

Choi, S. J., & Youn, H. Y. (2005). An Efficient Key Pre-Distribution Scheme for Secure Distributed Sensor Networks. In *EUC Workshops, LNCS* (Vol. *3823*, pp. 1088–1097).

Chor, B., Goldwasser, S., Micali, S., & Awerbuch, B. (1985, May 6-8). Verifiable Secret Sharing and Achieving Simultaneity in the Presence of Faults (Extended Abstract). *Proceedings of the 17th Annual ACM Symposium on Theory of Computing*, Providence, Rhode Island, USA (pp. 383– 395). ACM Press.

Cocks, C. (2001). An Identity Based Encryption Scheme Based on Quadratic Residues. *Cryptography and Coding - Institute of Mathematics and Its Applications International Conference on Cryp-tography and Coding, Proceedings of IMA 2001*, 360-363.

Coron, J.-S., Lepoint, T., & Tibouchi, M. (2014): Scale-Invariant Fully Homomorphic Encryption over the Integers. Proceedings of IACR Cryptology '14 (pp. 311-328).

Cowie, J., Dodson, B., Elkenbracht–Huizing, R. M., Lenstra, A. K., Montgomery, P. L., & Zayer, J. (1996). A World Wide Number Field Sieve factoring record: On to 512 bits. In *Advances in Cryptography Asiacrypt '96, LNCS* (Vol. *1163*, pp. 382–394). doi:10.1007/BFb0034863

Cramer, R., & Damgard, I. (2004). Multiparty Computation: An Introduction. Retrieved from http://citeseerx.ist.psu.edu/viewdoc/download?doi=10.1.1.91.6488&rep=rep1&type=pdf

Cramer, R., Gennaro, R., & Schoenmakers, B. (1997). A secure and optimally efficient multi-authority election scheme. In Advances in Cryptology EUROCRYPT '97.

Cramer, R., & Shoup, V. (2003). Design and Analysis of Practical Public Key Encryption Schemes Secure Against Chosen Ciphertext Attack. *SIAM Journal on Computing*, *33*(1), 167–226. doi:10.1137/S0097539702403773

Crepeau, C. (1988). Equivalence between two flavors of oblivious transfers. In Advances in Cryptology CRYPTO '87, LNCS (Vol. *293*, pp. 239–247). doi:10.1007/3-540-48184-2_30

Damguard, I. (1989) A Design Principal for Hash Functions. *Proceedings of CRYPTO '89, LNCS* (Vol. 435, pp. 416-427). doi:10.1007/0-387-34805-0_39

Denis, T. S., & Rose, G. (2006). *BigNum Math Implementing Cryptographic Multiple Precision Arithmetic*. Syngress.

Desmedt, Y., & Wang, Y. (n. d.). Efficient Zero Knowledge Proofs for Some Practical Graph Problems. Retrieved from webpages.uncc.edu/yonwang/papers/zkip.pdf

Diffie, W. (1988). The first ten years of Public-Key Cryptography. *Proceedings of the IEEE*, *76*(5), 560–577. doi:10.1109/5.4442

Diffie, W., & Hellman, M. (1976). New Directions in Cryptography. *IEEE Transactions on Information Theory*, *2*(6), 644–654.

Diffie, W., & Hellman, M. E. (1976). New Directions in Cryptography. *IEEE Transactions on Information Theory*, *22(6)*, 29–40.

Diffie, W., & Hellman, M. E. (1976). New Directions in Cryptography. *IEEE Transactions on Information Theory*, *22*(6), 644–654. doi:10.1109/TIT.1976.1055638

Digital Signature Standard. (n. d.) Retrieved from http://www-2.cs.cmu.edu/afs/cs/academic/class/15827-f98/www/Slides/lecture2/base.024.html

Digital Signature Standard. (n. d.). *Digital Signature Algorithm.* Retrieved from http://home.pacbell.net/tpanero/crypto/dsa.html

Dixon, J. D. (1981). Asymptotically Fast Factorization of Integers. *Mathematics of Computation, 36*(153), 255. doi:10.1090/S0025-5718-1981-0595059-1

Dodis, Y., & Yampolskiy, A. (2005). A Verifiable Random Function with Short Proofs and Keys. In *Public Key Cryptography 2005, LNCS* (Vol. *3386*, pp. 416–431).

Dolev, D., Dwork, C., & Naor, M. (1991). Non-malleable cryptography. *Proceedings of the 23rd annual ACM Symposium on theory of computing* (pp. 542-552). doi:10.1145/103418.103474

Dolev, D., Dwork, C., & Naor, M. (2000). Non-malleable cryptography. *SIAM Journal on Computing, 30*(2), 391–437. doi:10.1137/S0097539795291562

Dorrendorf, L., Gutterman, Z., & Pinkas, B. (2007). Cryptanalysis of the Random Number Generator of the Windows Operating System. Retrieved from http://eprint.iacr.org/419.pdf

Du, W., & Atallah, M. J. (2001). Secure Multi-party computation Problems And Their Applications: A Review and Open problems. Retrieved from http://www.cis.syr.edu/~wedu/Research/paper/nspw2001.pdf

Dube, R. (2008). *Hardware-based Computer Security Techniques to Defeat Hackers, From Biometrics to Quantum Cryptography.* John Wiley & Sons. doi:10.1002/9780470425497

Dwork, C., & Naor, M. (1996) Method for message authentication from non-malleable cryptosystems. U. S. Patent no. 05539826.

Dwork, C., Naor, M., & Sahai, A. (1998). *Concurrent Zero Knowledge. Proceedings of the 30*[th] *STOC* (pp. 409–418).

Elgamal, T. (1985). A public-key cryptosystem and a signature scheme based on discrete logarithms. *IEEE Transactions on Information Theory, 31*(4), 469–472. doi:10.1109/TIT.1985.1057074

Erkin, Z., Beye, M., Veugen, T., & Lagendijk, R. L. , (2012). Privacy-Preserving Content-Based Recommendations through Homomorphic Encryption. *Proceedings of the 33rd WIC Symposium on Information Theory in the Benelux and The 2nd Joint WIC/IEEE Symposium on Information Theory and Signal Processing in the Benelux* (pp. 71-77).

Even, S., Goldreich, O., & Lempel, A. (1985). A Randomized Protocol for Signing Contracts. Communications of the ACM, 28(6), 637-647.

Federal Information Processing Standards Publication 186. (n. d.). Retrieved from http://jbr.org/articles.html

Feige, U. (1990) *Alternative Models of Zero Knowledge Proofs.* [Ph.D. Dissertation]. Weismann Institute of Science.

Ferguson, N., Schroeppel, R., & Whiting, D. (2001, August 16-17). A simple algebraic representation of Rijndael. In S. Vaudenay & A. Youssef (Eds.), *Selected Areas in Cryptography: 8th Annual International Workshop SAC '01*, Toronto, Ontario, Canada, LNCS (Vol. 2259, pp. 103-111). Springer-Verlag. doi:10.1007/3-540-45537-X_8

Floyd, S., Jacobson, V., Liu, C., McCanne, S., & Zhang, L. (1997). A reliable multicast framework for light-weight sessions and application level framing. *IEEE/ACM Transactions on Networking, 5*(6), 784–803. doi:10.1109/90.650139

Fujioka, A., Okamoto, T., & Ohta, K. (1992). A practical secret voting scheme for large scale elections. In *Advances in Cryptology AUSCRYPT '92.*

Galbraith, S. D. (2002). Elliptic Curve Paillier Schemes. *Journal of Cryptology, 15*(2), 129–138. doi:10.1007/s00145-001-0015-6

Galil, Z., Haber, S., & Yung, M. (1988) Cryptographic computation: Secure fault-tolerant protocols and the public-key model (extended abstract). In Advances in Cryptology CRYPTO '87, LNCS (Vol. 293, pp. 135–155).

Garrett, S. L. (2008). *On the Quadratic Sieve* [Master's Thesis]. University of North Carolina at Greensboro.

Gauravram, P. (2003). Cryptographic Hash Functions: Cryptanalysis, design and Applications [Ph.D. thesis]. Queensland University of Technology, Brisbane, Australia.

Geetha, J. S., & Amalarethinam, D. I. (2015). ABC-RNG For Public Key Cryptography for Random Number Generation. *International Journal of Fuzzy Mathematical Archive, 6*(2), 177–186.

Gentry, C. (2003). Certificate-based encryption and the certificate revocation problem. Advances in Cryptology – EUROCRYPT 2003, 272-293. doi:10.1007/3-540-39200-9_17

Gentry, C., & Silverberg, A. (2002). Hierarchical ID-based cryptography. Advances in Cryptology – ASIACRYPT 2002, 548-566.

Gentry, C., Sahai, A., & Waters, B. (2013). Homomorphic Encryption from Learning with Errors: Conceptually-Simpler, Asymptotically-Faster, Attribute-Based.

Ghebregiorgish, S. T. (2012). *Quadratic Sieve Integer Factorization using Hadoop* [Master's Thesis]. University of Stavanger.

Goldreich, O. (2004). Foundations of Cryptography (Vol 2. Basic Applications). Cambridge University Press.

Goldreich, O., Micali, S., & Wigderson, A. (1987). How to Play any Mental Game A Completeness Theorem for Protocols with Honest Majority. Proceedings of 19th STOC (pp. 218-229).

Goldreich, O., & Oren, Y. (1994). Definitions and Properties of Zero Knowledge Systems. *Journal of Cryptology, 7*(1). doi:10.1007/BF00195207

Goldwasser, S., & Micali, S. (1984). Probabilistic Encryption. *System Sciences, 28*, 270-299.

Grigoriev, D., & Ponomarenko, I. (2006). Homomorphic public-key cryptosystems and encrypting boolean circuits. *Appl. Algebra Engrg. Comm. Comput, 17*(3-4), 239–255. doi:10.1007/s00200-006-0005-x

Haitner, I., Harnik, D., & Reingold, O. (2006). Efficient Pseudorandom Generators from Exponentially Hard One-Way Functions. Proceedings of ICALP (Vol. 2, pp. 228-239). doi:10.1007/11787006_20

Halevi, S., & Krawczyk, H. (1997). MMH: Software Message Authentication in the Gbit/Second Rates. *Proceedings of Fast Software Encryption FSE'97, LNCS* (Vol. 1267).

Handschuh, H., & Naccache, D. (2000). SHACAL (Submissions to NESSIE). *Proceedings of the First Open NESSIE Workshop.*

Hellman, M. E. (1980). A cryptanalytic time-memory tradeoff. *IEEE Transactions on Information Theory, 26*(4), 401–406. doi:10.1109/TIT.1980.1056220

Hirt, M., & Sako, K. (2000). Efficient Receipt-free voting based Homomorphic Encryption. In *EUROCRYPT '00.*

Hoffman, P. (2012). *Elliptic Curve Digital Signature Algorithm (DSA) for DNSSEC.* RFC6605. doi:10.1007/978-3-642-20542-2

Hoffstein, J., Pipher, J., & Silverman, J. H. (1998). NTRU: a ring based public key cryptosystem. *Proceedings of ANTS-III*, 267–288. doi:10.1007/BFb0054868

Huang, Y. (2012). Practical Secure Two-party Computation [Ph.D. Dissertation]. University of Virginia.

Iwata, T., & Kurosawa, K. (2003). OMAC: One-Key CBC MAC. *Proc. of FSE'03, LNCS* (Vol. 2887).

Jacobsen, T., & Knudsen, L. (1997). The The interpolation attack against block ciphers. In E. Biham(Ed), *Fast Software Encryption: 4th International Workshop FSE'97, LNCS* (Vol. 1267, pp. 28-40). Springer-Verlag.

Jansen, P. L. (2005). *Integer Factorization* [Master's Thesis]. University of Copenhagen.

Jarecki, S., & Shmatikov, V. (2007). *Efficient two-party Secure Computation on Committed Inputs*. EuroCrypt. doi:10.1007/978-3-540-72540-4_6

Joux, A. (2004). Multicollisions in Iterated Hash Functions. Application to Cascaded Constructions. *Proceedings of CRYPTO'04 (Vol. 3152*, pp. 306-316).

Joux, A., Odlyzko, A., & Pierrot, C. (2014). The Past, Evolving Present and future of Discrete Logarithm, In Ç.K. Koç (Ed.), Open Problems in Mathematics and Computational Science (pp. 5-36). Springer.

Joux, A. (2004). A one round protocol for tripartite Diffie-Hellman. *Journal of Cryptology, 17*(4), 263–276. doi:10.1007/s00145-004-0312-y

Joux, A. (2009). *Algorithmic Cryptanalysis*. Chapman/Hall &CRC. doi:10.1201/9781420070033

Joye, M., Lenstra, A. K., & Quisquater, J.-J. (1999). Chinese remaindering based cryptosystems in the presence of faults. *Journal of Cryptology, 12*(4), 241–245. doi:10.1007/s001459900055

Juang, W., & Lei, C. (1997). A secure and practical electronic voting scheme for real world environment. *IEICE Trans. On Fundamentals, E80-A*(1).

Juang, W., Lei, C., & Yu, P. (1998). A verifiable multi-authorities secret elections allowing abstaining from voting. *Proceedings of the International Computer Symposium*, Taiwan.

Junod, P. (2005). Statistical Cryptanalysis of Block Ciphers, *Doctoral dissertation*, Lusanne, EPFL.

Kelsey, J., & Kohno, T. (2006). Herding hash functions and the nostradamus attack. In S. Vaudenay (Ed.), *Advances in Cryptology, LNCS* (Vol. 4004, pp. 183–200). doi:10.1007/11761679_12

Kerry, C. F., & Gallagher, P. D. (2013). *FIPS PUB 186-4, Digital Signature Standard*. National Institute of Standards and Technology.

Kilian, J. (1988). Founding Cryptography on oblivious transfer. *Proceedings of the Twentieth ACM symposium on Theory of Computing* (pp. 20-31).

Kim, Y., Perrig, A., & Tsudik, G. (2000). Simple and fault-tolerant key agreement for dynamic collaborative groups. *Proceedings of 7th ACM Conference on Computer and Communications Security* (pp. 235–244). ACM Press. doi:10.1145/352600.352638

Kim, Y., Perrig, A., & Tsudik, G. (2001). Communication-efficient group key agreement. *Proceedings of IFIP SEC '01*.

Kizhvatov, I. (2011). Physical Security of Cryptographic Algorithm Implementations [Ph.D Dissertation]. University of Luxemborg.

Kleinjung, T., Aoki, K., Franke, J., Lenstra, A., Thome, E., Bos, J., ... Zimmermann, P. (2010). Factorization of a 768-bit RSA modulus (Cryptology ePrint Archive, Report 2010/006).

Knudsen, L. (1998). Contemporary block ciphers. In I. Damgard, (Ed.), Lectures on Data Security Modern Cryptology in Theory and Practice, LNCS (Vol. 1561, pp. 105-126). Springer-Verlag.

Knuth, D. E. (1981). Art of computer programming: Vol. 2. *Seminumerical Algorithms* (2nd ed.). Reading, Massachusetts: Addison-Wesley.

Koblitz, N., & Menezes, A. (2010). *Intractable Problems in Cryptography*. International Association for Cryptological Research. Retrieved from: http://eprint.iacr.org/2010/290.pdf

Koblitz, N. (1987). Elliptic Curve Cryptosystems. *Mathematics of Computation, 48*(177), 203–209. doi:10.1090/S0025-5718-1987-0866109-5

Kocarev, L. (2001). Chaos-Based Cryptography: A Brief Overview, (Invited paper). *IEEE Circuits and Magazine, 1*(3), 6–21. doi:10.1109/7384.963463

Kocarev, L., & Lian, S. (Eds.). (2011). *Chaos-Based Cryptography Theory Algorithms and Applications*. Springer.

Kocher, P. (1996) Timing attacks on implementations of Diffie-Hellman, RSA, DSS, and other systems. In N. Koblitz (Ed.), Advances in Cryptology - CRYPTO '96, Santa Barbara, California, LNCS (Vol. 1109, pp. 104–113). Springer.

Kocher, P., Jaffe, J., & Jub, B. Differential power analysis. In M. Wiener (Ed.), Proc. of Advances in Cryptology – CRYPTO '99, LNCS (Vol. 1666, pp. 388–397). Springer-Verlag.

Koeune, F., & Standaert, F.-X. (2005). A Tutorial on Physical Security and Side-Channel Attacks. In Foundations of Security Analysis and Design III, *LNCS* (Vol. *3655*, pp. 78–108). doi:10.1007/11554578_3

Ko, K. H., Lee, S. J., Cheon, J. H., Han, J. W., Kang, J., & Park, C. (2000). New public-key cryptosystem using braid groups. In *Advances in cryptology, LNCS* (Vol. 1880, pp. 166-183). Springer.

Kommerling, O., & Kuhn, M. G. (1999). Design principles for tamper-resistant smartcard processors. *Proc. of USENIX Workshop on Smartcard Technology (Smartcard '99)*.

Krawczyk, H. (1994). LFSR-based Hashing and Authentication. *Proc. of CRYPTO '94, LNCS* (Vol. 839). Springer-Verlag.

Lamport, L. (1979). *Constructing digital signatures from a one way function*. Technical Report SRI-CSL-98, SRI International Computer Science Laboratory. Retrieved from http://research.microsoft.com/en-us/um/people/lamport/pubs/dig-sig.pdf

Laskari, E. C., Meletiou, G. C., & Vrahatis, M. N. (2005). Problems of Cryptography as Discrete Optimization Tasks. *Nonlinear Analysis, 63*(5-7), 831–837. doi:10.1016/j.na.2005.03.003

Laud, P., & Kamm, L. (2015). *Applications of Secure Multiparty Computation*. IOS Press.

Lauter, K., Naehrig, M., & Vaikuntanathan, V. (2011) Can Homomorphic Encryption be Practical? *Proceedings of the ACM Cloud Computing Security Workshop CCSW '11*, Chicago, IL, USA (pp. 113-124).

Lee, P. P. C., Lui, J. C. S., & Yau, D. K. Y. (2007). SEAL: A secure communication library for building dynamic group key agreement applications. *Journal of Systems and Software, 80*(3), 356–370. doi:10.1016/j.jss.2006.04.016

Lenstra, H.W., Jr. (1987). Factoring integers with elliptic curves. *Ann. of Math, 126*, 649–673.

Lenstra, A. K. (2000). Integer Factoring, Designs. *Codes and Cryptography, 19*(2/3), 101–128. doi:10.1023/A:1008397921377

Lenstra, A. K., & Lenstra, H. W. Jr. (1993). The development of the number field sieve. In *Lecture Notes in Mathematics* (Vol. 1554). Berlin, Heidelberg: Springer-Verlag. doi:10.1007/BFb0091534

Lenstra, A. K., & Manasse, M. S. (1990). Factoring by electronic mail. In *Advances in Cryptology, Eurocrypt '89, LNCS* (Vol. *434*, pp. 355–371). doi:10.1007/3-540-46885-4_35

Lindell, Y., & Pinkas, B. (2004). A Proof of Yao's Protocol for Secure Two-Party Computation. *Proceedings of the Electronic Colloquium on Computational Complexity*.

Lindell, Y., & Pinkas, B. (2007). *An Efficient Protocol for Secure Two-Party Computation in the Presence of Malicious Adversaries*. EuroCrypt. doi:10.1007/978-3-540-72540-4_4

Lucks, S. (2004). Design Principles for Iterated Hash Functions. Retrieved from http://eprint.iacr.org/2003/253

Magyarik, M. R., & Wagner, N. R. (1985). Lecture Notes in Computer Science: Vol. 196. *A Public Key Cryptosystem Based on the Word Problem*. Berlin: Springer.

Maimu, D., Patrascu, A., & Simion, E. (2012). Homomorphic Encryption Schemes and Applications for a Secure Digital World. *Journal of Mobile, Embedded and Distributed Systems*, *4*(4).

Malka, L. (2008). *A study of Perfect Zero Knowledge Proofs* [Ph.D. dissertation]. University of Victoria.

Massacci, F., & Marraro, L. (2000). Logical Analysis as a SAT Problem, Encoding and Analysis of the U.S. Data Encryption Standard. *Journal of Automated Reasoning*, *24*(1/2), 165–203. doi:10.1023/A:1006326723002

Massierer, M. (2006). Provable Secure Cryptographic Hash Functions [B.S. thesis]. University of New South Wales.

Matsumoto, T., & Imai, H. (1988). Public quadratic polynomial-tuples for efficient signature verification and message-encryption. Advances in Cryptology, 419-453.

Matyas, S. M., Le, A. V., & Abraham, D. G. (1991). A Key-Management Scheme Based on Control Vectors. *IBM Systems Journal*, *30*(2), 175–191. doi:10.1147/sj.302.0175

Maurer, U. M., & Wolf, S. (1998). Diffie-Hellman, Decision Diffie-Hellman, and discrete logarithms. *Proceedings of the IEEE Symposium on Information Theory*, Cambridge, USA.

Maurer, U. (2006). Secure Multi-party Computation made simple. *Discrete Applied Mathematics, Elsevier*, *154*(2), 370–381. doi:10.1016/j.dam.2005.03.020

McEliece, R.J., (1978). A Public-Key Cryptosystem based Algebraic Coding Theory. *DSN Progress Report*, 42-44.

McEliece, R. J. (1978). A Public-Key System based on Algebraic Coding Theory, *Jet Propulsion Lab. DSN Progress Report*, *44*, 114–116.

Meletiou, G. C., Triantafllou, D. S., & Vrahatis, M. N. (2015). Handling problems in cryptography with matrix factorization. *Journal of Applied Mathematics and Bioinformatics*, *5*(3), 37–48.

Menezes, A., Van Oorshoot, P. C., & Vanstone, A. (1996). *Handbook of Applied Cryptography*. CRC Press. doi:10.1201/9781439821916

Merkle, R. C. (1979). Secrecy, Authentication and Public Key Systems [Ph.D. thesis]. Stanford University, Stanford, USA.

Merkle, R. C. (1989). A Certified Digital Signature. *Advances in Cryptology, CRYPTO '89 Proceedings,* 218-238.

Merkle, R. C. (1989). One Way Hash Functions and DES. *Proceedings of CRYPTO '89, LNCS* (Vol. 435, pp. 428-446).

Merkle, R., & Hellman, M. (1978). Hiding Information and signatures in trapdoor knapsacks. *IEEE Transactions on Information Theory, IT-24*(5), 525–530. doi:10.1109/TIT.1978.1055927

Microsoft. (2006) Factoring large numbers with quadratic sieve. *Microsoft developer.* Retrieved from https://blogs.msdn.microsoft.com/devdev/2006/06/19/factoring-large-numbers-with-quadratic-sieve/

Microsoft. (n. d.) Applications of Digital Signature. Retrieved from https://technet.microsoft.com/en-us/library/cc962021.aspx

Miller, S. V. (1985). Use of Elliptic Curves in Cryptography. In *Advances in cryptology: CRYPTO'85* (pp. 417–426).

Mitsunari, S., Sakai, R., & Kasahara, M. (2002). A New Traitor Tracing. IEICE Trans. Fundamentals, E85-A(2), 481-484.

Mohassel, P., & Franklin, M. (2006). Efficiency Tradeoffs for Malicious Two-Party Computation. *Proceedings of the International Conference on Theory and Practice of Public Key Cryptography* (pp. 458-473).

Mohr, A. (2007). A survey of Zero Knowledge Proofs with applications to Cryptography. Retrieved from austinmohr.com/work/files/zkp.pdf

Mollin, R. (2003). *RSA and Public-Key Cryptography*. Chapman &Hall/CRC.

Montgomery, P. L. (1995), A block Lanczos algorithm for finding dependencies over GF(2). *Proceedings of the 14th annual international conference on theory and application of cryptographic techniques* (pp. 106-120). Springer-Verlag.

Montgomery, P. L. (1987). Speeding the Pollard and the Elliptic Curve methods of factorization. *Mathematics of Computation, 48*(177), 243–264. doi:10.1090/S0025-5718-1987-0866113-7

Myasnikov, A., Shpilrain, V., & Ushakov, A. (2008). *Group-based Cryptography*. Birkauser.

Nakkala, N.K., Ram Mohan, C., & Rao, N.V. (2014). Generating Private Recommendations Efficiently Using GAE Datastore and Data Packing. *International Journal of Advanced Research in Computer and Communication Engineering, 3*(2).

Naor, M., & Yung, M. (1990). Public-key cryptosystems provably secure against chosen ciphertext attacks. *Proceedings of the 22nd Annual ACM symposium on theory of computing* (pp. 427-437). doi:10.1145/100216.100273

Naor, M., & Reingold, O. (1997). Number Theoretic constructions of efficient Pseudo-random functions. *Proceedings of FOCS'97* (pp. 458-467). IEEE Computer Society Press. doi:10.1109/SFCS.1997.646134

Naor, M., & Yung, M. (1989). *Universal One-Way Hash Functions and their Cryptographic Applications* (pp. 33–43). STOC. doi:10.1145/73007.73011

Nevelsteen, W., & Preneel, B. (1999). Software Performance of Universal Hash Functions. *Proc. of Eurocrypt '99, LNCS* (Vol. 1592).

Nielsen, J. B., Nordholt, P. S., Orlandi, C., & Burra, S. S. (2011) A New Approach to Practical Active-Secure Two-Party Computation. Retrieved from http://eprint.iacr.org/2011/091

NIST. (2001). NIST Special Publication 800-38A, Recommendation for Block Cipher Modes of Operation - Methods and Techniques.

NIST. (2005). NIST Special Publication 800-38B, Recommendation for Block Cipher Modes of Operation: The CMAC Mode for Authentication.

NIST. (n. d.) Digital Signature Standard. Retrieved from http://www.itl.nist.gov/fipspubs/fip186.htm

Okamoto, T. (1997). Receipt-free electronic voting scheme for large-scale election. *In Security Protocols (pp. 25-35).*

Okamoto, T., & Pointcheval, D. (2001). The gap-problems: A new class of problems for the security of cryptographic schemes. In Public Key Cryptography, LNCS (Vol. *1992*, pp. 104–118). doi:10.1007/3-540-44586-2_8

Okamoto, T., Tanaka, K., & Uchiyama, S. (2000). Quantum Public-Key Cryptosystems. In *Advances in Cryptology: CRYPTO 00* (pp. 147–165).

Paillier, P. (2007). Impossibility proofs for RSA signatures in the standard model. Proceedings of CT-RSA 2007, LNCS (Vol. 4377, pp. 31–48). Heidelberg: Springer.

Paillier, P., & Villar, J. L. (2006). Trading one-wayness against chosen-ciphertext security in factoring-based encryption. Proceedings of ASIACRYPT '06, LNCS (Vol. 4284, pp. 252–266). Heidelberg: Springer. doi:10.1007/11935230_17

Papadopoulos, J. (2012). MSIEVE 2012. Retrieved from http://sourceforge.net/projects/msieve/

Pass, R. (2004). Alternative variants of Zero Knowledge Proofs. Retrieved from http://www.cs.cornell.edu/~rafael/papers/raf-lic.pdf

Patarin, J., & Goubin, L. (1997). Trapdoor one-way permutations and multivariate polynomials. *International Conference on Information Security and Cryptology, 356-368.* Retrieved from http:// citeseer.nj.nec.com/patarin97trapdoor.html

Patarin, J., Goubin, L., & Courtois, N. T. (1998). Improved algorithms for isomoprhisms of polynomials, *Advances in Cryptology, 184-200.* Retrieved from http://www.minrank.org/ip6long.ps

Patarin, J. (1986). *Hidden Fields Equations (HFE) and Isomorphisms of Polynomials(IP): Two new families of Asymmetric Algorithms.* Springer-Verlag.

Pathan, A. S. K., Hong, C. S., & Suda, T. (2007), A novel and efficient bilateral remote user authentication scheme using smart cards. *Proceedings of the IEEE International Conference on Consumer Electronics* (pp. 1-2). doi:10.1109/ICCE.2007.341503

Patra, A. (2010). *Studies on Verifiable secret sharing, Byzantine Agreement, and Multiparty Computation* [Ph.D. Thesis]. Indian Institute of Technology, Madras.

Pollard, J. M. (1974). Theorems on factororization and primality testing. *Proceedings of the Cambridge Philosophical Society, 76*(03), 521–528. doi:10.1017/S0305004100049252

Pollard, J. M. (1975). A Monte Carlo method for factorization. *BIT Numerical Mathematics, 15*(3), 331–334. doi:10.1007/BF01933667

Pomerance, C. (1982). Analysis and Comparison of Some Integer Factoring Algorithms, in Computational Methods in Number Theory, Part I. In H.W. Lenstra, Jr. And R. Tiejdeman, (Eds.), Math, Centre Tract 154, Amsterdam (pp. 89-139).

Pomerance, C. (1985) The quadratic sieve factoring algorithm. In T. Beth, N. Cot, & I. Ingemarsson (Eds.), Advances in cryptology: EUROCRYPT '84, LNCS (Vol. 209, pp. 169–182). Springer-Verlag.

Preneel, B. (2003). Analysis and design of cryptographic hash functions [PhD thesis]. Katholieke Universiteit Leuven, Belgium.

Purohit, R., Mishra, U., & Bansal, A. (2013). A survey on Recent Cryptographic Hash Function Designs. *International Journal of Emerging Trends and Technology in Computer Science, 1*(1), 117–122.

Quisquater, J-J., & Samyde, D. (2002). Eddy current for magnetic analysis with active sensor. *Proc. of Esmart '02.*

Rabin, M. (1981). How to Exchange Secrets by Oblivious Transfer (Tech. Memo TR-81). Aiken Computation Laboratory, Harvard University.

Racko, C., & Simon, D. (1991) Noninteractive zero-knowledge proof of knowledge and Chosen ciphertext attack. In Advances in cryptology, crypto '91 (pp. 433-444).

Radwin, M. J. (1995). An untraceable, universally verifiable voting scheme. Retrieved from http://citeseerx.ist.psu.edu/viewdoc/download?doi=10.1.1.9.1758&rep=rep1&type=pdf

Rankl, W., & Effing, W. (1997). *Smart Card Handbook.* John Wiley & Sons.

Rivest, R. (1992a). The MD4 Message Digest Algorithm, IETF RFC 1320.

Rivest, R. (1992b). The MD5 Message Digest Algorithm, IETF RFC 1321.

Rivest, R., Shamir, A., & Adleman, L. (1978) A method for obtaining digital signatures and public-key cryptosystems. Comm. of the ACM, 21(2), 120-126. doi:10.1145/359340.359342

Rivest, R. L., Shamir, A., & Adleman, L. (1978). A Method for Obtaining Digital Signatures and Public-Key Cryptosystems. *Communications of the ACM, 21*(2).

Rompay, B. V. (2004). Analysis and Design of Cryptographic Hash functions, MAC algorithms and Block Ciphers [Ph.D. thesis]. Electrical Engineering Department, Katholieke Universiteit, Leuven, Belgium.

Rujaskova, Z. (2002). Electronic Voting Schemes [Diplomova Praca dissertation]. Comenius University, Bratislava.

Sadehi, A.-R., & Steiner, M. (2001). *Assumptions related to Discrete Logarithms; Why Subtleties Make a Real Difference. In Eurocrypt 2001, LNCS* (Vol. *2045*, pp. 243–260). Springer-Verlag.

Sahai, A., & Waters, B. (2004). *Fuzzy Identity Based Encryption.* IACR ePrint Archive, Report 2004/086. Retrieved from http://eprint.iacr.org/

Sako, K., & Kilian, J. (1995). Receipt-free Mix type voting scheme- a practical solution to the implementation of a voting booth. In *Advances in Cryptology EUROCRYPT '95.*

Seibert, C. (2011). Integer Factorization using the Quadratic Sieve. *Proceedings of MICS '11.* Retrieved from micsymposium.org/mics_2011_proceedings/mics2011_submission_28.pdf

Shamir, A. (1999). Factoring Large numbers with the TWINKLE Device. Retrieved from http://link.springer.com/content/pdf/10.1007%2F3-540-48059-5_2.pdf

Shamir, A. (1979). How to share a secret. *Communications of the ACM, 22*(11), 612–613. doi:10.1145/359168.359176

Shamir, A. (1984). A polynomial time algorithm for breaking the basic Merkle-Hellman Cryptosystem. *IEEE Transactions on Information Theory, IT-30*(5), 699–704. doi:10.1109/TIT.1984.1056964

Shamir, A. (1984). Identity-Based Cryptosystems and Signature Schemes. *Advances in Cryptology: Proceedings of CRYPTO 84, Lecture Notes in Computer Science, 7*, 47—53.

Shannon, C. (1949), Communication Theory of secrecy systems. *Bell System Technical Journal, 2894*, 656-719.

Shen, C. H., & Shelat, A. (2011). Two-output Secure Computation With Malicious Adversaries. Proceedings of EUROCRYPT.

Sherman, A. T., & McGrew, D. A. (2003). Key establishment in large dynamic groups using one-way function trees. *IEEE Transactions on Software Engineering, 29*(5), 444–458. doi:10.1109/TSE.2003.1199073

Shoenmakers, B. (1999). A simple publicly verifiable secret sharing scheme and its application to electronic voting. In Crypto 1999, LNCS (Vol. *1666*, pp. 148–164). doi:10.1007/3-540-48405-1_10

Shoup, V. (1999). On formal models for secure key exchange. *Cryptology eprint archive report*. Retrieved from http://eprint.iacr.org

Shoup, V. (1998). *Why chosen ciphertext security matters. Technical Report RZ 3076*. IBM Research.

Shpilrain, V., & Ushakov, A. (2005) Thompson's group and public key cryptography. In ACNS '05, LNCS (Vol. 3531, pp. 151-164). doi:10.1007/11496137_11

Shpilrain, V., & Zapata, G. (2006b). Using the subgroup membership search problem in public key cryptography, *Contemp. Math., Amer. Math. Soc., 418,* 169-179.

Shpilrain, V., & Zapata, G. (2006a). Combinatorial group theory and public key cryptography. *Appl. Algebra Engrg. Comm. Comput., 17*(3-4), 291–302. doi:10.1007/s00200-006-0006-9

Singh, S. (1999). *The Codebook*. DoubleDay.

Skorobogatov, S., & Anderson, R. (2002). Optical fault induction attacks. In B. S. Kaliski et al. (Eds.), *CHES-2002, LNCS* (Vol. 2523). Springer-Verlag.

Smart, N., (Ed.) (2010). ECRYPT II yearly report on algorithms and keysizes. *ECRYPT II deliverable, Revision* 1.0. Retrieved from http://www.ecrypt.eu.org/documents/D.SPA.13.pdf

Sobti, R., & Geetha, G. (2012). Cryptographic Hash Functions: A Review. *International Journal of Computer Science Issues, 9*(2), 461-479.

Stallings, W. (2013). *Cryptography and Network Security Principles and Practice* (7th ed.). Prentice Hall.

Steiner, M., Tsudik, G., & Waidner, M. (1998). CLIQUES: A New Approach to Group Key Agreement. Retrieved from http://www.isi.edu/div7/publication_files/cliques_a_new.pdf

Steiner, M., Tsudik, G., & Waidner, M. (1996). Diffie Hellman key distribution extended to group communication. *Proceedings of ACM CCS '96* (pp. 31-37). doi:10.1145/238168.238182

Steiner, M., Tsudik, G., & Waidner, M. (2000). Key agreement in dynamic peer groups. *IEEE Transactions on Parallel and Distributed Systems, 11*(8), 769–780. doi:10.1109/71.877936

The Trusted Computing Group. (2003, October). TPM Main: Part 1 Design Principles. Retrieved from https://trusted-computinggroup.org/wp-content/uploads/TPM-Main-Part-1-Design-Principles_v1.2_rev116_01032011.pdf

The Trusted Computing Group. (n. d.) Retrieved from: http://www.trustedcomputinggroup.org

Tsudik, G. (1992). Message Authentication with One-Way Hash Functions. In INFOCOM (pp. 2055-2059).

Wagner, D. (1999). The boomerang attack. In L. Knudsen (Ed.), *Fast Soft-ware Encryption: 6th International Workshop FSE'99*, Rome, Italy, *LNCS* (Vol. 1636, pp. 156-170). Springer-Verlag. doi:10.1007/3-540-48519-8_12

Wallner, D., Harder, E., & Agee, R. (1999). Key management for multicast: Issues and architectures.

Wegman, M. N., & Carter, J. L. (1991). New hash functions and their use in authentication and set equality. *Journal of Computer and System Sciences, 22*(3), 265-279.

Wong, C. K., Gouda, M. G., & Lam, S. S. (2000). Secure group communications using key graphs. *IEEE/ACM Transactions on Networking, 8*(1), 16–30. doi:10.1109/90.836475

Wu, H., & Wang, F. (2014). A Survey of Noninteractive Zero knowledge Proof system and its applications. *TheScientificWorldJournal*. doi:10.1155/2014/560484 PMID:24883407

Yao, A. (1986) How to generate and exchange secrets. Proceedings of the 27th FOCS (pp. 162-167).

Yao, A. C. (1982). Protocols for Secure Computations. *Proceedings of the 23rd Annual IEEE Symposium on Foundations of Computer Science*.

Zheng, Y., & Seberry, J. (1992). Practical approaches for attaining security against chosen-ciphertext attacks. Retrieved from http://coitweb.uncc.edu/~yzheng/publications/files/crypto92-immunize.pdf

Zhu, H. (2001). *Survey of Computational Assumptions Used in Cryptography Broken or Not by Shor's Algorithm* [Master's Thesis]. McGill University, Canada.

About the Contributors

Kannan Balasubramanian received the Ph.D. degree in Computer Science from University of California, Los Angeles, and the M.Tech degree in computer Science and Engineering from IIT Bombay India and his Msc. (Tech) degree in Computer Science from BITS., Pilani, India. He is a Professor in Mepco Schlenk Engineering College, Sivakasi, India. His research interest includes Network Security, Network Protocols, Applications and Performance.

Rajakani M. is currently working as Senior Grade Assistant Professor in Mepco Schlenk Engineering College. Research interests are Remote Sensing, Data Mining and Information Security.

* * *

Ahmed Mahmoud Abbas is a Senior Project Manager who received his BSc in 2001 and MSc in 2009 from the Department of Computer Science and Engineering at The American University in Cairo, Egypt. He has long experience in software development using Java programming language and IBM technologies; while currently is managing software products development. He is Agile certified and has firm knowledge of CMMI processes and PMI practices. His research interests include Software Project Management, Enterprise Portal Development, Computer Security, Cryptography and Open Source Software Development.

D. Sumathi Doraikannan is presently Associate Professor, Department of Computer Science and Engineering, PPG Institute of Technology, Affiliated to Anna University Chennai, Tamil Nadu. She received the B.E degree from Bharathiar University in 1994 and M.E degree from Sathyabama University in 2006, Chennai and completed her Ph.D. degree in Anna University, Chennai. Her Research interests include Cloud computing, Network Security and Theoretical Foundations. Mrs. D. Sumathi has published papers in international journal and conference papers and has been involved in many international conferences as Technical Chair and Tutorial Presenter. She is an active member of ISTE.

Index

A

adversary 29-30, 44-47, 56, 58, 62-63, 68, 71, 88, 90, 118-119, 131, 134-141, 143-144, 146, 148-153, 156-158, 161-162, 164-166

anonymous channel 126-130, 132

arbitrarily long integers 197-198

authentication 1, 4, 12, 28, 55-56, 58, 66-67, 71-74, 76, 78, 83-84, 115, 135, 152, 168, 175, 177-178, 180, 184

authorities 56, 124-126, 128-130, 132-133, 174

B

BGN CRYPTOSYSTEM 104

BigInteger 197, 225

Bit Commitment 122

blind signatures 124-125, 128, 130, 132

Botnets 177, 185

broadcast channel 157, 163

brute-force attack 38

B-smooth 230, 245, 250, 252

Buffer Overflow Attacks 171, 185

C

certificates 12-13, 15-16, 174, 178-179, 183

Certification Authority 85

chosen ciphertext attack 45-47, 134-136, 139, 143

chosen-ciphertext attack 53, 139

ciphertext 11-12, 21, 23, 29, 39, 44-47, 53, 72, 88, 97-98, 101, 104-105, 110, 118, 131, 134-144, 194

Classical Encryption 194

Closest Vector Problem 27, 39

codes 5, 21, 27, 66-67, 71-73, 76, 168, 175, 181

collision resistance 2, 76

commitment schemes 110, 116

compression function 70-71, 76

computational Diffie-Hellman 40-41, 50, 53

confidentiality 1, 13, 21, 28, 53, 56, 59, 66, 81, 105, 167

Covert Adversaries 153-154

covert adversary 164

Cryptanalysis 23, 29, 33, 36, 39, 66, 88, 92, 191-192, 194

D

decisional Diffie-Hellman 40, 42-44, 53

decisional Diffie-Hellman assumption 42-44, 53

decryption oracle 45-46, 134-136, 139-140, 143-144

deniable encryption 129, 131-132

Differential Evolution Method 28, 39

Diffie-Hellman 23, 26, 36, 39-45, 48-55, 61, 64-65, 190, 195-196

Diffie-Hellman assumption 41-44, 49, 53-54

Diffie-Hellman Key Exchange 23, 55, 64-65, 190

Diffie-Hellman problem 26, 36, 39-45, 48-50, 52, 54

digital signature 2, 76, 78-85, 194

Discrete Logarithms 1, 23, 25-26, 39, 41, 50-51, 53, 81, 141

E

Electro-Magnetic Attacks 96

electronic voting 124, 126-127, 129, 131, 133

Elgamal Digital Signature 81

Elliptic Curve Discrete Logarithms 1

Elliptic Curve method 228-229, 231, 239

encryption 2, 8-12, 15-16, 18-19, 21-22, 26-27, 31, 33, 44-47, 52-54, 56-57, 65-66, 72-74, 76, 81, 83, 88, 94, 97-103, 105, 107-110, 124-125, 128-142, 144, 147, 171, 181, 183, 194, 231

environment 14, 87, 155, 157-158, 165-166, 168, 170-171, 174-175, 178, 185

F

factor base 233-235, 250-252

Stay Current on the Latest Emerging Research Developments

Become an IGI Global Reviewer for Authored Book Projects

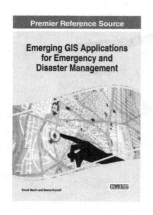
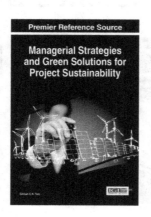

The overall success of an authored book project is dependent on quality and timely reviews.

In this competitive age of scholarly publishing, constructive and timely feedback significantly decreases the turnaround time of manuscripts from submission to acceptance, allowing the publication and discovery of progressive research at a much more expeditious rate. Several IGI Global authored book projects are currently seeking highly qualified experts in the field to fill vacancies on their respective editorial review boards:

Applications may be sent to:
development@igi-global.com

Applicants must have a doctorate (or an equivalent degree) as well as publishing and reviewing experience. Reviewers are asked to write reviews in a timely, collegial, and constructive manner. All reviewers will begin their role on an ad-hoc basis for a period of one year, and upon successful completion of this term can be considered for full editorial review board status, with the potential for a subsequent promotion to Associate Editor.

If you have a colleague that may be interested in this opportunity, we encourage you to share this information with them.

Information Resources Management Association

Advancing the Concepts & Practices of Information Resources Management in Modern Organizations

Become an IRMA Member

Members of the **Information Resources Management Association (IRMA)** understand the importance of community within their field of study. The Information Resources Management Association is an ideal venue through which professionals, students, and academicians can convene and share the latest industry innovations and scholarly research that is changing the field of information science and technology. Become a member today and enjoy the benefits of membership as well as the opportunity to collaborate and network with fellow experts in the field.

IRMA Membership Benefits:

- **One FREE Journal Subscription**
- **30% Off Additional Journal Subscriptions**
- **20% Off Book Purchases**
- Updates on the latest events and research on Information Resources Management through the IRMA-L listserv.
- Updates on new open access and downloadable content added to Research IRM.
- A copy of the Information Technology Management Newsletter twice a year.
- A certificate of membership.

IRMA Membership $195

Scan code or visit **irma-international.org** and begin by selecting your free journal subscription.

Membership is good for one full year.

Printed in the United States
By Bookmasters